Birds of Passage

Birds of Passage

Five Englishwomen
in Search of America

Richard Mullen

St. Martin's Press

New York

To
my sisters,
Anne Mary and Nora

E
165
.M9
1994

All rights reserved. For information, write:
Scholarly and Reference Division,
St. Martin's Press, 175 Fifth Avenue,
New York, NY 10010

First published in the United States of America in 1994

ISBN 0-312-12228-4

Library of Congress Cataloging-in-Publication Data

Mullen, Richard.
    Birds of passage : five Englishwomen in search of America /
Richard Mullen.
        p.   cm.
    Includes bibliographical references (p.) and index.
    ISBN 0-312-12228-4
    1. United States–Description and travel.   2. English–Travel
–United States–History–19th century.   3. Women–Travel–
United States–History–19th century.   4. United States–Foreign
public opinion, British–History–19th century.   5. Public opinion
–England–History–19th century.   I. Title.
E165.M9 1994
917,304–dc20   94-14200
                                                                            CIP

Printed in Great Britain

Contents

Plates

(between pages 118 and 119)

1. Rebecca Burlend
2. Edward Burlend
3. The Levee in New Orleans
4. Cartoon from Major Walter Wilkey's *Western Immigration* (1839)
5. Frances Wright
6. Frances Wright and her husband, William Phiquepal D'Arusmont
7. Cartoon mocking Frances Wright as a lecturer
8. The Marquis de Lafayette
9. Frances Wright's settlement at Nashoba in Tennessee
10. Frances Trollope and Frances Wright in a milliner's shop
11. A crowded American stage-coach
12. Frances Trollope, painted by Auguste Hervieu
13. Frances Trollope's Bazaar in Cincinnati
14. Mrs Trollope visits a gallery in Philadelphia
15. American behaviour at the theatre
16. An American attack on Frances Trollope
17. American caricature of the Trollope family in Cincinnati
18. Illustration by Hervieu for Frances Trollope's anti-slavery novel, *The Life and Adventures of Jonathan Jefferson Whitlaw*
19. The ascent to the Capitol Building in Washington, D.C.
20. Lady Emmeline Stuart Wortley
21. Niagara Falls, drawn by Lady Emmeline
22. A northern Virginia plantation home
23. Confederate troops crowded onto trains
24. Civilians sheltering from the bombardment of Charleston
25. Harper's Ferry, Virginia

Acknowledgments

While working on this book I have been greatly helped by many people on both sides of the Atlantic. I wish to thank the staffs of: the Berkshire Record Office; the Bodleian Library, Oxford, especially those of Rhodes House Library and Duke Humfrey; the Manuscript Room of the British Library; the General Register Office, Somerset House; the Greater London Record Office; the Hampshire Record Office; Houghton Library, Harvard University; the Archives of John Murray, Publishers; the Library of Congress; the Lilly Library at the University of Indiana; the New York Public Library for the Arents Collection; the Staffordshire Record Office; the Taylor Collection at Princeton University Library and the University of Illinois at Urbana-Champaign.

I am also grateful to Mr Arthur Bantoff, Chairman of the Barwick-in-Elmet Historical Society, Mrs Virginia Wright Durrett of the Spotsylvania Historical Association in Virginia and Mrs Martha C. Carter, Director of that Association, Mr David J. Coles, Reference Supervisor of the Florida Department of State's Division of Library and Information Services, Mr Robert H. Hirst, General Editor of the Mark Twain Project at the University of California at Berkeley, Mr James H. Hutson, Chief of the Manuscript Division in the Library of Congress, Miss Virginia Murray at John Murray, Publishers, Hilda A. Parks of the United Methodist Church's General Commission on Archives and History, Miss Alison Peacock, Methodist Church Archivist at John Rylands University Library, Manchester, Mr Christopher Sheppard, Sub-librarian of the Brotherton Collection, Leeds University Library, and officials of the Royal Literary Fund.

Finally, I would like to thank Deborah Blake, my editor at Duckworth, for her help and patience, Mr John Burlend for keeping me informed about the descendants of Rebecca and John Burlend, the late Mrs Vera Bradbury Munson for telling me of the life of the Old South, the late Captain Eugene Wild for guiding me round numerous Virginia plantations, the late Alan Haydock who produced my BBC dramatised features on Mrs Burlend and Mrs Trollope, Mrs Muriel Lass, who helped with my work on Cincinnati, the late Mr Louis Stark, for his help in understanding Rebecca Burlend's experiences in America, Dr Richard Carwardine of the University of Sheffield, who often gave me the benefit of his great knowledge of the growth of the anti-slavery movement in America, and Dr James Munson, who first suggested the idea to me and has been a constant help ever since.

Chronology

1851	Lady Emmeline Stuart Wortley's *Travels in the United States Etc.* published.
1852	Victoria Stuart Wortley's *A Young Traveller's Journal* published
	Uncle Tom's Cabin published in book form
	Frances Wright dies
1854	Lady Emmeline Stuart Wortley's book, &c., published
	Catherine Hopley arrives in America
1855	Lady Emmeline Stuart Wortley dies
1857	Second edition of Rebecca Burlend's book published as *The Wesleyan Emigrants*
1858	First transatlantic cable laid but soon ceases to work
1859	John Brown's raid at Harper's Ferry
1860	Catherine Hopley goes to Virginia
	Lincoln's election in November
	Secession begins in December
1861	Civil War begins
1862	Catherine Hopley goes to Florida and then returns to England
1863	Catherine Hopley's *Life in the South* and *Stonewall Jackson* published
	Frances Trollope dies
1865	End of Civil War
1866	Second transatlantic cable laid and works successfully
1867	The Second Reform Act
1871	Rebecca Burlend dies
1911	Catherine Hopley dies

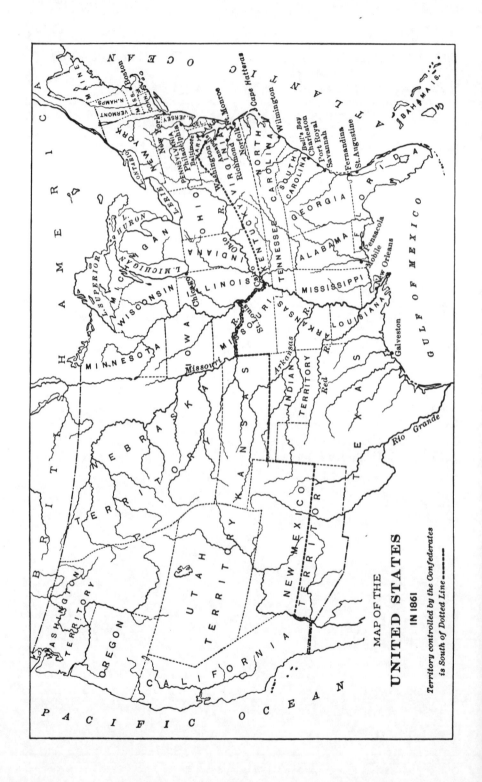

MAP OF THE
UNITED STATES
IN 1861

Territory controlled by the Confederates
is South of Dotted Line

Introduction

On 2 August 1837 the eighteen-year-old Queen Victoria, then only six weeks on the throne, invited the American envoy, Andrew Stevenson, and his wife to dinner at Buckingham Palace. The Queen had met very few Americans and, with the intolerance of youth, she was somewhat perplexed by Mrs Stevenson's behaviour, which differed from that of ladies bred up in court etiquette. After dinner the monarch drew the Marchioness of Salisbury aside and 'observed in a low voice on the American *tournure* and manners of Mrs Stevenson, and seemed much diverted with her'. The young Queen 'thought the Americans must be a very disagreeable people, and that it was impossible to see any of them without being reminded of the books ... lately written about them and which she was afraid were all true in the main points'.[1]

Queen Victoria, like so many of her subjects, had been influenced by reading, or reading about, 'lately written' books describing American travel. The most famous of these was Frances Trollope's *Domestic Manners of the Americans*, which had caused an immense sensation on both sides of the Atlantic when it was published in 1832. It remains the best remembered, or most notorious, of the English books on America. Even today, many people assume that Mrs Trollope's hostile work was typical of English attitudes. This is, in fact, far from the case. During the early nineteenth century hundreds of English travellers wrote books about their visits to America. The President of Harvard, Josiah Quincy, referred to these writers as 'Birds of Passage' – people who, like migrating birds, flew over America only to leave with a superficial view of what was wrong with the country.[2] Yet there were other writers who were full of praise for the new nation, and there were even some who were judicious enough to see both good and bad. Some travel books focused on specific aspects of American life and manners, ranging from geology to Methodism. But the books that influenced people in Britain were general accounts of American life and manners. Such books formed an image of the young Republic and its citizens in the British mind. They also created a conviction in American minds that all visitors from the Mother Country had come to make a profit out of critical books. Both views affected Anglo-American relations for decades to come, and traces of them can still be found today.

Travel books had long been one of the most popular forms of writing in England.[3] The end of the Napoleonic wars saw an upsurge in them as Englishmen flocked in their thousands to see recent battlefields or older attractions. However, there was another and more important consequence of the end of the conflict: British society turned in upon itself to consider domestic and constitutional questions. Such questions inevitably called up the example of America, the only country in the world that had a more democratic government than Britain. Those who favoured and those who opposed change in British government and society both pointed to America. Those who believed reform would bring unlimited blessings held up America as a beacon of liberty and progress. Those who saw reform as the first step in a descent to democratic doom pointed to America as the embodiment of mob rule, anarchy and hypocrisy. As John Stuart Mill observed in 1840, 'For many years, every book of travels in America' had been seen as 'a party pamphlet' or a work 'fallen among partisans, and ... pressed into the service of one party or the other'.[4]

In the half-century from Waterloo in 1815 to the end of the American Civil War in 1865, almost all of the ideas that still reverberate round the world were developed either in Britain or in America. America was in many ways a vast laboratory where the British gene of democracy could be studied or altered. Like many laboratories it was isolated, and that isolation only encouraged interest. In the days before the transatlantic cable, it took weeks for news to travel back and forth between Britain and America. English families wanted to know something of American life: many had relatives or friends who had gone there; many more talked about venturing across the sea to start a new life in the new world. They were thus avid for travel books about America. As we shall see, the husband of Rebecca Burlend – the first woman in this book – thought nothing of walking many miles just to read a letter describing American life so that he and his wife could decide whether to move there.

Families like the Burlends often lost contact once they were separated by a great ocean. The full force of this came home to me only recently when I came across a letter to my great-great-grandfather, George Wild. He left his native Cheshire at about the same time as the Burlends left Yorkshire and went to America where for many years he received no news of his family. Then, in 1847, a brother-in-law sent him a short letter with news that his mother had died, his father was 'poorly' and one of his sister's babies was 'likely for dying'. In these days of instant communication, few people receive so much bad news all at once. The transatlantic cable was finally secured in 1866, the year after the end of the Civil War. One year later Parliament reluctantly agreed to the Second Reform Act, which put Britain on an irreversible path towards democratic government. America was no longer the isolated laboratory of democracy. Travel writing, which flourishes best when a country is isolated and seems innocent, was a victim of this progress.

Most English travellers in this half-century were men, but most of those whom we remember were women. Many people today, whether in Britain or in America, can only recall one Englishman who wrote about America in the nineteenth century, Charles Dickens, but they also remember and read Mrs Trollope, Fanny Kemble and Harriet Martineau. Is this sheer co-incidence or did women writers have qualities men lacked? To some degree it was a matter of luck: Frances Trollope's book happened to appear at a crucial moment which meant that it was widely noticed. But there is more to it that this. Men tended to go to America for business or professional reasons: Charles Dickens to give public readings from his novels; Sir Charles Lyell to study geology; John Cassell to promote his publishing interests, and George Combe to stir up interest in the 'science' of phrenology. Women, usually free of the business commitments that restricted Victorian men, tended to have less specific tasks and could stay longer. Men may have learned more about commerce, science or politics, but women learned more about life. As one reviewer commented about one of the women in this book, 'the governess photographs much which a man would either not observe or would erroneously pass over as unworthy of narration'.[5]

Many of the women who wrote about their American travels set up house there. This brought them into contact with all segments of American society: neighbours, shop-keepers, servants and slaves. They learned about manners, food, houses, shopping, dress, education, language and transport, amusements, children, family life and religion. These were the topics they knew at home and about which they wrote when they went abroad. As Mrs Trollope observed, social behaviour 'and the minutiae of which it is composed, suits better the minute and lynx-like optics of the female'.[6] These were also the topics about which most people in England really wished to know. Indeed they are the things which most of us want to know about today. Those who want learned disquisitions about the Constitution of the state of Massachusetts or the water supply of New York City can find them in the travel books of Victorian men. Those who want to know about how people lived will find this in the books of Victorian women travellers. These women also paid great attention to the lives of their American sisters, in contrast to an author like Captain Basil Hall, who dealt with the position of American women in one part of one chapter of a three-volume work. Other male writers seemed only interested in deciding which American city boasted the most beautiful women. Many male authors did scant justice to women writers: the novelist Nathaniel Hawthorne referred in 1850 to 'the damned mob of scribbling women'.[7] Yet today anyone with an interest in the history of women could find few better sources than the travel books of these 'scribbling women'.

✳

For many years I have read widely in travel literature. To read the travel literature of another century is to go on two journeys: the first in place, the second in time. One starts as a tourist, completely dependent on a guide, but in time one becomes a traveller and begins to see for oneself. Yet even

the most experienced of travellers carries the luggage of his own life with
him. Like all travellers, I think my luggage is particularly useful. Having
lived half of my life in America and half in Britain, I think I have a good
understanding of the ways in which Britons and Americans react to one
another. When I was working my way through stacks of travel books, I
often found that other people had the same reactions as I had to both my
homes. Yet I did not just wish to pick authors with whom I agreed; I wanted
to pick authors who expressed many of those basic attitudes that are still
with us today. Nor did I wish to have a constant debate with dead authors
because their judgements or values are not considered politically, morally,
or linguistically correct by me or by the age in which I live. I wanted to find
women writers whose opinions and books were strong enough to stand on
their own. I soon found there were not too few but too many of them, and
my task was to select the best.

I finally selected five women, all of whom wrote vivid accounts of their
time in America. As I researched into their backgrounds, I quickly discovered that the colourfulness of their books derived from equally colourful
lives. They represented a cross-section of British society, yet each was able
to make her own mark on the world in which she lived; every one of them,
from a wealthy Duke's daughter to a pioneer in a log cabin, managed to
take a dominant role in an age that is thought to have been overwhelmingly
masculine. As my researches went on, I began to see that the story of these
five women said as much about Britain in the nineteenth century as about
the United States. Every one of them was able to do what she wanted with
her own life, albeit sometimes at considerable cost to herself and to others.
All were deeply influenced by their time in America: often the country's
impact on them determined the course of their lives. Few of the English
men who wrote about America were so affected. In most of their cases a
prominent and successful English man went to America, enjoyed his visit,
returned home, wrote his book and carried on with what he had been doing.
Of course thousands of ordinary English men did go to America and were
profoundly changed by the experience, but these were rarely the sort of
men who were able to produce books. These five women, on the other hand,
were changed and were able to write about that change. They demonstrate
better than any other writer the effect that America had on England, as
well as the effect England had on America. America was not just another
country: it was a product of England's past and a vision of her future.

Rebecca Burlend tells us in her straightforward Yorkshire manner what
it was like to settle on the frontier. People like her made America the
country it was and her history gives perspective to the more 'intellectual'
accounts that follow. She became part of the America that others visited,
analysed and described. Her story is the best introduction to actual
American life and that is why I have placed her first even though two of
the other women stepped ashore before her.

Frances Wright personifies the radical response to the vision of America.

From her girlhood she felt it to be her spiritual home and she sought to use her great wealth and even greater abilities to eradicate what she saw as the one great blot on its otherwise perfect society: slavery.

Frances Trollope, still the most famous, or infamous, English writer on America, exemplifies the critical reaction of an English conservative to the rough democratic manners of the frontier. Yet beneath the surface of her sarcasm there are many profound reflections that are as true today as they were 150 years ago.

Lady Emmeline Stuart Wortley's account differs from those of the other women in that she did not begin her book with the idea of promoting a cause. While she believed fervently in Anglo-American friendship, the main purpose, as well as achievement, of her book is to describe her extensive American travels which took her through more of the country than those of any other woman in this book. An added feature of her visit is that her twelve-year-old daughter, Victoria, also wrote a book about America which probably makes her the youngest author on the subject.

Finally we have Catherine Hopley's account of her life as a governess on Southern plantations in the first years of the Civil War. No other Englishwoman saw as much of the daily life on slave plantations and in Southern cities. Her departure from an America torn apart by war marks the end of an era whose beginnings were seen by Fanny Wright when she first arrived in New York in 1818. The end of the Civil War marked a great change in the English image of America and also the end of the great period of travel writing about the United States.

❋

These five were not the only Englishwomen of the period to write about America, but they are the best and, as a group, they represent all shades of opinion in Britain. Some may wonder why I have not included two of the best known: Harriet Martineau and Fanny Kemble. Harriet Martineau has been excluded because the sheer volume of her American writings would have made this book unmanageable and unbalanced: in addition to six volumes she wrote numerous articles. Her approach to America is, as Allan Nevins commented, highly 'philosophical'; as she herself pretentiously put it, her American books mark 'the highest point of the metaphysical period of her mind'.[8] Her views, as well as her approach to American society and government, are better contrasted with Tocqueville than with the women in this book. I did not include Fanny Kemble for the simple reason that I do not trust her. She used her writings about America to carry on a private war with her American husband. Her much-quoted *Journal of a Residence on a Georgia Plantation in 1838-1839* has roused much admiration and much criticism since its appearance, but for me it failed on two accounts. I wanted to write about authors whose books reflected both their immediate reactions and their extensive experiences.

Kemble's book about American slavery was based on fifteen weeks of plantation life and she waited until 1863 to publish it.

To exclude Fanny Kemble is hardly to exclude any discussion of slavery, for it intrigued all visitors to America and is always present in this book. Long before the appearance of Harriet Beecher Stowe's *Uncle Tom's Cabin* in 1852, English men and, even more, English women, were fascinated by slavery. The anti-slavery novel was not invented by the American Mrs Stowe in the 1850s but by the Englishwoman Mrs Trollope in the 1830s. Almost every Briton of the time would have agreed with the *Quarterly Review*'s description of the United States as 'a land which doggedly retains millions of human beings in the most degrading state of slavery in direct defiance of the opinion of the world'.[9] Almost all English travellers attacked slavery in theory, though some did not find it as objectionable when they saw it in practice. Women saw it from a different perspective than men. They were better able to compare the distinctions in treatment and behaviour between English servants and American slaves, a point which attracted few men. On the other hand, women were less aware of the financial aspects of the question. To radicals like Fanny Wright, slavery was the tragic disgrace of America, but no matter how horrible it was, it did not negate America's essential greatness. To conservatives like Mrs Trollope, slavery was the most glaring example of American hypocrisy in which greed overcame the principles of the Declaration of Independence.

One other aspect of American life annoyed almost all British visitors as well as many American writers such as Longfellow and Emerson. This was the loathsome habit of tobacco-spitting. In the early nineteenth century, tobacco, in whatever form, had yet to enter its brief period of respectability. In America the most devoted worshippers of the weed spent much of their energy in chewing the stuff. The chewer in due course had to dispose of the exhausted 'wad': he did so by spitting it out, accompanied by a stream of brown saliva, onto the earth or the floor, whether it was the floor of a house, of a steamboat or of the United States Senate. If he – and it was almost invariably a 'he' – was lucky, he would aim successfully at the nearest spittoon; if not, so be it. Women, with the long dresses that fashion prescribed, could scarcely avoid the horrible consequences. No single facet of American life was so firmly fixed in English minds as that of a nation of 'chewers and spitters'. I can just remember spittoons from the barbershops of my childhood in 1950s New Jersey, and only a few months ago I noted the latest in the long line of English commentators on America describing an encounter with a man in Arizona 'who said nothing, but could spit with deadly accuracy'.[10] Longfellow said that he would forgive all the hostility of English travel writers if they helped to eradicate this disgusting practice. Undoubtedly the constant criticism did help to reduce it if not to abolish it altogether.

Was Longfellow correct in thinking that English writers as a group were hostile? Of the women in this book only Mrs Trollope can be regarded as such and even she had many good things to say about America. But *any* criticism by English travellers was resented. An American friend explained this national sensitivity to Frances Wright in 1819:

> We are young, and therefore, perhaps despised: we are a people fast growing in strength and prosperity, and therefore perhaps envied. We have, doubtless, errors; I never yet saw a nation that had them not; but it is equally certain that we have many virtues. An enemy will see only the former; the friend will point to both.

The friend went on to say: 'Cutting words cut deep; and I fear that we are human enough to feel ourselves gradually estranged from a nation that was once our own, and for which we so long cherished an affection ... had not the *pen* yet more than the sword destroyed it.'[11]

English criticism was resented not so much because it was criticism but because it was English. Just as a growing adolescent resents parental criticism, so the young Republic was peculiarly sensitive to any fault-finding by the Mother Country. Fanny Kemble, herself something of an expert on divided families, wrote in 1864 that 'the two nations, mother and daughter though they be, can no more understand each other than I and my children can'.[12] Although she was being overly pessimistic, Americans were, and continue to be, quick to resent anything that was, or could be imagined to be, English superciliousness. Winston Churchill (the American novelist, not the great statesman), pointed to 'that smile of superiority which to us is the Englishman's most maddening trait'. Englishmen, for their part, disliked American boasting, and understandably still do. The one bad trait often led to the other, and both led to misunderstanding. 'We are two people, but we are of one family,' thundered *The Times* in 1846.[13] Because of this, any criticism had the added venom of a family quarrel. The wide circulation of books and periodicals, printed in one country and read in the other, only helped to raise tempers when criticisms were made. The press often selected the most unfavourable anecdotes from books by travellers to stir up emotions. The Americans were also sensitive because they felt not only that they were a new nation but that they were a nation with a particular message for the whole world. The English, on the other hand, paid little attention to criticisms by travellers from America or anywhere else. One English journal put it well: 'The English are a proud nation; the Americans, a vain one. The English care little what foreigners think or say of them; the Americans care a great deal.'[14]

We must also remember that this was an age of supreme confidence which often slid into conceit on both sides of the Atlantic. All the progress of the age seemed to come from, and to work for, the English and the Americans. Humility was not their greatest virtue. Richard Cobden, a paragon of Victorian pomposity, was horrified on a visit to Rome to discover that the Pope did not know the name of a minor official of the Anti-Corn Law League back in England. J.L. Motley, in his travels through Europe as an American diplomat and historian, was often astonished that Europeans seemed ignorant about the personalities of the American Senate. Often misunderstandings between Englishmen and Americans sprang from this shared propensity to provincialism, buttressed by invincible arrogance. Because they shared so much, they resented minor differences and minor criticisms. Tocqueville, with his usual incisiveness, saw this clearly: 'America gives the most perfect picture,' he wrote in his notebooks, 'for good and for ill, of the special character of the English race. The American is the Englishman left to himself.'[15]

The five women in this book illustrate, both by their books and by their lives, the continuous interplay between Britain and America. Today we can see that relations between the two countries were for the most part friendly. This was often obscured at the time because of what Alistair Cooke has rightly called the 'one constant' in Anglo-American relations: the 'hypersensitiveness of the Americans and the British to criticisms of each other, a three-hundred-year-old neurosis that was spawned when the first father saw his son sail away knowing he would not stay, and then was miffed to find that he did stay and – what is worse – prospered'.[16] Our reactions to the views and prejudices of these five women will be as conditioned by our own views and prejudices as were their impressions of America. Their reactions, as well as our reactions to them, are part of this continuing saga of the English-speaking peoples.

Oxford, 1993   Richard Mullen

Note

It is always difficult to give relative values of money between two countries. From the recognition of American independence in 1783 to 1830 the pound was rated at about $4.50. After 1830 and until the beginning of the Second World War, the exchange rate stood at $5 to the pound. This meant that each shilling was worth twenty-five cents. However, in an age when travellers had far fewer ways of transferring money than we have today, few travellers would have got that high an exchange rate.

To relate this in some way to the life of ordinary people it might be worth knowing that male industrial workers in Paterson, New Jersey earned $5 a week in 1828 while women earned $2.37. Power-loom workers in Manchester in 1834 earned 12s 7d a week. Prices varied throughout the period and America, in particular, had tremendous regional variations. Nevertheless it is still somewhat staggering to be told by Mrs Trollope that she could buy the best beef in Cincinnati in the late 1820s for four cents a pound, or less than one English penny.

1

The Settler: Rebecca Burlend

THE DECISION TO EMIGRATE

Rebecca Burlend, a Yorkshire farmer's wife, was but one of millions of Britons who left the shores of their homeland to settle in the New World. Unlike those nameless others whose struggles, failures and achievements are unrecorded in history, she left behind her a unique record. Her book, *A True Picture of Emigration*, brought her neither fame nor profit. This is unfortunate as it is both an adventure story of the first order and one of the best accounts of life on the American frontier. Because it was written to describe her own experiences, to present the facts and to serve as a guide for those who had decided to follow her, there is no hidden message. Yet few could read her book 150 years later without being moved at the experiences of this simple and quietly great woman.

The rapidly expanding extent and wealth of America were due to the efforts of pioneers like the Burlends. As we shall see, frontier life left little time or inclination for social niceties or elegant manners. The lack of these in many parts of America infuriated some English travellers, including Fanny Trollope. Yet it is only by reading about people like the Burlends that we can put such criticisms into proper perspective.

The story of this Yorkshire family is a record of the kind of life faced by the vast bulk of British emigrants to America in the early part of the nineteenth century. Emigration underwent various fluctuations in the first fifty years of the century and tended to rise or fall in response to economic conditions in the British Isles. In 1830, the year before the Burlends left, almost 57,000 people left Britain and Ireland for North America: the majority went to Canada. In 1850, two years after Rebecca's book appeared, the number had risen almost fivefold to over 280,000; of these, 223,000 went to the United States. The Burlends' story is to a large extent the story of America.

A True Picture of Emigration: or Fourteen Years in the Interior of North America; Being a Full and Impartial Account of the Various Difficulties and Ultimate Success of An English Family who Emigrated from Barwick-in-Elmet near Leeds, in the Year 1831 is a long title for a short book of some 150 pages.[1] It was written when Rebecca Burlend returned to England for a visit in 1846. She described her experiences to her eldest child, Edward, who had stayed in England when the family went to America. Edward, a schoolmaster, actually wrote the book, but the account was, as he himself tells us, 'delivered to him *viva voce* by his mother'. Every so often this otherwise perfectly straightforward and clear account is interrupted by a sprinkling of pretentious learning. But this is a small flaw in an otherwise delightful and well-written account.

The Burlends were a good example of a class that suffered severely after the Napoleonic wars. We are so accustomed to hear of the horrors of the manufacturing system, both real and exaggerated, that we often forget that this period was also a time of great hardship for farmers. The Burlends had a farm in the West Riding of Yorkshire, near Barwick-in-Elmet, a village four miles east of Leeds. It was and still is famous for its maypole. (The Barwick-in-Elmet maypole song has provided in our own day the signature tune for BBC Radio's long running drama series, *The Archers*.) Barwick, with a population under 200, was a farming village: over half the population were either farmers or farm-labourers. The Burlends seem to have been one of the oldest resident families: parish records show Burlends living there in the 1630s. They had followed the usual practice of tenant farmers and taken their land on a fourteen-year lease. When they took out their lease the price of wheat, as of all other cereals, was high due to the prosperity brought by the war. Within a few years, however, prices had plummeted and farmers faced hard times. Not surprisingly, as their lease drew to a close in 1831, Rebecca and John Burlend began to consider other ways of surviving, if not of prospering, as farmers. If they stayed in Barwick, he might have to give up the farm and become a labourer on another man's land. Yet with agriculture facing so many difficulties, it could well prove difficult for a man of his age to find even such a miserable job as that.

John and Rebecca were devout Wesleyan Methodists and shared a serious approach to life. When John first thought of going to America he was anxious to obtain proper information. Rebecca says that they had no wish to be like a poor fellow-countryman who was so totally ignorant of America when he arrived in New York that he simply asked the first person he met to point him in the direction of the frontier. John heard that a Yorkshire emigrant, Charles Bickerdike, who had gone to Illinois, had written some letters to a brother describing pioneer life. John walked miles to read these letters and must have liked what he read about life in Illinois, for by the end of August 1831 he, his wife and family were ready to leave their farm.

Rebecca Burlend was not a young woman when we consider the task she was about to undertake, the life expectancy of the early nineteenth century and the fact that she had endured eleven pregnancies. She was thirty-eight, and her husband about eleven years older. Behind them they left their two eldest children. Their seventeen-year-old son, Edward, was anxious to leave farm work to establish himself as a schoolmaster. He eventually became a teacher of 'classics, mathematics and other branches of science and literature' in a boarding school in the nearby village of Swillington.[2] Their eldest daughter, Mary, like the daughters of many other farmers, was already in domestic service. The other five children – John, nine, Hannah, eight, Sarah, three, Charlotte, one, and the infant, William – went with their parents. Behind them they left four others who had died in childhood. Years later Edward, the son who remained in England, wrote a novel, *Amy Thornton*, which contains a scene in which a girl looks at Barwick as she is leaving it. Rebecca Burlend also must have had a sad final look at her village before Barwick 'with all its associations, save the grey old [church] tower and the maypole, were hid from the travellers'.

None of the family had ever been further than forty miles from home, so the journey from Leeds to Liverpool to take ship was in itself an adventure. The trip was made by waggon and by that new phenomenon, the railway. When they arrived in Liverpool they found, as have so many other travellers, that life in ports (as today in airports) was quite expensive. Their small, dingy room cost them two shillings a day, not including a fire. Liverpool was building up a notorious reputation: the American novelist, Herman Melville, would write in 1849: 'Of all the seaports in the world, Liverpool perhaps most abounds in all the variety of land-sharks, land-rats and other vermin.' The problem was great enough to warrant Parliamentary investigation, and in time emigrant guide-books would warn people of the dangers they faced.[3]

The Burlends, however, had no guide as they sat in their cold room, and they began to lose the hope with which they had set out from their farm. Soon despair overwhelmed them at the 'throes of leaving England and all its endearments'. Rebecca recalled that 'even our children participated in our disquietude'. Her husband, 'who before had displayed nothing but hardihood, on this occasion had almost played the woman. After a deep silence I not unfrequently observed his eyes suffused with tears, which though unnoticed by him, fell in quick succession down his sunbrowned cheeks.' The family spent six days in their room, although John Burlend 'did not spend six hours of the time in the forgetfulness of sleep'.

After their six days of waiting the day dawned on which the ship was to set sail. Like many before and since, they were seized by panic. Since they had first mooted the idea in their Yorkshire farmhouse, John Burlend had been the driving force. It was Rebecca who had feared the unknown and hesitated at the thought of leaving her beloved England. Now he turned to his wife when only hours stood between them and a new life or disaster and cried, 'O Rebecca, I cannot do it, I cannot do it!' John Burlend did not fear so much for himself as for his family: 'Should anything befall me, what will become of you and my children on the stormy ocean, or in a strange land and among pathless woods. Bad as our prospects are in England we must go back!' Rebecca was nothing if not a truthful and forthright woman. She frankly admits to her readers that 'sentiments like these a few months ago would have been hailed with delight, and even then I must confess I felt a sort of inward satisfaction'. So they began to move their luggage back to the waggon with an air of 'mournful silence'. Yet even as they were lifting their meagre goods, Rebecca turned her thought to Him 'who sitteth above the water-floods' and reminded her husband that 'the Almighty is as able to preserve us and our children across the sea or in America as He is in England'. As a practical Yorkshirewoman she also reminded him that all their furniture had been sold. Her husband took heart and once again removed their luggage from the waggon and took it back to their quarters. The family spent the rest of the day buying food and cooking utensils for the voyage.

At four o'clock in the afternoon of 2 September 1831, John, Rebecca and their five children sailed out of Liverpool harbour and committed themselves 'to the care of Him "whom earth and seas are ready to obey" '. The Burlends were now steerage passengers on the *Home*, headed for New Orleans. They had chosen this port because it would enable them to sail up the Mississippi River with their large family and scant possessions to Illinois without the need to cross the mountains that separated their new home from the better-known eastern ports such as New York or Boston.

The great benefit of Rebecca Burlend's book lies in its detailed and straightforward account of the trials and adventures faced by so many of her countrymen. We do not turn to her for a commentary on American manners, or the lack thereof: for that we have Mrs Trollope. We do not look to her for the exotic adventures of the social reformer: for that we have Fanny Wright. The Yorkshirewoman's great strength lies in telling us what it was like to venture across the Atlantic and to clear the wilderness. Few other accounts give us such a first-hand account, an account which begins with the departure of the *Home*. Her crossing was worse than that faced by any of the other women in this book for she alone came as millions after her would come: in steerage.

Throughout her book, Rebecca makes it clear that she always considered herself an Englishwoman in America and not a new American. She was fervently patriotic about the land of her birth, which remained the land of her heart and loyalty. We must remember that she left England when she was thirty-eight and that she had lived there through some of the greatest days in English history, days which included Waterloo and the defeat of 'Boney'. We can picture her and her husband on the deck of their ship, like the couple in the famous painting by Ford Madox Brown, 'The Last of England', who gaze for the final time on the receding sight of their native soil. The Burlends were leaving behind not just their home but their two eldest children and the graves of the four they had lost. Rebecca, despite her sadness, had still been impressed by the magnificence of Liverpool's harbour with its 'unwieldy instruments of commerce crowded like forest trees on the sea further than the eye could reach'. A good wind carried the ship quickly down the Mersey, yet 'the eye with unwearied vigilance kept steadily fixed on the few eminences which remained visible, till they gradually waned into obscurity, and at last disappeared altogether'.

Rebecca Burlend admits that her readers 'may think me needlessly precise in naming this circumstance; but ... there were many on board who ... felt a gratification in gazing at the naked rocks that projected from the land that had given us birth'. When it was finally announced that England was no longer visible, 'there was not a person in the ship who would not have heartily responded Amen to the prayer, "God bless it" '. Rebecca was deeply moved at leaving all she had been 'wont to prize', and as the inappropriately named *Home* left English waters she gazed with envy at those ships headed towards the land she had left.

THE VOYAGE OUT

Rebecca Burlend would not have been such a fervent Methodist if she had not known that work was the best cure for depression. She went below deck to begin preparing a meal. Passengers in steerage provided their own food and did their own cooking with their own utensils. One fire sufficed for all steerage passengers. The Burlends had provided themselves with oatmeal, flour, bacon, biscuits, tea and coffee. They were a dignified couple and were appalled by their fellow steerage passengers who surrounded the single fire: 'A half-a-dozen sturdy rustics, as busy boiling, roasting, and frying as if their lives depended upon a single meal.' Rebecca had wished to preserve regular meal times, as such things were always important to her, but she soon found it best to cook whenever she could get a free spot at the fire. Nor was the actual cooking easy, for the continual rolling of the ship caused frequent burning either to the food or, more often, to the cook.

As the *Home* made her way through the Irish Sea and towards St George's Channel the sea turned unusually rough, even for those tempestuous waters. Soon all aboard were sick and deadened by fear as the 'huge foaming waves came dashing against the sides of the vessel, as if they had been let loose to destroy it'. 'Sometimes', she recalled, 'we appeared about to leave the waters, and become inhabitants of aerial regions; then again one might suppose the ship was instantaneously descending into the caverns of the deep, overwhelmed by the mass of waters which on all sides encompassed it.' She feared the *Home* would actually sink, for the storm 'carried all before it, and often laid our masts nearly level with the main; when suddenly regaining her upright position' the ship would right herself. Despite the activity of the crew, 'terror and dismay were on every hand'. The captain alone 'preserved his serenity; his orders were delivered in a loud but unfaultering [*sic*] tone; he might have been a divinity of the waters so dignified and majestic was his deportment'.

As the storm continued, the devout Rebecca noted that those 'who yesterday could not conclude a sentence without the usual flourish of an oath [were] now on their knees'. It was the worst night she had ever spent and she vividly recalled the creaking timbers and the moans of the passengers. Her own family crowded into a 'corner of the cabin, my husband at my right hand, which he often clasped in his, and our dear little children huddled around us, giving us their little hands to fondle over and caress'. She told those of her readers who were mothers, 'thou mayest in part conceive what my feelings were; but there are sensations', she added, 'which no description can embody; there are emotions which nothing but experience can explain'.

As the morning dawned the sleepless mass in steerage gazed up through the hazy glass cover which alone gave them a sight of the outer world. Suddenly the hatch was flung open and the fearful throng rushed round the captain. He told them simply, 'The danger is past.' The danger had indeed been severe as the storm had driven them off course and into the Bay of Biscay. The captain's assurance was repeated throughout the ship and Rebecca noted the effect the good news had on those hastily made acts of repentance:

> Forgotten or disregarded were all the pious vows which had been made the preceding night. 'They ate and they drank and they rose up to play'; but few could be seen in the attitude of praise. The storm had indeed abated; and, such is human nature, religion had vanished at the same time.

Fortunately, this was the only storm they encountered. The worse dangers during the rest of the voyage were illness and ever-present boredom. For her part Rebecca was never easily bored: there were five children to look after, meals to prepare, clothes to be washed and darned and, of course, her daily Bible reading. She also had a reflective side and, as befitted her generation, she was given to Romantic reveries. Thus, one evening, when the ship was in mid-Atlantic and she was alone on deck, she beheld the moon in its full glory rising over the horizon. To her it was an old friend, the same moon that had been part of her Yorkshire life. She tells her reader that her 'whole soul was overpowered with ecstasy. Bear with me, kind reader, bear with a woman's weakness, if I tell thee I looked upon her as an old companion, and addressed her as a bosom friend' who reminded Rebecca of the 'many delightful and happy hours I had spent under her auspicious beams in my native land'. She then turned her thoughts to the ship, the 'poor feeble bark' which 'a single wave could undo'. Lastly she turned to herself. 'The contrast', she said, 'was sickening; human pride could not bear it; I cast my eyes once more upon the moon, and returned into the cabin.'

Not everything was as inspiring as the moon or her own reflections. There were more mundane sights: her fellow passengers, for instance. After the voyage was half over the passengers began to get more restless: one can observe the same behaviour in an aeroplane on a transatlantic flight today. Gradually little groups began to emerge in the steerage as people sought to relieve the boredom, 'sometimes by cracking jokes at each other, sometimes by relating portions of their histories or celebrating the matchless heroism or strength of their kindred'. The Burlends did not join in any of these groups; undoubtedly they found some of the humour too racy. Also they did not wish to share in any common cooking arrangement as they were concerned to preserve their own supplies, perhaps recalling the biblical parable of the five wise virgins and their carefully guarded supply of oil. Rebecca admitted that they probably would have been happier if they had joined in the general companionship but they were too worried about what the future held for them.

Occasionally accidents relieved the tedium. Once Rebecca saved a stowaway from burning to death and on another occasion she spotted her nine-year-old son, John, fast asleep on the bowsprit, the spar which ran out from the ship's stem. The least movement could have plunged him into the ocean. Rebecca found her husband, who eased his way onto the sprit and rescued the still sleeping lad. Near the West Indies the *Home* came close to another ship, which rumour soon magnified into pirates, but the passengers were relieved to find, after several hours of suspense, that it was only another English vessel.*

The day after the incident with the suspected pirates, land was sighted and the voyagers raced onto the deck. The weather was excessively hot and a large sail-cloth was spread above the deck to give shade to the excited passengers. Within a few days they entered the mouth of the Mississippi and the *Home* hung a large lantern from its mast to let the pilot know that they needed his services to guide them into New Orleans harbour. The next morning the pilot was rowed out to the ship: it was 1 November 1831. They had left Liverpool on 2 September.

FROM NEW ORLEANS TO THE FRONTIER

The Burlends landed in New Orleans on a Sunday, and nothing more shocking to Yorkshire Methodists could be imagined than New Orleans on the Sabbath. The city, with its French and Spanish heritage, had few sabbatarian traditions, and Rebecca was outraged to find shops and stalls open for business. The noisy city appeared to be in the midst of a fair. She was especially struck with the inhabitants for 'their appearance was

---

* Their fear was well-founded for the waters of the Gulf of Mexico had a long tradition of piracy. In her rough draft of *Domestic Manners* Mrs Trollope wrote that her ship had been chased by pirates in December 1827, although the incident was omitted in the published version. Just over five months after the Burlends set sail in the *Home*, the *St George*, also sailing from Liverpool to New Orleans, was boarded by Spanish pirates near the coast of Cuba. Passengers and crew were robbed of valuables and navigation equipment. One Englishwoman who was emigrating to America has left an exciting account of the incident (C.R. King [ed.], *Victorian Lady on the Texas Frontier: The Journal of Anne Raney Coleman* (n.d.), pp. 55-8).

exceedingly peculiar, their complexions varying almost as much as their features; from the deep black of the flat-nosed negro to the sickly pale hue of the American shopman'. (In the early nineteenth century Englishmen said that Americans were pale while Americans claimed that the English all had rosy complexions.) Rebecca was also appalled at slavery when first she saw it in 'its grossest forms'. This is hardly surprising when we remember that Yorkshire had been the scene of some of the fiercest campaigns against slavery in the British Empire. Henry Brougham, one of Yorkshire's four MPs, had risen to his great influence by his oratory against slavery, and he was only following in the Yorkshire tradition of William Wilberforce. As followers of John Wesley, a strong opponent of slavery, the Burlends, along with other Nonconformists, would not have been any more sympathetic to America's 'peculiar institution' than they had been to slavery in Britain's own West Indies. Many Nonconformists, including Methodists, refused to use slave-grown products such as West Indian sugar, and even today it is claimed that in parts of Cornwall, where Methodism was strong, sugar consumption is markedly below that of the rest of England. Not surprisingly, then, Rebecca was horrified to see 'slaves linked together in chains, and driven about the streets like oxen under yoke', for the city acted as a 'clearing house' where slaves were bought and sold.* Rebecca, like so many other English settlers in the 1830s, had no desire to live in a state that tolerated slavery.

The Burlends had to wait in New Orleans until there was a steamboat going up the Mississippi to St Louis. The family now took stock of their money and found they had spent about £23 since leaving Yorkshire. This included their trip to Liverpool, their expensive stay there, their supplies and the cost of steerage passage for seven. They had spent the night waiting for the steamboat aboard the *Home* and it was with heavy hearts that they left their last link with England. The captain gave each of the children a small gift or 'token of approbation'. The Burlends were not sorry to leave New Orleans even though the journey to St Louis would mean a voyage of 1,300 miles made even longer by the need to stop frequently to collect wood for the steamboat's boilers. Rebecca was struck with the tropical beauty that she saw on the extensive plantations which fronted both sides of the great river. She found them 'exceedingly beautiful' and wrote that 'if anything could have made me forget that I was an unsettled exile, the scenery ... bordering this river must have done it'. Yet once again the ever-present reality of slave labour blighted even the beauty of the landscape.

She liked the steamboat much more than she had expected and expressed none of the criticisms that Mrs Trollope would frequently and bitterly make of them. Indeed, she tells us that because she helped various

---

* The American Census of 1830 showed that there were 2,009,031 slaves out of a total population of 12,866,020.

people on the boat she was presented with much free food. The Burlends naturally sought out information about Illinois from fellow passengers, and the answers to some small extent reassured the fearful travellers. Not everyone aboard the boat was so friendly. A crewman, knowing the family was going to settle in Illinois, assumed they had a good deal of money. During the night he 'came to the side of our berths and began to search under my pillow, so softly indeed as not to awake me'. When the man began to do the same with Mr Burlend he was surprised to find him awake. The Englishman disarmed him completely when he told him that he could get the black man 'anything he wanted'. 'Such an unexpected kindness', Rebecca recalled, 'was immediately understood, and the villain disappeared in a moment.'

It took twelve days to sail up the river to St Louis. Here the Burlends had little time to explore their second American city. Rebecca only noted their surprise at finding that so many of the dwellings were made of wood and not brick or stone. This is something that still surprises the English when they visit America. They now had to board yet another boat that would take them the final 120 miles up the Illinois River through the middle of the state to their final destination, Philips Ferry. Accommodation on their last boat was 'very inferior' and their apprehensions began to grow once more. One frosty midnight, in the middle of November, the boat stopped and the Burlends and their few meagre possessions were rowed ashore. They had arrived at their new home. When they reached the shore they could not find a single dwelling nor any sign of life. There was no one to ask. All they knew was that this was the spot to which 'Mr B.', the Yorkshire emigrant whose letters John Burlend had walked miles to read, had directed them. As the steamboat's lights disappeared into the darkness, it is easy to imagine the distress of the Burlend family. They were alone and lost in a strange, cold wilderness at midnight with no one to ask for help or even for directions. 'My husband and I looked at each other', Rebecca recalled, 'till we burst into tears, and our children observing our disquietude began to cry bitterly.' She wondered at such a reception after their 'long, painfully anxious and bereaving voyage'. 'In vain did we look around us hoping to see a light in some distant cabin.' A degree of confidence returned and the Yorkshirewoman added tersely, 'It was not, however, the time to weep.'

John Burlend set forth into the night to see what he could find. This, of course, only increased Rebecca's fears. What if her husband should be lost in the vast darkness? Looking back after fifteen years she tells us, 'When I survey this portion of my history, it looks more like fiction than reality.' She put the four eldest children down on one of the beds they had brought with them, made them as warm as she could and held the baby. She then 'knelt down on the bare ground, and committed myself and little ones to the Father of mercies, beseeching him "to be a lantern to my feet, a light unto my path, and to establish my goings" '. She rose from her prayers 'considerably comforted' in spirit although now alarmed by the sound of two dogs barking. The dogs' appearance, however, heralded the return of her husband with a stranger. John Burlend had found a cattle track which led him to a log cabin and soon the Burlends were happy to be in the rude shelter of the cabin of a family called Philips where at least the glowing embers of the fire gave some warmth and welcome.

The next morning, while John was examining the soil and enquiring into farming methods, Rebecca was asking questions about keeping house on the frontier. Her hostess was a small woman, 'exceedingly fond of smoking, as the Americans generally are, particularly the females'. Rebecca had been told much about American hospitality but she now found that it had its well defined boundaries, like all advertised virtues. Americans, she said, 'are exceedingly hospitable to gentlemen who may be making a tour, likewise amongst themselves as neighbours, but when they know a person really must trouble them, they appear to be aware they are conferring a favour, and expect an equivalent'. Part of this behaviour was no doubt due to the close margin of life as lived on the frontier. Generosity normally requires the means with which to be generous. Thus, when Mrs Philips told Mrs Burlend that she could have the water in which the Philips' cabbage had been boiled to feed her children, that may well have been all that she had to give. From her new acquaintances Rebecca learned 'the peculiarities of Illinois politeness'. Every man, no matter 'how long so ever the time since his small-clothes were new' was called 'Sir' while every woman was called 'Madam'. This sounded strange to her but she soon adapted herself to local practice. (Like most people, Rebecca defined 'English custom' according to her own time and background. The American use of 'Sir' and 'Ma'am' was, and remains today mainly in the Southern states, essentially a continuation of eighteenth-century use which was dying out in England in Rebecca's time. Dr Johnson remains its most frequently cited proponent.) One custom Rebecca did like was that by which people left the table as soon as they had finished a meal: to stay longer implied unsatisfied hunger.

Rebecca gives us a full description of the Philips' log cabin, which was typical of frontier life. There were only two rooms, although each measured about thirty to forty square yards. The rooms were divided by a log partition but the many crevices prevented real privacy. Under one room was a sort of cellar. In the summer one of the two doors was always left open to allow fresh air to enter as there were no windows. The Philips had gathered stones from their land and with clay as mortar they had made a chimney. This fire, at one end of the house, provided heat for both rooms. Although she called it a 'log house', the walls were actually constructed of 'layers of strong blocks of timber, roughly squared and notched into each other at the corners; the joints filled up with clay'. The walls were then covered with oak shingles which also made up the floor. Altogether Rebecca found that the structure did not equal an English cottage for comfort. (In

England the Burlends would most likely have had a much larger and more comfortable house which came with their rented land. Yet as tenant farmers in Yorkshire they had owned neither land nor house and any improvements they made only increased the value of their landlord's property.) The furniture in the cabin was very crude: a shelf secured to the wall served as a 'sideboard'. The candlestick was fashioned from an ear of Indian corn. Herbs and bacon hung from the roof and under the bed were several large pots of honey which the family used to sweeten their coffee. In the second room were two more beds and a hand-loom while in the cellar were tubs of lard and a store of home-grown tobacco, 'in appearance sufficient to serve an ordinary smoker his life'.

Within a few days John Burlend had located 'Mr B.' who sent over his pair of oxen to drag the Burlends' possessions to his own house. Here they were again shocked, for it was his letters describing Illinois as a land flowing with milk and honey that had encouraged them to emigrate. But, Rebecca assured her 'patient reader', Mr B.'s 'appearance would have led any one to suppose that he gathered his honey rather from thorns than flowers. He was verily as ragged as a sheep: too much so for decency to describe.' His home was not much better: it was 'more like the cell of a hermit ... than the cottage of an industrious peasant'. In her first night there she 'almost perished' from the cold. John heated a flat iron, wrapped it in flannel and put it next her feet to warm them. The fastidious Rebecca could scarcely be content to reside long in the slovenly hovel of a bachelor whose only pair of trousers were so badly torn that he feared venturing away from his farm.

The Burlends therefore decided to acquire their own land as quickly as possible. The public lands on the western frontier had been divided by the government into eighty-acre plots; each plot sold for $100 or $1.25 an acre. Anyone could buy plots although purchase could only be completed after basic improvements had been made to the property within a specified period. It was common to find restless men who would buy or even 'squat' on some land, make some improvements and then hand over their right to purchase for the value of the improvements. A Mr Oakes, hearing that there were some new settlers in the neighbourhood, came to sell John Burlend some venison at a halfpenny a pound. Oakes also told the Burlends he was anxious to move on and would let them take over his rights to his eighty-acre plot, along with his house, for $60. This came to £12 in the days when the exchange rate was about five dollars to the pound. In addition they paid $100 or £20 to the government to acquire absolute ownership or, to use a term they would have been used to, the freehold. This is something they would have had little if any likelihood of ever doing in Yorkshire. Oakes' land had some 400 sugar maple trees and the Burlends had also bought from him the equipment needed to tap them. Rebecca tells us that she thought maple sugar would soon replace cane sugar in America; the thought would have pleased her as sugar maple trees did not grow in those Southern states where sugar cane was harvested by slave labour. Oakes had also broken up the soil on about twelve acres of which three were already sown with wheat while the other nine were ready for oats or 'Indian corn' (maize) to be sown in the spring.

The Burlends moved into the cabin, which was similar to the Philips' dwelling. The only furniture they had consisted of two beds, two large boxes and a few cooking utensils. The food they had bought in England was gone and they had left only a few of the biscuits they had purchased in New Orleans. Their supply of money was almost exhausted after the payment to Oakes and they were lucky to be able to buy a bushel of ground Indian maize or corn-meal. They disliked the taste of it but it was the cheapest food to be had. They had no oven, no yeast and no flour, so Rebecca could not bake bread. She therefore followed frontier practice and mixed some of the meal with water, heating it in a frying pan over the fire. They were able to buy some milk from a neighbour but, because of the intense cold, it arrived in frozen lumps. Fortunately they still had some of the venison they had bought from Oakes. It was a difficult time to move into a new house and there was little that John Burlend could do in mid-winter save cut wood for the fire. He spent more of their diminishing capital in acquiring a few animals: a cow and a calf cost \$14 (£2 16s); two pigs and a young mare cost \$20 (£4). Rebecca also acquired a 'skellit', a slender iron dish which, when covered with hot ashes in the fireplace, formed a make-shift oven.

When Rebecca later looked back on this period she contrasted the food of the English peasantry with that of Illinois pioneers. She was somewhat surprised that Illinois farmers had only three meals a day. Almost all their meals featured bread, butter, bacon and coffee although settlers, unlike English farmers living in or near villages with their butcher's shops, had no fresh meat. However the farmers did have their own livestock which they salted after killing. At times they would distribute portions of this meat among their neighbours, knowing that in due course others would share their supply with them. Chickens and turkeys provided some occasional relief from the monotony. As so often with the nineteenth-century diet, there seems to have been a dearth of vegetables and this undoubtedly contributed to the frequent illnesses so prevalent on the frontier. Indeed, it is hardly surprising that the whole Burlend family soon came down with a disease known as the 'Illinois mange'. Their bodies became covered with little spots and they all suffered from intolerable itching. Worse still, they had to spend part of their money, when they had only five dollars left, to buy sulphur to cure the complaint.

THE FIRST YEAR ON THE FRONTIER

The family was now faced with the problem of getting through the winter with sufficient food not only for themselves but for their new stock of animals. They soon learned that Indian corn was a most useful product. As we have seen, they shared the normal English dislike of it although Rebecca did admit that 'nothing can be more beautiful than a field of Indian corn in full blossom, and perhaps nothing in nature displays the munificence of Providence more strikingly than this matchless plant'. In England and in Europe in general, there was a strong repugnance to the idea of eating maize. Thus, when the potato famine broke out in 1845, the Irish resisted attempts by the London government to substitute maize for the blight-striken potatoes which made up the bulk of their diet. To this day, anyone examining the papers of Sir Robert Peel in the British Library will find maize seed mixed in with the Prime Minister's correspondence for the anxious years of 1845 and 1846. Several concerned Americans had sent him the seeds to try to alleviate the distress.

The Burlends overcame their prejudice and cut down part of the field of maize for their own use, letting their animals feed off the uncut remains. They killed their two pigs to provide a supply of meat and lard and as a way to avoid using up their slender stock of maize as animal feed. John Burlend also used the winter months to make some furniture: he constructed a stool for himself and his wife and he squared a long log for the children to sit on in front of the fire. He formed a table out of a tree stump by nailing some planks to the top. As they had no candles they put some lard in a saucer with a lighted rag as a wick: this was 'troublesome' because the rag often fell into the saucer. They also lost several saucers because of the heat. This was 'much to be regretted' because crockery of any sort was quite valuable. The family was also in desperate need of soap: here again the pigs provided the answer. Rebecca first took ashes which, by frequent burnings and then boilings, were reduced to potash. The difficulty was that this solution was so caustic that it could take the skin off her fingers in a minute. Then to the potash she added all the waste bits and entrails of the slaughtered pigs and from this formed a substance which, however offensive in odour, was still soap.

In addition to disease and dirt there was the cold. The Burlends had never known cold as severe as that which they experienced during their first winter on the frontier. John was kept busy cutting enough wood just to keep the fire going round the clock. For two or three months every liquid was frozen, even the milk, as soon as it left the cow's udder. This made it impossible to separate out the cream in order to churn butter. But one of the most attractive aspects of Rebecca Burlend's character was her ability to see some good amidst the bad. Thus, although the nights were 'inexpressibly cold' they were also 'poetically fine'. 'The sky', she wrote, 'is almost invariably clear, and the stars shine with a brilliancy entirely unknown in the humid atmosphere of England.' She would often 'stand at the door of our cabin, admiring their lustre and listening to the wolves, whose howlings, among the leafless woods ... are almost unceasing'.

Rebecca's poetic nature was of great benefit to her and she was fortunate to be able to take such comfort from her wild surroundings. She had few neighbours; the nearest was half a mile away. The closest shop was several miles distant and it was there that they would barter some of their crops once they had harvested the wheat and tapped the maple sugar. An even greater trial was the fact that the only church was five miles distant. For such a devout family this was a sore trial, yet every Sabbath was scrupulously observed with careful Bible reading and meditation and, of course, an absence of manual labour.

As the Burlends' first American winter drew to its close, Rebecca admits they much regretted their move. Here they were, in a strange land, with scarcely any money and nearly frozen with the cold. They were even deprived of tea, while the small supply of coffee had to be parcelled out sparingly and could only be made after they had thawed the water. John found that the lack of a rifle severely restricted his hunting although he did manage to trap some quail and rabbits. He also caught what he took to be a turkey, and his wife and children, rejoicing in the prospect of an alteration in their monotonous diet, were about to feast off his catch when the fortunate appearance of a neighbour kept them from devouring a buzzard! As always there was wood to chop: any extra was kept for fencing.

Like most people, the family's hopes revived with the coming of spring and the prospect of actually beginning to farm. Yet Rebecca warns us in a philosophical aside: 'Man's career in prospective is always brilliant; and it is providentially ordered that it should be so. Could we have foreseen our destiny, the prospect would have thrown us into despair.'

Rebecca's main task was to tap the maple trees to extract their sugar. By her hard work they got over three hundredweight of sugar plus a barrel of molasses. They sold most of the sugar at the shop and with the credit they earned (at seven cents a pound) they bought much-needed maize seed, flour, coffee and some hoes. As Rebecca's son, Edward, added when writing down her account: '*Labor omnia vincit* was our motto.'

But if work did conquer everything in general, it still left one overwhelming problem: how was John to prepare the soil when he had no plough? Even if he had one, the mare was about to foal and he dared not risk her precarious life. So Rebecca, John and their nine-year-old son set to work and within three weeks they had tilled and sown forty acres, using only the hoes that had been meant for weeding. She tells us that they would have done even more but for the extremely severe weather, with its frequent and violent rainstorms. They were also attacked by swarms of mosquitos. Many a night Rebecca could not sleep as they invaded the house and she had to keep them off her face by waving a handkerchief. At times these insects grew so troublesome that the Burlends built a large fire near the door of the house. On this they could place enough green leaves to create a smoke-screen to keep the pests away.

In addition to sowing the already cleared land, the Burlends had to work hard to clear the remaining virgin fields. Having chopped down the trees they then had to cope with the stumps: some were left to rot while others were burnt out. The wood was set aside for next winter's fires and for fence rails. In the midst of all this work their mare died while foaling, but fortunately her offspring survived. As June approached the family found themselves out of money. They were not yet able to harvest a crop but were lucky because they could get credit from the local shop to supply their wants. For under a dollar's credit they were able to get enough flour to feed the family for six weeks. Nevertheless, even such a small debt was a trial for the thrifty and proud Burlends.

By the end of June the settlers could harvest their first crop of wheat. But, like everything else on the frontier, this presented a problem. They had no sickles. Again they were lucky, at least for a while, because 'Mr B.' came to their rescue with the loan of two. Although these were not very sharp they were able to give John Burlend a severe cut to his knee when he stumbled while carrying them home. It was all poor Rebecca could do to get him back: he bled profusely before fainting. The next day the wound got much worse and a severe fever set in, accompanied by rapid swelling. This was, perhaps, their greatest crisis yet. 'My situation requires no comment: I could not but perceive I was likely to lose my dearest earthly friend, and with him all visible means of supporting myself, or maintaining my family. I was almost driven to frenzy.' Despair 'began to lay hold of me with his iron sinews: I longed to exchange situations with my husband; there was no one near to assist or encourage me.' Only the eldest child understood what was happening and 'the poor boy went up to his father's bed, and with affectionate and child-like simplicity said, "Don't die, father, don't die." ' When the knee had swollen to an alarming degree Rebecca fomented the swelling with a warm poultice and this produced sweating: the crisis of the illness passed and the inflammation subsided. His leg at last began to heal.

Rebecca now had a new burst of hope, but as her husband was still too weak to work she had to take his place. With her son she went into the fields although it was so hot that she was 'almost melted'. She and the boy, with their two borrowed sickles, harvested the wheat by themselves. Of course they had no waggons or horses to carry the crop away from the heat of the sun. So she and young John gathered the corn into sheaves and then laid a few across two boards: by this method they were able to carry the wheat indoors. By this time John Burlend could hobble out of doors on a crutch to give instructions about stacking. Between them Rebecca and her son harvested and stacked three acres of wheat: it was an incredible feat for a woman close to forty and a boy under ten. For her part, Rebecca's health had improved in America. The drier climate seemed to relieve her of the asthma she had suffered in England. In Illinois the climate tended to be more extreme, whether hot or cold, but at least the greater heat did allow them to cultivate certain crops that would not grow as quickly, if at all, in England. They were even able to grow enough tobacco for their own use. This they could never have done back in England where both the climate and, although Rebecca does not say so, the law forbade growing the crop.

Harvesting the wheat was not enough. They now had to winnow it by hand in order to separate out the small weed called 'cheat' which was intermingled with it. Their three acres produced about eighty bushels, but a quarter of this was ruined by the 'cheat'. Of the good wheat they were able to sell only about fifty bushels at fifty cents (2s) a bushel to the local shop. With the $25 they had earned – in credit, not cash – they were able to settle their debt. Out of the balance they had to buy new shoes for all the family: as goods were so expensive, they were forced to spend about a fifth of their whole crop, about five dollars, just on these. They still had enough to buy a plough and two milking bowls. They also bought some flour and coffee at four pounds for a dollar: with these purchases the profits from their first American wheat were almost exhausted.

The Burlends now had only a few dollars left and had to pass several weeks without meat. They managed to barter one of their china teacups for a few chickens. They wanted to keep some money aside to buy some pigs but by the autumn they were faced with the need to sow next year's wheat. Although they now had a plough they still had no horses for it. They asked a neighbour if they could use his team in return for one-fifth of the crop. The neighbour refused and this, as well as several other stories, calls into question the legends of frontier neighbourliness.* Fortunately, however, the unhelpful neighbour spotted John Burlend's English pocketwatch and offered to do the ploughing himself in return for the watch. This neighbour also sold him three pigs for a dollar each, and within a month careful feeding had fattened them to about 140 pounds each. The three dollars had, therefore, been wisely spent. In addition to the bacon and other meat the pigs provided, the family had a good crop of potatoes with which to face its second Illinois winter.

The beauties of nature provided some solace in the midst of their constant struggles. Rebecca Burlend was a keen observer of the differences in animal life between England and America, and the summer months now gave her some opportunity to look about her. There were so many animals

* This un-named neighbour personified in his unhelpfulness one of the characteristics of the 'Pike characters', stereotyped frontiersmen said to originate in Pike County, ironically, the county where the Burlends settled. No one was sure in which state the fictional Pike County was located – Illinois, Missouri, Arkansas or Texas. The writer and poet, Bayard Taylor, described the type in his *At Home and Abroad*, published in 1860, as 'the Anglo Saxon relapsed into semi-barbarism'. John Hay's *Pike County Ballads*, which were published in 1871, were set in the Illinois county and personified the character in one Jim Bludso.

in America that she had never seen in England or, in the case of birds, heard. While she missed cuckoos and robins she enjoyed the great variety of American bird life: the jays, humming-birds, whip-poor-wills and wild parrots. She found the butterflies more colourful and the snakes more plentiful, and when she first saw a 'fire-fly' or 'glow-worm' she thought it portended some great catastrophe. What the fire-flies, along with the croaking of the bull-frogs at night, did do was to remind her of the work at hand when daylight returned.

SETTLER LIFE

The first Sunday in November was the first anniversary of their landing in America: it was a time for reflection, and Rebecca tells us that 'this was one of the gloomy days in our history'. A large share of the gloom was due to the fact that the children had fewer warm clothes with which to face the winter than when they first arrived. Indeed, the lack of clothes prevented them from attending chapel and for such loyal Methodists this was a great trial. It was natural that their thoughts should turn to the home they had left and to those lines by Cowper:

> When I think of my own native land,
> In a moment I seem to be there;
> But alas! Recollection at hand
> Soon hurries me back to despair.

After wallowing awhile in their poetic grief the Burlends reflected that in most ways their situation had improved. They had four more acres of wheat sown than in the previous year. Their cattle had increased in number and size. They had a plough even if they had no team to pull it. Both John and Rebecca had managed to overcome bouts of 'the ague', the prevalent fever that attacked new settlers, normally in the autumn. This was thought to be caused by the damp arising from a forested countryside teeming with the rotting vegetation of millennia. Finally, they owned their own land.

Once again the Burlends now faced several months of struggling against the cold. As in their first winter, they found that there was little they could do except to feed the cattle, chop firewood and split rails. They soon had another chance to increase their herd when a neighbour offered to sell them a cow and two steers, but they had no money and the deal could only be completed if the owner would wait for payment. He agreed but then charged them the frontier interest rate of 25 per cent. (By the time Rebecca's book appeared the rate had fallen to 12 per cent.) The Burlends agreed to pay $30 (£6) for the cattle plus the interest but within a few days they were served with a writ threatening seizure of all their cattle as well as their land in order to meet the debt. Once again they turned to 'Mr B.' for help. John walked to see his friend to ask for a second loan with which to pay off their debt but returned home empty-handed: he broke the news to Rebecca that 'Mr B.' could not help them. She was so distressed that, pious as she was, she could not pray. The next morning they heard a knock at the door. It was 'Mr B.' who had not been able to sleep and now loaned them the $30. With the money in hand they were able to meet the demand of their unscrupulous neighbour.

Once again the Burlends turned with renewed hope to their work, anxious to clear their debt to 'Mr B.'. With much hard work they were able to obtain 350 pounds of sugar from their maple trees. By using part of their profit from this they were able to repay 'Mr B.' $15 in cash. To pay off the balance John Burlend agreed to work five days each year for his friend until the other $15 had been paid off. The cash obtained for about forty pounds of sugar (if they had taken credit from the shop they would have got more) allowed them to buy a sow and her litter. Their lifestock now consisted of two milch cows, two steers ready to be yoked to the plough, one heifer, one calf, the young mare and the pigs.

There was, however, no end to the difficulties of frontier life as epito-mised in the struggles of the Burlends. They were next faced with the problem of sowing their Indian corn because their steers were still too young to be yoked to the plough. They were therefore delighted to look out one morning to see a neighbour busy ploughing the field for them. This unasked-for help enabled them to plant twelve acres of maize. It is somewhat surprising that it was only now, well over a year after their arrival in Illinois, that they started a vegetable garden.

As the principal purpose of Rebecca Burlend's book was to recount the family's experiences for other English families who were considering emigrating, she never neglected an opportunity to give necessary advice. In so doing she gives us insights into frontier life found nowhere else. Thus she tells her readers that there were few items that her husband missed more than 'a good Yorkshire scythe-stone and a wrag wetstone' to sharpen his scythes. Because he could not sharpen his tools it took them much longer to harvest the corn, which was difficult enough at the best of times. One day during the harvest she was startled by the appearance of a full-grown rattlesnake. Although horrified she preserved enough presence of mind to strike it several times on the head until it was dead. She knew that they travelled in pairs so she waited till the mate came, when she dispatched it in like manner. Her children proudly carried the remains home as a sign of their mother's prowess.

The following day there was an even greater scare and a timely reminder of the narrow margin of survival allowed frontier settlers. One of the little girls was playing too near one of the outdoor fires and her clothes caught light. The terrified child ran into the fields of wheat which had been cut and bound into sheaves, awaiting winnowing. Fortunately her father got to her quickly enough to put out the flames but not before she had set the wheatfields alight. The Burlends were now faced with absolute disaster:

they saw their whole wheat crop, dry and ready for harvesting, going up in flames. At first they tried pouring water on the fire but they could not get enough to do any good. Then they decided to create a divide between the burning wheat and that yet untouched by the flames. They dragged the sheaves of wheat away and those they could not remove quickly enough they threw onto the fire. Their divide left a space where the fire could die out.

The Burlends lost about an acre of wheat but, by their prompt action, preserved the hard-won produce of some seven acres. But the event was in its way a milestone. Although Rebecca admits that as soon as they were assured the fire was really out they 'sat down and wept', their tears were 'if I may use the expression, tears of thanksgiving'. 'We called to mind the various difficulties through which we had successfully struggled and we looked upon this as another pledge of ultimate success. We may indeed date the commencement of a moderately comfortable existence from this occurrence.' The Burlends managed to harvest a wheat crop of about 220 bushels, of which only forty were unsaleable because of the 'cheat'. Our admiration for Rebecca's constancy and courage during the long harvest is only increased when we learn that in September she was safely delivered of twins. Even so, the perilous nature of frontier life meant that had they not put out the fire they could have been ruined.

Now, as things began to improve and as the family settled into a routine of life, they began to make plans about ploughing their own land with their own team of steers. They could now buy the harnesses necessary to yoke them properly. They were also able to buy some salt as well as some clothing from the proceeds of their wheat. Their herd increased as cows tended to calf sooner in Illinois than in Yorkshire, a fact which Rebecca attributes both to the climate and to the custom of allowing the herd to range at large in the summer. As things began to improve, the Burlends decided on acquiring more land. One of their neighbours was a Mr Paddock, of whom Rebecca had a low opinion: 'Like many persons in Illinois, this individual wanted industry, as he rarely worked more than half of his time.' Mr Paddock wanted to sell the rights to his land as he had no desire to finish the necessary improvements required by law before purchase could be completed. Paddock was evidently one of those restless frontiersmen who moved from one unimproved plot to another, collecting and then selling their options. He offered John Burlend the rights to his land, which lay next to the Burlends' farm, for $50. The price included what work he had done, a house and some fourteen or fifteen acres already broken up for sowing. Paddock accepted John Burlend's offer of 'a good cow, a heifer and seventy bushels of wheat'.

There was, however, a suspicious character in the district, one Mr Carr, who had a claim to the land. In order to prevent him from interfering with their rights, the redoubtable Rebecca and some of the children moved into Paddock's house. Eventually Carr laid siege to the house and was able to force his way inside, but he was unable to eject Rebecca: brave as ever, she stood her ground by retreating to one room with her children and her Bible. Rebecca was not simply maintaining their rights but was engaged in a 'delaying tactic', for John was secretly on his way to the Land Office at Quincy, some fifty miles away. Carr and his family took possession of the other room and Rebecca was left 'exposed to the jeers and taunts of a malicious man who left no means untried, short of personal violence, to expel me from the house'. On the third day of her imprisonment, which happened to be a Sunday, Rebecca settled down to read her Bible. This infuriated Carr who roared that he 'would be both rid of me and my cursed religion before long'. Some of Carr's friends now arrived to help him, but his wife checked their vociferous attacks. Otherwise, Rebecca admitted, 'I should have been obliged to withdraw'. It was now time for Rebecca's reinforcements to act: some of her friends came to comfort her and she was able to speak to them through a hole in the wall which passed for a window. Her male friends forced an entry into the house for their wives and in time the Burlend forces celebrated their victory with a *Te Deum*, or at least a Bible service. Carr, non-plussed till then, found this too much and 'entirely left the premises'. Victory was theirs and it was only confirmed when John returned with the news that Carr's claims were based on lies. Rebecca warned future settlers: 'The peculiarity of the American law respecting the purchase of land, although framed originally with the view of assisting new settlers, is not infrequently a source of strife.' Two years later the Burlends had another legal dispute, this time over a water mill.

Rebecca Burlend's recollections differ from those of the better-educated women we shall be considering in that she makes few general observations. However, she does seek to explain the causes of some of these legal wrangles. She traces them to the settlers' conditions of life, for

> ignorance is a predominating feature in their character, indeed it can hardly be otherwise; not that they are less gifted than the Europeans from whom they have originated, but because their opportunities for cultivating their minds are so limited; besides, their pursuits and manner of living do not require much intellectual training; a really learned man would be in solitude amongst them.

Of course, the same might well have been said of many Yorkshire tenant farmers. Her experience of American life was, after all, very limited, while her generalisations applied to 'inhabitants of the western world'. Other than her time in Illinois, her travels in America were limited to her trip up the Mississippi and Illinois Rivers and her journey to New York in 1846 en route for England. She is neither the first nor the last writer to base a pound of generalisation on an ounce of experience.

Set against Rebecca's criticisms of American land law are her praises of the American government for providing public lands to maintain education. It should be recalled that there was as yet no state educational system in England. (One recent attempt by a Tory government to introduce one had been destroyed by the fierce hostility of English Nonconformists who hated the thought of Anglican religious instruction in state schools. In England, Exchequer grants were paid to elementary schools, the bulk of which were established by the Church of England.) The Americans, freed of the mother country's religious rivalries to a considerable degree, established a superb system of secular state education, at least on paper. In practice there was great trouble in securing teachers, even when the only requirement was an ability to spell. Not surprisingly, teaching was a good way to begin on the frontier. Stephen A. Douglas, who arrived in Illinois exactly two years after the Burlends, came with only five dollars which he supplemented by selling a few books. He started by teaching and within twenty-five years was a wealthy man, a Senator and perhaps the most controversial politician in America.[4]

Mrs Burlend and her schoolmaster son in Yorkshire, who put her recollections down on paper, had no reason to doubt the age-old connexion between Christianity and education. Their attitude was part of the average Victorian's approach to learning. Naturally, therefore, her account of American education led her to a discussion of American religion. Her views are of interest because the other Englishwomen whose writings on America we shall be looking at were either Anglicans like Mrs Trollope or agnostics such as Fanny Wright. Rebecca Burlend was the only Nonconformist and her account is therefore an important and somewhat rare record, especially given the importance of Nonconformist emigration to America.[5]

Rebecca had been a Wesleyan Methodist for almost twenty years before leaving England and, as we have seen, was genuinely distressed at not finding a Methodist chapel near her when she arrived in Illinois. When eventually a Methodist 'Class Meeting' was established in a house some two miles away Rebecca attended but found that the gathering was 'by no means congenial to my views and sentiments'. As religion had spread westwards it shed many of the restraints originally brought over from England. In this case the Class Meeting began with the whole congregation joining hands and dancing round the leader who then gave an extemporaneous prayer 'not indeed in language or style the best selected'. After this the congregation would wait until someone shrieked, 'I feel it.' This would often lead to convulsions and other manifestations of religious ecstasy. This behaviour was not exactly what John Wesley had intended and it did not please Rebecca, who ceased attending. Wesleyan worship in England, which was still based largely on the Prayer Book, had little if anything in common with such carryings-on. Although Rebecca found the American devotion to 'liberty' praiseworthy in many ways, she felt it had gone too far, especially in religion. In particular she objected to the continuous growth of new sects despite the fact that her own denomination was the product of a schism from the Church of England. Just as Mrs Trollope would denounce 'camp meetings' in Ohio, so Rebecca disliked the same meetings' 'very irregular manner'. She also found that many of the frontier preachers had far too little religion.

When the Burlends' neighbour, Charles Bickerdike – 'Mr B.' – died, the brother to whom he had written about the glories of Illinois frontier life came to America to see if he could claim any part of his brother's estate. The Burlends proudly showed the family's achievements to their fellow Yorkshireman. The house now had new furniture to replace the primitive pieces John had made during their first winter. Rebecca tells us that while their home was no better than most cottages in England, there was one great difference: they owned their home. Their stock of animals had grown to twenty horned cattle and seven horses, as well as pigs, sheep and chickens. They now owned 360 acres, half of which was under cultivation. Indeed, they had two other small farms which they let to tenant farmers at a dollar an acre. They had come full circle and were landlords with tenants of their own.

Rebecca was also proud that a dozen years after they had arrived they were among the most prosperous of the farmers in the district, an achievement she attributes mainly to their own unremitting hard work. But the Burlends had not been the only people at work in Illinois. When they arrived in the 1830s the area had been a wilderness, but by the 1840s small villages had sprung up and they were no longer so cut off from many of the comforts of life. By the late 1840s improved farms of from 60 to 150 acres, fenced in, cultivated and with a dwelling, were selling at 15s to 40s an acre.[6] At 30s an acre the Burlends' 180 acres of cultivated land were worth £270. The undeveloped land, cattle and standing crops would have increased their wealth. Theirs was a considerable achievement.

A BRIEF VISIT TO ENGLAND

'Mr B.'s brother decided to go back to England to bring his family out to Illinois to occupy the land he had inherited. For Rebecca this was a marvellous opportunity to return 'home', even if only for a short visit. She left Illinois on 20 April 1846 and arrived in England on 19 June, fifteen years after her original departure. While back in Yorkshire she told her tale and with her eldest son put it down in writing. Edward was faithful to his mother's story and if he occasionally paraded his learning, he had worked hard to obtain it. The book was published in 1848 and had a considerable influence on the growing tide of emigration to North America which, since the early 1830s, had been increasingly to the United States. In Leeds alone, some 2,000 copies were sold, and in 1856 Edward Burlend brought out a second edition with a somewhat expanded title: *Wesleyan*

Christianity Tested and Exemplified being an Authentic Narrative of Striking Events in the History of a Wesleyan Family of Yorkshire Emigrants in the Back Woods of America.

At the end of her book Rebecca Burlend made an impassioned plea to those wanting to emigrate to consider her account and then, after careful thought, to decide. She does not presume to tell readers which way to choose, perhaps because in her own mind she had never decided whether her course had been the correct one. In a somewhat defensive tone she rejects with scorn one argument against emigration: to leave England, she insisted, was not to cease to love her. How, Rebecca asks, could such a small island continue to feed and employ a population that was expanding as rapidly as England's without emigration? Secondly, English manufacturing and exports depended on the American market and English emigrants to America were supporting their mother country by developing that market. Emigration had its strongest appeal to people like the Burlends who wanted to improve their lives and that of their families. Another Englishwoman, writing at about the same time as Rebecca Burlend's book appeared, put it quite tersely: 'If you are possessed of rank and money, stay in England; no where are there advantages so available. If you have neither rank nor money get away as fast as possible.' [7]

✻

After three months in England Rebecca returned to America. With her came her daughter Mary and her family and one or two others from Barwick. Edward remained in England. In 1855 he continued his new career as a writer with *A Catechism of English History* and three years later produced a volume of poems, *Village Rhymes*. In 1862 he published a novel, *Amy Thornton; or, the Curate's Daughter*, a typical mid-Victorian story filled with consumption, orphans, the workhouse, contested wills and charges of illegitimacy. The story is mainly set in Barwick and features an uncle who emigrates to America. There are scenes set in Charleston, South Carolina, presumably because Charleston's importance during the American Civil War made it a familiar as well as an exotic city.

Back in Illinois Rebecca was pleased that in due course three or four other families left Barwick to join what had become a settlement with religious overtones. At last she was able to see the establishment of the type of Methodism she favoured. Her family continued to prosper and towards the end of their lives both John and Rebecca went to live with their eldest daughter who had settled near them. Rebecca spent her final years rocking in front of the fire and smoking her pipe: a grandson, who preserved her favourite chair, observed that its rockers were worn out by her continuous moves to get close enough to the fire to re-light her pipe. It was many years since she had spent her first night in a log cabin where she had observed that the Americans were fond of smoking, 'particularly the females'. One grandchild remembered Rebecca as a slight woman with a commanding expression, while another said rather that she was tall and heavy: so much for the reliability of oral history. John Burlend, all agreed, was both tall and heavy and a man fond of practical jokes: he died in April 1871 at the age of 88 and Rebecca followed him only ten months later, in January 1872. John and Rebecca were buried in Bethel Cemetery, surrounded by the graves of numerous Englishmen who had followed them to America after reading her book. Local history has it that the cemetery also contains the grave of 'Mr B.'.

The Burlends' eldest child, Edward, the only one to remain in England, survived his mother by only three years and died on 6 April 1875. The inscription on his tombstone, which for once has a ring of truth, testifies to those virtues he had inherited from his parents: 'Under social disadvantages and under extreme delicacy of constitution, he taught with marked success a competent knowledge of classics, mathematics, and other branches of science and literature. As an original thinker his prose works, and as an elegant writer, his poetry will long remain evidence of his power and ability. Cautious, peaceful and retiring by nature, he lived respected, and his end truly deserving the character of a just man.'[8] Edward's greatest service to history went unrecorded: in writing down his mother's recollections he left us a deeply moving story of one English family's experience as they established themselves in America. Millions of families, who had no one to record their struggles, would do the same. In so doing they not only peopled a new country but laid the foundation for the 'special relationship' which has done so much to preserve the values they took with them across the Atlantic.

In concluding her tale Rebecca Burlend gave a balanced summary of their success, and any hint of boastfulness was tempered by an honest warning of the price demanded by the frontier: 'If our success has been ultimately greater than at one time we anticipated, or even than that of many of our neighbours, as indeed it has, it must be borne in mind that our industry and perseverance have been unremitting.'

2

The Enthusiast: Frances Wright

CHILDHOOD AND EARLY LIFE

A wealthy young woman, landing in New York today, armed with enthusiastic revolutionary views, would hardly be a cause for comment. Things were different in 1818 when Frances Wright arrived: from then until her death in 1852 she was to be the subject of much praise, of even more controversy but, most of all, of outrage and denunciation. She became one of the best-known, indeed notorious, women in nineteenth-century America. Yet today few remember her. Such is so often the fate of those whom their contemporaries think unforgettable.

Frances Wright was born on 6 September 1795 in Dundee where her father, James, was a linen-merchant as well as a considerable collector of rare coins; his collection is now in the British Museum. He was also a convinced radical who supported the ideas of Thomas Paine. This was a particularly risky stance to take in Scotland in the years following the French Revolution, and it is said that he was under surveillance by the government. He even carried his radical politics into his collecting, for he despised 'the silly morsels of heraldry' that appeared on so many coins. Years later his daughter was amazed to find how many of her own radical views were the same as those held by the father she had scarcely known. James Wright was related by family and friendship to many of the leading figures of what was known as the Scottish Enlightenment. His wife, Camilla, was connected with the outer fringes of the aristocracy. She was the daughter of Major General Duncan Campbell of the Royal Marines and the niece of Richard Robinson, an Archbishop of Armagh who had been raised to the peerage as Baron Rokeby. It is somewhat ironic that Frances Wright, who would be known as a revolutionary and atheist, had among her antecedents a Major General and an Archbishop. However, Camilla Wright was also the great-niece and god-daughter of Elizabeth Montagu, a well-known author and famous hostess. She was called the 'Queen of the Blues' because her house was one of the first places where women and men were encouraged to take part in intellectual conversation on an equal footing. Dr Johnson greatly admired her and proclaimed: 'Mrs Montagu is a very extraordinary woman; she has a constant stream of conversation, and it is always impregnated; it has always meaning.'[1] Frances Wright did resemble at least one of her family.

Yet for the young Frances, her family was a source of misery, not of
happiness or security. In 1798, before she was three, both her parents died.
She was separated from her brother, Richard, and her younger sister,
Camilla, and sent to London to live with her grandfather and her young
aunt, Frances Campbell. She remembered her grandfather as a cynical
and idle man, but her real detestation was reserved for her aunt.[2] Unfortunately no evidence has emerged of what they thought of her. Her brother
was killed at the age of fifteen in a naval battle with the French when he
was on his way to India. Yet another family death, that of her uncle, a
Major in India, left the two Wright sisters as heiresses to a considerable
fortune. Eventually she was re-united with her sister, Camilla, when they
were taken by their despised aunt to her country house near Dawlish in
Devonshire.

The young Frances, or Fanny as she was often known, was a moody
child, given to reading Byron's poetry and to writing imitations in suitably
Byronic style. Her education was somewhat haphazard and in later years
she came to feel that such a lack of method in studying hurt many women,
few of whom had the opportunity to attend school. Girls from wealthy
backgrounds studied at home, often under a governess. There were two
great advantages to this type of education: it encouraged a love of books
and a highly developed power of imagination. When she was sixteen she
stumbled across a book that was to determine her life's course. Rarely has
one book so influenced anyone. In the library of her aunt's country house
she found a work by Carlo Botta, an Italian radical historian who had held
office under Napoleon. *Storia della Guerra dell' Independenza degli Stati
Uniti d'America* was a history of events that had taken place twenty years
before her birth. By chance she had found the 'first standard account' of
the American War of Independence written for 'Americans of all parties'.
John Adams felt that it was the best history while his successor as
President, Thomas Jefferson, called it 'the common manual of our Revolutionary History'.[3] She did not know that Botta had invented eloquent
speeches for the characters in his story, though one suspects that such a
discovery would not have dampened her spirits unduly.

It is a good insight into her great abilities and enthusiasms as well as
into her fragmented education that while she could read Italian she could
never remember having heard of America. She was not even certain if the
book recounted actual events. In a fragment of an autobiography written
in the third person in 1844 she says that from that moment she awoke 'as
it were to a new existence ... There existed a country consecrated to
freedom, in which man might wake to the full knowledge and full exercise
of his powers. To see that country was, now at the age of sixteen, her fixed
but secret determination.'[4] She was delighted with her new-found determination to escape the routine luxuries of a country house existence for
this new land of liberty. Suddenly, she says, 'a panic terror seized her'. She
hurried to find an atlas which could tell her where this marvellous new

country was. Indeed, she wondered, did it actually exist? The first atlas she looked at contained no such country, nor did several other works she consulted. Finally she found a more up-to-date atlas that included the 'United States'. The story she had read in Italian was confirmed in English, in a history of George III by the Dissenting writer, William Belsham, who was sympathetic to the Americans' cause. This revealing little incident shows the basic trait that was always to be characteristic of her: warm sentiments always came before solid facts. It was to be the tragedy of her life that facts tend to influence events more than emotions.

The discovery of Frances Wright's new-found spiritual homeland was one of the few remembered joys of what she calls a 'singularly calamitous' childhood.[5] In her book on America, when speaking of the Indians, for whom she evinced little sympathy, she makes an obvious reference to her own childhood when referring to those 'who have known the feelings of an orphan, when in a house and country foreign to his race'. Yet even as a child she had those characteristics that were to mark her life-long quest: a deep sympathy for the poor and a passion for truth. She tells us that on one occasion she was talking with a 'deep and shrewd mathematician and physician' who told her that some questions were too dangerous for children. She replied, 'Can Truth be dangerous?' He answered, 'It is thought so.' The young Frances 'learned in this experience two things: the one, that Truth had still to be found; the other, that men were afraid of it'.

In 1813, she staged her first recorded rebellion when she took herself and Camilla away from her aunt and went to Glasgow to live with their great-uncle, James Mylne. He was Adam Smith's successor as Professor of Moral Philosophy in the University of Glasgow. In his well-stocked library she settled down to a serious course of reading. This was supplemented by many trips to the University library where she was able to pore over the large collection of pamphlets on America. Her reading now included much philosophy and, under the influence of Epicurus, she rejected such Christian belief as she still held and hovered between deism and outright atheism. She was delighted to discover a modern philosopher who would later become a mentor and friend but who just now gave her a new faith. Jeremy Bentham's slogan of the greatest good for the greatest number became her personal motto. Armed with her new-found philosophy and with much leisure, it is hardly surprising that she began to write various articles which formed the basis of later published works. She also appears to have written some political pamphlets and even to have sent a play about the Swiss struggle for liberty to the great actor, Charles Kemble. He returned it without comment.

One of the great sights in Glasgow in her youth was the many ships leaving for America. Glasgow had long been a centre of American trade, particularly the profitable tobacco from Virginia. Fanny quickly developed a great sympathy for the poor emigrants crowded into steerage. Many of these people were Scottish crofters turned off the land in the agricultural depression that followed the Napoleonic wars, as we saw in the case of the Burlends in Yorkshire. Fanny Wright swore a secret oath 'to wear ever in her heart the cause of the poor and the helpless; and to aid in all she could in redressing the grievous wrongs which seemed to prevail in society'. These generous sentiments remained with her all her life and although many would laugh at some of her absurdities, good intentions always motivated her.

The stirring sight of the great sailing ships moving down the Clyde towards the open sea swelled her desire to see the wonderful New World about which she was reading. She had now found a friend who could give her some personal recollections of America. James Mylne had married the daughter of another professor, John Millar. The Mylnes and the Millars formed one large family of radical intellectuals. Among them was Robina Craig Millar. At the time of the French Revolution, her husband, like his friend, Fanny Wright's father, was a radical. When the British political climate began to prove too hot for him, he left for America, where another form of climate attacked him. Robina Millar soon returned to Scotland as a widow after her husband died of sunstroke. She rapidly became the mother the young Fanny had never known. Stimulated by their talks, Fanny Wright decided that the time had come to visit the land of her studies and dreams. Her younger sister, Camilla, would accompany her. Fanny confided her plans only to Professor Mylne and Mrs Millar, for she and Camilla were probably afraid lest other relatives try to prevent the wealthy young heiresses from leaving. Not only would their family be horrified by the dangers of the trip itself but by their desire to visit a strange land. It was a shocking thing for two young ladies to set off on an unchaperoned day-trip, let alone a quixotic adventure that could last months or even years.

LIVERPOOL TO NEW YORK

In August 1818 the dream that had been born over an Italian book in a Devonshire country house library came true when Fanny and Camilla boarded a ship in Liverpool bound for New York. During the voyage and the two years that she spent on her first visit to America, Fanny wrote a regular series of letters to Robina Millar. Writing a book in the form of letters was a favourite device of travel writers. To take but one example, Henry Fearon, who was returning from America at the same time that Fanny Wright was preparing to leave for it, produced his *Sketches of America* in a series of long letters and this was published by the same firm that would bring out her book. Not only do letters give a book a sense of the author's first impressions (though of course these may have been polished before publication), they also give the reader a greater sense of movement, a sense of almost sharing the difficulties and delights of travel. After the Wright sisters returned to England, Fanny went through her letters to Mrs Millar and arranged them into a book with only a few changes, such as the removal of some personal passages. *Views of Society and Manners in America* by Frances Wright was published in 1821.[6] It is a colourful and enthusiastic account by a romantic twenty-two-year-old. Its main fault is its ever-present delight in almost everything American. While there is little attempt at objectivity there is, on the other hand, no descent into diatribe. In the book we can grasp in all its colour the vision and the hope that the United States raised in young liberals throughout England and Europe. Fanny Wright's account, with a few trifling exceptions, also presents the view that Americans had of their own country. Perhaps no other British traveller so conveyed that mood.

The two young women sailed rather appropriately on an American ship named *Amity*, and Fanny used the voyage to discuss politics and history with the crew. 'I never came from the conversation,' she wrote in her first published letter from New York, 'without having gained some useful information, or without having conceived a higher idea of the country.' Both the American navy and merchant marine had a reputation at this time for literate sailors and she was not alone in commenting on the fact that every one of these 'sons of Neptune' could read and write.[7] The crossing took thirty days, which was fairly good for the time. Almost all travellers to America were agreed on one thing, the beauty of New York harbour, and Fanny Wright was no exception. She was lost in amazement at 'the purity of the air, the brilliancy of the unspotted heavens, the crowd of moving vessels, shooting in various directions ... across the bay ... and the forest of masts crowded round the quays'. 'There is something in all of this,' she continued, 'in the very air you breathe, and the fair and moving scene that you rest your eye upon, which exhilarates the spirits, and makes you in good-humour with life and your fellow creatures.' She gives a long and lingering description of the beauty of the young men who rowed out to collect the post, even before the ship had docked. She was pleased to note that 'all spoke good English with a good voice and accent'.

The modern traveller may perhaps envy her luck or question whether her enthusiasm did not exceed her accuracy. She assures us that the porters who unloaded her luggage, in itself no small task, 'smiled a good welcome to the city'. (Her compatriot, Henry Fearon, who arrived in New York almost exactly a year before, had noted that a boy who fetched him a carriage at the dock rejected a tip of an English shilling as 'too little'. The boy was only pacified when an American passenger – no less than John Quincy Adams, returning from his post as Minister in London to become Secretary of State and eventually President – satisfied him with a half-dollar.) 'There was,' Fanny writes, 'in the look and air of these men, though clad in working-jackets, something which told that they are rendering civilities, not services; and that a kind *thank ye* was all that should be tendered in return.'

One of the most important requisites for any serious and well-born traveller was a collection of letters of introduction. These could open a whole social and political world to a tourist from abroad. People like the Burlends had to venture into a virtually unknown land with no introductions until they made contact with their fellow Yorkshireman in Illinois, but the Wright sisters were spared that. Although Fanny arrived with several letters, written by Mrs Millar, she claimed she only delivered three. One was apparently to the man to whom she later dedicated her book, Charles Wilkes, who, as we shall see, was one of those men who would play a key role in facilitating Anglo-American travel and friendship. Because he stood at the centre of a network of friendships, letters of introduction to him were a great help to any visitor. He was the nephew of the famous English radical, John Wilkes, who had championed the cause of the American colonies. Undoubtedly this connexion helped the younger Wilkes when he first arrived in the newly independent country in 1784. He became head cashier of the Bank of New York and eventually its president. He paid frequent visits to Britain as well as to France and his daughter married Lord Jeffrey, the Scottish jurist and highly influential editor of the *Edinburgh Review*. Charles Wilkes was evidently a kindly man and was always anxious to help British visitors to his adopted land.[8] (Somewhat ironically, it was the precipitate and illegal action of Wilkes' kinsman, Captain Charles Wilkes, in seizing the Confederate diplomats, James Mason and John Slidell, from a British ship that nearly brought Britain and the United States to war in 1861.)

Unfortunately Fanny Wright's book tells us virtually nothing of her friends or her activities in New York, for it was not meant as a personal memoir. Yet it is interesting to follow her career in the city. Through Charles Wilkes she met such people as the painter, John Trumbull, best known for his 'Signing of the Declaration of Independence', as well as politicians like Cadwallader Colden, soon to become the Mayor of New York. As she tells us nothing of her life in New York the casual reader might have wondered why she lingered so long there. She had brought with her the manuscript of a play, *Altorf*, which presumably was the same play that Charles Kemble had rejected. She now asked Wilkes about the state of the theatre in New York. His comment was similar to those made by American critics from time to time ever since: 'Nothing can be – as far as I can judge – more degraded than our stage. The only passport to success here seems to be success in London.'

However, the budding playwright was luckier in New York than she had been back home and the play was put on at the Park Theatre on 19 February 1819, about five months after her arrival. She had set the action in fourteenth-century Switzerland and it dealt with the battle for independence from Austria. Nothing could be more timely for a young radical. Rousseau had popularised Switzerland as the home of liberty and Swiss themes were popular at the time, as in Rossini's *Wilhelm Tell*. No country was more detested by young Radicals like the Wrights than Austria for the role that Empire had played in Napoleon's downfall and the re-establishment of conservative rule throughout Europe.[9] *Altorf* proved moderately successful, especially for such an inexperienced playwright, although the *New York Evening Post* felt that it had too much talk and too little action. Nevertheless the *Post* was delighted that the anonymous author, whom they of course assumed to be a man, 'trusted his work ... to the unprejudiced liberality of an American audience ... the only nation where the cause of freedom dare be asserted'.[10] After three performances in New York there was a fourth in Philadelphia. It was then published in Philadelphia under her own name. The published version had a preface which acclaimed America as the only land of liberty and truth left on the earth. The play was dedicated to Mrs Millar, who, however, was not wholly pleased. She took exception to a line which referred to 'The burning kisses we have mixed together.' This was, she said, 'not in character ... and from a young female author will be thought improper, and more than improper'. About a year later Fanny received praise from an omnivorous reader in Virginia. Thomas Jefferson wrote to say that he had found *Altorf* to have 'that excellent moral which gives dignity and usefulness to poetry ... He prays Mrs [sic] Wright to accept the assurance of his high respect.'[11] One can well imagine her thrill at receiving a letter from the hand that had drafted her beloved Declaration of Independence. The play was also important in another sense. It had carried a preface by a new friend who was to have a further influence on her radical and, indeed, revolutionary sentiments.

When the Wright sisters had first arrived in New York they had not been able to find suitable lodgings, and Mrs Millar had written from Scotland about her concern that they were spending too much money. To Mrs Millar's relief, they moved into the boarding-house of a Scotswoman, Martha Wilson, the widow of Wolfe Tone, the Irish revolutionary who had committed suicide after being condemned to death for his part in trying to lead French invasions of the British Isles. His son, William Theobald Wolfe Tone, lived with his mother in New York. He was four years older than Fanny Wright, had been educated at the expense of a grateful French Republic and had served in the French Army under Napoleon. He had resigned when the Bourbons were restored to the throne. Young Tone and Fanny became close friends and, as he was also a writer, they had much in common.

When not busy with her play, she spent much time in New York, wandering round the city, enjoying the wide streets and admiring some of the splendid private houses. She had little time for public buildings: 'There is not a public building worth noticing', she admitted, save for the City Hall. She also claimed that New York was free from slums: there were no 'dark alleys ... no hovels, in whose ruined garrets, or dark and gloomy cellars, crowd the wretched victims of vice and disease, whom penury drives to despair, ere she opens to them the grave'.

The two sisters also paid visits to friends of Charles Wilkes who lived in the surrounding countryside, visits which were much enjoyed. There Fanny found several lovely but, she is quick to reassure us, not lordly, houses. Like so many of the other women writers on America, she had a strong feeling for nature and especially admired the large willow trees. However, she did complain that there were no old trees remaining on Manhattan Island itself. She was evidently relieved when an American friend told her that they had all been cut down for fire-wood by British troops during the Revolution. After this she could look with increased respect at the young trees in 'the land which freedom has regenerated'.

Fanny Wright distributed her warm praises to all classes in America and claimed after two months that there seemed 'to be neither poor nor uneducated'. Remarks like this, and those about slums, do cause one to wonder just how deeply she had seen into her new-found land. She constantly stressed the kindness and courtesy she encountered everywhere, a trait often found among tourists after a pleasant holiday. As she was herself a kind and courteous woman, and a remarkably beautiful one, it is likely that she was well received almost everywhere she went at this stage of her life. She frequently denounced those Englishmen 'who complain ... of being elbowed in the streets, and scowled at in the houses, and made uncomfortable everywhere'. 'I have not yet found,' she says, 'even the servants, a race of beings peculiarly quarrelled with by our grumbletonians, either morose or impertinent.' She recounts one incident where a New Yorker helped her to find a particular address but as he was carrying a heavy basket of shopping he simply set it down until he could return. She assures us that as New York was much more honest than any English city, there was no fear about leaving the basket. Here we have a good example of her constant propensity to leap to unfounded conclusions. She had, probably, no way of knowing whether the man had found his basket on his return.

It comes as no surprise to learn that she was equally delighted with the politics of the United States and the readiness with which Americans discussed their government and history. It was with unabated joy that she heard Americans speak of 'our' president and how 'we' passed legislation in Congress. 'To speak in short,' she writes, 'I should say that it were impossible for a people to be more completely identified with their government, than are the Americans. In considering it, they seem to feel, *it is ours: We created it*.' Things were so perfect, she asserts, that there were virtually no political parties nor any great, divisive issues.

This statement is not quite so naive as it might appear for, with the end of the War of 1812, the United States entered upon the 'Era of Good Feelings'. By arriving in 1818 the young enthusiast had chosen the best possible time for her first view of the land of which she had read and dreamed. If she found it a supremely contented nation of almost ten million people it was not merely her optimism that led her to this conclusion.

Sectional tension was at its lowest for years and the veteran American statesman, Albert Gallatin (who would become her close friend) wrote that the War of 1812 had 'renewed and reinstated the national feelings which the Revolution had given'. The people, he claimed, were 'more American; they feel and act more like a nation'. By the following year, 1819, things had begun to change and two issues which were to divide public opinion and dominate politics appeared. In 1819 there was a financial panic and, even more importantly, debates over slavery began to appear in Congress.

By February 1819, after five months in the country, Fanny Wright was becoming somewhat more observant. As with nearly all women writers on America she was more critical of American women than men and, in particular, young women. She found their costume ill-adapted for the rigours of a New York winter and her criticism was echoed by later and more conservative visitors such as Mrs Trollope and Lady Emmeline Stuart Wortley. (In later years Fanny Wright became an advocate of dress reform and was among the first women to appear in public in a form of trousers.) Like other observers she commented on the beauty of American girls but said their beauty ended when they were about twenty-five due to their complexions being ruined by an 'envious sun' and the cares of family life.

It is hardly surprising that she also disapproved of early marriages which she felt were bad for both sexes, though, naturally, worse for the women: 'Men have necessarily in all countries greater facilities than women for the acquirement of knowledge.' When she maintained that American men spent many hours philosophising about the virtues and beauties of Republicanism we can only assume that her male acquaintances were still mainly limited to those she met through Charles Wilkes or young Tone. Perhaps her definition of philosophy was somewhat broad. She advocated more educational opportunities for women so that America could advance even faster and further. American girls, she wrote, have good manners 'equally removed from the studied English coldness and indifference, and the no less studied French vivacity and mannerism', but they needed more intellectual training in order to play a proper role in their country's life. She was somewhat surprised to find that fashions, both in dress and dancing, seemed based more on the French model than on the English but she reassured worried readers that 'the bosom never forgets its screen'. American youth, she found, as would almost all nineteenth-century observers, was far too solemn.[12]

Fanny Wright makes her own radical sentiments plain when she notes how Irish exiles had risen to positions of leadership in New York – no doubt she was thinking of Theobald Tone. This observation provides her with an opportunity to deny the assertion by many previous travellers that America did not welcome foreigners. To her, there was only one reason for this assertion and, indeed, for almost any criticism of the young Republic: the 'disappointed vanity' of the European when set against the Americans' 'provoking soundness of judgment' and 'straight-forward common sense'. These had seen through the pomposity of earlier visitors whose stories had, she felt, done great harm in spreading false tales about America.

PHILADELPHIA, WEST POINT AND NIAGARA

In May, after eight months in New York, the Wrights felt it was time to see more of the country and set out to visit Philadelphia. Fanny did not find the city so welcoming as New York, probably because she had fewer contacts. She had looked forward to seeing the Quakers in the city they had founded but was disappointed not to see one 'drab-colored son of Penn'. Yet she was delighted when she was told that this was because American Quakers had abandoned the distinctive dress and speech that their brethren still used to a large extent in England. Like Tocqueville, she admired the enlightened concepts of justice that prevailed in Pennsylvania, concepts which she traced to the Quaker influence. She was particularly relieved to find that capital punishment had been abandoned in favour of solitary confinement except for premeditated murder.

While in Philadelphia Fanny Wright began to think about a subject that would come to dominate her life: slavery. At first her interest was not strong. We may presume that some of it was due to the debate in Congress, beginning in 1819, on whether Missouri should enter the Union as a 'free' or 'slave' state, a decision which could affect the sectional balance of power in the Senate. She praised the Quakers' opposition to the slave trade and to slavery itself although she erred when she claimed that slavery only existed in those colonies where the Church of England had been established. She was anxious to defend, if necessary, and praise, if possible, all things American. Thus on slavery she comments: 'The history of African slavery is at once the disgrace and honor of America, the disgrace she shares in common with the whole civilised world – the honor is all her own.' The 'honor' consisted in the various protests made by the colonies to the mother country against the slave trade which England had 'forced' on them. She pointed out that the United States could claim to be the first country to end the slave trade even though the Congress which did this included many slave-owners. She failed, however, to point out that Britain had abolished the slave trade in 1807 and that as far back as 1772 Lord Mansfield (whom she would have detested as a benighted Tory) had ruled that English law neither allowed nor approved the 'odious' practice. Under Mansfield's decision, slaves, when in England, were regarded as free men.

Furthermore, Fanny Wright argued, as did most writers of the time, that slavery would die out in the South as it already had largely done in the North. In the South, where it was 'engrafted in the soil', emancipation would be a slower but still an inevitable prospect for 'the evil yet needs years of patience, the more perfect understanding of the mischief to the master, or the more universal feeling of the injustice to the slave'. She pleaded for a greater understanding of the plight of slave-owners in the South and was pleased that many Americans understood this. Virginia, she said, had every right to expect this because of the great services of that valiant state to the patriotic cause. However, she maintained that Americans saw that slavery was a complex problem while Europeans, particularly Englishmen, merely used it as a weapon with which to berate America. There is some truth in this, as we shall see when we come to consider Mrs Trollope. Later, a more mature Wright would insist that English attacks on American slavery had their highly principled side as well as their hypocritical one.

Fanny Wright was, however, perceptive enough to see one aspect in the anti-slavery attacks by both Americans and Englishmen. She recognised that their opposition to Negro slavery sprang as much from dislike of the Negro as from dislike of slavery. We find this in many English travellers of whom Dickens would become the most prominent. We shall see how it affected the attitude of Catherine Hopley in the midst of the war that would eliminate American slavery. We also find it in speeches by politicians such as Lincoln.* Frances Wright well describes this racialist attitude of those who disliked the slave as much as slavery itself:[13]

> When he sees a crowd of black faces assembled at the corner of a street, or descries the sable cheeks and clumsy features of a negro girl under a pink silk bonnet, the sight offends him in its ugliness, and an immediate distaste at the country, defaced by a mixture of so novel and unseemly a population, takes possession of his mind.

She held that in time much of the slaves' condition could be improved and that a gradual emancipation could lead to a greater equality. Here she points to the condition of the freed slaves in the New England states and concludes: 'Nothing indeed is here necessary but his own exertions to raise him in the scale of being.'

Satisfied, at least for a time, that slavery was not an insoluble problem, she used much of her time in Philadelphia to wander round the streets and to observe the historical places connected with the War of Independence, which she had first read about in Botta's history. As she revered past Americans, so she generalised about those she now saw. Earlier and in common with almost all European travellers and even many American writers – Henry James would be a prime example – she had criticised American men for being too serious. Now she would have none of this. She was delighted that in her travels in America, i.e., in the ninety-two miles from New York to Philadelphia, she had seen no leisured class. 'Every hand

---

*In 1858 during the famous Lincoln-Douglas debates, Lincoln would make it clear that 'We profess to have no taste for running and catching niggers'; his aim in politics was to keep the undeveloped western territories as 'an outlet for *free white people every where*, the world over'.

is occupied,' she wrote, 'and every head is thinking, not only of the active business of human life (which usually sits lighter upon this people than many others) but of matters touching the general weal of a vast empire.' Americans were also 'very good talkers, and *admirable listeners*'. No doubt she gave them ample chance to prove the correctness of her latter assertion. If other travellers had not found Americans good at conversation it was because they avoided all light topics: 'good sense' alone is the American's concern. She herself had felt this: 'I know no people who sooner make you sensible of your own ignorance. In conversing even with a plain farmer, it has seemed to me, that I had been nothing but a foolish trifler all my life, running after painted butterflies.'

In June she crossed the Delaware River and made her way eastwards into New Jersey where she travelled the short distance to Bordentown, a small village which sheltered a famous exile. Here Joseph Bonaparte, Napoleon's elder brother, was living in comfortable retirement after the collapse of his family's imperial world. Fanny had always taken a great interest in French affairs and, like many radicals, had a great sympathy for Napoleon. Joseph Bonaparte was perhaps the most pleasant, indeed, perhaps the only pleasant member of his remarkable family. He had first been installed by his brother as King of Naples and then later promoted to King of Spain. The wily Joseph had managed to escape the final downfall of the Bonapartes in 1815 and had arrived in neutral America with a considerable fortune. He adopted the name of Count Survillier and was much liked by his neighbours in his rural retreat. He possessed probably the finest art collection in America, famous for the various busts of his family by Canova and portraits such as David's 'Napoleon Crossing the Alps'. His collection, drawing on Spain's royal palaces, would have been even greater if the Duke of Wellington had not captured his loot-filled waggons as they trundled out of the Spanish capital.

The young Republican evidently enjoyed her visit with the ex-King who always retained some of the liberal ideals that his more famous brother had come to scorn. It is said that he turned down a proposal to occupy the new throne of Mexico, feeling that he had occupied enough thrones already. He told his visitor that he found America 'a country for the many, and not for the few; which gave freedom to all and power to none, in which happiness might better be found than any other'. In spite of all that, 'King Joseph' returned to Europe after the death of Napoleon made it safe for Bonapartes to reappear. Even after his departure his house remained one of America's major tourist attractions for years.[14]

After this enjoyable visit Fanny Wright travelled northwards, back into New York state. Here she started up the Hudson River to visit West Point, the American military academy some forty-five miles north of New York City. The Academy, started in 1802, had already played its role in providing officers for the War of 1812 and it is not surprising that while Fanny found European militarism bad, the American republican version was acceptable. She found that the main virtue of the Academy, and the military it served, was the creation of a sense of national unity. She felt that the young cadets 'necessarily forget all those paltry jealousies and selfish interests which once went nigh to split these great republics, and to break down the last and noblest bulwark of freedom erected on this earth'. Such noble sentiments would take on an ironic ring when we remember that it was the graduates of this same Academy who would lead their respective nations in the War Between the States some forty years later.

For Fanny not only was America superior to all existing countries but it surpassed even the ancient republics. The Roman Republic had been ruined by an 'arrogant and artful' nobility who had given too much power to an ambitious military. Naturally she maintained that kings were to blame for all the modern wars as the people themselves never desired violence. The example of the blood-thirsty mobs of the French Revolution had had no effect on her opinions. She was able to rest assured that the youth of West Point could not be infected with a military spirit because they had a true knowledge of liberty and 'knowledge is the bugbear of tyranny'. To her, in 'this union of knowledge with liberty lies the strength of America'. Liberty and education were always to be her two gods.

She continued her travels in upstate New York to Niagara Falls. This was, in many ways, the main tourist attraction in America. It was then the largest waterfall known to Europeans and the tremendous force of the water had a great appeal to romantic intellectuals of the age of Wordsworth, Byron and Turner. Of course, the means by which she reached the Falls were more primitive than those used by the other women writers in this book. They had the advantage of steamboats and, sometimes, trains, but the Wright sisters had only two choices in the second decade of the nineteenth century. They could rent a Dearborn carriage or use the public stage-coach. Fanny was always a hearty traveller and was prepared for discomfort. Characteristically she preferred the stage-coach as it would allow her to meet more people. Camilla, as always, did what her elder sister thought best. Here we see an essential difference between Fanny Wright and other travellers. Whereas Frances Trollope gives us lengthy descriptions of the discomforts of American stage-coaches or the boorishness of fellow passengers, Fanny Wright is more concerned to point out that all her fellow travellers were distinguished by 'good-humour and intelligence'. It is true that at times her boundless optimism can lead a reader astray, but there are few authors who give a better sense of the sheer excitement of visiting a burgeoning land.

Her travels also gave her time to speculate on the relative positions of English and American farmers. She was writing at one of the bleakest periods in British agricultural history. She had grown up in Devon where farm workers were among the worst paid in the country and she had also seen Scottish crofters being forced off the land, men whose only option was to emigrate to the New World. (In England, families like the Burlends were drawn to America because they wanted to get on in farming and to avoid being pushed into the new, industrial order of the expanding cities. We shall see how Mrs Trollope's finances were ruined by the agricultural collapse, this time in Middlesex.) As Fanny Wright bounced along in her stage-coach she found it impossible to 'conceive man placed in a more enviable position' than an American farmer. The English farmer was being ruined by high taxes and tithes, and for once her views would have met with a hearty 'Hear, hear' from many Tories. Of course, while she was reflecting on these topics, she was able to observe some of the best agricultural land under cultivation in America.

The favourable prospects for American agriculture did much to encourage westward migration. On her first visit she did not see the frontier, although much of the country through which she passed on her way to Niagara Falls was not far removed from frontier conditions. She must also have had considerable opportunities to discuss pioneer life with her fellow passengers and the people she met. She became one of the first writers to recognise the importance of this frontier to American history and the developing American character: 'The position of this country, its boundless territory, its varied soils and climates, its free institutions, and ... the rapid increase of its population, – all combine to generate in this people a spirit of daring enterprise, as well as of proud independence.' During her stay in New York City she realised the commercial importance of that new American invention, the steamboat. She foresaw the spreading of commercial links into the expanding western states as a bond between the north-east and the new states and territories in the Mississippi valley. Once again she defends Americans from any European sneer at the westward movement. She rejects any suggestion that this migration is just an excuse to extend slavery or that it is only the worthless who move west. Rather, she claims, 'it is generally the best' who go to the frontier. Americans, she says, 'spurn at little hindrances in narrow room and prefer great difficulties in a wide horizon'.

Fanny Wright noticed, as well, a different physique between Englishmen and Americans. She was annoyed with an earlier English traveller, Lieutenant Francis Hall (not to be confused with the more famous Captain Basil Hall), when he attributed the greater height that he had noticed, especially in Western Congressmen in Washington, to 'the absence of mental irritation'. While it is undoubtedly true that some Congressmen then, and perhaps even now, have not been unduly irritated by mental strain, his explanation seems somewhat spurious. Wright, who often praised Lieutenant Hall's writings, puts forward a much more sensible view, and one not quite so obvious then as now, namely that the cause of the greater height was better diet, exercise and climate. She also noticed that this increased height was as prevalent in the older states as in the new. What she did not know, for she did not visit the frontier, was that its climate was often actually bad for health. She, like the Burlends and Mrs Trollope, would only learn this hard lesson when she came to live on the frontier in later years.

The native American Indians presented her with a more complicated problem. As a radical believer in freedom and as a good Romantic, she should have been stirred by their 'free spirit' and tragic fate at the hands of white men. Like slavery, the Americans' harsh treatment of the Indians provided arguments for those who wished to attack the moral pretensions of the new republic. The Romantics' image of the American Indian had been established by Chateaubriand's tale of *Atala* at the beginning of the century. One of Wright's strong points is her absolute honesty: if she has a moral problem she does not resolve it in private but shares it, and her conclusions, with her readers. Thus she freely admits that the 'falling greatness' of the Indians at first excited her indignation and sympathy. But along with her devotion to liberty went the nineteenth-century liberal's faith in progress and so, she announces with evident relief, 'such regrets are scarcely rational'. After all, 'the savage with all his virtues, and he has some virtues, is still a savage'.

Here we have the Utilitarian ideas of Jeremy Bentham conquering Fanny Wright's natural generous impulses because the Indians' decline led to a greater good for the greater number or, as she herself puts it, 'the triumph of peace over violence'. She is prepared to admit that the earlier settlers may have been guilty of the occasional injustice but then they themselves were suffering under English rule and influence. There is always a sense of relief in her writing when she can blame her native land for any fault in her new-found country. For her the Indians' problems of vice, disease and death (which were hardly uniquely Indian) were caused mainly by alcohol, and she comments that the republican government, wise and virtuous in all things, has banned the trade in spirits while monarchial Canada has not. She had, however, little hope for the Indians' future, and felt they would disappear under the dictates of Utilitarian logic. Unlike the slaves who, she repeats, could rise by freedom, 'with scarcely an exception, the Indian, on emerging from the savage state, sinks, instead of rising in the scale of being'.[15]

She was quick to dismiss any suggestion that religion could help in 'civilising' the Indian or indeed, the slaves. She appears to have been totally unaware of the work with Indians undertaken by French Jesuits or Spanish Franciscans. Here again we see not only the influence of Bentham but of her other rationalist reading as she proclaims: 'A practical philosopher were the best tutor in this case.' She does not explain how such a philosopher could help civilise the Indians when she has just proved, at least to her own satisfaction, that the Indians were not worth helping by the rules of practical philosophy. She does admit that if any help could be given by religious people it would best come from Quakers or Moravians.

The worst possible helpers would be Methodists or interdenominational itinerant preachers.

Niagara Falls offered another opportunity to British travellers. As the best views of the mighty falls then as today are from the Canadian side of the border, almost all tourists crossed over to enjoy the view. Their brief trip also allowed some hasty comparison between the republic and the colony. There is, perhaps, no better guide to writers' true opinions of America at this time than their comments on Canada. To conservative writers like Mrs Trollope or Basil Hall, there was no question but that British rule was superior. Naturally, Fanny Wright took the other view: Canada, she pronounced, was 'the most useless' of British colonies, although it was the only British colony she had visited at that time. The original French settlers were 'in ignorance and infatuated superstition' under the control of their priests while recent British settlers 'are often sent so far into the interior and at so great a distance one from another as to be exposed to insurmountable difficulties and labour'. When speaking of Canadian distrust of America she neglects to say that part of the reason for it was that many of the earlier settlers were dispossessed American loyalists whose lands had been confiscated during the Revolutionary War or people who had suffered from the atrocities that occurred on both sides of the border during the War of 1812.

Fanny Wright does attribute great importance, however, to the War which led, as we have seen, to a consolidation of American nationalism. Once again she repeats in her letters that the War ended party feuds and that true unity was now permanently established. Of course, she reasoned, there was no real need for party squabbles because all agreed on the excellence of the Constitution. To her, the American Constitution had one particular excellence: 'That while an able statesman has it in his power to promote the public good, he must ever find it difficult to work public mischief.' Thus Alexander Hamilton, whose support for aristocratic principles did not please her, was enabled to do some good work at the Treasury because he followed the Constitutional rules. We are left to assume that if he had not been killed in a duel in 1804, the same Constitution would have prevented him from doing any harm. Naturally her sympathies are with Hamilton's great rival, Thomas Jefferson, and the more liberal ideas associated with him. Yet, ever anxious to defend anything American, she is careful to say that Hamilton's party, the Federalists, were not bad people. Here she falls back on an old radical argument: 'Their errors were those of judgment, we may say of education.'[16] This is a strange argument when we recall that the Federalists tended to appeal to the better educated while their leaders, men like Hamilton, John Adams, Gouverneur Morris and John Jay, were men conspicuous for their learning. It is obvious that her real sympathy is thoroughly with the party of Jefferson and his 'venerable successor', Madison, and that she really could not understand Federalism.

One frequent complaint made against the American Constitution by informed English critics was that it produced weak government. Fanny Wright would have none of this. She maintains that the American government is strong because it is so closely united with the people and the people in their turn are united because they are free from 'the taint' of aristocracy. America is, in short, 'a country where the dreams of sages, smiled at as utopian, seem distinctly realized; a people voluntarily submitting to laws of their own imposing'. Can such a superb example offer any guidance to Europe? She admits that the attempt to transplant American ideals to France failed and that 'the same causes may produce the same failure elsewhere; but surely it is proposed to force the same *attempt* elsewhere'. She is obviously writing with Britain in mind, for by this time she had received news of 'Peterloo'. This famous 'massacre' occurred on 16 August 1819 when soldiers opened fire on demonstrators who had gathered in St Peter's Fields in Manchester. The crowd had been demanding parliamentary reform and when magistrates ordered the arrest of the principal speaker, 'Orator' Hunt, a wild panic ensued in which eleven people were killed by the soldiers and hundreds of the demonstrators were injured. Many were alarmed that this could be the spark to set off an English revolution, and Robina Millar wrote to her young friend about her own fears.[17] To Fanny Wright, it only proved that an army was incompatible with liberty. Yet it is obvious that her real interest was not in reform or in revolution in England. Tocqueville and Mrs Trollope might use America as an interesting study or a dire warning for their own countries: Fanny Wright was now in her own country.

VIEWS ON THE SOUTH, EDUCATION AND RELIGION

By February 1820 Fanny and Camilla Wright, of whom we unfortunately hear very little, had been in America for almost eighteen months. Although they had spent almost all their time in the north-east, mainly in New York and Pennsylvania, Fanny was genuinely interested in other sections of the country and was carefully gathering information both from friends and from her own reading. As we have seen, she did allude to the role of the frontier and was particularly interested in the South. Anyone reading travellers' books on nineteenth-century America becomes familiar with attacks on the South, especially if the traveller is a liberal or radical. Fanny Wright, however, is the exception to the rule. She was possessed of an unbounded admiration for the South, by which (like many of her contemporaries) she usually means Virginia. This emotional attachment to Virginia, the 'Old Dominion', would be felt by both Frances Trollope and Catherine Hopley. Fanny Wright's book resounds with praise for the role of Southerners in the formation of the republic and their guidance of it during its youth. The account she gives of the South in *Views of Society and Manners in America* is far more favourable than her private views, as we shall see.

Jefferson's Democratic party, which enjoyed her particular support, was
led mainly by Southerners and drew its most prominent support from the
South, so it is hardly surprising to find her praising the South, 'whose
policy', she declared, 'has uniformly been liberal and patriotic ... Whatever
be the effect of black slavery upon the moral character of the Southern
population, and that upon the mass it must be deadly mischievous there
can be no question, it has never been felt in the national Senate.' This was
a somewhat strange comment to make in the very year that slavery was
to become such an explosive issue in Congress. Yet she remained full of
praise for Southern planters because of their 'liberal sentiments and
general philanthropy'. Her habit of leaping to conclusions before she had
much information is shown in her claim that most of the South's planters
had travelled widely in Europe and were therefore cultivated men. When
she wrote this she had yet to visit the region and her knowledge was
derived from reading about men like Jefferson and from meeting a few
cultivated men who had passed through New York. It was only later in life
that she realised that such men were the exception rather than the rule.

Most visitors to America were interested in its newspapers and had
mixed feelings about them; Fanny Wright was no exception. She was
impressed with both their number and variety: 'It would be impossible for
a country to be more completely deluged with newspapers than this is.' In
New York she was amazed to find both French and Dutch papers 'and some
will probably soon appear in Spanish'. Naturally she lauded the idea of a
free press but, like many before and not a few since, she was concerned
that in practice it was too inclined to attack her heroes such as Jefferson.
Here she uses a timely metaphor which shows how she attempted to keep
abreast of scientific developments: 'An unrestricted press appears to be the
safety-valve of their free constitution ... they no more regard all the noise
and sputter that it occasions, than the roaring of the vapour on board their
steam-boats.'

Fanny Wright closely followed the Congressional debates in the newspapers and claimed that American reporting standards were very high
and, of course, superior to those in England. She found the tone of
Congressional debate 'worthy of the Roman Senate in its best days'. She
had not as yet visited Congress nor did she seem well informed on several
violent incidents that had occurred in both chambers. She perhaps did not
know that some speeches were given to newspapers before they were
delivered and in some cases handed to official recorders without a word
having been uttered in Congress. She was likewise ignorant of the more
eccentric habits of some members, such as John Randolph of Roanoke in
Virginia, who would bring his hunting dogs into the House of Representatives to growl at his opponents.[18] She does maintain that Congress
is superior to Parliament because it has no regular majority and minority
that follow party lines on every issue. While she exaggerates the extent to
which this was the case in early nineteenth-century Parliaments – there

was cross voting, for example, on the contentious 1829 Catholic Emancipation Bill – she did spot a key difference that has continued to fascinate political commentators as party control of MPs has grown in strength.

As we have seen, she had a concern for education. As she was always conscious of her own handicaps in this regard she would devote her life to education in a variety of ways. Here again she was a good Benthamite radical, for education seemed to be the answer to every ill, much as government intervention would be to later generations. Education was more important in a free country than in one she did not deem free, for 'Liberty and knowledge ever go hand in hand'. She was impressed with the public education of the New England states but did wonder if the rapidly growing number of smaller colleges might not prevent the establishment of a few truly distinguished universities – a problem that has continued to plague American education. Here she was perhaps influenced by reading that President Madison had advocated, in at least four annual messages to Congress, the establishment of a national university.[19] But Fanny Wright, at this stage of her life, could not long maintain any criticism of American institutions and she went on to point out that American education was not concerned with the few 'very learned' but with educating young men to fulfil their calling as free citizens. We must remember that when she wrote, English universities were still confined to Oxford and Cambridge and, unlike those in Scotland, were primarily devoted to the training of clergymen. She was annoyed and surprised to discover that the Germans and Dutch in America seemed reluctant to leave what she quaintly calls 'the temple of ignorance'. She was not the last outraged radical to find that ethnic groups preferred to remain loyal to their own heritage rather than be absorbed in any 'melting pot' inspired by reformers raised in the tradition of English radicalism.

Naturally she was particularly concerned with the education of women, a topic on which most of our writers touched. She noted that New England women were better read than those of New York but does not give any details to sustain this conclusion. For that matter, she does not seem to have travelled extensively in New England before making this observation. She urged political education for women not on the grounds that they should play a direct role in politics but because they should be better able to prepare their sons for such a role. She disapproved strongly of girls being taught such fashionable and 'feminine' subjects as French, drawing and dancing while men studied history and economics. Here we can hear the voice of the girl who could read Italian but who could not find America on the map.

While Fanny Wright believed women were not playing the role they should in America, they were still far more advanced than their European sisters. At this phase in her life, when her feminist views were in their early stage, she did not think that American men were opposed to women's playing a larger role in social and public debate. 'The women,' she writes,

'are assuming their place as thinking beings not in despite of the men, but
chiefly in consequence of their enlarged views and exertions as fathers and
legislators.' She found it impossible to imagine any place where women
stood in higher estimation than in the United States. This gave her 'as
much surprise as pleasure'. American women, she continued, never did
any field labour: her compatriot, Mrs Burlend, would have been amused
to read this! Here again the restricted extent of Fanny Wright's visit is
evident. Had she visited the frontier to the west or the plantations and
farms to the south she would have written otherwise. She also felt that
while women were held in such high regard in America, their position in
England was actually getting worse. Unfortunately she does not expand
on this assertion other than to say that English women were taught to see
men as seducers. She does make one final suggestion – a somewhat rare
one for the time – about the education of women. Such education should
not simply concentrate on the mind but on women's bodies which should
be strengthened through activities like swimming and shooting.

Religion was a topic that interested almost all British travellers to
America, a country which had no nationally established church and was
in law a 'secular' state but not, like revolutionary France, an atheist one.
As we have seen, Fanny Wright had abandoned any shred of Christian
belief by the time she sat down to write yet she was careful, at this stage
in her career, to avoid any full-scale attack upon it. She did not find any
lack of religion in America; indeed, in New England, she decided they had
too much of it – but at least the older Calvinism was giving way to a more
palatable and comfortable Unitarianism. With these changes came a
decline in the churches' hold on people: she quotes a naval officer who told
her that in the New England of his youth it would have been better to have
picked someone's pocket on a Saturday night than to have smiled on a
Sunday. Now, one could smile all the week long. While the young visitor
did not care for organised religion in any form, she had to admit that it
was less offensive in America – excluding, that is, her old enemies the
Methodists, whom she detested as too emotional. 'American religion,' she
wrote, 'of whatever sect (and it includes all the sects under heaven) is of a
quiet and unassuming character; no way disputatious, even when more
doctrinal than the majority may think wise.' But, she went on, 'I do not
include the strolling Methodists and shaking quakers, and sects with
unutterable names and deranged imaginations.' From what one can
gather, she did not appear to have visited many churches. We must
conclude that her views of American religion came from her reading, her
friends or her prejudices. Part of her dislike of the Methodists was as much
due to their conservative social and political views in England as to their
enthusiastic services in America. By attacking the 'shaking quakers' she
was not withdrawing her earlier praise for the descendants of Fox and
Penn but was criticising the 'Shakers', a group of religious enthusiasts best

known for their celibacy and their furniture. Because of their devotion to the former they are now mainly remembered for the latter.

WASHINGTON AND VIRGINIA

By April 1820, Frances Wright was preparing her twenty-eighth and last letter to Robina Millar. She had come to the capital of the young republic. Most travellers were disappointed with the city of Washington in the nineteenth century. Like St Petersburg before or Brasilia afterwards, the city had been conceived and planned on a vast and noble scale, but such a scale made the realisation of the plans all the more difficult. Such things did not, of course, disturb Fanny Wright, to whom the plan was always more important than the fulfilment. The fact that there were few public buildings delighted her and her only worry for the virtue of the Republic was when and if Washington ever became a 'sumptuous metropolis' with 'the form and magnificence of an imperial city'. She was like a devout pilgrim who has reached a holy shrine when she entered the Capitol building, and her ecstasy knew no bounds: 'While this edifice stands, liberty has an anchorage from which the congress of European autocrats cannot uproot her.' This was, of course, a blow at the Congress of Vienna and the succeeding Congresses which sought to establish and maintain a peaceful and conservative Europe.

If she had arrived in Washington much earlier she would not have been able to see the Capitol functioning as the seat of the legislature. After British troops had burned the building in August 1814, Congress had been forced to meet elsewhere and the two houses only returned in December 1819. The building she saw was, of course, a far cry from the noble structure familiar today.[20] When she returned a few years later she was delighted with the great improvements that had taken place. On her first visit she was finally able to hear, and not just to read, congressional debates and she was particularly struck with the oratory of Henry Clay. She did, however, criticise some of the younger members of Congress for speaking too much and for 'coining new words when old ones do not occur to them'. Some things, at least, never change.

A high point of Fanny Wright's first trip was an introduction to President James Monroe, who had become the fifth President in 1817. In her comment on her meeting she could not resist a sneer at her own sovereign, George IV, thinly disguised with the quaint eighteenth-century fiction of asterisks: 'How would the courtiers of C*RLT*N H**S* look upon a chief magistrate of a country who stands only as a man among men; who walks forth without attendants, and lives without state?' Her information was somewhat out of date for George IV, who had become King only a few months before she wrote, had left Carlton House for Buckingham Palace.

One benefit of a trip to Washington for most British visitors was that it allowed a quick glimpse at slavery. They could have seen it while passing through Maryland on their way to Washington, yet most seemed unaware of its existence in that state. Slavery existed, of course, in Washington itself but only in the form of house servants. There seemed little difference in these servants and those most British visitors would have left at home, save that of race. One aspect of 'slavery' that visitors could see in Washington was the slave trade, although it was considered unseemly for a lady to attend a slave auction.

Fanny Wright was forced to make a quick dash across the Potomac River to spend a day or two in Virginia to see slavery 'first hand'. Not surprisingly such rapid visits did not give a foreign visitor a very detailed understanding. This was due not just to the shortness of the visit but to the peculiar circumstances affecting northern Virginia. Virginia's great tobacco plantations of the eighteenth century had died out with the exhaustion of the soil and many Virginians had followed George Washington's example and turned to wheat farming. To some visitors, like Dickens, the exhaustion of the soil was attributed to slave labour: in the event this was only one among many causes; far more important were the demands of the plants on the soil and the state of agricultural knowledge. The decline of tobacco farming on a vast scale had made many of the slaves in Virginia redundant and they were instead used as workers on smaller farms or as house servants. When English visitors encountered these house servants they were often struck with the strong bond between master and 'servant' – the term 'slave' was seldom used. But just as northern Virginia showed examples of the least offensive side of slavery, so it also showed some of the most, for some of the redundant slaves were shipped to the lower South to work on the expanding cotton, rice and sugar farms of Alabama, Mississippi and Louisiana. Visitors to Virginia, therefore, saw a glimpse of the 'peculiar institution' they had come to see: the little they saw was normally enough to confirm the views with which they had arrived.

Some of the visitors' reluctance to journey far into the South was due to the heat, the poor transport and the paucity of large cities. But there was one other reason, a 'secret reluctance' as Fanny Wright honestly described it. 'The sight of slavery is revolting every where, but to inhale the impure breath of its pestilence in the free winds of America is odious beyond all that the imagination can conceive.' At this point she refrained from 'idle declamation, either against the injustice of the masters, or upon the degradation of the slave' and therefore gave no examples of either. Few English travellers would provide a more incisive and honest explanation of their attitudes than she did. It is interesting that only at the end of her book does she come to consider at any length this vexed subject, the one great blot upon her utopia. She admitted that the difficulties of 'emancipation' were enormous yet she was convinced that Southerners would soon feel 'the reprobation of their northern brethren, and the scorn of mankind'. Here, again, she was perceptive for she predicted the tremendous growth of anti-slavery sentiment both in the North and in England. But she was wrong in her conclusion: rather than stimulating Southerners towards emancipation it strengthened them in their hostility to it.

After her brief visit to Virginia she concluded that the Virginians were good and mild masters but 'to break the chains would be more generous than to gild them'. She had, however, also observed that freed blacks in Maryland as well as in Virginia were in a dreadful condition, worse either than Southern slaves or Northern freed Negroes. To her this was the result of unthinking emancipation: many prominent Virginians such as George Washington had freed their slaves in their wills. But emancipation was a serious and difficult business and to Frances Wright it was bound up with education. It 'neither can nor ought to be done too hastily. To give liberty to a slave before he understands its value is, perhaps, rather to impose a penalty than to bestow a blessing.' One can sense her deep agony in the last few paragraphs in her book as she tries to come to terms with this glaring evil in her otherwise perfect vision of America. Her devotion to the rationalist ideas of the eighteenth century came into conflict with her strong passion for liberty. She expressed this well when she told Robina Millar: 'This [slavery] is a subject upon which it is difficult to reason, because it is so easy to feel.'

Yet her American experience had shown her the crucial question that bedevilled those who wanted to end slavery. Many British and European opponents of slavery never troubled themselves with the question of how America could come to terms with a large population of former slaves. Even at this early stage in her life, Frances Wright knew that truth compelled her to mention this dilemma. She felt that emancipation could never be successful where there was a mixed black population, part slave and part free. She hoped that Virginians, as always, would give a lead on this great and complicated question. She was delighted to end her book with the words that President Monroe had addressed to her at their meeting, especially as he was a Virginian and a slave-owner: 'The day is not very far distant,' the President had said, 'when a slave will not be found in America.'*

In her book Fanny Wright was not particularly concerned, as was Mrs Burlend, with giving hints to would-be emigrants. When she does do so her hints are so evidently intended for her own class as to be next to useless for ordinary people. Her principal concern when advising emigrants is what they should do with their servants. Coping with the 'servant problem' was a contentious topic which almost all women writers on America discussed. Most male travellers barely mentioned it. It does not appear

---

* Monroe, like his friend, Jefferson, was perplexed by the problem of freed slaves. When he was Governor of Virginia in 1800, the state legislature asked him to find western territories in which to settle freedmen. Monroe also supported the work of the American Colonization Society which created Liberia as a home for freed blacks; the capital, Monrovia, was named in his honour.[21]

odd to us that a Duke's daughter like Lady Emmeline Stuart Wortley discussed servants but it does appear so when an upper-middle-class radical like Fanny Wright tackles the question. We must remember that few middle-class ladies, let alone aristocrats, would venture forth in the nineteenth century without a maid. Indeed, more than anything else, a lady's maid made the lady both in status as well as in constructing the complicated dress of the period. Servants were a necessity for the running of any middle-class home and it was the woman's task to manage them. It was therefore only natural for women writers to be concerned with the subject.

Fanny Wright warned European emigrants not to bring their own servants, as they could not adjust to American ways. (Readers of Henry James' *The Europeans* will remember the problem faced by the baroness's maid.) It was difficult for a European servant to adjust to the balance between the American ideal of equality and their own position. It was not a problem for American servants, for 'those bred up under it, can perceive and acknowledge the distinctions which education and condition place between the gentleman and the laborer'. She found that there were servants available in the North, drawn mainly from Irish immigrants but some British as well. Unlike many British travellers, Fanny Wright was well disposed towards the Irish in America: 'There is something about the Irishman that every where seems to attract sympathy.' She had at least found it so with young Tone. People with money could also hire Negro servants and such work frequently gave employment to freed slaves now living in those northern states which allowed Negroes to reside within their borders. Yet she complained that 'their faults are indolence, and an occasional tendency to intemperance and petty dishonesty'. She warned Europeans not to assume that these Negro servants were not as fiercely proud of their country as white Americans.

Part of her concern in the little advice she did offer to emigrants was her belief that the worsening economic conditions in England and the increasingly repressive measures of Lord Liverpool's Tory government, as symbolised in the 'Peterloo Massacre', would cause Englishmen to flock to America. She had found most of the English emigrants in America 'vulgar and illiterate' while the French and Irish were better educated because many of them were political exiles. Yet now she felt that changed conditions were forcing 'Hampdens' – radicals of independent means like the Parliamentarian leader of the seventeenth century, John Hampden – from England and by 1819 she knew of thirteen English families who had arrived recently with £500 each.[22] This was the minimum she felt that families should bring, showing how far removed she was from the reality of normal life in Britain. (The thrifty Burlends, it may be remembered, spent £30 to get to America and a further £35 to buy their eighty-acre farm. They had very little left.) The policies of the British government, about which Fanny Wright appears to have had little detailed information, would soon make England, like Spain, a land of 'beggars and princes'. It was to the English middle-classes that she addressed her book in the hope of describing a land where they could be both prosperous and happy.

PUBLICATION AND CRITICAL RECEPTION

The Wright sisters left America in May 1820 after a stay of some twenty months. It had been a pleasant and useful trip for Fanny. She had seen her play produced with a moderate success and both she and Camilla had been well received by important people wherever they travelled. They had made many friends; after years of loneliness, the world seemed to be opening up for both of them. By following Fanny Wright's activities in the years after her first American trip we shall be able to place her first visit in its proper perspective. Her book about this trip was only the beginning of America's influence on her as well as of her influence on America.

The best source of information about the years after her return to Europe lies in a collection of letters written by Fanny Wright to Julia and Harriet Garnett, daughters of a prominent English radical, John Garnett, who had settled in America. Garnett had been Sheriff of Bristol from 1782 to 1792 but, like Robina Millar's husband, had left England when the government began suspecting radicals during the French Revolution. Garnett had settled at a farm on the Raritan River near New Brunswick, New Jersey, not far from New York City.[23] His two daughters were only slightly older than Fanny Wright and became her closest friends. Julia Garnett was twenty-six and Harriet was a year younger. They were to play a key role in her life and in the life of another woman in this book, Frances Trollope. Indeed, the Garnetts would emerge as the centre of a large network of radical sympathisers with links in New York, Washington, London and Paris. Frances and Camilla Wright spent many happy days with the Garnetts at their New Jersey house – a house that still bore scars of the Revolutionary War. John Garnett was one of the first in a long line of elderly radicals whom the orphaned Fanny Wright made into substitute fathers. In her book she speaks with great emotion of her 'almost filial affection' for this 'philosopher of the world and friend of man'. His friendship also provided her with valuable introductions. Ironically one of his close friends had been a fellow refugee and neighbour, Baron Hyde de Neuville, a royalist émigré from revolutionary France. Garnett had fled from England because of his support for the Revolution that forced Hyde de Neuville from France. By the time Fanny Wright visited America, France had had another of its periodic revolutions and Hyde de Neuville was no longer a refugee. He was sent to represent the restored Bourbon monarchy in Washington and it was through him that the Wrights met Henry Clay, then Speaker of the House of Representatives, and other American politicians. This was one of John Garnett's last services to the

Wrights. He died 'almost before' Fanny was 'out of sight of the American
shores', and this made her sing his praises all the more effusively in her
book.

It was not only Garnett's death that made Fanny Wright depressed as
she sailed for her native land. She had made some attempt to become an
American citizen, but decided she must return to Britain. It is hardly
surprising that she felt ill as the ship sailed eastward, and the Captain
had to make a mad dash to a chemist's shop when they arrived in Liverpool
to get some gum-arabic to relieve the congestion of her lungs. (Her career
would be punctuated by a series of illnesses and nervous collapses.) The
two sisters went to stay with Mrs Millar in Cumberland, there to await
the Revolution they expected in the wake of the 'Peterloo Massacre'. By
October, when the cool breezes of autumn had blown away the hot summer
winds of revolution, Fanny Wright was plainly getting restless. She wrote
to the Garnetts that she might settle on the Continent although she was
also considering a return to the United States to 'follow the bent of my
heart in becoming a citizen of the only country to which I acknowledge an
attachment'. Her love for America was almost equalled by her 'aversion'
to England's climate, government, society and, most of all, 'the recollections which make all these doubly offensive to me'. Some might, she agreed,
find her 'madly prejudiced against this island' which 'contains much of good
and something yet of happiness'. Yet the sight of beggars upset her and
she was disgusted with what she regarded as political and religious
hypocrisy: 'Whatever be the condition of the nations on the Continent, they
are at least *improving*. Here all is *retrograde*.' It is plain that at least some
of her devotion to her new country was based on hatred of her old one.[24]

In the midst of her letter to the Garnetts there is an outburst that gives
her true feelings about America. Her private thoughts were far more
troubled than she had admitted in her book:

> My Harriet I love your feelings towards your country. You may well be proud
> of it; you may well exult in its prosperity and its freedom, and you may well
> too sigh when you throw your eyes Southward, and see liberty mocked and
> outraged and that by a race of free men, who while they have her name in
> their mouths, ay and her energy in their souls, grasp the chain of oppression
> in their hands, denying to the wretched sons of Africa that holy birth-right
> which they themselves declare man holds of God. When my thoughts turn to
> America the crying sin of her slavery weighs upon my heart; there are
> moments when this foul blot so defaces to my mind's eye all the beauty of her
> character that I turn with disgust from her, and in her from the last and only
> nation on the globe to which my soul clings with affection, pride and hope.

She was sure that the South 'can only *delay*' emancipation as the slave
was, she claimed, anxious for freedom as 'already he feels the chain, and
he who *feels* will soon *snap* it'.

Her increasing interest in slavery was certainly a topical one. Had she glanced at a current issue of the *Edinburgh Review* she would have seen a lengthy review of a book of American statistics which showed the tremendous advances the United States had made in less than fifty years of independence. While praising the achievements, the reviewer – the fact that it was Sydney Smith soon became known – attacked the Americans for their constant boasting that 'they were the greatest, the most refined, the most enlightened, and the most moral people upon earth'. Smith, who in many ways was friendly to Americans, warned them – in words that are still heard today – that this boasting appears 'unspeakably ludicrous on this side of the Atlantic'. He then concluded with a well-aimed blow which would have unsettled Fanny Wright if she had read it: 'Under which of the old tyrannical governments of Europe is every sixth man a slave, whom his fellow creatures may buy and sell and torture?'[25]

Throughout her travels, Fanny Wright had been annoyed when she heard of attacks upon America by English travellers. Her enthusiasm made her anxious to write her own account based on her letters to Robina Millar. She told the Garnetts not to expect too much from anything she published about her trip: 'I grow more doubtful of my fitness for the task every day.' Nevertheless she was delighted to hear that she had made such an impression during her visit to Washington that Henry Clay had cited her as 'a distinguished foreign lady'. She carried on with revising her letters into a book and, when she had finished, sent it to Longmans who, as mentioned earlier, had recently published Henry Fearon's book on America. Fearon had gone to America with strong radical opinions, but he was soon convinced it was not 'the political Elysium ... which the imaginations of many have fondly anticipated'.[26] Fanny Wright knew Fearon's book and made several criticisms of it in her own, but his book showed that Longmans had an interest in America. The Garnett sisters may also have sought the help of an English author who managed their father's property in England. Henry Milton, who had written a book on art for Longmans, was the son of an old friend of John Garnett and was also the brother of a woman who had many friends in the literary world, Frances Trollope. One of her sons later recalled that his father had had correspondence with Longmans about Frances Wright's book.[27]

Views of Society and Manners in America; in a Series of Letters from that Country to a Friend in England, during the Years 1818, 1819, and 1820 by an Englishwoman was published in 1821. The author remained anonymous in this edition. The book, as we have seen, is a highly personal and emotional account of a young radical's love affair with the country of her dreams. The work was not intended to be a book either of reflections, such as Tocqueville's, or of personal achievement, such as Mrs Burlend's, but an exciting love story of one young woman's rapturous devotion to her vision of America. Fanny Wright described the book's publication in her autobiography: its appearance, she said, 'changed the tone, and somewhat corrected the views, of leading periodicals, while they revived, on the

European Continent, old reminiscences of the country of Franklin and Washington'.[28] This pardonable exaggeration does not allow for Tory attacks such as that launched by the powerful *Quarterly Review*, which denounced this 'impudent attempt to foist into public notice under a spurious title, namely that of an Englishwoman' this 'ridiculous and extravagant panegyric' on America. The *Quarterly* resented 'the grossest and most contemptible calumnies against this country that folly and malignity ever invented'. An 'Englishwoman with the proper spirit attached to that proud title would blush to be thought the author of such a work'. The periodical refused to believe that 'one so lost to shame exists among us'. The book must be the work of 'one of those wretched hirelings who under the assumed name of travellers, &c., supply the radical press'.[29] Her book was, of course, praised by radical publications and received a warm welcome in America, although at least one critic in the *North American Review* hinted gently that it was, at times, a shade too optimistic.

Neither adulation nor criticism was important to the author: what was important was the way the book made her a figure in radical circles. 'I want to talk with you about Miss Wright. I am in love with her, and I suspect that you are.' Jeremy Bentham had not even met Fanny Wright when he wrote these words to the American Minister in London, Richard Rush. He had been so impressed with her book that he had obtained the address of the anonymous author from Longmans and had then invited her to visit him: 'During your stay in London my hermitage, such as it is, is at your service, and you will be expected in it. I am a single man, turned seventy, but as far from melancholy as a man need be.' Once again luck seemed to be with her: as a young woman she had studied Bentham's writings and now she was to live in his house and meet such famous radicals as Francis Place, 'the radical tailor of Charing Cross'. (Anyone who is interested to see what Bentham looked like at this time can still see him at University College London. He sits there in an 'auto-icon' of his own devising – that is, a wax dummy dressed to resemble him and displayed in a glass case like some obscure Sicilian saint.) Fanny Wright could look forward to long hours of discussions of radical philosophy and the delights of inventing constitutions. Yet, as so often would be the case in her life, reality proved more difficult than hope.

As Bentham was stone deaf, it was difficult to carry on conversation and her visit was not altogether a success. As she herself put it, 'an hour's conversation with my Socrates leaves me more fatigued than does a walk of six miles'.[30] Bentham was in touch with many leading liberals and radicals on the continent, but their governments kept a close watch on such correspondence. When he heard that the Wrights planned to visit France, he asked Fanny to arrange safe ways for him to write to his friends. As he told his brother, she was 'trusty, intelligent, and diligent'. He added, in a somewhat snide comment, 'she is in petticoats (and you will see they are no small ones) *quite* the *man* of business'.[31]

The friendship with Bentham was only a prelude to the most important relationship in her life, which began when Fanny and Camilla decided to spend some time in France. The two Garnett sisters and their mother had moved to Paris after their father's death. It was delightful to be reunited with such old friends, but it was her meeting with a new friend that provided Fanny with a purpose. A few days before her twenty-sixth birthday, the ardent radical broke down in tears when she met a Marquis in his mid-sixties. Marie Joseph Paul, Marquis de Lafayette, was known as 'the hero of two continents'. As a young aristocrat in the 1770s, he had gone to America and offered his help to the rebels. He became an honorary son to George Washington and played an important role in the ultimate American victory at Yorktown. Yet his later career had been one long disaster both for himself and for his country. He took a conspicuous part in the momentous events of 1789 and for a while it seemed that he might be able to guide France into some form of constitutional monarchy. His limited abilities could not prevent the Revolution's rapid descent into tyranny and bloodshed. His own family suffered: on one day his wife lost her mother, grandmother and sister to the rapacious guillotine. After the final overthrow of Napoleon in 1815, Lafayette was seen once again as the leader of liberal opposition to the restored Bourbon monarchy, and he was a symbol of liberty throughout Europe. Yet those who observed him first hand saw a more complicated figure. By this time his much-loved wife had been long dead, but the Marquis was no inconsolable widower. Stendhal, who shared his dislike of the Restoration, often observed him in the salons of Paris. With his waspish wit, the novelist sketched a devastating portrait of the way the Marquis appeared within a month or two of Fanny Wright's encounter with him:[32]

On top of this tall body [was] an impassive countenance, cold, insignificant as an old family portrait ... Fresh as I was in 1821 ... I perceived ... that M de Lafayette was quite simply one of Plutarch's heroes. He lived from day to day, without too much intelligence ... Meanwhile, despite his age ... his unique occupation was to press his hand on a pretty girl's skirt from behind (*vulgo*, to feel her bottom), and to do so frequently and without too much restraint. While awaiting the great deeds which do not present themselves every day, and the chance of placing a hand on a young women's skirts ... M de Lafayette ... has the same fault as I. He is frantic over a young Portuguese of eighteen ... the friend of his grandchildren ... he imagines, with this young Portuguese and with all other young women, that she singles him out; he dreams only of her, and what is pleasant is that he is often right in his imaginings ... his eyes light up when they encounter the start of a well-curved breast – all goes to make him pass his last years gaily, to the great scandal of women of thirty-five.

Fanny Wright had sent a copy of her book to Lafayette shortly after it was published. It delighted him as it brought back the scenes and the ideals of his youth and his days of unsullied glory. He sent her a fulsome reply, as well as a private message, with a Frenchman visiting London. She waited only a day after her arrival in Paris before leaving for his château, only to find that he was travelling in the opposite direction; this slight contretemps only made their meeting all the more emotional. She described the scene to Bentham: 'Our meeting was scarcely without tears (at least on my side) and whether it was that this venerable friend of human liberty saw in me what recalled to him some of the most pleasing recollections of his youth (I mean those connected with America) or whether it was only that he was touched by the sensibility which appeared at that moment in me, he evidently shared my emotion.' They talked for over an hour and then he came back that evening and stayed till after midnight. She assured the elderly sage in London that the 'main subject of our discourse was America'.[33]

Fanny Wright's formidable intelligence and fervent sincerity, not to mention her great height, did not appeal to many men of her own age. Yet older men, like Garnett, Bentham and now Lafayette – who was himself tall – revelled in the company of such a zealous disciple. She was soon installed at Lafayette's château, La Grange, which became her 'consecrated dwelling'. The cynical habitués of Parisian salons no doubt smiled knowingly at yet another conquest by the aged Marquis. No one can really say what was the nature of the relationship between them. Whatever it was, it was intense. She decided she wanted to write his biography, which meant many months of delightful research at the elegant château with an almost permanent house party of liberal luminaries. She also began to assist the Marquis in his ineffective plots not only against the French government, but also against the far more reactionary Spanish Bourbons and some of the small monarchies of Italy. Once, when he was absent for a short while in Paris on political business, she wrote to him as 'my friend, my father, and if there be a word more expressive of love, and reverence, and adoration I would fain use it'. 'I am only half alive', she groaned, 'when away from you. You see you have spoilt me ... in truth I love you very, very much ... I put my arms round the neck of my paternal friend and ask his blessing.' The paternal friend more than equalled her outpourings when replying to 'ma bien aimée, adorée Fanny, la tendre fille de mon choix'.[34] She was fortunate in that she got on well with other members of Lafayette's family, especially his son, George Washington Lafayette.

She was also busy working on a French translation of her book, aided by the American Minister to France, yet another elderly admirer, the Swiss-born Albert Gallatin. By January 1822 *Voyage aux Etats-Unis D'Amerique* was ready and this edition, unlike the first English one, acknowledged its authorship '*Par Miss Wright*'. Of course she also frequented the salon the Garnetts had established for visiting Americans and

Englishmen. Here she became so close to that old friend of the Garnett family, Frances Trollope, that she invited that rather proper English visitor and her somewhat intractable husband to spend time at Lafayette's château. This in itself shows how well-established Fanny Wright had become: she was now issuing invitations and acting as the virtual *châtelaine* of La Grange. Even Lafayette's remarkably tolerant daughters began to worry about gossip. However, there was a far greater threat to his reputation. One of his anti-Bourbon plots went disastrously wrong and some of the plotters were executed. It suddenly seemed an excellent time for the Marquis to take up a long-standing invitation to pay a ceremonial visit to the Republic where he was venerated.

TO AMERICA WITH LAFAYETTE

For Fanny Wright nothing could be more delightful than another visit to America and one in the company of her hero. Naturally the ever-patient Camilla would accompany them. Lafayette's family seems to have demurred, perhaps because there was talk that the Marquis planned to adopt his young disciple as a daughter. He left for America and arrived in New York in August 1824. The Wrights arrived one month later and throughout the hero's triumphal tour they followed him almost everywhere. Fanny Wright's book had made her an admired figure in America, but her almost constant presence at Lafayette's side caused much speculation and considerable criticism. Since, to Americans, Lafayette could do no wrong, the blame for this curious relationship was visited on Fanny Wright and it is hardly surprising that her most vehement critics were other women. Her most determined enemy was Eleanor Parke Custis Lewis, the granddaughter of the Washingtons, who had been one of the first of Lafayette's honorary daughters. She was genuinely horrified at the thought that he might become the subject of ridicule and she marshalled her innumerable connections among the 'First Families of Virginia' to keep the Wrights from the most important celebrations. 'The fair Ws did not go to Mt V——n with the Gen'l ... or [to] Alexandria', boasted Nelly Lewis. 'Do I not deserve well of my country for this good deed ... I know that but for me they would have now be[en] tarnishing his glory by their presence. They were resolved to go, & he could not say *no*, until I taught him how to set his mouth & pen to a negative position.'[35]

Although the Wrights were kept from two of the great pageants, Lafayette's visit to Mount Vernon to honour the memory of George Washington and his spectacular reception in the near-by town of Alexandria, where he went to call on the widow of his old companion, 'Light Horse Harry' Lee, they were present at many other celebrations in Virginia. Naturally Fanny Wright exulted in the wild enthusiasm which greeted her hero. Yet, 'amid all the politeness I see and attention I receive my heart is sick', she wrote to the Garnetts in Paris. Her problem was that she was seeing far more of slavery than she had on her first visit. 'I have not yet seen my fellow creatures sold in the market place and God forbid I should see it, for I really cannot answer for what I might say or do, but I have seen them manacled when sold on board a vessel bound for New Orleans.' 'Our steamboat,' she wrote, 'brushed past her swiftly which perhaps prevented my committing what could only have been folly.' Sitting in Virginia's beautiful capital city, Richmond, she brooded on slavery: 'They who so sin against the liberty of their country – against those great principles for which their honored guest poured on their soil his treasure and his blood are not worthy to rejoice in his presence.'[36]

Yet for Fanny Wright the highlight of this Grand Tour was the six weeks that Lafayette spent as the guest of Thomas Jefferson at his home, Monticello. Even before this, Jefferson, as we have seen, had begun a correspondence with the young Scotswoman and he thoroughly approved of her book on America. Lafayette, mindful no doubt of the snide criticisms of her position, had written to Jefferson:

> You and I are the two Men in the world the esteem of whom she values the Most. I wish much, My dear friend, to present these two adopted daughters of mine to Mrs Randolph [Jefferson's daughter] and to you; they being orphans from their Youth, and preferring American principles to British Aristocracy, Having an Independent, tho not Very large fortune, have passed the three last Years in Most intimate Connection with My Children and Myself and Have Readily Yielded to our joint Entreaties to make a second Visit to the U.S.

As an experienced general, Lafayette had obviously fortified himself against all the possible attacks of his or Fanny's critics. For the Wright sisters, this visit not only gave them a chance to marvel at Jefferson's clever contrivances which made Monticello so fascinating a house, but it gave them the best opportunity to study the workings of a slave plantation. Fanny had some serious talks about slavery with her host, who had long agonised to discover a practical plan for gradual emancipation. We can get a flavour of the conversation because among Jefferson's slaves was a remarkable man called Israel, who waited at table and sometimes drove the visitors and Jefferson about the estate in a carriage. Israel listened to their conversation and long remembered Lafayette's saying that he had fought for the Americans because they battled for 'a great and noble principle – the freedom of mankind', but some people 'were held in bondage'. Lafayette stressed the importance of educating the slaves and Jefferson gave partial agreement, saying that he wanted them to learn to read, but he did not approve of their learning to write lest they forge documents.[37] From Jefferson and other Virginians, Fanny Wright realised that emancipation in itself could not solve the problem. Slavery was not just an economic system, but also a racial one. 'The prejudice, whether absurd or the contrary, against a mixture of the two colors is so deeply rooted in the American mind,' she wrote to the Garnetts, 'that emancipation without expatriation seems impossible.'[38]

Jefferson explained to her that any plan for emancipation had to cope with this near universal dread of 'miscegenation'. A decade earlier he had written that 'the amalgamation of whites with blacks produces a degradation to which no lover of his country, no lover of excellence in the human character, can innocently consent'.[39] She heard a similar view from James Madison, whom she visited later in her trip. He had succeeded his friend and neighbour, Jefferson, as President and now, eight years after leaving office, he also was retired from politics. She must have enjoyed this opportunity to talk with the 'Father of the Constitution'. Their meeting gave her a further opportunity to discuss slavery with someone whose views were the same as Jefferson's. Madison and Wright must have made a striking sight as they talked: the shortest President in American history conferring with the tall Scotswoman.

There was one other man who would deeply influence her developing ideas about emancipation. When she returned to Washington, she heard a lecture by a fellow Scot, Robert Owen. After a highly successful career as a manufacturer, he sought to find a way to alleviate the problems of the working class. His socialist message soon began to attract many followers. To promote these ideas he was in the midst of establishing a utopian community at New Harmony, Indiana, a village developed by a German religious sect. If Owen's ideas could help the 'white slaves' of industrial England and New England, perhaps they might also offer some hope for the black slaves of the South. Certainly party politics seemed to offer little hope for Fanny Wright, especially after she observed that rare occasion in American history when the House of Representatives picked a President after no candidate had a majority in the Electoral College. For her, this was a blatant attack upon democratic principles. She had many splendid opportunities to study the workings of politics for she discussed political ideas with the third and fourth Presidents in Virginia, met the fifth President in Washington, watched the election of the sixth and within a few months would be seeking the advice of Andrew Jackson, who would become the seventh.

The *Washington Gazette* reported the visit of 'the celebrated English authoress, Miss Wright and her sister' to Congress when Lafayette was presented with a grant of $200,000 (£40,000) and an estate of 24,000 acres. For once we hear from the normally silent Camilla, who wrote to tell the Garnetts that Fanny had sent an account of their visit to 'our dear Mrs Trollope'. But dear Mrs Trollope was not to give such a flattering account in her own book, written several years later. She would then write that a lady in Washington told her that the Wrights 'very frequently attended the debates, and that the most distinguished members were always crowded round them'. The Congressmen justified their behaviour by arguing that if American women would attend the debates, Congressmen might visit *them* in the galleries. To be fair, Mrs Trollope's comment was made almost ten years after the visit and after her friendship with Fanny Wright had soured. In a city like Washington, even in its youthful days, rumours spread quickly – in this case, about the elderly hero and his fervent disciple. Some of this gossip was picked up by a German visitor, the Duke of Saxe-Weimar, who commented in his own travel book: 'I was told that this lady with her sister, unattended by a male protector, had roved through the country in steamboats and stages, that she constantly tagged about after General Lafayette, and whenever the General arrived at any place Miss Wright was sure to follow next day.'[40]

THE NASHOBA EXPERIMENT

However, the sisters did part from Lafayette when he continued further South. The Wrights went west – and away from slavery – to visit two Utopian communities established by British radicals: Owen's New Harmony and an abolitionist colony of English Quakers in Illinois. Fanny Wright was impressed with Owen's plan and the educational work of a French physician, William Phiquepal D'Arusmont, which seemed to offer some practical ideas on emancipation. She now began to see her life's work taking shape. She wrote *A Plan for the Gradual Abolition of Slavery in the United States Without Danger or Loss to the Citizens of the South*, which was published in Baltimore in 1825. Her plan was to set up utopian colonies throughout the South where slaves could work to purchase their freedom. The slaves would also be educated so that they could use this freedom properly. She was also influenced by talks with Quaker abolitionists like Benjamin Lundy. Fanny Wright avoided the violent denunciations of slave-owners as sinners so common among later abolitionists. Her idea was to win converts by presenting a reasonable plan to reasonable men. Surely, as Bentham had taught, this was the proper way.

She sent a copy of her pamphlet to her recent host, Madison. His reply is, perhaps, the best analysis of the problems she would face. The former President readily admitted: 'The magnitude of this evil among us is so deeply felt, and so universally acknowledged, that no merit could be greater than that of devising a satisfactory remedy for it.' Yet, Madison continued, 'Unfortunately the task, not easy under any other circumstances, is vastly augmented by the physical peculiarities of those held in bondage, which preclude their incorporation with the white population.' This only confirmed the view that she herself had reluctantly come to accept. The other problem was how to replace slave labour, as it was impossible to get whites to do their work. Nevertheless Madison said her plan had two excellent points: it envisaged both the voluntary co-operation of the slaveholders and the removal of the freed slaves. He then, however, pointed to the rock upon which her plan was to crash: would the slaves be able to produce enough to purchase their freedom? Madison accepted the idea that they should be educated for their eventual freedom, but he doubted whether the ideas of utopian communities were good models for her work as they were based on religious convictions.[41]

Fanny Wright was even more anxious to secure public support from Jefferson. She sent him a copy of her plan, but did not receive a reply for several months because the aged statesman was suffering excruciating pain from a prostate condition. However, he studied her pamphlet and his eventual reply was encouraging. 'At the age of eighty-two, with one foot in the grave, and the other uplifted to follow it', he explained that he could not take any part in her experiment. Nevertheless, he encouraged her in her work for emancipation:[42]

> The abolition of the evil is not impossible; it ought never to be despaired of. Every plan should be adopted, every experiment tried, which may do something ... That which you propose is well worth of trial. It has succeeded with certain portions of our white brethren, under the care of ... an Owen, and why may it not succeed with the man of color? ... You are young, dear Madam, and have powers of mind which may do much in exciting others in this arduous task.

Buoyed by this letter, she set about her 'arduous task'. For once she was not accompanied by the faithful Camilla, but by a new friend, George Flower, an Englishman who had been involved in the anti-slavery cause in Illinois. Flower also had practical experience of organising a settlement for English radicals. Fanny Wright's most authoritative biographer thinks that Flower became her lover on this trip. They stopped at the plantation of Andrew Jackson, the future President, and from him learned that there was some cheap land available in his own state of Tennessee. In November 1825 she paid $480 (£96) for 320 acres on both sides of the Wolf River near Memphis. She named the settlement Nashoba, after the Indian word for wolf. She spent more of her money in her most painful act by purchasing ten slaves in Nashville. If she was to train slaves for freedom, she had to buy them first, horrible though the process was. She acquired some others when a supporter from South Carolina sent a pregnant slave with five small children – not really a very helpful donation to the struggling community.

Her plan was not as absurd as it might seem today. Tennessee had the first anti-slavery newspaper in the South as well as twenty-five anti-slavery societies.* If Nashoba proved a financial success and avoided outraging local opinion, it could attract more converts to the cause. Unfortunately Flower did not long remain at Nashoba, and when he left there

---

* The first Mayor of Memphis, a man with the resounding name of Marcus Brutus Winchester, had openly married a freed black woman. He was the son of Andrew Jackson's business partner. Fanny Wright stayed with the Winchesters while work was going on at Nashoba, and they named their daughter after her. Several years later, Mrs Winchester was barred from Memphis by an ordinance against freed blacks.[43]

was no one with practical experience or common sense. Fanny Wright had the help of a fellow Scot and radical, James Richardson, who would act as overseer to ensure that the slaves worked for their freedom. There was also a young Quaker, Richesson Whitby. Fanny Wright threw herself into the work with her customary enthusiasm. Although she had probably never done any physical labour in her life she now worked incessantly in clearing the fields and in doing work much like that done daily by Rebecca Burlend. Unfortunately she fell ill from sun-stroke and malaria and returned to New Harmony to recover her health. While there she formed a close friendship with Owen's son, Robert Dale Owen, and renewed her acquaintance with D'Arusmont. When the New Harmony community began to show signs of collapse, young Owen became increasingly pre-occupied with the Nashoba experiment. However, Fanny Wright suffered more ill-health when she returned to Nashoba and decided that a trip to Europe might give her time to recover as well as to recruit more supporters. The fact that young Owen was also making a visit to Europe offered the prospect of many long conversations about Nashoba and their other projects.

Her health seemed to recover once she was back in France, by July 1827. Lafayette, by now re-established in his château, was interested in her plans. He had himself tried and failed in a similar experiment with some of his own slaves in the French West Indies. She was not very fortunate in gathering new recruits or additional funds either in London or in Paris. Her attempts to win over Mary Shelley, widow of the poet, came to nothing, but she had better luck with the Garnetts' friend, Frances Trollope. The eldest Trollope child, Thomas Adolphus, then a schoolboy at Winchester, was impressed by the zealous young reformer, as he recalled sixty years later:

> She was very handsome in a large and almost masculine style of beauty, with a most commanding presence, a superb figure, and stature fully masculine. Her features both in form and expression were really noble. There exists ... a large lithographed portrait ... She is represented standing, with her hand on the neck of a grey horse ... and if I remember rightly, in Turkish trousers.

The reasons why Mrs Trollope and some of her children left for America will be discussed later, but they can be simply summarised by saying that she was tired of both her husband and his financial difficulties. Neither Tom Trollope nor his brother, Anthony, the future novelist, accompanied their mother. By November 1827 Fanny Wright and the Trollope party were on their way to New Orleans. They had hoped to return to America with Robert Dale Owen but they arranged their travel so hurriedly that he had to follow in another vessel. From her ship, as it lay on the Thames by Tower Stairs, she issued an 'Address to the Liberal Youth of France' and, as she crossed the Atlantic, she penned another, this time an 'Address to the Friends of Human Improvement in All Countries'.[44]

When the party finally arrived at Nashoba everything was in disarray. Richardson had run off with his slave-mistress and some of the other female slaves had been raped, a crime made easier by the rule that cabin doors could not be locked. (This was to teach the slaves a sense of responsibility.) Another principle of the colony was that the whole institution of marriage was wrong. Fanny was therefore particularly shocked to find that Camilla, who had hitherto seemed particularly keen on this theory, had married young Whitby. On one of the few occasions in which Camilla had been left alone she had done something of her own devising.

The story of Nashoba is complicated and depressing and it is not our purpose to follow its collapse in any detail. The Trollope party fled after ten days and all the warnings that Madison had given were now fulfilled. For once, Camilla should be allowed the last word. She wrote in November 1829 to Julia Garnett, 'Having after a four year experiment ascertained that the Slaves at Nashoba, *cannot* at the low state of agricultural produce which has prevailed from their first arrival there, raise a sufficiency for their food and clothing and far less lay by a surplus fund for their emancipation and are moreover a constant source of anxiety and pecuniary loss', Fanny had come to the 'decision of freeing herself from all farther responsibility regarding them, by their removal to a free country'. To her credit, Fanny Wright acted responsibly towards her slaves. She planned to take thirty of them to Haiti where they would be freed and placed under the care of the President of that black republic. She had lost at least $16,000 (£3,200) of her own money by the Nashoba experiment.[45]

OTHER CRUSADES

The journey to Haiti was delayed by Fanny's involvement in other causes that were gaining her a notoriety that still clings to her name today. At that time there were the stirrings of a 'Christian Party' in American politics. To the atheistic Wright this was a threat to the ideals of liberty. She therefore set out on a course of public lectures in 1828 to attack this development. These lectures rapidly expanded into an assault on Christianity and then on religion itself. From that she moved on to attack the concept of matrimony and to advocate birth control and sexual equality. She was fearless in her attacks as she toured most of the northern states giving lectures. Because of these she quickly became identified in the public mind with the idea of 'free love'; the exaggerated accounts of the scandals at Nashoba, which now began to appear in newspapers, confirmed the popular view.

Mrs Trollope was in Cincinnati, Ohio when her erstwhile friend made her first public appearance as a lecturer. The idea of a woman lecturing, Mrs Trollope recalled, would have been strange enough in Europe but it was even more shocking in America 'where women are guarded by a

seven-fold shield of habitual insignificance'.* Mrs Trollope well knew
Fanny Wright's ability as a talker with a wide vocabulary and a lovely
voice. She went on to describe her old friend: 'It is impossible to imagine
any thing more striking than her appearance. Her tall and majestic figure,
the deep and almost solemn expression of her eyes, the simple contour of
her finely formed head ... her garment of plain muslin, which hung around
her in folds that recalled the drapery of a Grecian statue.' As she confided
to a friend in England, the writer Mary Mitford: 'Wild and often mischievous, as her doctrines are she is a thing to wonder at, and you must see
her if you can.'46

One American journalist recalled years later that Fanny Wright had 'no
inconsiderable success' and that she won many young intellectuals, at least
temporarily, to some of her views. She even managed to interest the young
Walt Whitman who later recalled: 'She has always been to me one of the
sweetest of sweet memories, we all loved her; fell down before her; her very
appearance seemed to enthrall us.' He described her as 'beautiful in bodily
shape and gifts of soul. I never felt so glowingly towards any other woman
... she possessed herself of my body and soul.' The Owenite community at
New Harmony had become her latest cause. To head its school she tried to
recruit Bronson Alcott, who had given up his career as a pedlar to become
a progressive schoolmaster. He rejected her tempting offer of $1,200 (£240)
a year because he did not think New Harmony would last, although he did
believe that she 'may be and *is* right in many of her views, but their party
are not wise enough to understand her, or good enough to apply her
precepts'. In the privacy of his journal he reflected on her attacks on
marriage and her seeming advocacy of free love. He wondered 'whether the
intercourse of the sexes in a reasonable state of society will be wholly
promiscuous or whether each man will select for himself a partner to whom
he will adhere, as long as that adherence shall continue to be the choice of
both parties'. After such a convoluted contemplation the New England
sage concluded: 'It is by no means necessary that the female with whom
each man has sexual intercourse, should appear to each the most
deserving and excellent of her sex.'47 It seems a very different world to
that of *Little Women*, which Alcott's daughter, Louisa, would write in
the 1860s.

To promote her views, Fanny Wright established, appropriately enough
on Thomas Paine's birthday, the 'Free Press Association' which quickly set
up local branches. Its appeal went beyond intellectuals like Whitman and
Alcott. In the growing industrial city of Paterson, New Jersey, some sixteen
miles from New York, there was, for example, a 'Paterson Free Reading

* The Library of Congress has an 1829 coloured lithograph done by James Akin and
printed in Philadelphia. It is entitled 'A Downwright Gabbler, or a Goose that Deserves to be
Hissed'. It shows Fanny Wright as a goose dressed in black and lecturing while a simpering
male holds her hat.

Association'. In February 1829 the Paterson Association was delighted to have a visit from its leader, which she described in a letter to Camilla. Characteristically she sees this one minor success as the harbinger of major triumphs: 'The whole country is waking up – invitations pour in from every town ... Last week I went to Paterson, Passaic Falls, under the escort of the libs.' who had sent a carriage to collect her in New York. They had also insisted that she have a carriage and four horses for her return. She was given the same four horses that had pulled General Jackson's carriage and was pleased to discover that the stable manager, who would not normally let the horses out at night at any price, refused to charge her supporters.[48]

Parts of her career at this stage sound remarkably familiar to late twentieth-century ears. A wealthy young idealist, fresh from a radical commune, upset by the sermons of fundamentalist preachers, rushes round America giving lectures on every cause she can collect. It should not come as a surprise, therefore, that when she settled down briefly in a house near New York she used the opportunity to take up vegetarianism and to give up tea and coffee. (Bronson Alcott, like many of her associates, was a vegetarian. Thomas Carlyle described him as 'bent on saving the world by a return to acorns'.) She was apparently gathering her strength before returning to Nashoba to wind up its tangled affairs. Camilla, who was by this time both pregnant and separated from her husband, hastened to join her in Tennessee. The Wrights were beginning to lose some of the friends they had made on their first visit to America. Charles Wilkes, who had managed Fanny's fortune since she first arrived in New York eleven years before, now broke with her: 'The united opinions of all the females of my own family and of my connections prescribed to me one course – that of breaking off the intercourse between our families.' Few bankers are in the habit of associating with 'notorious' women – at least publicly. As word of her activities drifted back to Europe, even Lafayette was upset. He wrote to Robert Dale Owen that 'my love for her cannot be impaired' and that he still honoured her ideals and talents. Yet he worried about her total disregard of public opinion. Lafayette was himself a religious sceptic but he never could forget the deep piety of his late wife. He therefore particularly resented Fanny's 'exhibition of herself as a female lecturer in a whirlwind of anti-religious propaganda'.

Her career in America now came full circle as she hired the same theatre where her youthful play, *Altorf*, had been put on some ten years before. Now she wanted it to give lectures attacking religion and marriage. She met considerable hostility and felt it necessary to have protection on the stage by surrounding herself with a guard of Quaker ladies. We can only wonder what their tactics would have been in the midst of any attack! The press was particularly hostile. The *New York Evening Post*, under the editorship of the poet, William Cullen Bryant, declared that 'female expounders of any kind of doctrine are not to our taste'. She bought a disused church in New York's Bowery district and converted it into a 'Hall of Science'. Ironically, years later her grandson would serve as an Episcopal priest in the same area. In the basement of the church D'Arusmont and his pupils from New Harmony printed her newspaper, the *Free Enquirer*. She also took a great interest in promoting the Working Man's Party in New York. In addition she launched attacks on banks in good Jacksonian fashion, much to the undoubted horror of Charles Wilkes, who blamed Robert Owen for infecting his 'deluded' friends with such radical views. The party soon became known as 'The Fanny Wright Party' and although she worked enthusiastically for it, her presence did it no good. For these and other reasons, including the death of Camilla's baby, she decided to leave America, at least for a while. Philip Hone, who had recently been Mayor of New York, exulted as did many other conservatives when the *Hannibal* sailed eastward:

> Miss Frances Wright and her sister Mrs Whitby sailed for England ... These ladies came to this country soon after the arrival of Gen. Lafayette, and Miss Wright seemed at that time desirous of uniting her fame with that of the veteran republican, and it appeared that a matrimonial union would not then have been disagreeable to her. The good old man was, however, saved from the disgrace of such a connection.

Hone went on to record her connection with Robert Owen and to denounce her lectures as intended 'to break down the moral and religious ties which bind mankind together and bring into disrepute the institutions which have been revered by all good men'. Nevertheless he admitted that 'she is eloquent, bold, and singular in her opinions and the novelty of her doctrines has given her a degree of celebrity'. In London, Thomas Carlyle was not very impressed. He and his wife took time out from planning their move to Great Cheyne Row to attend one of Fanny Wright's lectures in the Freemasons Hall. In writing to his brother he appears not to have taken her too seriously: 'A poor Fanny Wright goes lecturing over the whole world; before sight, I will engage to lecture twice as well; being ... "the more gigantic spirit of the two".'[49]

MARRIAGE AND LAST YEARS

Hone did not know that Fanny had another companion as well as her sister. D'Arusmont, the French educational theorist, who had accompanied her on the trip with her freed slaves to Haiti, would be her companion on her transatlantic journey. Fanny Wright, now thirty-five, and D'Arusmont, fifty-two, found that they shared many interests and ideas, and she was soon pregnant. For the next year, her life was dominated by her desire to keep her pregnancy and the birth of a daughter secret. She avoided her friends and wrote hardly any letters. Even the outbreak of the 1830 revolution in France, in which Lafayette played a prominent role, does not seem to have sparked much interest in her. Her old hero was, however, one of the witnesses at her marriage to D'Arusmont in Paris in July 1831, some months after the birth of their daughter, Sylva. Old enemies, such as the *Quarterly Review*, exulted that the 'lecturer itinerant against Christianity, and Matrimony ... now alas! for philosophy! a mother, – and, we have been told, – (though we forget the new name) – a wife.'[50] The American writer, James Fenimore Cooper, saw her and wrote to tell Charles Wilkes that she now looked 'haggard and much changed for the worse'. Cooper's reaction was the same as Wilkes' had been: he would be insulting his own wife if he even met Fanny Wright, whose opinions on 'free love' had made her an outcast. If they had known that she had advanced beyond the realm of theory into that of practice, their horror would have been so uncontainable that they would have scarcely been able to write about it.[51]

Somehow Madame D'Arusmont never seemed to have the vivacity of Miss Wright. In February 1831 Camilla had died in her sister's arms; she had never really recovered her strength after the break-up of her strange marriage at Nashoba and the death of her son Francis. It may well be that Fanny blamed herself – and not without cause – for the tragedy of Camilla's life. For the rest of her own life she was preoccupied with an attempt to fool the world about the illegitimacy of Sylva. When a second and legitimate daughter died as an infant, the unhappy mother gave the younger child's birthdate to Sylva, who was about one year older. Naturally this made her more anxious to avoid friends who might notice that a child who looked like a two-year-old girl was officially only a few months old. Even the Garnetts saw little of their old friend. It was several years before the D'Arusmonts returned to America, where Fanny resumed her political activities, particularly in New York. She became an eloquent advocate for the increasing numbers of industrial workers who flocked in their thousands to hear her. When the Mayor of New York would not allow her to speak in public buildings, she held her rallies outdoors in the rain. At one point the entire police force of New York City had to be sent to protect her from outraged opponents.

Fanny Wright now seemed less interested in slavery; indeed she argued that the North must first rid itself of industrial slavery before it could criticise Southern slavery. In her lectures and speeches she continued to attack religion, particularly the way in which powerful Evangelical preachers such as Lyman Beecher used it to cloak their political programmes. In return she was attacked as 'the Red Harlot of Infidelity'. The founder of the Woman's College in Cincinnati, Catherine Beecher, Lyman's daughter, unleashed a fierce broadside at her:

Who can look without disgust and abhorrence upon such a one as Fanny Wright, with her great masculine person, her loud voice, her untasteful attire, going about unprotected, and feeling no need of protection, mingling with men in stormy debate, and standing up with bare-faced impudence, to lecture to a public assembly ... There she stands, with brazen front and brawny arms, attacking the safeguards of all that is venerable and sacred in religion.

It was almost constitutionally impossible for a member of the Beecher family to restrain a well-oiled torrent of personal abuse, so when Catherine paused to pay a compliment, it was but a mere prelude to further invective. She accepted that Fanny Wright – few opponents ever used her married name – was sincere and 'amiable', but that only made her 'folly' the 'more pitiable'. Wright's 'talents' only made her more offensive. Miss Beecher closed in for the kill: 'Her freedom from private vices, if she is free, only indicates ... that she has thrown off all feminine attractions. I cannot conceive any thing in the shape of a woman, more intolerably offensive and disgusting.' The Rev. Lyman Beecher must have glowed with paternal pride as he read his daughter's *Letters on the Difficulties of Religion*. Fanny Wright's biographer, Celia Morris, sees this as 'the prototype of the attacks that conservative American women launch on women who differ'.[52]

In the last fifteen years of her life, Fanny Wright became an almost regular transatlantic commuter. Since she clothed so many of her movements in secrecy, we only know of some of her trips from her opponents. In the nineteenth century the names of prominent passengers were noted in the newspapers on each side of the Atlantic. Thus, in 1839, Philip Hone happily underscored in his diary the words *'Fanny Wright's Gone'* as he read the passenger list of one packet ship and exulted: 'Mme Frances Wright D'Arusmont, better known as Fanny Wright, the quondam friend of Lafayette ... the apostle of infidelity, the idol of the Loco-focos. Let her go home or go to the Devil, so that she never visits us again.'[53]

Yet Hone was wrong. Fanny Wright had been 'home' ever since she first landed in New York more than twenty years before. Throughout the 1840s she supported various radical movements, but ill-health and family quarrels kept her from any sustained activity. From time to time she took up a new cause, as when she presented a petition to the U.S. Congress about the reform of land law. Perhaps she was thinking of those unhappy labourers whom she had seen about her aunt's Devonshire house forty years before when she gave one reason why America must support land reform: 'As the people of Great Britain are now fast turning their attention to the recovery of their long lost right to the soil, it would give them encouragement in their object and enable them the sooner to furnish happy homes for the thousands who otherwise would come among us as exiles.'[54] Gradually her name faded from public consciousness, for public opinion always demands a fresh subject to discuss and to dissect. No doubt for some politicians it was convenient to forget about her. In 1844 there was a debate in the House of Representatives about military chaplains. One Democrat said that he knew that anyone who spoke against chaplains would be accused of espousing 'Fanny Wright principles', but Congressman Wentworth denied that she had any role in this. In fact, he asked, who was she? 'I never saw her. I never saw a person who said he had seen her, nor did I ever read a line of her writings or even see a person who said he had ever read them ... [e]ven now her spectre haunts the imagination of politicians in want of capital.'[55]

Phiquepal D'Arusmont overflowed with ideas for educational improvements, but he was a vile husband and 'ultimately a suspicious and headstrong man' as Robert Dale Owen, who knew him well, said.[56] When his wife inherited yet another fortune in Scotland – Camilla's had already been added to her own – D'Arusmont not only cheated her out of her money, but turned their daughter, Sylva, against her. Fanny Wright settled in Cincinnati, the home of her enemies, the Beechers, where she had commenced her public career as a lecturer. She eventually divorced her husband. Sylva visited Cincinnati, but only to start a legal fight to gain her mother's land at Nashoba. Worn out by all these struggles, Fanny Wright died on 13 December 1852 after a fall on the ice. In her last days she read *Uncle Tom's Cabin* by Catherine Beecher's sister, Harriet, as a distraction from her physical and other suffering. The novel won millions to support the cause for the abolition of slavery, a cause which she had served decades before it became fashionable.

D'Arusmont did not long enjoy the money he had filched, for he died in Paris within a few years. Their daughter put up monuments to both of them; D'Arusmont's is in Montparnasse. In Spring Grove Cemetery, Cincinnati she raised an obelisk with a truly dreadful profile of her mother. It proclaims the basic dates of 'Frances Wright Phiquepal d'Arusmont'. At least Sylva selected two ringing quotations for the monument: 'I have wedded the cause of human improvement, staked on it my fortune, my reputation and my life' and 'Human-kind is but one family. The Education of its youth should be equal and universal.' The daughter, for whom she had sacrificed so much, turned against her mother's 'infidel trash' and became an active Christian. She even testified before a Congressional Committee about the question of female suffrage. 'As the daughter of Frances Wright whom the Female Suffragists are pleased to consider as having *opened* the door to their pretensions', she asked the legislators, 'to *shut* it forever, from the strongest convictions that they can only bring misery and degradation upon the whole sex, and thereby wreck human happiness in America'.[57]

＊

Some might find it easy to laugh at Fanny Wright. Yet her life is in so many ways a tragedy. She had beauty, wealth, charm and intelligence. She had noble aims and ideals. Yet she lacked that rarest of gifts: common sense. Rather than concentrate on what she came to see as her life's work in America, gradual emancipation, she became an advocate of every cause she could find and ended up doing more harm than good. President Madison summed this up when he wrote to Lafayette in 1828: 'With her rare talents and still rarer disinterestedness she has I fear created insuperable obstacles to the good fruits of which they might be productive by her disregard or rather defiance of the most established opinion and vivid feelings.' He continued: 'Besides her views of amalgamating the white and black population so universally obnoxious, she gives an eclat to her notions on the subject of Religion and of marriage, the effect of which your knowledge of this country can readily estimate.' The harm to her reputation done by her 'notions' was not confined to America. Her fellow Scotswoman, the canny Jane Welsh Carlyle, wrote to her husband in 1845, eleven years after the Freemasons Hall lecture he had scorned, and referred to Fanny Wright as someone who had devoted her life to 'boiling up individuals into the *species*'; Wright's views were the 'lost gilt lacker [*sic*] of other people's *"isms"* '. Van Wyck Brooks, the twentieth-century literary critic who shared most of Wright's radicalism, concluded that she suffered from 'that sclerosis of the temperament which often goes with humanitarian activities'.[58]

Throughout her restless life Fanny Wright had remained faithful to the vision of the America she had first found in an Italian history in her aunt's country house in Devon. The United States, the country she so deeply loved and so confusedly sought to serve, has almost totally forgotten her. If she is remembered at all it is as an eccentric, dressed in her Turkish trousers and described by one New York newspaper in a song to be sung to the tune of 'Oh! Put the Onions to Your Eyes':[59]

> E'en mother Lee has nothing to
> Our little Fanny Wright.
> For she had gold within her purse,
> And brass upon her face;
> And talent indescribable,
> To give old thoughts new grace.
> And if you want to raise a wind,
> Or breed a moral storm
> You must have one bold lady-man
> To prate about reform.

The heady atmosphere of young America provided her not only with a platform but with an inspiration, things she could not have found in any other country or time. America was the laboratory and she was one of the most renowned of those amateur chemists who worked there. Her vision of America and her life there remain part of the American experience. It was the great freedom found in that burgeoning land that allowed Fanny Wright on the one hand, and Rebecca Burlend on the other, to create the life of which each had dreamed. The descendants of Rebecca Burlend continue to provide the mainstream of American life; the descendants of Fanny Wright continue to provide their critics.

3

The Critic Abroad: Frances Trollope

On Christmas Day 1827 a ship slowly made its way into the mouth of the Mississippi River and headed for New Orleans. Among its passengers was an exotic party that had left London on 4 November. Now, after seven dreary weeks at sea, they stood on deck to watch the semi-tropical foliage unfold before them. One of the passengers was Fanny Wright, who had brought with her a middle-aged Englishwoman with her two daughters, one son, one man-servant, a maid and a French artist who was also a family friend. Why the forty-seven-year-old Frances Trollope accompanied Fanny Wright to America baffles people today as much as it did her friends at the time. She later claimed that she had gone to America to recoup family finances but, as we shall see, there was more to it than that. As a financial venture her time in America would prove a disaster and when she finally left the country in 1831 she was not only an embittered woman but a poorer one. Yet she would carry with her the manuscript of her first book, a book that was to mark a change in her fortune, create a new career for herself and her family and leave a permanent mark on Anglo-American relations. The publication of *Domestic Manners of the Americans* in 1832 caused more bitterness and misunderstanding than any other book on America: after 150 years it is still remembered as one of the most critical works ever written about the United States.

What had driven this English lady from the drawing rooms of London into the mouth of the Mississippi in the company of 'the notorious Fanny Wright'? Frances Trollope – like her friend she too was often called Fanny – was the daughter of a clergyman, the Rev. William Milton. She was born in 1779 and in 1809 she married a clergyman's son, Thomas Anthony Trollope, a barrister who had hopes of inheriting a considerable fortune, along with a sizeable country estate, from an uncle. Trollope was one of those unlucky men who proliferate on the borders of nineteenth-century literary history. His prospects of inherited wealth evaporated when his widowed uncle took a second wife and begat an heir: some said the old man was annoyed at his nephew's liberal politics. Whatever the reason, Trollope lost his hope of settling into the comfortable life of a country squire. He had an irascible temper and quarrelled with his clients: as a result he had fewer with whom to quarrel. In the meantime he had leased a farm in

Harrow so that his family could have the benefit of a country retreat and
he could enjoy the extra income from farming. Again he was unlucky: the
decline of agricultural prices meant that he never made enough from the
farm even to pay the rent, let alone make a profit. By 1830 his losses had
reached £5,000, a tremendous sum at the time. He should have listened to
his wife, who had long predicted that any attempt to make money from
farming would be 'precarious'.[1]

Both in London and in Harrow the Trollopes enjoyed entertaining
various political radicals along with literary and theatrical figures, while
the occasional foreign revolutionary added a diverting *frisson*. However, it
was a long-standing family friendship that lay behind Mrs Trollope's
quixotic adventures in the New World. Decades earlier her father had put
forward some plans to improve the Bristol docks, and he received much
encouragement from John Garnett, the Sheriff of Bristol. Their friendship
continued even after Garnett moved to America. As we know, this link was
of use to Fanny Wright when she was seeking a publisher and Mrs
Trollope's brother, Henry, seems to have helped her find a home for the
book at Longmans. Harriet and Julia Garnett moved to Paris and it was
in their salon that the Trollopes became increasingly friendly with Fanny
Wright who invited them to pay a visit to Lafayette. The Trollopes had a
delightful time at the château of La Grange, even though their hostess
forgot to come. They listened to the Marquis's radical talk while eight
liveried footmen lifted delicacies from silver salvers. This was the type of
'radical chic' Mrs Trollope enjoyed, and her normally morose husband even
abandoned his customary reserve and flung himself into a dance with
Lafayette's peasants. Thomas Trollope was no revolutionary, but he had
a strong contempt for the Tory politicians who had dominated Britain for
three decades. The hospitable Marquis not only discoursed on the iniqui-
ties of Louis XVIII's government, but on recent history in which he had
played a conspicuous role. He admitted to Mrs Trollope that the murder
of Louis XVI was the great tragedy of the French Revolution as the King
'really was one of the best of Kings'.[2]

Mrs Trollope's activities and opinions in the 1820s were diametrically
opposed to the opinions expressed in her book on America. Unlike her
friend, Fanny Wright, whose views sprang from within herself, Fanny
Trollope was always influenced by the world in which she moved. Her
youngest son, Anthony, recalled in his *Autobiography* that 'she had loved
society, affecting a somewhat liberal *rôle*, and professing an emotional
dislike to tyrants, which sprung from the wrongs of would-be regicides and
the poverty of patriot exiles'. He went on:

An Italian marquis who had escaped with only a second shirt from the
clutches of some archduke whom he had wished to exterminate, or a French
prolétaire with distant ideas of sacrificing himself to the cause of liberty, were
always welcome to the modest hospitality of her house. In after years, when

marquises of another caste had been gracious to her, she became a strong Tory, and thought that archduchesses were sweet.

The 'Italian marquis' was General Guglielmo Pepe, who had fled Naples after the failure of the Revolution he had led. The Neapolitan general visited the Trollopes both in London and in Harrow and was soon involved in conspiracies with Fanny Wright and Lafayette.[3]

Anthony Trollope, always a keen analyser of character, went on to comment on his mother's political views. His analysis would be echoed by most perceptive readers of her book on America: 'With her, politics were always an affair of the heart, as, indeed, were all her convictions. Of reasoning from causes, I think she knew nothing.' One 'affair of the heart' which had a profound effect on Mrs Trollope was a growing fascination for Fanny Wright. We often think of the early nineteenth century as a time of emotional friendships between men, such as Tennyson and Hallam, but the Romantic Age saw similar friendships between women who were so often isolated from the outside world of politics and business. Freed by servants from the drudgery of domestic chores, many talented and frustrated ladies turned their abilities and passions into female friendships, often nurtured by a wonderful gift for letter writing. One can still sense the outpouring of emotion as one turns over pages of carefully written letters with their tightly squeezed words in the surviving correspondence between Fanny Trollope and the Garnetts. They kept her informed of the activities of the Wright sisters when they followed Lafayette to America in 1824, and both the Wrights also wrote to 'our dear Mrs Trollope'.

As we have seen, Fanny Wright returned to Europe in 1827 seeking new recruits for Nashoba. She particularly wanted a 'female companion' who shared her delight in ideas and books. She first tried her hand with Mary Shelley, widow of the poet and creator of Frankenstein, but she could not leave her young son. Nor did the Garnetts seem entirely anxious to abandon their Parisian salon for the utopian rigours of Nashoba. Worn out by this dithering, Fanny Wright retreated to La Grange and there met Mrs Trollope who was once again visiting France. Here she had more luck, for Frances Trollope was ripe for adventure. For some years she had been urging her husband to abandon the Harrow farm so that they could live comfortably on the continent where English families found that their income went twice or even three times as far as at home. His refusal was just one of the many tensions between them. Her husband's headaches, increasingly 'dreadful' temper and the family's declining fortunes made her a willing listener. Fanny Trollope was also motivated by a growing sense of frustration. She was older than both the Wrights and the Garnetts and yet these younger women seemed to have accomplished so much more. All she had done was to circulate amusing verses about her local vicar's refusal to give a public burial to Lord Byron's illegitimate daughter. She had some reputation as a hostess, but even that could no longer continue since her husband had recently told her that they could no longer maintain their comfortable home in Harrow. She would soon have to undergo the humiliation of moving into a near-by farmhouse. Two of her sons were ensconced in public school, but the middle son, Henry, then sixteen and more than a bit feckless, was proving a problem. He was in Paris, where he was endeavouring with little success to be a banker. He found Fanny Wright and her enthusiasm for all things American far more fascinating than the intricacies of foreign currencies. The combination of all these factors led Mrs Trollope to take an impulsive decision to accompany Fanny Wright to America. 'Will it be possible', she asked the Garnetts, 'to let this "angel" ... depart without vowing to follow her? I think not. I feel greatly inclined to say "where her country is, there shall be my country". The more I see of her ... the more I feel convinced that *all* her motives are right.' For her part, Fanny Wright had been aware of the weaknesses of her 'dear but infatuated friend' for some two-and-a-half years before Mrs Trollope left England; it appears that she also did not trust her to keep a secret.[4] For Fanny Trollope, the first task was to tell her husband in Harrow of her somewhat quixotic notion.

Not surprisingly, Mr Trollope opposed the idea of his wife's going off to America. While he later complained that Fanny Wright had 'induced' his wife to leave, Fanny Wright told the Garnetts in a letter written aboard ship as it entered the mouth of the Mississippi: 'I wrote you also it was settled Trollope shd. pay us a visit next autumn twelvemonth.' In a later letter she referred to 'the consent of Mr Trollope' which implies he had been won over to whatever plan they had adopted. Lafayette thought the idea ridiculous and wrote to Charles Wilkes in New York: 'You will be not a little surprised to hear that Mrs Trollope, after a full explanation of the Nashoba experimental system has ... determined to become with her daughters and son, members of the society and to give up the habits and comforts to which I thought her peculiarly attached.' Even Wright herself wondered if her friend was the right person for the 'forest adventure' and wrote to the Garnetts, 'I at first used every argument to dissuade her from an enterprise for which I thought her unfit', but, 'she being decided, I aided her of course as a friend should'. It appears that Mrs Trollope's was a rushed decision, made only five days before the ship sailed: this may have been partly because she wanted to force her husband's hand. Fanny Wright's reference to having 'aided' Mrs Trollope might mean that she helped with her fare.[5]

In her book, Mrs Trollope was rather coy about the reasons for her trip to America although she says she planned to pass 'some months' with Fanny Wright at 'the estate she had purchased in Tennessee' which makes this exotic foray sound like a holiday jaunt to some titled relative in Lincolnshire. Later in the book she says that she intended to visit Cincinnati where she would wait for her husband in order to 'fix our son there, intending to continue with him till he should feel himself sufficiently established' in what she called a 'commercial speculation'. She told Charles Wilkes in New York that she had 'fixed upon it [Nashoba] as a residence for a year or two during which from motives of economy, we had decided upon residing abroad. – but most assuredly we were altogether deluded by the picture her imagination drew.' With her, Frances Trollope had taken three of her five children: Henry, of course, Cecilia, aged eleven and Emily, aged nine. At least, as she wrote from the ship to Harriet Garnett, America offered her and her children 'frequent intervals of tranquillity in the absence of Mr Trollope'. The children's drawing master, Auguste Jean Hervieu, a thirty-three-year-old French revolutionary, had been promised a post as teacher at Nashoba and he accompanied them. (His being in the party was one reason for the secrecy surrounding Mrs Trollope's departure from Harrow.) As we have seen, Mrs Trollope also brought her maid, Hester Rust, and a manservant named William Abbott, a young farmer who had been employed by her husband for some years.[6] Even in Utopia, Fanny Trollope would expect personal service. Although she later wrote that she began wondering about Fanny Wright's mental balance aboard ship, she remained optimistic and carried with her many of her hopes, most of her remaining capital and some of her children. Her other two sons, Thomas Adolphus and Anthony, remained at school in England, unaware of their mother's departure and of the plan for their father to join her in due course if the venture proved successful.

Mrs Trollope spent three days in New Orleans where, like Rebecca Burlend, she was struck by the 'large proportion of blacks seen in the streets, all labour being performed by them; the grace and beauty of the elegant Quadroons; [and] the occasional groups of wild and savage looking Indians'. As a disciple of Fanny Wright she arrived with a fierce hostility to slavery and, with the skill of a future novelist, she frequently wove romantic little tales about the origins and sufferings of the slaves she saw. During the course of her trip her attitude towards slavery was to modify although she always remained hostile. Her real hostility blazed forth when she returned to England and wrote one of the fiercest fictional denunciations of American slavery in her novel, *The Life and Adventures of Jonathan Jefferson Whitlaw: or Scenes on the Mississippi.* In New Orleans Frances Trollope also had her first meeting with another aspect of America that she came to detest: equality. Ironically her introduction to egalitarian manners came in a millinery shop run by a fellow Englishwoman and associate of Fanny Wright, Mary Carroll. Mrs Trollope was surprised to find Miss Carroll conversing with her customers on philosophical questions. She did not like this mix of bonnets and politics. As an English lady of the early nineteenth century she expected deference rather than a disquisition from her milliner. It was gratifying no doubt to listen to a Marquis preach equality in his château, but one did not expect the same theories in a hat shop.

However, her real introduction to American life came when she boarded a steamboat to travel up the Mississippi River to Memphis. For many people today the great old 'River Queens' are symbols of a world of lost elegance where graceful ladies in crinoline dresses accompanied by elegant gentlemen sipped mint-juleps. Mrs Trollope, however, hated American steamboats and their rough passengers and said so with her accustomed frankness: 'I declare, that I would infinitely prefer sharing the apartment of a party of well conditioned pigs.' (The boats that she took were quite primitive compared to those of legend.) This voyage also introduced her to two other aspects of American society that were to infuriate her throughout her travels. The egalitarian atmosphere was constantly broken by the use of military titles. On the American frontier many men claimed the rank of 'Major' and 'Colonel' in the militia, a custom which survives today in the 'Kentucky Colonels'. Secondly, she was horrified by the nearly constant chewing of tobacco and 'the loathsome spitting, from the contamination of which it was absolutely impossible to protect our dresses'. In the world Mrs Trollope knew in England, it was still uncommon for a gentleman to smoke, let alone to smoke in the presence of a lady.

From the first, her main interest in America was the lack of those little habits of courtesy which she believed showed the true nature of any society far more than its political or economic systems. In this approach her account of America differs fundamentally from that of Fanny Wright, who relished democratic familiarity and the assumption of equality. Frances Trollope immediately noted and hated 'the total want of all the usual courtesies of the table, the voracious rapidity with which the viands were seized and devoured, the strange uncouth phrases and pronunciation'. She was horrified by the 'frightful manner of feeding with their knives, till the whole blade seemed to enter into the mouth; and the still more frightful manner of cleaning the teeth afterwards with a pocket knife'. These were complaints she would repeat constantly.

Worse was in store for poor Mrs Trollope when, after leaving the steamboat and enduring a trek through a primeval forest, she finally arrived at Nashoba with its dispirited slaves, its feuding whites and its squalid log cabins. 'Desolation was the only feeling,' she wrote, 'the only word that presented itself.' Naturally the English party was hungry but Mrs Trollope was dismayed to see Fanny Wright settling down to a meal of corn-bread washed down by a cup of rain water. 'The Frances Wright of Nashoba, in dress, looks, and manner, bore no more resemblance to the Miss Wright I had known and admired in London and Paris than did her log cabin to the Tuileries or Buckingham Palace.'[7] Mrs Trollope had travelled 5,000 miles to discover the obvious! She was even more horrified when she talked to the recently married Camilla Wright who warned her that the place would ruin the health of her children.

Fanny Wright seemed oblivious to the squalor surrounding her: this was because, as Mrs Trollope wrote in her first draft of *Domestic Manners*, she was so absorbed in the life of the commune that 'all her other faculties were in a manner suspended'. She later came to the conclusion that Fanny Wright was suffering from the effects of 'brain fever' which had attacked her in 1827. The two friends shared a bedroom without a ceiling in one of the log cabins, but after ten days Mrs Trollope had had enough. Her sleep had been interrupted by the rain which came through the roof and she announced she was leaving. The illusions of a Parisian salon had vanished in the rain-soaked reality of a Tennessee log cabin. Fanny Wright, generous as ever, advanced her $300 (£60) to help her find 'some place in the western world better suited' for her and her children. The ever-unlucky Henry was dispatched to the school at the Owenite settlement of New Harmony. The school had been founded by a wealthy Scottish philanthropist, William Maclure. He was well described by Fanny Trollope: 'This venerable philosopher, like all of his school that I ever heard of, loved better to originate lofty imaginings of faultless systems, than to watch their application to practice.' In time he left for Mexico. The school could also boast the services of another educationalist and friend of Fanny Wright, the French scoundrel, D'Arusmont, who would in time, as we know, cheat Wright out of her various fortunes. While Henry experienced the blessings of progressive education on the Indiana frontier, his mother and sisters would find some more settled place to wait until money came from Mr Trollope. For Hervieu, Fanny Wright had come to feel nothing but contempt: he was 'totally unsuited for anything but his art'. For his part Hervieu was furious when he found there was no school awaiting his services. In truth there was little need for the slaves to be educated in the polite accomplishment of drawing, although some French would have proved useful to them when they eventually went to Haiti. In revenge the Frenchman used his talent to make a realistic drawing of the desolation of Nashoba for Mrs Trollope's book. For her erstwhile friend, Fanny Wright retained good feelings: as she explained to the Garnetts, Mrs Trollope 'has a heart good enough to correct her head'.[8]

ESCAPE TO CINCINNATI

Once again the Trollope party embarked on one of the hated steamboats and made their way up the Mississippi, a river she had come to dislike, and onto the Ohio, which she considered one of the most beautiful of rivers. Indeed, she admits that the scenery was so 'sweet' that she was tempted to copy her uncouth fellow travellers in 'their voracious rapidity for swallowing' so that she, too, could hurry back onto the deck to see the unfolding beauty of the unspoilt countryside. We may rest assured that *she* preserved her dignified table manners: even ten days in Nashoba could not erase the training of a lifetime. On 10 February 1828 she reached her goal: Cincinnati. This city had grown from virtually nothing at the beginning of the century to a population of some 20,000 people. Another Englishwoman, Mrs Basil Hall, who passed through with her husband in

June of that same year was pleased both with its beautiful setting and its appearance of 'bustle and business'.[9] Its status as the most important city on what was then the western frontier had been symbolised in a visit a few years previously by Mrs Trollope's friend, Lafayette.

As the first problem was finding a place to live, Mrs Trollope responded to a notice from an agency which promised houses for new arrivals. She soon realised that the boy sent to guide them was simply leading her through the streets, looking for any house with 'To Rent' signs. After getting rid of the useless boy by giving him a dollar, she found a house and started to settle in. She was appalled at the lack of pumps and drains, but even more outraged by her landlord's explanation of rubbish disposal: 'Your help will just have to fix them all into the middle of the street, but you must mind, old woman, that it is in the middle. I expect you don't know as we have got a law what forbids throwing such things at the sides of the streets, they must just all be cast right into the middle, and the pigs soon takes them off.' The steamboats had made Cincinnati the centre for the trade in pig-meat and by 1849 over 400,000 hogs would be slaughtered there each year. It soon became famous – or to Mrs Trollope, infamous – as the 'Porkopolis of the West'. Not surprisingly, pork was the city's principal meat.[10]

Mrs Trollope was miserable almost from the outset of her time in Cincinnati and her chapters on the frontier city form the largest and the most bitter section of *Domestic Manners of the Americans*. This has given the book a far more caustic reputation than it deserves. As time passed things did not improve: no money came from England to pay for their return passage. After much pleading, poor Henry was taken out of his radical school: his health had broken down because of the forced labour in the fields which was part of Maclure's theory of progressive education. The boy then turned to that ever-faithful remedy which well educated Englishmen always seek to apply when in pecuniary distress: tutoring. The *Cincinnati Gazette* soon sported an advertisement that Mr Henry Trollope, from 'the Royal College of Winchester (England)' was prepared to teach Latin to 'gentlemen at their own houses'. Budding classicists were assured that 'Mr H. Trollope flatters himself he shall be able to give a competent knowledge of the Latin tongue in a much shorter space of time than has hitherto been considered necessary.' This elegant accomplishment could be acquired for a mere fifty cents an hour.

Sadly, the gentlemen of Cincinnati (unlike the heroic Roman from whom their city ultimately derived its name) were not prepared to leave their ploughs or their pigs to learn Latin, even by the quickest methods available. However Henry's linguistic skills were soon put to profitable use. The proprietor of the Western Museum persuaded Mrs Trollope to superintend an entertainment called 'The Invisible Girl at the Western Museum'. Groups of a dozen people paid to gaze at a stage featuring an Egyptian temple where exotic animals and wax bandits glided against painted transparencies. The audience could then ask an invisible oracle any question. From off-stage came a voice with a smattering of Latin, French and English giving a suitably 'Delphic' reply. The 'invisible girl' was none other than young Henry. One can understand why his eleven-year-old sister Cecilia wrote, 'Cincinnati is a very pretty little town, but I heartilly hope papa will come and take us away from it.'[11]

In the autumn of 1828 'Papa' and his eldest son, Thomas Adolphus, finally arrived from England. They had had a dreadful crossing of the Atlantic as Mr Trollope's inveterate penny-pinching led him to take places in steerage. As a result he spent 38 nights confined to a miserable bunk surrounded by all the loathsome smells that so disturbed Rebecca Burlend, while the hearty young Tom slept on the deck to avoid the horrors. In New York the ever-kindly Charles Wilkes performed his usual function of advising so many of the travellers in this book, carefully explaining how much he disapproved of the whole Nashoba 'experiment'. Mr Trollope's purpose in coming was to escort his wife and children back to England, but by the time he made his wearisome way across primitive roads to Cincinnati, she was ready with a new scheme to re-establish the family on its feet. She planned to erect 'a very elegant building' which would become 'the chief lion of the city'. The ground floor would be a 'bazaar' which she would let to various small shops selling a variety of expensive goods. (She would later claim that this part was Mr Trollope's idea.) The bulk of the building, however, was designed as something like a modern 'leisure centre' with a variety of facilities including reading rooms, coffee room, bar, promenades, ball-room, saloon for ices, and areas for exhibitions and lectures. The top would be crowned with a rotunda housing a 'Panorama' or one of those large circular paintings then very fashionable: Hervieu's vast painting of Lafayette's landing at Cincinnati would be the *chef d'oeuvre* that would make art truly accessible. Mrs Trollope believed that her building would provide the growing city with sadly needed cultural opportunities. Cincinnati offered little in the way of leisure except religious revivals and talks by visiting lecturers such as Fanny Wright.[12] Although Mr Trollope was not keen on the idea he had little power as the money his wife wanted to use was her own, part of her inheritance from her father. She would remain in Cincinnati for a while after which Henry would take over the management. Her scheme would also act as an excuse to keep the Atlantic between herself and her irascible husband.

Within a short time the most extraordinary building Cincinnati had ever seen began to rise. The style Mrs Trollope chose would today be called something like 'eclectic pastiche'. Her son, Anthony, first depicted it as 'a showy building' which he then changed to 'a sorry building' in his *Autobiography*. Others have been less charitable and it became the fashion to deride the building. A New England historian, who saw it in 1846, described it as 'a most ridiculous piece of architecture, in utter defiance of taste and common sense'. One English visitor, Captain Thomas Hamilton, called it a 'large Graeco-Moresco-gothic-Chinese looking building – an architectural compilation of prettiness of all sorts, the effect of which is eminently grotesque'.[13] It was loosely based on an Egyptian mosque and even featured a large crescent on the top of its central dome. As Mrs Trollope had frequently complained about the wide diversity of religious cults in America one wonders if she wanted to add the gentle blessings of Mohammedanism to the spiritual riches of Cincinnati. The Bazaar proved a total failure within six months, as much due to bad luck as to the town's prejudice against her. Eventually it cost her $24,000 (£4,800) of which she managed to pay half. Her husband's impractical nature, which had helped to bring on the family's collapse in England, contributed to the failure. Instead of spending £150 on a limited range of expensive goods he spent $4,000 (£800) on 'trumpery goods' on which the duty in New York exceeded any profit that could be made. A French economist who visited Cincinnati a few years later commented that the city had 'general ease but little wealth' and therefore no desire for 'the little luxuries of a more refined society'. Not only did Mrs Trollope have goods she could not sell, but the money she had set aside to pay off the builders was gone.[14] She was also forced to compete with existing shops in selling goods no better than those already on sale. The inevitable happened and the sheriff seized her goods to satisfy her debt to the builders. Her dream, parts of which had made some economic sense, had turned into a nightmare.

After so many horrible experiences, it is hardly surprising that Mrs Trollope's dislike of Cincinnati turned into something far stronger or that both her health and Henry's collapsed. Occasionally a strong emotion can give a sharpness and insight to a writer which a detached objectivity cannot, and this was the case with Fanny Trollope. In her portrayal of life on the western frontier she gives us a valuable and, on the whole, accurate picture, even if her pen was often dipped in acid. The general accuracy of her view of Cincinnati was borne out by many other observers, even those who came a few decades later. Francis Parkman, the American historian, arrived in Cincinnati in 1846 on his way west to write his classic, *The Oregon Trail*, and he wrote home to his mother in New England descriptions that sound like Mrs Trollope's: 'The boat ... was filled with a swarm of half-civilized reprobates, gambling, swearing ... The great annoyance of these boats is the absurd haste of everybody to gulp down their meals ... The case is much the same here in the best hotel in Cincinnati ... such a set of beasts are these western men.' A distinguished American Presbyterian minister, the Rev. Charles Colcock Jones, also described many features of the town in terms similar to those of Mrs Trollope, noting as she had done the sight and smell of the streets which even a quarter-century later retained the 'filthy custom' of relying on pigs to cope with rubbish.[15] Her great weakness lay in seeing a bustling frontier city as the embodiment of American social life. Most British and European writers arrived in Boston and New York and took their earliest views of America from cities with both history and culture. Fanny Trollope virtually began her journey in the midst of the frontier and that is what gives her book its strength and its weakness. While her hostility emerged in her descriptions of the citizens of Cincinnati, she did express open admiration of their town's economic growth which she attributed to the pervading spirit of enterprise. If she saw no gentlemen, neither did she see beggars. 'Every bee in the hive is actively employed in search of that honey of Hybla', she wrote, anxious to parade her classical knowledge, 'vulgarly called money; neither art, science, learning, nor pleasure can seduce them from its pursuits.'

One factor in this amazing economic growth was low taxation which Mrs Trollope envied in common with other English commentators. She was writing at a time of tremendous concern about the soaring cost of government, especially local government and the poor laws in England. These had particularly affected the 'landed interest' and her husband was on the outer fringes of this group. However, she is perceptive enough to note that if the English paid higher taxes they also got more from government. She admits that she had accepted the radical demand for retrenchment in government spending before leaving England. America, however, had cured that as it had her radicalism in general: 'Were I an English legislator,' she wrote, 'instead of sending sedition to the Tower, I would send her to make a tour of the United States. I had a little leaning toward sedition myself when I set out, but before I had half completed my tour I was quite cured.' The influence of Fanny Wright and the allurements of 'sedition' had vanished in Nashoba and 'Porkopolis'.

The lack of good servants no doubt caused Mrs Trollope to turn away from 'sedition' and to pine for the delights of a deferential society. Fanny Wright had warned English visitors to America that they would have difficulty in getting servants, and Mrs Trollope found that here, at least, her friend was right. It was inconceivable for someone like Mrs Trollope to imagine living without servants and indeed it was virtually impossible to maintain a middle-class household without a maid or two. One of her sons remembered that although his parents might scrimp on the number of candles used at night, they insisted on maintaining a manservant in the family livery. (In 1834 when the Trollopes were forced to flee England because of their debts, one of the first things they did was to hire two maids for their Belgian home.) Fanny Trollope was amused that Americans used the word 'help' rather than 'servant' because 'it is more than petty treason to the Republic, to call a free citizen a *servant*.'* When Mark Twain took her book with him as he revisited the scenes of his boyhood he noted in his

---

* Mrs Trollope would perhaps have been amused to know that in late twentieth-century democratic Britain 'help' is now firmly established as the socially correct word. Most of the middle classes who use this term would be horrified to learn that it was yet another example of 'Yankee talk'.

marginalia, 'A fair shot'.[16] In Cincinnati finding 'help' did prove one of her greatest headaches. She found it impossible to engage young women on a yearly basis and several only agreed to work long enough to buy some more clothes.

The lack of servants forced Mrs Trollope to do some of her own shopping and she was pleasantly surprised at her experience: 'For excellence, abundance, and cheapness' the Cincinnati market 'can hardly ... be surpassed in any part of the world.' The beef was excellent and sold for no more than four cents a pound; in her unpublished notebooks she wrote, 'I am decidedly of opinion that to whomever abundance of cheap beef steaks can be ... enjoyment, Cincinnati must be the happiest spot on earth.'[17] She did not find the lamb or veal as good as in England although the poultry was of a fine quality and cheap. A full-sized chicken sold for twelve cents and a large turkey or goose for fifty. Fish, eggs and butter were remarkably cheap. If America lacked some of the more exotic fruits of European markets it had tomatoes, still virtually unknown in England. These were 'the great luxury of the American table in the opinion of most Europeans'. The vegetables won her praise as well, although she was surprised not to find either cauliflower or broccoli. For the fruit, however, she, like many later English visitors including her son Anthony, had little praise.

If American food largely came up to her severe standards, American methods of amusement, or rather the dearth of them, did not. 'I never saw any people who appeared to live so much without amusement as the Cincinnatians.' Public balls were restricted to six during Christmastide. This naturally upset her as the Bazaar had a large ball-room for hire, but she was discreet enough not to mention this important factor in her criticism. As a devoted player of whist, she also missed games of cards which formed such an important part of the leisurely pursuits of the English lady during the long interval after dinner parties when the gentlemen lingered over their port and politics. In Ohio, anyone who sold a pack of cards could be fined fifty dollars.

Nor is it surprising that Mrs Trollope, the friend of the playwright, Mary Mitford, and the actor, William Macready, deplored the state of the theatres in this 'triste little town'. Here again her criticisms were not wholly without self-interest. Just as she had mounted amateur productions of French plays for her children in Harrow, so in Cincinnati she had attempted to stage various theatrical performances which had proved failures. She frequently rebuked the Americans for their manners, or rather their lack of them, in theatres. There was constant talk during performances and, generally speaking, American audiences were boisterous. But so, too, were English audiences of the same period, as indeed were those that first went to see Shakespeare or Sheridan. A German prince who was in England when she was in America was horrified when he went to the theatre in London: 'The most striking thing to a foreigner in English theatres is the unheard-of coarseness and brutality of the audiences.'

Europeans often complained about the behaviour of English visitors to continental theatres. Mrs Trollope, however, was not one for subtle comparisons. The exotic poses in which the audiences or rather the men in the audience sprawled across the seats were even more annoying than the noise and the spitting. Hervieu, in his illustrations for her book, drew one picture of an American 'gentleman' lounging in a box, displaying his 'entire rear' while propped on the box's rail. Two American reviews took her to task for this: not only was it indelicate to mention gentlemen's 'entire rears' but the picture, they claimed, showed that the rear in question was not American at all, but English. Unfortunately the reviewers do not tell us exactly how one recognised a true 'John Bull rear'. Nevertheless no other part of her book had so much influence in America as her comments about behaviour in theatres, and it was an influence for good.

We can get a good idea of how well known Fanny Trollope's book became in America from the frequent allusions to this particular criticism. Within a few months of *Domestic Manners'* appearance in America, the *New York Mirror* said that her name had become a 'by-word in taverns and in the pit of the theatres, which, we doubt not, pleases her vastly ... Spitters and chewers, look to it; and ye indolent beings, who lounge on two chairs with your feet on the mantel-piece, remember Mr. Herview's [sic] sketches, and be no more guilty of a *Trollope!*' While a few years later an American novelist describes men 'with legs *à la Trollope*, upon the tables' in a hotel bar in New Orleans. Dr T.L. Nichols, a distinguished American journalist with a wide knowledge of mid-western America, wrote that in the following two decades it was common to hear the cry of 'Trollope! Trollope!' if a man 'in the boxes placed his feet upon the rail or turned his back to the stage'. Even the acerbic Henry T. Tuckerman in his book, *America and Her Commentators*, written with great bitterness in the midst of the War Between the States, was forced to admit:

> Until recently, the sight of a human foot protruding over the gallery of a Western theatre was hailed with the instant and vociferous challenge, apparently undisputed as authoritative, of 'Trollope!' whereupon the obnoxious member was withdrawn from sight ... [thus] this best abused writer on America was a beneficent, practical reformer.

Throughout her book Mrs Trollope continuously commented on Society, or rather the lack of it, in America. By 'Society' she meant the elegant conversation of the cultured. She believed that there could be no true 'Society' in America because of the pervasive vice of equality and she certainly had found none in Cincinnati. What, however, did the inhabitants of Cincinnati think of this eccentric Englishwoman who had erected 'Trollope's Folly' in their midst? Some understandably wondered about her connexion with the young French artist, Hervieu. In fact it was perfectly respectable, but one so concerned with others' 'domestic manners' could hardly blame them for enquiring into her own. The fullest description of Mrs Trollope in Cincinnati came from the Rev. Timothy Flint, a Congregational minister and the town's leading and virtually only literary figure. Flint, born in Massachusetts in 1780, was one of those men who went to the new north-western states like Ohio to transplant New England culture. (The most famous of these would be Lyman Beecher, father of Harriet Beecher Stowe, who came to Cincinnati in the year Mrs Trollope's book was published.) Flint was a writer, who by 1829 had published four novels based on his own wide travels. For four years, from 1827 to 1830, he published a literary journal, the *Western Monthly Review*, designed to report cultural progress to New England. Mrs Trollope liked his works and praised them, along with his son's poems and his daughter's manners.

Flint, however, was critical of his one-time friend. After her book appeared he reviewed it and described her as 'a short, plump figure, with a ruddy, round Saxon face of bright complexion'. Her appearance was 'singularly unladylike, a misfortune heightened by her want of taste and female intelligence in ... dress'. He also found her 'robust and masculine in her habits' and remembered that 'she had no fear of the elements'. He attributed her frequent fevers to her habit of walking even in bad weather. She was 'voluble as a French woman, shrill and piercing in the tones of her voice, piquant and sarcastic in the tenor of her conversation', but despite this, 'her conversation was remarkably amusing' especially as she claimed to know all the celebrities of England and Europe. (She did have letters of introduction from Lafayette which she had used, to little avail, in Cincinnati.) She was, he added, kind to the poor and sick to whom she appeared as a 'Lady Bountiful'. This description is excessively kind when compared to that of another American who saw her at Flint's house: 'In one corner of the room sat the veritable old Trollope herself,' he recalled, 'rough-cast and misshapen – of coarse and vulgar expression, and a head, viewed phrenologically, of the very lowest order.'[18]

In Mrs Trollope's view any attempt at 'Society' was hindered not just by the pervasive presumption of equality but by puritanical religion. 'I never saw, or read,' she wrote, 'of any country where religion had so strong a hold upon the women, or so slight a hold upon the men.' When we consider her religious views we should recall that as a daughter of a country clergyman of the Church of England she looked with dismay on the many dissenting sects that had sprung up in England and blossomed in America. For her, such bodies were not only heretical, but also inescapably vulgar. In her travels she was a great attender of various churches. Strangely, the only church she virtually ignores is the Episcopal, the American branch of her own Church. Unlike many Englishmen of her day she was remarkably tolerant of the Roman Catholic Church and exempted it, along with the Episcopal Church, from her strictures. (She would become more hostile in later novels such as *Father Eustace: A Tale of the Jesuits*.) She found the behaviour of American Methodists and Presbyterians shocking but her particular ire was reserved for the Methodists, something shared by Rebecca Burlend. There had been, it is true, two or three in the village in which she had grown up but, as her elder son, Tom, later wrote, they had been regarded as if they were 'Chinese settled among them'. She added the Methodist term, 'class leader', to her list of peculiar 'Americanisms' and made the common mistake of assuming as 'American' usages with which she was unfamiliar. The term had actually been used by English Methodists since 1742.* It should also be remembered that she was writing for English Tories who were, almost to a man, members of the Established Church. By the time her book appeared, they were increasingly worried about the growing demand among radical dissenters for the disestablishment of the Church of England. As one of the leading authorities on Anglo-American religious history says, 'Mrs Trollope provided fodder for establishmentarians'.[19]

Frances Trollope particularly disliked 'revivals' which have been a staple part of the American religious scene from colonial days. It was, after all, the religious revivals of the 1820s that had sparked Fanny Wright's lecture tours. This was the period of the 'Second Great Awakening' when Evangelical Protestants doubled their membership within a few decades. One of Mrs Trollope's longest descriptions was an account of a 'camp meeting' where thousands came to attend revivals that went on for days. Fortunately she was able to drive there in a carriage provided by some other English visitors who had come to witness the spectacle. She saw what happened when the restraining power of an established church and of an educated clergy was removed and she did not like what she saw. 'But how', she asked, 'am I to describe the sounds that proceeded from this strange mass of human beings? I know no words which can convey an idea of it. Hysterical sobbings, convulsive groans, shrieks and screams the most appalling, burst forth on all sides. I felt sick with horror.' She was surprised that among the many tents was one reserved exclusively for the freed blacks, where 'a youth of coal-black comeliness, was preaching with the most violent gesticulations, frequently springing high from the ground, and clapping his hands over his head'. As usual, she drew a moral for her readers at home: 'Could our missionary societies have heard the trash he uttered, by way of an address to the Deity, they might perhaps have doubted whether his conversion had much enlightened his mind.' She came to believe that this evangelistic ranting drove almost all cultivated Americans into 'the cold comfortless stillness of Unitarianism', which had gained

---

* Mrs Trollope was shocked to hear Americans use the expression 'God damn' and listed seventeen occasions when she heard it. (She wrote it 'G-d d-mn'.) Even today it remains a standard exclamation for Americans in much English writing. Ironically, ever since the Middle Ages, Frenchmen had adopted the exclamation used by English soldiers to identify Englishmen. Her son, Henry, had complained that when walking in Paris, street urchins had called after him: '*Voici, le petit goddamn.*' Once again it was the Americans who were being faithful to old Anglo-Saxon usages.

such strength in New England. It is amusing to note that while Mrs Trollope, as an English lady, was horrified by the way women participated and were manipulated at these camp-meetings, a Frenchman, Michael Chevalier, found this the most attractive aspect of the revivals. They reminded him of Catholic religious festivals. Indeed he wanted the French to return to such festivals and to abandon the dullness which was only 'suited to the climate of Great Britain'.

Mrs Trollope continued her observations of American religion when she reached Philadelphia later in her travels. Here she was taken to a Quaker meeting house where their worship, 'if worship it may be called, where all prayer is forbidden', was preferable to that of the Methodists and Presbyterians. It is interesting to see how American critics reacted to this aspect of her comments. The *American Quarterly Review*, for example, which was quite critical of the rest of her book, agreed with much of her view of American religion. Like her, they saw 'the undue and sometimes improper influence' of the clergy on women as hindering the development of innocent forms of culture and amusement such as good theatre. Instead of resorting to such diversions, the reviewer alleged, many Americans became heavy drinkers.[20] Others, of course, looked to their religion to provide their entertainment.

Although Mrs Trollope saw fundamentalist religion as one of the most important factors hindering the growth of Society in America, she pointed to the pervasive spirit of equality as the real culprit. She thoroughly detested the presumption of equality she found in America and she was not the first, nor the last, to note that the realities of life did not always come up to the theory. The belief that any man's son could become the equal of anyone else's was 'a spur to exertion' but it was also 'a spur to that coarse familiarity, untempered by any shadow of respect, which is assumed by the grossest and the lowest in their intercourse with the highest and most refined'. From time to time Mrs Trollope felt compelled to read her countrymen a lecture and to point out a lesson based on her own experiences. No doubt remembering some of her own dinner parties she warned that

> the theory of equality may be very daintily discussed by English gentlemen in a London dining-room, when the servant, having placed a fresh bottle of cool wine on the table, respectfully shuts the door, and leaves them to their walnuts and their wisdom; but it will be found less palatable when it presents itself in the shape of a hard, greasy paw, and is claimed in accents that breathe less of freedom than of onions and whiskey. Strong, indeed, must be the love of equality in an English breast if it can survive a tour through the Union.

It is appropriate that Mrs Trollope saw Andrew Jackson on his triumphant journey to take office as President in 1829, for he epitomised the frontier spirit of equality and democracy she was finding so distasteful.

His victory marked a great change in American political history towards a more popular democracy. The Founding Fathers had had little use for equality either in principle or in practice, whereas Jackson continually preached and often practised it. Strangely, Mrs Trollope actually praised him for looking like a 'soldier and a gentleman' and no one can deny that Jackson was a considerable soldier. Perhaps her unusual kindness owed something to the fact that her husband enjoyed the President-elect's company when they both took the same steamboat, Jackson on his way to Washington and 'Mr T.' on his way back to England. Jackson was in mourning for his recently deceased wife and this formed the basis of a conversation which 'painfully grated against' the 'European feelings' of Mr Trollope, who later described the conversation to his wife. She put it to good use as an example of how 'equality' destroyed manners. Her skill in recording such conversations, reminiscent at times of Boswell, did more than anything to make her book such a sensation. English readers would particularly enjoy the examples of 'Yankee talk' such as the ubiquitous 'I guess'.[21] Mr Trollope told his wife that a 'greasy fellow' demanded to be introduced to General Jackson. The following exchange took place:

> 'General Jackson, I guess?' The General bowed assent. 'Why they told me you was dead.' 'No! Providence has hitherto preserved my life.' 'And is your wife alive too?' The General, apparently much hurt, signified the contrary, upon which the courtier concluded his harangue, by saying, 'Aye, I thought it was the one or the t'other of ye.'

To Mrs Trollope the position of women in American life was the final factor, after religion and the spirit of equality, which accounted for the low state of social manners and development. She made frequent comments about women in the course of her travels. While she was far from being a 'feminist' in the modern sense, she did believe that there was too much separation of the sexes in America. On her first steamboat trip she had been horrified to find even husbands and wives segregated from one another. However bad that was, worse was to come when she attended a George Washington Birthday Ball in Cincinnati. First she was astounded to find that almost 'every full-dressed *beau*' was the 'master or shopman' that she had seen 'lolling at the door of every shop in the city'. Having put the tradesmen in their place, the proprietor of Cincinnati's most fantastic and most unsuccessful bazaar turned to survey the ladies. She was furious to discover that while the gentlemen had a large banquet spread for them in one room of the hotel, the ladies had to dine in a separate room on sweetmeats, cakes and creams although afterwards they concluded their delicate repast with pickled oysters and iced cream. This segregation was justified on the ground that the men preferred it. Mrs Trollope commented:

> I am led to mention this feature of American manners very frequently, not only because it constantly recurs, but because I consider it as being in a great

degree the cause of that universal deficiency in good manners and graceful
demeanour, both in men and women, which is so remarkable.

It is somewhat ironic that she was making the same complaint against the
Americans that many Europeans made against the English. Continental
travellers continually attacked the English custom whereby ladies with-
drew after dinner to the sitting room to leave the gentlemen at the table
to discuss politics over their port or, to quote Mrs Trollope, over their 'wine
and walnuts'. Indeed, when Mrs Trollope's son, Anthony, attended the
great banquet given to Dickens in London in 1867 before his second trip
to America, the ladies were confined to a balcony from where they could
view the gentlemen merrily eating and drinking their way through toast
after toast.

Mrs Trollope lamented that 'with the exception of dancing' all the
'enjoyments of the men are found in the absence of the women'. She claimed
that with some few exceptions in the larger Eastern cities, all American
women occupied themselves with domestic duties, even in the 'slave
states'. The situation was even worse among the lower classes. The wives
of small farmers had lives of 'hardship, privation, and labour' and few of
them retained any beauty after thirty. Even the girls were thin and
haggard from their work as 'domestic slaves'. The only escape was 'the still
sadder burdens' of marriage. She noted that these girls were often resent-
ful of parental authority and this, perhaps, encouraged them to marry
early. She disapproved of early marriage, having herself not married until
she was twenty-nine, and embarked on one of those flights of purple prose
on which she prided herself. In 'no rank of life', she wrote, 'do you meet
with young women in that delightful period ... between childhood and
marriage, wherein, if only tolerably well spent, so much useful information
is gained' and a strong character is created. In America, 'the slender,
childish thing ... is made to stem a sea of troubles that dims her young eye
and makes her cheek grow pale, even before nature has given it the last
beautiful finish of the full-grown woman'. Of one thing she was absolutely
convinced, as she wrote in her notebook: 'The American people will not
equal the nations of Europe in refinement till women become of more
importance among them.'

Mrs Trollope herself had 'a sea of troubles' to make even her cheeks grow
pale throughout 1829. She had no news of her husband and eldest son after
they left Cincinnati in January on their way back to England. She was
worn out by constant disputes with the builders of the Bazaar and by
worries about money. She had frequently been warned that Europeans ran
a great risk to their health during a second summer in America and this
prediction came true. Like Rebecca Burlend and Fanny Wright, she 'fell
low before the monster that is for ever stalking through that land of lake
and rivers, breathing fever and death around'. While she was seriously ill
for over two months she embarked on a wild course of novel-reading – apt

preparation, had she but known it, for her future career. She read contemporary American fiction and found that the novels of James Fenimore Cooper were too violent. (Ironically at the same time in England her son, Anthony, was seeking to solace his loneliness by reading and re-reading Cooper's *The Prairie*, but unlike his mother he remained devoted to the works of the American novelist.) She claimed that she also read the whole of Sir Walter Scott's works, and one might be excused the suspicion that either her illness or her reading must have been exaggerated.

She may also have used the time to look over the observations she had been scribbling in half-used school notebooks abandoned by her sons. Ever since 1823 she had jotted down notes about her experiences and in June 1828, after five months in Cincinnati, she told her eldest son: 'I amuse myself by making notes, and hope some day to manufacture them into a volume. This is a remote corner of the world, and but seldom visited and I think that if Hervieu could find time to furnish sketches of scenery, and groups, a very taking little volume might be produced.' At first she thought she might write a book for an American publisher and asked Charles Wilkes to see if he could find one in New York, but this, like so many of her hopes, came to naught. After six months she had not made much progress and in January 1829 admitted to her old friend, Mary Russell Mitford, 'O! My dear friend, had I but the tenth of an inch of the nib of your pen, what pictures might I draw of the people here! – so very queer, so very unlike any other thing in heaven above or earth below!'22 Any idea for a book was upset by her own financial problems and by Henry's succumbing to the fever in the spring of 1830. As she put it in *Domestic Manners*, she now accepted the 'not very agreeable conviction ... that our Cincinnati speculation for my son would in no way answer our expectation', that is, the Bazaar had proved a failure and Mrs Trollope was ready to throw in the towel. A final humiliation awaited her when the sheriff, who had earlier seized the goods at the Bazaar, now took away furniture from her rented house. She had to take refuge with a friend and there shared a bed with her daughters while Henry and Hervieu made do with the floor. Somehow she scraped together enough money to send Henry, who now looked like a 'walking corpse', back to his father. Once again Charles Wilkes appears in this saga as he gave Henry money when he reached New York. This was just enough for him to take passage to Liverpool and there to get a coach to London. Shortly after midnight on 18 April 1830, the Harrow Weald farmhouse was disturbed by loud banging at the door. Poor Henry, lacking any more money, had had to walk the final sixteen miles of his journey. His father could now listen to a first-hand account of what had happened since he left Cincinnati.

BALTIMORE AND WASHINGTON

Early one March afternoon in 1830 Fanny Trollope, her two daughters and the ever-faithful Hervieu boarded the steamboat, *Lady Franklin*, and left Cincinnati after a two-year stay. 'The only regret', she wrote, 'was that we had ever entered it; for we had wasted health, time, and money there.' Behind her she left her memorial, 'Trollope's Folly'. When her son, Anthony, visited the city thirty-two years later he heard that the Bazaar had become a 'Physico-medical Institute'. 'It was under the domination', Trollope was told by the landlord, 'of a quack doctor on one side, and of a college of rights-of-women female medical professors on the other.' The landlord doubted if anyone, including himself, had made any money out of the jinxed building. Frances Trollope would have shared her son's dislike at the Bazaar's occupation by female medical professors, yet we cannot help but feel that she would have preferred them to one of its many intermediate uses as a Presbyterian church.

Mrs Trollope did not leave 'Porkopolis' empty-handed, for she had her notebooks and the idea for a travel book based on her experiences. On 12 March she wrote to her friend, Julia Garnett, 'I have long ago written every thing about it [Cincinnati] that I think worth putting in *my book*'. Her pleasure at quitting Ohio was evident: 'Every thing I have seen since I began to climb the Alleghany mountains has delighted me – and to confess the truth it is the first time I have been delighted since I came to America.'[23] She enjoyed her three-day cruise down the beautiful Ohio river to Wheeling, then part of Virginia, although she much resented being confined to the ladies' quarters. When the boat arrived at Wheeling at 2 am she was impressed with the speed and efficiency that saw her quickly accommodated in a fine hotel and seated before a roaring fire. Indeed, she was so content that for once she praised slavery. This passage in her book shows that she wrote as she went along and was honest enough to retain passages which would conflict with her final judgment. In the hotel she found that 'sedulous attention which in this country distinguishes a slave state'. As to slavery as an abstraction, 'I conceive it to be essentially wrong, but 'its influence is far less injurious to the manners and morals of the people than the fallacious ideas of equality ... so fondly cherished by the working classes of the white population of America'. In the northern states, service was rendered 'grudgingly, and ... with no appearance of cheerful good-will on the one side, or of kindly interest on the other'. This was because it was based solely on payment by one with money to one without. She always knew when she was in a 'slave state' for 'I was immediately comfortable, and at my ease, and felt that the intercourse between me and those who served me, was profitable to both parties and painful to neither'.

After resting for two days in Wheeling, Mrs Trollope resumed her journey with her first ride in an American stage-coach. While English coaches were world-famous for their design and craftsmanship, American coaches had a deservedly dreadful reputation. The lack of steps forced Mrs Trollope, a rather short woman, to climb a ladder. The coach could carry nine people in three rows of seats, but as there were only six on this journey, 'we were for some miles tossed about like a few potatoes in a wheelbarrow. Our knees, elbows, and heads required too much care for their protection to allow us leisure to look out of the windows.' This infuriated her because as the uncomfortable coach entered the Alleghany mountains she increasingly grew enchanted with the natural beauty along with the increasing signs of civilisation: 'The whole of this mountain region, through ninety miles of which the road passes, is a garden ... I really can hardly conceive a higher enjoyment than a botanical tour among the Alleghany mountains.' Yet natural beauty, as much as she might revel in it, was not enough to please her. At their first stop in Pennsylvania they found a clean and comfortable hotel where the servants were slaves hired from neighbouring Virginia. Further along the road she encountered a 'surly' white maid in a hotel who muttered something about the difficulty of 'fixing English folks'. One can but assume that Mrs Trollope was not the easiest guest to 'fix' after hours of bouncing along in a miserable coach.

Mrs Trollope left us some of the most colourful pictures of the unspoilt beauty of nineteenth-century America. She described the 'Alleghany Alps' in the Romantic prose of the age: 'It is a world of mountains rising around you in every direction, and in every form; savage, vast, and wild; yet almost at every step, some lovely spot meets your eye, green, bright, and blooming.' The journey was through 'kalmias, rhododendrons, azalias, vines and roses; sheltered from every blast ... while in every direction you have a back-ground of blue mountain tops, that play at bo-peep with you in the clouds'. Although the mountains had come to an end as her coach neared Baltimore, Maryland, she was comforted by the thought that she was nearing the Atlantic. She was pleased to see a large city: 'If we had not arrived in London or Paris, we had, at least, left far behind the "half-horse, half-alligator" tribes of the West, as the Kentuckians call themselves.' Most visitors to America liked Baltimore, as it seemed less hectic than New York or Boston and its Catholic heritage gave it a somewhat European atmosphere. Many Americans had assured her that the Catholic Cathedral was the grandest building in the country, but she found it a pale copy of European architecture. She was, however, struck with 'the beauty and splendid appearance of the ladies who filled it'. Seeing a favourable opportunity to show how well travelled she was, she engaged in some powerful name-dropping: 'Excepting on a very brilliant Sunday at the Tuileries, I never saw ... any where so many beautiful women at one glance.' It was common practice for nineteenth-century travel writers to pronounce on the appearance of women in any particular city. Captain Thomas Hamilton, who rattled through a few months after Fanny Trollope, believed this city had the most beautiful women in America as 'the fair Baltimoreans are less remarkable than American ladies usually are

e absence of a certain fulness'. American travel writers performed in
ar fashion when visiting Britain. James Fenimore Cooper in his book
on England agreed that Englishwomen have 'the advantage in the bust,
shoulders, and throat' but American women are 'superior in general
delicacy of outline' as well as having smaller hands and feet.[24] Needless to
say, men were rarely subjected to such cursory examinations.

Yet even in Baltimore, Mrs Trollope found that prevalent seriousness
of life that so annoyed her in America: 'I never saw a population so totally
divested of gaiety ... They have no fêtes, no fairs, no merry-makings, no
music in the streets, no Punch, no puppet-shows.' If Americans saw a
comedy or a farce 'they may laugh at it; but they can do very well without
it; and the consciousness of the number of cents that must be paid to enter
a theatre, I am very sure turns more steps from its door than any religious
feeling'. She was not alone in this complaint and many American writers
agreed with her. When Frederick Law Olmsted returned from his visit to
England, he concluded: 'I do believe the people of the United States have
less of pleasure and less of actual suffering than any other in the world.
Hopefulness, but hope ever unsatisfied, is marked in every American's
face.'[25]

Although the land route from Baltimore to Washington, her next stop,
was the quicker one, she decided to continue her travels with her old
enemy, the steamboat, in order to see the scenery on the Chesapeake Bay.
She was delighted to catch sight of the cypress tree that waved over the
grave of 'this truly great man', George Washington. If she disapproved of
what had been done in his country she shared the nearly universal esteem
in which Washington was held by almost all Englishmen. (Even in the War
of 1812, British ships had fired a salute as they passed by the grave of the
first President.) Unlike many English visitors, however, she also very
much liked the city named after him and was pleased to be in a place where
she could avoid 'all sights, sounds, or smells of commerce'. She was much
impressed with the Capitol which was larger than it had been when Fanny
Wright had seen it. Mrs Trollope rebuked European and American critics
who thought it too large and imposing. An additional and welcome feature
of the city was the foreign embassies, Senators and Congressmen who gave
a tone to Society that she had so missed elsewhere.

She visited the State Department where she admitted that the examples
of American workmanship on the seals of treaties and other state documents far surpassed all European examples. She wished that such good
taste was prevalent in other things: 'Let America give a fair portion of her
attention to the arts and the graces that embellish life, and I will make
her another visit, and write another book as unlike this as possible.' When
she was shown two documents bearing the signature of Napoleon she quite
frankly recorded: 'I longed to steal both.' This is one of the most refreshing
aspects of Mrs Trollope: she was as truthful in setting down her own flaws
as she was in noting those of others. She also visited the Bureau of Indian

Affairs where she admired the portraits of the chiefs who had come to negotiate with the 'Great Father', the President. Jackson, himself an old Indian-fighter, had little sympathy with the Indians but no less than the average American she met. She used this visit to the Indian Bureau to point out what was to her one of the most glaring examples of American hypocrisy. She found it 'impossible for any mind of common honesty not to be revolted by the contradictions' in America's principles and practices. Americans 'inveigh against the governments of Europe, because, as they say, they favour the powerful and oppress the weak'. Visitors could hear this view 'declaimed upon in Congress, roared out in taverns, discussed in every drawing-room, satirized upon the stage, nay, even anathematized from the pulpit'. One saw Americans, she wrote, 'lecturing their mob on the indefeasible rights of man' in one hour and in the next, 'driving from their homes the children of the soil, whom they have bound themselves to protect by the most solemn treaties'.

Her passionate denunciation of the treatment of the Indians led Mrs Trollope to make one of her most cutting criticisms: 'Had I, during my residence ... observed any single feature in their national character that could justify their eternal boast of liberality ... I might have respected them, however much my taste might have been offended by what was peculiar in their manners and customs.' This powerful attack might surprise those who think of Mrs Trollope as a hide-bound reactionary fortified by the passion of the convert from earlier, liberal sentiments. Yet many English Tories had long attacked American hypocrisy on both slavery and the treatment of Indians. That most characteristic of Tories, Dr Johnson, had thundered in 1775: 'How is it we hear the loudest *yelps* for liberty among the drivers of negroes?' Mrs Trollope was as sincere in her detestation of slavery and of the mistreatment of the Indians as she was in her attack on the American hypocrisy concerning them, but she also knew that these subjects provided convenient ammunition to undermine the claims made for American democracy. The purpose of her book was, we must remember, to warn an England caught in the riots and agitation over political reform of the hypocrisy and anarchy that frequently went hand in hand with the cry for 'Liberty!'.

Although her visit to the Indian Bureau did bring Mrs Trollope to make one of her fiercest political denunciations, the rest of her time in Washington, even her visit to Congress, could not bring her to involve herself in party politics. Indeed, she was more concerned with describing the funeral of a deceased Congressman than with discussing the work of a live one. Politics, as opposed to the moral questions involved in American attitudes towards slavery and the Indians, were for her an exclusively masculine concern. 'If I should occasionally make an observation' on the effects of politics, she wrote, it would only be a superficial one 'made in the spirit, and with the feelings of a woman, who is apt to tell what her first impressions may be, but unapt to reason back from effects to their cause'.

She therefore readily admitted what some of her critics would later claim, that she had no ability to reason from effect to cause. Her strength lay in observing and recording. In a later travel book, *Paris and the Parisians*, she complained: 'I often feel the most unfeigned longing to be out of reach of every sight and sound which must perforce mix up questions of government with all my womanly meditations on lesser things; but the necessity *de parler politique* seems like an evil spirit that follows whithersoever you go.'[26]

It is thus no surprise that when Mrs Trollope did attend debates in Congress, her concern was with the legislators' manners, not the substance of their arguments. The chambers impressed her and she was particularly delighted with the use of American products such as tobacco leaves in the decorations of the capitals of the marble columns. The behaviour of the members, however, shocked her. Almost all, saving the Virginians, were pronounced rude and loutish. (English visitors always had a special fondness for Virginians.) She was horrified to see members spitting on the floor, wearing their hats in the chamber and putting their feet on their desks. Here she showed her ignorance of her own country. It was common for MPs in the House of Commons to wear their hats throughout debates, though they sometimes took them off to use as portable desks. It was also said that Lord Brougham (who would become Lord Chancellor later that year) could be seen spitting on the 'fine carpet of the House [of Lords], and rubbing it with his feet'. Mrs Trollope could not have seen this at first hand as women could not then gain entry to the public gallery in the House of Commons. Some ladies were allowed to stand upon the steps of the throne in the House of Lords to admire their noble relatives' orations, but this led to understandable complaints that the large bonnets women wore blocked the view of any men on the steps.

Mrs Trollope's criticisms of Congressmen's hats and feet rankled with many American readers. When James Fenimore Cooper visited the House of Commons a few years later he noted that most Members wore their hats and counted six MPs each with one foot on the bench before them and three Members with both feet up. In fact, noted Cooper, the behaviour was 'a good deal resembling ... an American bar-room' and he thought that the legislators' agility with their feet showed a common 'tendency in the Anglo-Saxon race to put the heels higher than the head'. When another well-known American writer of the time was describing the delightful spa-town of Baden, just outside Vienna, he observed that the men danced with their hats on and added, 'Hear it ... Mrs Trollope!'[27]

In spite of her sartorial criticisms, Mrs Trollope's record of her visit to Washington still stands, on the whole, as a remarkably fair as well as enjoyable portrait, marked far more by praise than by censure. Yet it was her criticism that was remembered both in America and in England. She fixed firmly in the English mind the image of American legislators as hat-wearing, tobacco-spitting, mannerless louts who used such absurd phrases as 'go the whole hog'. Such an image, which was not entirely baseless, lingered long and bedevilled Anglo-American relations for decades. Some years later, when she had her first opportunity to view a European legislature, she decided that the deputies in Brussels were remarkably like those in Washington.

From the account that Mrs Trollope gave in her book we could never detect how crucial and how disappointing the trip to Washington proved. As so often with her American ventures, two factors had motivated this trip. With the first, the need to gather material for her book, she was quite successful. Concerning the second, the need to mend her perilous financial situation, she once again failed. Her finances remain difficult to disentangle. She was only able to get to Cincinnati after the debacle at Nashoba with a loan from Fanny Wright and once in Cincinnati she had to ask her New York banker friend, Charles Wilkes, for help. She left Cincinnati virtually penniless and her husband claimed he had no money to send her. Indeed, his own finances were steadily getting worse. He was never businesslike and sometimes would 'forget' to pay young Anthony's school fees. His reply to his wife's pleadings for funds to return home was that she should raise the money herself as it was she, not he, who had been financially incompetent.

The fact was that by the summer of 1830 the Trollopes in America were in a sad plight. They all made do with mended clothes and Mrs Trollope was forced to sell some of her own things to buy shoes for her daughter, Cecilia. She told Tom, 'As to other articles of dress, we should any of us as soon think of buying diamonds!'[28] Once again Hervieu came to her rescue. He used his ability as a portrait painter to earn enough for their keep, but sadly it was not enough to pay their passage back to England. When they left the Bazaar they had managed to salvage his vast painting, 'The Landing of Lafayette at Cincinnati'. The plan now was to exhibit it in the capital at a fee of twenty-five cents, a not inconsiderable sum at the time. They also hoped that a grateful Congress would buy the canvas as a suitably patriotic decoration for the Capitol. Once again their plans came to nothing.

Once in Washington the difficulty was to find a place to live. Frances Trollope knew she had an old acquaintance, an elder sister of Harriet Garnett, who was supposed to live in Washington, and she searched desperately for her in the hope that she might help. Her friend, Anna Maria Garnett, was now a widow, her English husband having died, and she was living not in Washington but in Stonington, in adjacent Maryland. Mrs Stone, as she now was, offered to take in Mrs Trollope and her two daughters as boarders but she could not offer them free hospitality as she was herself in reduced circumstances. The ever-generous Hervieu painted enough portraits of Washington worthies to pay the $8.25 (£1 13s) due each week. Mrs Trollope remained with her friend for almost five months and used her time to gather more information and to write. In a letter to her eldest son she explained that at least she did not need money for shoes for herself: 'I sit still and write, write, write, – so old shoes last me a long time.'[29]

This prolonged residence in Maryland allowed her more opportunities to observe slavery at first hand. As we have seen, she had arrived with a fierce hostility to America's 'peculiar institution', as was natural in a disciple of Fanny Wright. Yet after her long stay in the 'free state' of Ohio, she had been prepared to admit that she enjoyed the attention she had received in a 'slave state' when her coach passed through Virginia or when hired Virginian slaves waited on her in Pennsylvania. As she sat in her room in Maryland she pondered the subject and began to see the vastness and variety of the American Union. The differences between Maryland and Ohio, she came to feel, were as great as those between Amsterdam and St Petersburg, and slavery was the most obvious one. As she travelled about the homes of Mrs Stone's friends – many of them mere 'hovels' – Frances Trollope realised a point that escaped most commentators, then and since. She saw that the average slave lived on a small farm, not on an elegant white-pillared plantation nestling among whispering pines and weeping cypresses. In her travel she found that household slaves were normally well treated as part of an extended family's servants, something she would have been used to in her father's vicarage. Even so, 'they are rarely exposed to the lash and they are carefully nursed in sickness'. She felt that the slave's lot was often preferable to that of the American servant because 'they are more cared for and valued, and because their condition being born with them, their spirits do not struggle against it with that pining discontent which seems to be the lot of all free servants in America'. Yet the true horror of slavery was not the condition of the slave's life, but the fact that a slave could not change that condition. Her chief criticism of slavery as she came across it in Maryland and across the Potomac in Virginia was the constant fear slaves had of being 'sold South' to harsher conditions.

Mrs Trollope's attitude to slavery was similar to that held by many moderate Southerners at the time. Many Marylanders, for example, as well as Virginians, would have agreed with her, and it is likely that she took some of her opinions from them. Like Robert E. Lee, she believed that the worst effects of slavery were not on the slave but on the master, and although she claims that the worst masters were found among the smaller and poorer ones, the baneful influence of slavery affected all. Yet in the early 1830s it seemed quite possible that some of the states in the Upper South, such as Maryland and Virginia, were moving towards gradual emancipation. It was only when more than fifty white people were killed in a Virginia slave insurrection led by Nat Turner, which happened within weeks of Mrs Trollope's departure from America, that pro-slavery opinion began to harden and the hopes of gradual emancipation began to fade.[30] Mrs Trollope was, herself, against complete emancipation until the condition of the slaves had improved. Her views remained moderate, partly because she was in America before the debates over emancipation reached the heated level of later decades and partly because she was writing not just of a system but of individual situations she had personally observed. Unlike many English visitors she had no fear of or revulsion towards the slaves or towards black people. One day she heard cries that an eight-year-old slave girl had accidentally eaten a biscuit which had been covered with arsenic in an attempt to kill rats. Mrs Trollope immediately mixed a large cup of mustard and water, 'the most rapid of all emetics' she helpfully tells us, forced the child to swallow it and then cradled her in her lap till she was well.

It was only after she returned to England that she emerged as a great foe of slavery. In this, at least, she resembled Fanny Wright after her first visit. When she came to revise *Domestic Manners* for a fifth edition in 1839 her new preface gave her revised views on slavery. She said that if she were ever to travel again in America, something she claimed she could not do with safety because of her anti-slavery novel, *Jonathan Jefferson Whitlaw*, she would devote much more space to 'the peculiar institution'. The abolition of slavery throughout the British Empire in 1833 had focused even more attention on America. Fanny Trollope's hope in 1839 was that the northern states would secede from the Union and stay outside until the South had abolished slavery.

Slavery was not the only aspect of American life Mrs Trollope was able to study while in Maryland. A visit to the Chesapeake and Ohio Canal allowed her to comment on the condition of the workers and the poor. As we have seen, she had been very kind to those even worse off than herself: indeed, her own plight may have made her more conscious of their problems. She was anxious to counter the views of radicals like Fanny Wright, that America was a paradise for the poor. Mrs Trollope suggested instead that the poor would do better to emigrate to Canada. The workers she saw at the canal were, for the most part, Irish. Unlike most English writers she had no hostility to Irishmen but recognised that among the attitudes brought across the Atlantic from England was 'a strong feeling against the Irish in every part of the Union'. She added, however, that 'they will do twice as much work as a negro, and therefore are employed'. The canal workers were paid about ten to fifteen dollars a month and received, in addition, large allowances of free whisky to help them withstand the heat. Many fell victim to the 'fever' and had no one to care for them. She could not help but contrast their lot with that of the slaves she had seen: they had been better treated.

During her stay in Maryland she also had an opportunity to witness the Congressional election of 1830. Like many English commentators, she disliked 'the election fever which is constantly raging through the land'. Had America every other attraction, 'this electioneering madness would make me fly it in disgust'. The constant campaigning, she wrote, 'engrosses every conversation, it irritates every temper, it substitutes party spirit for personal esteem' and 'vitiates the whole system of society'. A similar analysis of the effects of electioneering was made by another lady at about the same time. This lady found that politics, or rather her opponents' conduct of them, 'have by the furious writing of their papers, excited the people into a perfect state of madness; the most disgraceful outrages have been in a manner sanctioned by the Govt., who take no pains to prevent or quell riots'. Those opposed to the cry for reform 'have not dared to appear out of their houses, candidates have been nearly beat to death who were anti-reformers'. This was not written by an American in Washington but by Harriet Arbuthnot, the Duke of Wellington's confidante, in London.[31]

This again illustrates a weakness in Mrs Trollope as in many of the other English travellers in America: they were often ignorant of those aspects of their own country which, when discovered in America, so shocked them. If Mrs Trollope had been in England from 1830 to 1832, she would have found it one constant round of politics, riots and elections. If she had been in Paris in 1830 she would have found the French engaged in one of their periodic revolutions, with her old friends, Lafayette and Pepe, playing their respective parts to unseat Charles X, bring in his cousin, Louis Philippe, and extend the revolution to Italy. Her view about excessive American concern with politics, as opposed to a more sensible and moderate British balance, continues today although it has no more validity now than in the 1830s. The amount of space British newspapers, radio and television devote to politics constantly increases and journalists no sooner see one government installed before they begin to unseat it. Because the stereotype that 'the Americans' are the only people obsessed with politics is a pleasing one, it is continued by those same people who in their daily effusions refute it.

To Mrs Trollope this American obsession with politics was part of a widespread and crass materialism. Almost all European commentators on America – including Tocqueville who wrote a month or two later – noted this.[32] She found more dishonest business dealings in America and, even worse, no general disapproval of them. Naturally, some of this was based on her own unhappy experience with the Bazaar. She felt that this dishonesty was due to a lack of knightly chivalry in America which caused this 'free-born race' to have so little regard for the 'vulgar virtue called probity'. This prevalent materialist outlook also ruined conversation. She quoted, with approval, a remark made to her by an Englishman long resident in America: 'In following, in meeting, or in overtaking, in the street, on the road, or in the field, at the theatre, the coffee-house, or at home, he had never overheard Americans conversing without the word DOLLAR being pronounced between them.' She added in a waspish aside: 'Such unity of purpose ... can ... be found nowhere else, except, perhaps, in an ants' nest.' The Yankees of New England, for example, were known for their sharp dealing and they were often accused of such tricks as selling wooden nutmegs. She was even more horrified at the open admiration given to such criminal abilities than at the practices themselves. This alone, she felt, destroyed the Americans' claim to be the most moral people in the world. By the end of her stay she had concluded that American morals were lower than those of Europe.

PHILADELPHIA

Mrs Trollope decided to gather more material for her book by visiting Philadelphia. The journey from Washington, now a short trip of a few hours, was for her a complicated journey by land and water. She went by road to Baltimore, impressed as ever by the beautiful flowers and trees that she saw round her and even more convinced that no country could surpass America in this regard. She then took a steamboat from Baltimore, leaving at six in the morning, and after six hours reached the Chesapeake and Delaware Canal where she had to walk a short distance to a 'pretty little decked boat, sheltered by a neat awning, and drawn by four horses'. This took her through the thirteen-mile canal that crossed the state of Delaware. At the end of this, passengers changed to another steamboat which, by four in the afternoon, was steaming into Philadelphia. In spite of all the changes she was impressed with the speed and efficiency of her journey. One wonders what she would have thought if she could have known that her future daughter-in-law and biographer would be born on one of these steamboats four years later.[33]

In her travels she had found that Americans seemed to regard their former capital Philadelphia as their most beautiful city, but she did not agree, preferring both Washington and New York. She praised Philadelphia's 'neatness' but found that the carefully planned streets gave it an 'almost wearisome regularity'. Here in the 'Quaker City' she had another encounter with American Puritanism. She had gone to the Pennsylvania Academy of Fine Arts only to find a screen blocking the open doorway to the 'Antique Statue Gallery' lest visitors see the contents. A woman guard hurried up to her saying, 'Now, ma'am, now; this is just the time for you – nobody can see you – make haste.' Mrs Trollope was annoyed when the guard grasped her arm to hurry her into the room. When she asked what this was all about she was told, 'Only, ma'am, that the ladies like to go into that room by themselves, when there be no gentlemen watching them.' Inside the gallery was a notice asking people not to write crude comments on the copies of ancient statues on display. Mrs Trollope sensibly adds that there would have been far fewer obscene graffiti on the naked statues if both men and women were allowed in together. This puritanical attitude long continued: twenty years later when her friend, the American sculptor, Hiram Powers, sent his famous – some said infamous – nude statue, 'The Greek Slave', to his native land, men and women were not allowed to view it together in some cities.[34]

A feature of American city life that Mrs Trollope noticed not only in

Philadelphia but in New Orleans, Baltimore, Washington and New York, was the lack of leisure. She even found that drinking in America was done standing up and in a hurry: English visitors still see this in the difference between American bars and English pubs. 'Excepting at church,' she wrote, the people 'never have the air of leisure or repose.' This was even more the case at night and this caused her to complain again about the American theatre and its audiences. One evening she went to the theatre to see 'The Living Skeleton', a man who was five feet four inches tall and weighed only fifty-four pounds. After this somewhat bizarre entertainment she commented on Philadelphia at night as a place where 'scarcely a sound is heard; hardly a voice or a wheel breaks the stillness. The streets are entirely dark ... no shops are open but those of the apothecary, and here and there a cook's shop.' It was a far cry from the hurly-burly of London street life, and Mrs Trollope 'listened in vain' for a note of music or the sound of laughter. 'This darkness,' she wrote, 'this stillness, is so great, that I almost felt it awful.' Even today her picture is an adequate description of many American cities at night: cities tend to be places where people work. Their homes, and now the 'more secure' suburbs, are where they seek leisure.

On the whole, Mrs Trollope liked the people of Philadelphia. As we saw earlier, she attended a Quaker meeting and was quick to note how the Quaker heritage had affected the city. Some earlier visitors as diverse as the English radical, Joseph Priestley, the French nobleman, Chateaubriand and the American President, John Adams, complained that the city had become too luxurious. Things as shocking as a Quaker with a gold snuff-box had actually been seen.[35] Presumably some of this outrageous luxury had declined when the Federal capital was moved to Washington in 1800, for Mrs Trollope was pleased with the simple sense of dignity she found during her visit: 'There is a quietness, a composure in a Philadelphia drawing-room ... characteristic of a city founded by William Penn.' Even the dress of the non-Quaker ladies was distinguished by an 'elegant simplicity' as compared to the 'gaudy splendour' of Baltimore.

In Philadelphia she was able to attend various parties that must have made a welcome break in her austere way of life. She used much of her time at these to observe American women and came to feel even more strongly than she had in Cincinnati that the principal faults in manners and in Society were due mainly to the position of women. She had earlier described women's position as being 'guarded by a seven-fold shield of habitual insignificance'. She was pleased to note that when she met cultivated ladies who knew how to converse, the whole tone of parties was raised. From this she drew a moral: if there were more cultivated women, men would not appear 'reeking with whiskey, their lips blackened with tobacco', convinced 'that women were made for no other purpose than to fabricate sweetmeats and gingerbread, construct shirts, darn stockings, and become mothers of possible presidents'. She concluded: 'Should the women of America ever discover what their power might be, and compare it with what it is, much improvement might be hoped for.' Yet she was anxious to reassure her readers that she was not another Fanny Wright, nor was she opposed to motherhood: 'The most important feature in a woman's history is her maternity.' Furthermore, Mrs Trollope doubted that women's influence would grow with increasing opportunities for formal education: 'It is in vain that "collegiate institutes" are formed for young ladies, or that "academic degrees" are conferred upon them.' It was after marriage, 'when these young attempts upon all the sciences are forgotten, that the lamentable insignificance of the American woman appears'.

Mrs Trollope also reflected on another favourite topic, women's dress. She thought American women spent more on clothes than European women, though she found that the expense produced little taste or sense in their dress. Pretty little bonnets were worn even in cold months, and she cited one young lady whose ear was frost-bitten because she did not dress warmly. She reserved her main criticism, however, for the way in which women used make-up to 'powder themselves immoderately, face, neck, and arms, with pulverised starch; the effect is indescribably dis-agreeable by day-light, and not very favourable at any time'. American women were also said to be 'most unhappily partial to false hair'. The use of false hair and pulverised starch arose from 'an indolent mode of making their toilet, and from accomplished ladies' maids not being very abundant'. Women also suffered from a 'universal defect in the formation of the bust, which is rarely full, or gracefully formed'. In addition, American women – and men as well – were pronounced to be bad walkers and the men were almost all round-shouldered. The women neither walked nor danced well, for their steps were too mincing. It is only fair to give some idea how this critic appeared herself. Cincinnati's *Mirror and Ladies' Parterre* returned the compliment, admittedly after her book was published: Mrs Trollope, it wrote, 'might be seen ever and anon, in a green calash, and long plaid cloak draggling at her heels ... walking with those colossean strides unattainable by any but English women'.* Two decades later one of her countrywomen who visited America found that 'the capabilities of English ladies are very much overrated. It is supposed that they go out in all weathers, invariably walk ten miles a day and leap five-barred fences on horseback.'[36]

While in Philadelphia Mrs Trollope visited the food market, which she found even more impressive than the one in Cincinnati. Her objection to American food did not concern its quality, which she found excellent, but the way in which it was eaten, which was not 'delicate'. Americans 'consume an extraordinary quantity of bacon. Ham and beef-steaks appear

---

* This view still survives in parts of America. A few years ago, when I was visiting my parents, my mother noticed a woman walking through a park. She said the woman must be English because she was walking so quickly. I rejected this as an old prejudice. A week later I spoke to the woman: she was English.

morning, noon, and night. In eating, they mix things together with the
strangest incongruity imaginable.' She recalled having seen eggs with
oysters, hams with apple-sauce, beef-steak with stewed peaches and salt
fish with onions. She singled out for particular condemnation the ubiquitous and 'horrible half-baked hot rolls'.*

If Mrs Trollope was impressed with the abundance and cheapness of
good food, she was not impressed with the development of American
literature. She had had little acquaintance with it before crossing the
Atlantic, save for stray meetings with James Fenimore Cooper and Washington Irving in Paris. Although Americans were 'great novel readers'
they were ignorant of the classics, of older English authors and of nearly
all European writers. When she was in Cincinnati she met a 'man of
reading' at one of Timothy Flint's literary gatherings and approached him
like a long-time wanderer in a desert hurrying towards an oasis. She had
a genuine love of literature and was, in truth, widely read. She was aghast
to hear 'the *serious* gentleman' denounce 'our poor Lord Byron', dismiss
Pope as 'entirely gone by' and smile as he pontifcated: 'We only know
Dryden by quotations, Madam.' The outraged Englishwoman summoned
her strongest artillery: 'And Shakespeare, sir?' 'Shakespeare, Madam, is
obscene, and, thank God, WE are sufficiently advanced to have found it out!
If we must have the abomination of stage plays, let them at least be marked
by the refinement of the age in which we live.' For once she was rendered
speechless, but she nursed her fury and allowed it to burst forth when she
wrote about American literature in her book.

Although she praised a few authors, such as Irving and Cooper, Americans, she said – and she was quite right at the time she was writing – had
produced 'few very good native novels'. She placed a large blame for what
she took to be the inferior state of American letters on the newspapers and
the 'immense exhalation of periodical trash, which penetrates into every
cot and corner of the country, and which is greedily sucked in by all ranks'.
'Where newspapers are the principal vehicles of the wit and wisdom of a
people,' she argued, 'the higher graces of composition can hardly be looked
for.' (Had she reflected she might have recalled that many of the penny
broadsheets and cheap newspapers published in London were little above
similar American publications.) It was, therefore, hardly surprising that
when her book appeared many American newspapers were not very kind
about 'Dame Trollope's Book'. She allowed that 'there are many among
them who can write well', but American writers had little option but to
become editors. She had little respect for serious periodicals when compared to their British rivals. She had in mind the two rival titans, the
Edinburgh Review and the *Quarterly Review*, which dominated British
literary and political life. There were several American reviews modelled

* These 'American' habits still fascinate many English visitors, but a country that can
seriously recommend 'spaghetti-on-toast' has little cause to bemoan eggs with oysters.

on them, but they lacked 'the playful vivacity and the keenly-cutting satire' of the British journals. Soon, however, Fanny Trollope would find the American reviews quite capable of satire, indeed for years she would be one of their favourite targets.

Mrs Trollope took the opportunity offered by her hurried excursion through American literature to level another blast at Thomas Jefferson, whose works were being republished at the time. No doubt she was also motivated by attending a lecture in Philadelphia by Fanny Wright and one suspects that Mrs Trollope's venom against Jefferson (who was praised by Wright in her lecture) provided a subtle way of attacking the woman who had lured her to America. She traced the American obsession with equality to his 'hollow and unsound' doctrines which were 'a mighty mass of mischief' full of 'hot-headed democracy'. Like Dr Johnson, Mrs Trollope was never satisfied with just one blast at a foe so, having attacked Jefferson's teaching, she proceeded to reflect, inaccurately, on his personal life. 'The great, the immortal Jefferson himself,' she wrote, 'he who when past the three score years and ten, still taught young females to obey his nod, and so became the father of unnumbered generations of groaning slaves.' (Mark Twain wrote, on reading this passage in her book almost thirty years later: 'It is within the possibilities at any rate.'[37]) She finished her attack by turning on his political theories: 'What was his matin and vesper hymn?' and answered that it must have been 'All men are born free and equal'. She asked: 'Did the venerable father of the gang believe it?'

The enduring popularity of Mrs Trollope's book has been an important factor in keeping alive the rumours of Jefferson's behaviour with female slaves. Mrs Trollope was only repeating stories that were current in America. Nor was hers the most outspoken attack upon Jefferson by a British traveller; at the same time Captain Hamilton was busy spreading some gossip he had picked up that Jefferson 'made money of his debaucheries' by arranging for his 'numerous offspring' to be sold at slave auctions. However, there is an interesting postscript to her story which shows how Mrs Trollope tried to be fair in her writings. In her third travel book, *Paris and the Parisians*, published in 1836, she remembered meeting an American diplomat who assured her that Jefferson was not the extreme democrat that she had depicted. She also included this additional material in a footnote to the fifth edition of *Domestic Manners* in 1839.[38]

After this trip to Philadelphia she returned to her friend's house in Maryland, but once again an American autumn brought her down with a serious fever. Mrs Trollope believed that she would not recover from this one. She was moved to the nearby town of Alexandria, Virginia as it had 'a skilful physician'. In spite of her fears, her strong constitution saved her once again. Soon she was picking her way through the icy streets of this 'pretty town' and staring in wonder at the 'noble winter landscape'. Today, of all the places Mrs Trollope visited in America, 'Old Town' Alexandria, with its elegant brick houses and English-style gardens, remains closest

to the world she knew. In this severe winter of 1830 the Potomac River –
more than a mile wide at this point – froze over and people and carts could
cross back and forth from Maryland and Washington to Virginia. In the
midst of all this icy splendour, Fanny Trollope marked the third anniversary of her arrival in America. She used her months in Alexandria to write
several chapters of *Domestic Manners*. As she re-read her early draft, she
'scrupulously challenged every expression of disapprobation'. She also was
prepared to contradict earlier portions of her book. Thus in Alexandria she
attended both the Episcopal and Catholic churches and found their services 'performed quietly and reverently'. This is similar to what she says in
the first part of her book, but her reactions to a Methodist service show a
marked change. In Alexandria she heard a sermon from a 'Picquot Indian'
and found it 'impossible not to be touched by the simple sincerity of this
poor man'.[39]

NEW YORK AND NIAGARA

After the mighty Potomac had thawed and Mrs Trollope's fever had
subsided, she began to plan her return to England. She needed to go to
New York, both to see the city and also to get some money from the
ever-helpful Charles Wilkes. After making their way to Baltimore, she and
her party boarded a steamboat to Philadelphia where they changed to yet
another boat to Trenton, New Jersey. Here they climbed into 'the most
detestable stage-coach that ever Christian built to dislocate the joints of
his fellow men'. The novelist that was waiting to be born in Frances
Trollope always emerged when confronted with the ludicrous, and on this
uncomfortable journey she observed some young dandies. Their tight high
neckcloths 'glimmered above coats made more elegant by the tight corsets
round their waists'. In the bouncing coach their costumes became instruments of torture and the young men, 'now crushed beneath their armour,
looked more like victims on the wheel, than dandies armed for conquest;
their whalebones seemed to enter into their souls, and every face grew grim
and scowling'. Nor did the young ladies, whose large bonnets were
crammed into the uncomfortable coach, look any happier. Mrs Trollope
made one of her forays into self-analysis: 'I looked into the altered eyes of
my companions,' she wrote, and was tempted to ask, ' "Look I as cross as
you?" Indeed, I believe that, if possible, I looked crosser still, for the roads
and the vehicle together were quite too much for my philosophy.'

    After this exhausting journey it is perhaps surprising that Mrs Trollope
was as enthusiastic about New York City as Fanny Wright had been, but
she was. 'I have never seen the bay of Naples,' she wrote, 'but my
imagination is incapable of conceiving any thing of the kind more beautiful
than the harbour of New York.' Her enthusiasm and her rapturous prose
were not restricted to the harbour. For the city itself she was full of praise:

New York was a 'lovely and noble city'. It was 'one of the finest cities I ever saw, and as much superior to every other in the Union'.

> To us, who had been so long travelling through half-cleared forests, and sojourning among an 'I'm-as-good-as-you' population, it seemed, perhaps, more beautiful, more splendid, and more refined than it might have done, had we arrived there directly from London.

People today are used to the adage that New York is a nice place to visit but not in which to live: not for Mrs Trollope. She was there for seven weeks and 'were it not so very far from all the old-world things which cling about the heart of an European, I should say that I never saw a city more desirable as a residence'. She was particularly struck with the beauty of Broadway for, like the main streets in Philadelphia, its shops had awnings which protected the well-dressed shoppers from the sun and rain. Yet, unlike Philadelphia, the streets were alive at night as people flocked to gas-illuminated shops that stayed open late.

Mrs Trollope also described the decoration of the mansions belonging to New York's wealthy citizens. She commented on the similarities and differences between New York and London. Furniture was frequently covered in silk or satin in New York, while in London people preferred chintz. She missed the extensive cultivation of flowers outside the houses but praised the bouquets that seemed to be everywhere inside. The interiors were cluttered with the various objects – she called them 'the pretty coxcomalities of the drawing-room' – that the nineteenth century loved even before Victoria ascended the throne and gave the age its name.

Mrs Trollope hastened to investigate the state of the theatre, and in New York there were three from which to choose. As always in her visits to American theatres, the audience interfered with her enjoyment. She had gone to see the play *Rienzi*, written by her friend, Mary Mitford, but 'observed in the front row of a dress-box a lady performing the most maternal office possible'. In addition, there were 'several gentlemen without their coats, and a general air of contempt for the decencies of life, certainly more than usually revolting'. Nor were things much better when she attended a performance of Rossini's opera *La Cenerentola*, for here she encountered her most detested foe when 'we saw many "yet unrazored lips" polluted with the grim tinge of the hateful tobacco, and heard, without ceasing, the spitting'.

Like Tocqueville and many other European visitors, Mrs Trollope was impressed with the prisons and public institutions she found in America. In New York she visited the Asylum for the Destitute where boys and girls were taught useful trades to lead them away from lives of crime. She noted that the boys were 'the finest set of lads I ever saw brought together; bright looking, gay, active, and full of intelligence'. The girls she found 'exactly the reverse; heavy, listless, indifferent, and melancholy'. She was told that the boys could improve when removed from evil influences while the girls, once fallen, had little hope.

Mrs Trollope also spent a 'delightful day' in New Jersey, just across the Hudson River to the west. She was greatly impressed with the Morris Canal which she thought could give English canal-builders lessons in saving money. The canal was then about one hundred miles long and, at one point, 'runs along the side of a mountain at thirty feet above the tops of the highest buildings in the town of Paterson', then one of the most important industrial cities in America. The scene so impressed her that she stopped to pay tribute to one point in the 'national character of the Americans' – the 'boldness and energy with which public works are undertaken and carried through':

> Nothing stops them if a profitable result can be fairly hoped for. It is this which has made cities spring up amidst the forests ... and could they once be thoroughly persuaded that any point of the ocean had a hoard of dollars beneath it ... in about eighteen months we should see a snug covered rail-road leading direct to the spot.

Mrs Trollope also noted some customs peculiar to New York. The city's Presbyterians had an annual 'spinning visit' when all the members of a congregation brought a wide variety of gifts to their minister's house. The poorer members left theirs in a basket by the door while the wealthier brought presents of food, china, glass and linen into the house where they were entertained to tea. On the first day of May another peculiar sight could be seen: on this day most leases fell in and the whole city seemed to be on the move as 'rich furniture and ragged furniture, carts, waggons, and drays, ropes, canvas, and straw, packers, porters, and draymen, white, yellow and black, occupy the streets'. Thirty years later, when the publisher John Cassell visited New York, he also commented on these two New York customs.[40] She went on to comment on the 'great number of negroes in New York'. They were, of course, all free by this time. 'Not even in Philadelphia,' she wrote, 'where the anti-slavery opinions have been the most active and violent, do the blacks appear to wear an air of so much consequence as they do in New York.' She singled out one theatre where all the performers were blacks and where the whites in the audience were segregated to one part of the house, which Mrs Trollope found a proper return for the opposite segregation in white theatres. Hervieu provided another of his drawings for a scene described by his patron in which she 'met in Broadway a young negress in the extreme of fashion and accompanied by a black beau, whose toilet was equally studied; eye-glass, guard-chain, nothing was omitted; he walked beside his sable goddess uncovered, and with an air of the most tender devotion'. She contrasted the pair with a group that she saw framed by a window in a handsome house on Broadway: there was 'a very pretty white girl, with two gentlemen beside her; but alas! both of them had their hats on, and one was smoking!'

Mrs Trollope found the hackney cabs expensive but 'the best in the world'. She was not the last visitor to complain of New York's cab drivers, warning future visitors to be alert to any financial trick. On her first trip in a New York cab she neglected to ask the fare and was charged $2.50 (10s) for a twenty-minute trip. When Mrs Trollope 'referred to the waiter of the hotel, he asked if I had made a bargain. "No." "Then I expect" (with the usual look of triumph) "that the Yankee has been too smart for you." ' Unfortunately Hervieu's gallant loyalty did not permit him to turn his skill to an illustration of that encounter.

Cab fares were no small matter to Mrs Trollope in the summer of 1831. Hervieu was able to earn enough by his portrait painting to keep them going but not enough for their return fare home. When asked for help, Mr Trollope said 'he had no money to send' and added that as she had got herself into this situation she could get herself out of it.[41] In spite of this rebuff, she knew that she had to see the great 'lion' of America, Niagara Falls. She did not feel that her book could succeed without a vivid description of it and so she scraped together enough money for a final journey by steamboat and stage-coach.

Mrs Trollope's poverty lessened neither her enjoyment nor her enthusiasm. As she travelled up the Hudson River she found that Americans had not exaggerated the beauty she found there: 'It is not in the power of man to paint with a strength exceeding that of nature, in such scenes as the Hudson presents. Every mile shews some new and startling effect of the combination of rocks, trees, and water.' At Albany her party took a stage-coach to avoid the Eire Canal's many time-consuming locks, but eventually they transferred to a canal boat where she found everyone behaving with 'unshrinking egotism'. Even the women entered the boat with a determination to grab the least uncomfortable place as soon as they could. 'In circumstances where an English woman would look proud, and a French woman *nonchalante,*' she wrote, 'an American lady looks grim; even the youngest and the prettiest can.' Eventually she found it less tiresome to walk along the tow-path, but the heat was so dreadful that she was forced to revive herself with iced water mixed with lemon juice and frequent dabs of *eau de cologne.*

Some days before the party reached Niagara they stopped at the smaller Trenton Falls. She was just about to join in the wholesale denunciation of those who had carved their names at such spots when someone pointed to one carving which read:

Trollope, England.

It appears that 'Mr T.' and Tom had stopped there on their return visit to England. Mrs Trollope is honest enough to record this anecdote, which many other writers would have omitted.[42] As her long trip continued, her comments became more acerbic. She found some amusement, as so many travellers did and indeed some still do, in the American custom of giving grand names to little places. One town, which consisted of a whisky store and a warehouse, was called Port Byron, while at Rome, New York, she found a shop named Remus. As she came close to Niagara Falls her patriotic fervour reasserted itself and she determined to cross to the Canadian side so that her first view could be under the British flag. As she and her daughters sailed across the Niagara River she was 'delighted to see British oaks, and British roofs, and British boys and girls. These latter, as if to impress upon us that they were not citizens [but *subjects* of the Queen], made bows and courtesies as we passed, and this little touch of long unknown civility produced great effect.'

Mrs Trollope was overwhelmed by the Falls as she drew near its thundering roar on a bright day in June. Today we are so jaded by being able to glance at the wonders of the world without leaving our television sets that it is difficult to understand the passion with which our ancestors encountered the glories of nature or of art. The visitor to the still awe-inspiring Niagara who wants to contemplate natural beauty is in perpetual danger of being trampled to death by bored honeymooners or hordes of jabbering tourists armed with loaded video cameras. We can only approach the sensations of earlier travellers through the flamboyant prose of a Romantic like Fanny Trollope:

> I trembled like a fool, and my girls clung to me, trembling too ... but with faces beaming with delight ... at one glance, I saw all I had wished for, hoped for, dreamed of ... wonder, terror, and delight completely overwhelmed me. I wept with a strange mixture of pleasure and of pain, and certainly was, for some time, too violently affected in the *physique* to be capable of much pleasure ... It has to me something beyond its vastness; there is a shadowy mystery hangs about it which neither the eye nor even the imagination can penetrate; but I dare not dwell on this, it is a dangerous subject.

Although she announced to her readers that she would not describe the 'loveliest thing I ever looked upon', she then spent several pages doing just that.* Years later it was rumoured in her family that 'the Hon. Mr Somebody' had fainted when reading her description. Three decades later her son, Anthony, in his travel book on America, advised visitors that to 'realize Niagara you must sit there till you see nothing else'. In this, as in so many things, he was following his mother's example. She stayed at the Falls for four 'delightful days of excitement and fatigue':

> We drenched ourselves in spray; we cut our feet on the rocks; we blistered

---

* A twentieth-century novelist has derived a similar feeling of 'spiritual strength' from one of the world's great waterfalls: in Muriel Spark's case it was the Victoria Falls (*Curriculum Vitae: Autobiography* [Penguin edition, 1993, pp. 128-9]).

our faces in the sun; we looked up the cataract, and down the cataract; we perched ourselves on every pinnacle we could find; we dipped our fingers in the flood at a few yards' distance from its thundering fall; in short, we strove to fill as many inches of memory with Niagara, as possible; and I think the images will be within the power of recall for ever.

A rival English travel-writer, Captain Thomas Hamilton, was gazing at the Falls along with the Trollopes. Perhaps he was annoyed by Mrs Trollope's challenge to capture Niagara adequately in prose, perhaps he was simply jealous, but he later wrote: 'From the odd appearance of matters, and her apparent poverty, which hardly admitted her and her daughters being decently dressed, it was conclusive against her being taken notice of by respectable ladies, or treated as one herself.'[43] No doubt 'the odd appearance' refers to the young French artist at the side of an English matron. Hamilton, as a younger brother of a baronet, would have considered himself licensed to look down at a mere wife of a baronet's cousin. Yet his waspish comment does provide us with the reason why Mrs Trollope did not frequent upper-class society in America.

After her rhapsodies at Niagara, she had to resume more mundane travelling as she passed through the city of Buffalo, 'the queerest looking' place she had seen. Here she noted a general feature of American life that has continued until the present: the rapid spreading out of towns. 'Surely', she wrote, 'this country may be said to spread rather than to rise.' As she rattled along in yet another uncomfortable coach she had one of her final encounters with American manners.

A new passenger tried to force a large box into the already crowded coach when one of Mrs Trollope's English companions objected. A group of 'whisky drinkers' appeared to contest this. Her account of this farce well shows her ability to re-create a scene and to entertain her readers with the peculiarities of American frontier dialect – or 'Yankee talk'. When informed that the box would not fit, the intruders replied: 'That's because you'll be English travellers I expect, but we have travelled in better countries than Europe – we have travelled in America – and the box will go, I calculate.' They had not calculated on Mrs Trollope: she now entered the fray and observed that none of the other passengers had put luggage inside the crowded carriage. 'Right!' her opponents replied, 'there they go – that's just their way – that will do in Europe, may be; it sounds just like English tyranny, now – don't it? but it won't do here.' Mrs Trollope then said that she assumed the law would never permit such offensive behaviour. '"Law!" exclaimed a gentleman very particularly drunk, "we makes our own laws, and governs our own selves."' '"Law!" echoed another gentleman ... "this is a free country, *we have no laws here*, and we don't want no foreign power to tyrannize over us."' In recording this incident she was repeating a point she had made earlier: 'All the freedom enjoyed in America, beyond what is enjoyed in England, is enjoyed solely by the disorderly at the expense of the orderly.' (Mark Twain's marginal comment by this passage reads, 'True yet'.)

   In addition to trouble on the coaches she also had to endure bad food as the stage-coach had no regular stops and halted at any inn or tavern that was available. She was 'amused by the patient manner in which our American fellow-travellers ate whatever was set before them, without uttering a word of complaint, or making any effort to improve it', a trait now sadly much more noticeable in England. Back in the coach, however, the Americans began their complaints, much as Englishmen do today as they return to their cars: ' " 'twas a shame" – " 'twas a robbery" – " 'twas poisoning folks" – and the like. I, at last, asked the reason of this, and why they did not remonstrate? "Because, madam, no American gentleman or lady that keeps an inn won't bear to be found fault with." ' Disregarding the food, Mrs Trollope concentrated on the beauties of the American countryside as the stage-coach rattled through the Mohawk Valley. She was more than ready to defend America from any European sneer that it was not a 'picturesque' country. A small incident on her return journey to New York City disturbed her enthusiasm over the scenery: a fellow traveller pointed out a vast tract of land that belonged to an English MP, Edward 'Bear' Ellice, son-in-law of the then Prime Minister, Lord Grey, and added that the land would only be properly developed when it passed into capable American hands.

   Mrs Trollope was delighted to find herself back in New York, where she passed her final fortnight in America. Money had finally arrived from Harrow after she tried a simple strategy: 'I wrote to Mr Trollope and told him that for my dear girls' sake I was *determined* upon returning to England – and that if he was unable to furnish me with the means, I would apply to his family for them – This brought eighty pounds.'[44] Before leaving she paid New York a final tribute: 'In truth, were all America like this fair city, and all, no, only a small proportion of its population like the friends we left there, I should say, that the land was the fairest in the world.' As she boarded the ship she had with her none of the illusions and few of the hopes with which she had arrived. Behind her lay the broken dreams of Fanny Wright's utopian colony and the shattered ruins of the Cincinnati Bazaar. Mrs Trollope had failed both as a social reformer and as an entrepreneur. Her family's finances were in a far worse condition than when she left. Yet ahead of her lay a memorable literary career, for among the few remaining possessions she carried onto the ship were 'my six hundred pages of griffonage'.

   The book's conclusion was probably written aboard ship. In it she did not mince words. 'I suspect that what I have written will make it evident that I do not like America.' She readily acknowledged that she 'met with individuals there whom I love and admire' and she accepted without doubt that the country was 'fair to the eye, and most richly teeming with the gifts of plenty'. Yet, despite its wealth and the good people she had met she still was 'led to ask myself why it is that I do not like it'. Why was it, she asked, 'that neither its beauty nor its abundance can suffice to neutralize, or greatly soften, the distaste which the aggregate of my recollections has left upon my mind'?

The reason for her dislike was the American people. She distinguished between the higher classes and the vast mass of the population but insisted that 'the small patrician band is a race apart; they live with each other, and for each other'. In making this distinction she seems to have assumed such separation existed only in America. One wonders how much she knew of the habits of the British or the European aristocracy, for surely such 'exclusive' behaviour by 'patricians' was hardly peculiar to America. Again, her view that such people kept apart from political life shows the limited nature of her travels in America; she did not visit South Carolina or Massachusetts where old families still played a powerful role. Having kindly excluded the minority, she returned to the majority and levelled the most outspoken blast in her book: 'I speak ... of the population generally, as seen in town and country, among the rich and the poor, in the slave states, and the free states. I do not like them. I do not like their principles, I do not like their manners, I do not like their opinions.'

She made no secret of her own opinions, opinions that had changed greatly during her 41 months in America. She knew that English advocates of radical reform frequently pointed to America as an example of a country, created and largely settled by the British, and still drawing on Britain for emigrants, where popular government marched hand in hand with a respect for private property and ordered society. With the zeal of the Tory convert, Mrs Trollope was anxious to defend English institutions from any democratic breeze that might be blowing her ship across the Atlantic. Although protesting that her concern was not with politics but with society, she showed how political changes affected life. This forced her to discuss politics: 'Both as a woman, and as a stranger, it might be unseemly for me to say that I do not like their government, and therefore I will not say so. That it is one which pleases themselves is most certain, and this is considerably more important than pleasing all the travelling old ladies in the world.' She admitted that American government both pleased Americans and was a fit government for them, but it was not so for other nations. When asked to specify the greatest difference between the two countries she did not answer that it lay in the difference between republicanism and monarchy but in 'the want of refinement'. Once again, Mark Twain, brought up in the egalitarianism of the frontier and famed for his 'folksy' image, concurred. He wrote simply: 'She hit it.' The levelling spirit of equality, ultimately based on political concepts of democracy, would, she felt, deny America true greatness just as it would real refinement.

Yet the final lines of *Domestic Manners of the Americans* held out some hope. Things might improve if only the Americans would turn away from their excessive worship of egalitarian manners:

If this ever happens, if refinement once creeps in among them, if they once learn to cling to the graces, the honours, the chivalry of life, then we shall say farewell to American equality, and welcome to European fellowship one of the finest countries on the earth.

PUBLICATION AND INFLUENCE

When Mrs Trollope and her daughters landed at Woolwich on 5 August 1831, they were returning to a much changed country from that which they had left in 1827. Only four days before, the new King, William IV, had opened the new London Bridge. A hot summer was being disturbed by yet hotter debates in Parliament over the Reform Bill, which everyone agreed would mark the beginning of a new era. The only disagreement was about what would follow if the Reform Bill passed. In Harrow one thing had not changed, the financial miseries of Thomas Anthony Trollope. Indeed, they were worse because the price of hay, his principal crop, had collapsed. The reason for his surly replies to her requests for money was that he was only able to pay his rent in instalments and, like his wife, he was facing the seizure of all his goods. The state of the tumbledown farmhouse at Harrow Weald – the prospect of which had been a main cause of her jaunt to America – was far worse than she imagined. There were not even pillows on the beds. Her three sons seemed 'perfectly without destination': Tom was lucky to find another Oxford college after a rude letter from his father to his Principal led to his being dismissed from Alban Hall; Henry was at Cambridge and thinking about trying the law as his latest career; Anthony, who was twelve when she left, was now a sullen sixteen-year-old who seemed interested only in flirting with a farmer's daughter. In between excruciating headaches, Mr Trollope drafted insulting letters to Lord Northwick, his landlord. 'Here we are,' Fanny Trollope informed the Garnetts, 'God knows what will become of us all!'

    She had little choice but to polish what she had written and to comb through the letters she had sent home for forgotten facts. By the end of the month the fifty-two-year-old author had completed her first book and, like almost all virgin authors, sought the advice of a published friend. Mary Mitford provided a letter to her publisher, Whittaker and Treacher, but she warned in words that are still heard: 'A first work must be given away to make a reputation but then will afterward bring money.'[45] Mrs Trollope was upset to hear that they had asked Captain Basil Hall to report on the book as she feared that he would regard it as a slight book by a frivolous woman. In the event he was delighted because it confirmed his own recent and much criticised account of American life. Like her, he had become a strong Tory through his experiences in America. A chapter of her book was devoted to praising his work and to giving an account of its reception in America. (The success of his *Travels in North America in the Years 1827*

1. Rebecca Burlend in old age.

2. Edward Burlend, the son who remained in England.

3. The Levee in New Orleans with slaves unloading bales of cotton from steamboats. This was the first sight of America for Rebecca Burlend and Frances Trollope. New Orleans was also visited by Frances Wright and Lady Emmeline Stuart Wortley (see pp. 15-16, 81, 159).

4. Cartoon from Major Walter Wilkey's *Western Immigration* (1839) showing a prosperous man going to Illinois and a disappointed family returning from the same state.

5. Frances Wright.

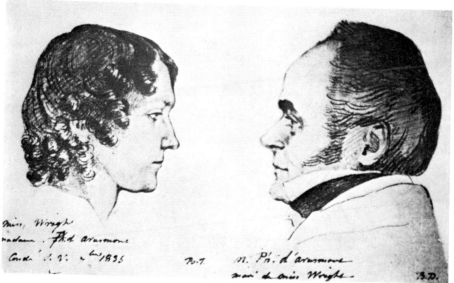

6. Frances Wright and her husband, William Phiquepal D'Arusmont.

7. Cartoon making fun of Frances Wright as a lecturer, 'A Down(w)right Gabbler, or a goose that deserves to be hissed' (see p. 70).

8. The Marquis de Lafayette.

9. Frances Wright's settlement at Nashoba in Tennessee, from an illustration by Auguste Hervieu in Frances Trollope's *Domestic Manners of the Americans* (see p. 83).

10. One of Auguste Hervieu's illustrations in *Domestic Manners of the Americans.* Mary Carroll is showing a hat to (from left to right) Frances Trollope, William Maclure and Frances Wright (see p. 81).

11. A crowded American stage coach, from *Harper's Weekly,* 13 August 1959 (see p. 115).

12. Frances Trollope
as painted by
Auguste Hervieu.

13. Frances Trollope's doomed
Bazaar in Cincinnati
(see pp. 85-6).

14. An illustration by Auguste Hervieu in *Domestic Manners of the Americans:* Mrs Trollope (centre) and one of her daughters (right) are being hurried into a nude statue gallery in Philadelphia when there are no men about (see p. 105).

15. An 'American rear' at the theatre. This drawing by Auguste Hervieu in *Domestic Manners of the Americans* caused great annoyance in America (see p. 89).

16. An American attack on Mrs Trollope from D.C. Johnston's *Trollopania*. The illustrator adhered to the American view that Englishmen could not pronounce their 'h's' (see p. 123).

17. Another American caricature of the Trollopes in Cincinnati: (from left to right) the Trollopes' two daughters, Mrs Trollope herself, Mr Trollope as a John Bull figure and their eldest son, Thomas Adolphus, in his Oxford gown and cap. Auguste Hervieu is painting a portrait of a local militia man as a uniformed soldier; the other portrait may be that of Lafayette.

18. An illustration by Auguste Hervieu in Mrs Trollope's anti-slavery novel, *The Life and Adventures of Jonathan Jefferson Whitlaw,* capitalising on the idea that Americans preferred 'lynch law' to common law (see p. 128).

19. The ascent to the Capitol Building in Washington, D.C., drawn by the English artist, William Henry Bartlett. All the women in this book except Mrs Burlend visited the Capitol.

20. Lady Emmeline Stuart Wortley. An engraving by F.C. Lewis after the portrait by Sir Francis Grant. (Reproduced by permission of the National Portrait Gallery.)

21. Niagara Falls, drawn by Lady Emmeline Stuart Wortley and used as a frontispiece to her oddly named book, &c. (see pp. 142-3).

22. A plantation house in Northern Virginia.

23. Confederate troops crowded onto trains; similar scene was described by Catherine Hopley (see p. 200).

24. Civilians sheltering during a Federal bombardment of Charleston, South Carolina. An illustration by Frank Vizetelly for the *Illustrated London News* of 5 December 1863 (see p. 202).

25. Harper's Ferry, Virginia, where the Potomac and Shenandoah Rivers meet. Catherine Hopley visited here after John Brown's raid (see p. 176). During the Civil War, the Catholic church on the right was protected from destruction by the Irish priest's flying the British flag.

and 1828, which she had read in July 1830, had played no small part in persuading her to write her own.) Within a few days Mrs Trollope was delighted to find a letter of praise from Hall, who also suggested the title of the book.

Domestic Manners of the Americans was published on 19 March 1832, the very day the third reading of the Reform Bill was passed by the House of Commons. The two volumes contained twenty-four drawings by Hervieu, all but two of which were even more harsh than her words. Having so many illustrations was unusual and they added greatly to the book's appeal. Shortly after publication, John Murray II, the most important publisher of the time, happened to be talking to Mr Trollope who had embarked single-handed on a vast work of scholarship, the *Encyclopaedia Ecclesiastica*, a projected four-volume reference work that would provide entries on every aspect of Christian history and liturgy. 'By the bye – Trollope,' said the publisher to his new author, 'Who the devil *is* Mrs Trollope? Her book is the cleverest thing I ever read. I have read it through. So spirited!' Poor old Thomas Trollope could only reply, 'The lady is my wife.' Murray answered, 'Why did she not bring it to me? It will sell like wildfire! She ought to have brought it to me. But I will help it all I can.'

Murray was true to his word. An enthusiastic review in his strongly Tory publication, the *Quarterly Review*, in July 1832 gave her wide publicity. The review was, as always, anonymous though we now know that it was by Captain Basil Hall. In a review of over forty pages, Mrs Trollope was lauded as 'an English *lady* of sense and acuteness'. He only quibbled on one point and that was her comment that the Americans were not charitable. He observed that she had gone to America under the guidance of the 'fanatical female', Fanny Wright, yet he pointed out how America had cured Mrs Trollope of her radicalism. Indeed, the good Captain saw an excellent opportunity to heap some praise on his own head, particularly as the same issue of the *Quarterly* carried a review of his newest book. Hall saw America as a valuable tool in opposing parliamentary reform. 'Almost every English liberal accustomed to the social habits of the upper classes in this country,' he wrote, 'who has recently travelled in the United States, appears to have come back a convert to the old-fashioned doctrines of Toryism.' For instance, he continued, 'Captain Hall went out with his head quite exalted as to the ineffable advantages of republican institutions – an ultra-Whig in Church and State', and 'we all know the results of his experience'. Even in his final tribute to Mrs Trollope he found room for another flattering reference to himself: 'We have now before us the story of a lady who also carried with her to the New World the most exaggerated notions of liberalism, and who seems to have returned, if possible, a stouter enemy of all such notions than the gallant captain himself.'

Mrs Trollope took the Captain's praise in her stride because she realised its value; by the end of 1832 she was said to have made about £1,000 from her writing. (This also included some payment for her first novel.) Perhaps of almost equal importance was the fame she secured in aristocratic Society. She, who had always roamed round the fringe of the literary and theatrical world of London, now found herself the centre of attraction. In a letter to Tom, Mrs Trollope boasted, echoing her hero, Byron, that she 'awoke one morning and found myself famous', but the precarious state of the family finances is seen in her celebratory treats: a quarter-pound of green tea and a half-pound of fresh butter. We can imagine her enjoying them and savouring the prospect of fame and financial salvation; even her harshest critic must admit that she had earned a good cup of tea. Yet the success of her book soon made such minor celebrations somewhat farcical. The Tory aristocracy was delighted with a book that exposed the fallacy of democratic theory and ridiculed the practice of democracy. Tory reviewers did all they could to promote it. 'The countess of Morley told me she was certain that if I drove through London proclaiming who I was, I should have the horses taken off and be drawn in triumph from one end of town to the other.' Lady Charlotte Lindsay 'implored' dear Mrs Trollope to carry on with her writing, and Lady Louisa Stuart told her that she 'had quite put English out of fashion, and that every one was talking Yankee talk. In short', she concluded, 'I was *overpowered* ... How strange all this seems!'[46] The praise was not confined to Society ladies, for such eminent Tories as Wordsworth and Southey were reported to be highly pleased – though the Tory wit and journalist, Theodore Hook, snarled that the book was too clever to have been written by a mere woman.

With the praise came a good deal of criticism, mainly by English liberals and radicals. Perhaps the most powerful attack was by William Empson in the Whig *Edinburgh Review* in an article entitled 'The Americans and Their Detractors' in July. Empson was amazed that 'an elderly personage' such as Mrs Trollope could be led to America by Fanny Wright, and he ironically praised the 'great dexterity' with which the commercial purpose of the trip was concealed. He scored an excellent hit by observing that if Mrs Trollope, or, one might add, the gallant Captain Hall, so easily abandoned their earlier radical views, one is free to question the stability of their newer, conservative ones:

> There is nothing so cheap, and at the same time nothing so intractable, as extremes. That a mind which the England of 1827 had diseased into sedition should also grumble over the real America, does not at all surprise us. The lowering down to themselves the few who are above them, is, we fear, practically, with many, a pleasanter sort of radicalism, than the raising up of the many who are below.

Empson also saw the book's essential weakness, a weakness missed by Mrs Trollope's admirers: so much of it was devoted to Cincinnati which 'can just as much represent the United States as a new flourishing port in the Orkneys would represent Great Britain'. He admitted that she had considerable skill in writing of her experiences: in perhaps one of the best summaries of her skills as a writer, he observed that 'Mrs Trollope describes better than she thinks'.

Her first American critic was someone who describes himself as the 'American editor' of the version of her book that was published in New York in June. Like most pirated editions it looked cheaper than its English original; the American book had only eight of Hervieu's twenty-four illustrations. The 'editor' poured scorn upon the 'inscrutable mystery' of Hervieu's role in the Trollope party. This self-appointed 'editor' then unleashed another sexist sneer. Like Theodore Hook, he could not believe that a woman was capable of writing such a book and he was ready with some literary gossip: 'I have ascertained beyond all reasonable doubt that the real author is no less a person than Captain Basil Hall or 'All, as he is called in the literary circles of London ... [Hall] is Mrs Trollope in breeches ... Mrs Trollope is Captain Basil 'All in petticoats.' No doubt he had confused the reviewer with the author. It was standard practice for Americans to rebut some of the English attacks upon them by insisting that no Englishman could pronounce the letter H.

American critics reacted with fury to *Domestic Manners*. Their ire was only increased by the praise of the *Quarterly Review*, with which they had long been at war. Many Americans only knew her book from reviews which tended to select her most unfavourable comments. Thus the most experienced American politician, John Quincy Adams – who had been President when she arrived in the country – wrote in his diary: 'Amused myself an hour by reading an article in the *Quarterly Review* ... The subject of it is a book written by a certain Mrs Trollop [*sic*] who has done much to justify her name.' He did however add: 'There is notwithstanding all the abuse a foundation of Justice in her remarks.'[47] Such a balanced judgment could hardly be expected from American literary magazines who vied with each other in the velocity of their response to this newly risen foe. English interest in American reactions to *Domestic Manners* was so great that some of the principal American reviews were republished in London in a shilling pamphlet, which allowed these literary cannonades to reverberate across the Atlantic.

The *American Quarterly Review* took the well-worn path of lofty condescension reinforced by time-honoured Anglo-Saxon prejudice: 'Her mistakes are numerous; but rather, we are disposed to think, the fault of her education – which appears to have been French and flippant, and by no means calculated for a comprehensive survey.' Her complaints were mainly 'evils of the tea-table and the toilet – subjects, we grant, of infinite importance among the young and budding of her sex'. Having put her in her place by virtue of her sex they continued by rounding on her age, which for some reason always seems to have outraged her critics. Why should minor things 'provoke the anger, or occasion the severe censure of an ancient and intelligent personage of Mrs Trollope's dimensions'? Like the *Edinburgh Review*, the *American Quarterly* pointed to the limited extent of her travels and knowledge: even in Cincinnati, people 'had no time for chat, and ... little taste for that of a garrulous woman, going about "taking notes" '. Nevertheless, the magazine did praise some of her observations, such as that on the undue influence of the clergy, and her account of the Methodists which, it said, was accurate and useful. It approved of her attacks upon the 'nauseous and unnecessary weed', i.e. tobacco, and said that it would forgive her all her errors if she could lessen the 'noxious indulgence' of spitting. The newly founded *New England Magazine*, while it agreed her denunciations of spitting, roundly censured her and had much sport with her unfortunate name: 'There is much ... in a name: if words are things, names are more than shades; the name of Mrs. Trollope, therefore, may be, at least, the shadow of a thing.'*

The *American Monthly Review* launched the fiercest assault on a book that was 'filled up to the brim with lies, for the sake of *making money* out of the prejudices of a certain party of the British public'. Like the *Edinburgh Review*, it wondered why 'Mrs. Trollope, educated, as we are given to understand, in all the refinements of the most polished circles of Europe, accustomed to all the luxuries of affluent life, should have left country, and home, and friends, and sense, and refinement, and every thing that makes life worth the having' to come to:

> a nation of spitters, and chewers, and smokers, and dram-drinkers, and majors, and colonels, and generals, and pigs, all alike swaggering republicans, boasting, bullying, bellowing, roaring, and squealing for liberty and equality under a government of tinkers and tailors.

Could her purpose have been, it asked, 'the sordid and peculiarly American purpose of "making a *spec*", as we Yankees call it'? Such a suggestion 'doth fill us with exceeding wonder'.

As Mrs Trollope had criticised American manners, it was only fitting that the *American Monthly Review* should criticise hers. 'Mrs. Trollope, we suppose, understands, or ought to understand, what belongs to the character and manners of a lady', it commented, but 'wherever she went, while in this country, the boldness, freedom, and coarseness of her bearing were such as would have excluded an American woman from the refined circles of her sex'. (Presumably the writer had heard that, despite her letters of introduction from Lafayette, she had not gained entry to the best circles in Cincinnati.) Finally the *Review* advised its readers to avoid the writings of both Captain Hall and Mrs Trollope, 'a conceited post-captain and an unblushing vixen'.[48]

---

* The name 'Trollope' attracted derision not only from critics of her books, but from schoolmates of her sons. The Trollope boys had a fanciful legend to explain their name. According to this, the founder of the family went hunting with William the Conqueror, who bestowed on him the name 'Trois Loup' after he had killed three wolves. The use of the word 'trollop' as a derogatory term for 'a shameless woman' seems to have survived more in the United States than in Britain.

Americans undoubtedly agreed with these attacks but they certainly did not take the advice to avoid reading the condemned book. Just as Mrs Trollope had taken note of the reception given to Captain Hall's book while in Cincinnati, another British traveller, a young subaltern named E.T. Coke, was in New York when her book appeared and has left us, in his own book of travels, a colourful account of its reception. 'The commotion it created amongst the good citizens is truly inconceivable ... and the tug of war was hard, whether the "Domestic Manners", or the cholera, which burst upon them simultaneously, should be the more engrossing topic of conversation.' At every street corner and newsagent one saw 'a large placard ... with "For sale here, with plates, *Domestic Manners of the Americans*, by Mrs. Trollope" '. At table, on board steamboats and even in the much maligned stage-coaches 'the first question was "Have you read Mrs. Trollope?" ' Of course, like all English books of the period, the American editions were pirated ones and Mrs Trollope received not a penny from the American sales, which were enormous. 'The more it was abused,' Coke recalled, 'the more rapidly did the printers issue new editions.' Although Coke did not entirely agree with Mrs Trollope's criticisms, he felt that her book was already having an effect in improving American manners within only a few months of publication. American travellers in Britain – gathering material for their own books – were naturally fascinated by Mrs Trollope's. Henry McLellan found that he and his English hosts were 'all laughing heartily at the silliness of Mrs Trollope's book which had just appeared'. The Scottish host of another American traveller, Charles Stewart, hid a copy of *Domestic Manners* lest it offend his guest. However, a son of the host told him about it: 'It is full of the funniest stories and the funniest pictures.' Washington Irving, her old acquaintance in Paris, read the book shortly after it appeared and privately agreed with many of her strictures. For many decades thereafter American travel books about England frequently contained a sneer against Mrs Trollope. Within the year, Grant Thornburn wrote an account of Britain for his fellow Americans. The title gave an indication of its sarcastic tone: *Men and Manners in Great Britain; Or, A Bone to Gnaw for Trollopes, Fidlers, etc.* (Thornburn was a Scottish nail-maker who had gone to New York and made a fortune as a seed merchant.) In America, Mrs Trollope was also ridiculed in cartoons and on stage. One cartoon showed her being knocked down by pigs in Cincinnati, while a strongly racialist one entitled 'Trollop at home in de fust color'd circles' showed her surrounded by fawning blacks serving her possum and cow heel. Given her strictures on American theatres, it is amusing to note that when an American comedy, *The Lion of the West*, was brought to London in 1833, a character called Amelia Wallop was added as a way to attack *Domestic Manners*.[49]

Of all of Mrs Trollope's assaults upon American manners none provoked greater outrage than her frequent denunciations of the habit of tobacco spitting. One New York newspaper burst forth with a poem a month after her book was published in America:[50]

> Mrs. Trollope is commendably bitter
> Against the filthy American spitter,
> For spitting his juice all about;
> While the English they (for so it is writ)
> Disgustingly in their handkerchiefs spit.

Yet sensitive Americans had a horror of this vile behaviour and were embarrassed when it was attacked. America's two best diarists in this era both discussed it. Philip Hone, a former Mayor of New York, wrote about 'the never-to-be-exhausted theme of English animadversion, our republican habit of *spitting*'. Although it was mainly a habit on the southern and western frontiers, he admitted it could also be found in the North. As much as he disliked it he wondered if it was all that much worse than 'the atmosphere which John Bull creates in the dark recesses of his porter house, redolent with the fumes of a hundred often smoked and never cleaned pipes'. Yet the Southern diarist, Mary Chesnut – arguably the greatest literary talent the Old South produced – knew the habit well and denounced it. She experienced it even in church: 'To think, there are men who dare so defile a church, a sacred sanctuary ... and we have to hold up our skirts and walk tiptoe, so covered is the floor, aisle, and pews with the dark shower of tobacco juice.' In a literary allusion that Mrs Trollope would have relished, she concluded: 'I know where Dante would place these – animals.'[51]

Domestic Manners naturally disturbed those who believed in good Anglo-American relations. Sir Augustus Foster, for example, had been the British envoy in Washington earlier in the century, but by this time had advanced to Turin whence he wrote to his friend, Josiah Quincy, President of Harvard: 'You have had enough of nonsense from Mrs. Trollope and other silly people, who saw nothing but the dark side, and who did not deserve such kind treatment as they met with, being merely land-jobbers or book-jobbers, instead of travellers for information.' President Quincy replied: 'I say nothing concerning the already perished travels of the Trollopes, the Fiddlers, the Halls, and the Hamiltons since you entertain so just an opinion of them.' But, like most people who promise to say nothing, this belligerent Unitarian continued: 'These birds of passage have skimmed over this country like vultures over the surface of the Carolinas, pouncing upon whatever is corrupt, and passing by whatever is sound or healthful, as adapted neither to their taste nor scent.' These somewhat outspoken words spurred the British diplomat to consider writing up his own recollections of his years in the United States. By this time he had perhaps forgotten that many of his own private letters contained complaints not at all dissimilar to those of Mrs Trollope. Sir Augustus assured

Quincy: 'I feel a spur in looking at the stupid assertions and reflections of so many book-makers who have visited your country full of prejudice and vulgarity, and who describe the fungous population of Irish and Germans, or Atlantic settlers at the West, as if they were natives.'[52]

Yet not all Americans shared either Foster's or Quincy's views in the years to come. Some thirty years later, one New York journalist looked back on the reaction of the America of his youth to Mrs Trollope's comments on its domestic manners. 'We were dreadfully angry at Mrs. Trollope,' he recalled, 'but we read her book all the same, or all the more, and profited in no small degree by its lessons.' Even so, Dr Thomas Nichols concluded: 'I fear that Americans will never be as thankful as they ought to their amusing monitress.' Longfellow was to say he would forgive all of Mrs Trollope's criticisms if she helped to suppress tobacco spitting. Another American who was grateful to Mrs Trollope was, as we have seen, Mark Twain. In the marginalia already quoted he was not uncritical and felt, for example, that she over-rated her ability to recreate conversations. This, he wrote, 'was woefully defective as to details'. Nevertheless he thought her 'very fair and thoughtful' when observing the life round her. In passages suppressed in the published version of his *Life on the Mississippi* he wrote: 'She knew her subject well, and she set it forth fairly and squarely, without any weak ifs and ands and buts. She deserved gratitude – but it is an error to suppose she got it.'[53]

Domestic Manners was soon translated into French, German, Spanish and Dutch, which made its author known throughout Europe. When she was in Brussels, the new King, Leopold, asked to meet her; in Vienna, where she went to do yet another travel book, she soon became a close friend of Prince and Princess Metternich, and in Paris she was granted an audience at the Tuileries by King Louis Philippe. The 'Citizen King' had spent some of his youthful exile in America and he enjoyed talking about it with Mrs Trollope, asking with a *soupçon* of malicious humour whether she dared re-visit America. According to family legend, Mrs Trollope – well knowing his shaky hold on his purloined throne, gave the apt riposte: 'And does Your Majesty?' It was all a far cry from the failed Bazaar. Certainly many Europeans, as well as Englishmen, had their notions of America formed by some report of what Mrs Trollope wrote or, more likely, of her opinions. A French economist, who visited America two years after the famous book appeared, commented: 'Cincinnati has been made famous by Mrs Trollope', while an Austrian who met Henry Clay in Washington immediately thought him ' "an American character" ' or 'the very type of what passes in Europe, ever since the clever caricatures of Mrs. Trollope'.[54]

For the fifth edition of *Domestic Manners* in 1839 the author – for an extra fee of £50 – added some notes and a new preface. She pointed to a few places where she said she had been wrong or where improvements were already taking place. She admitted her assertion that Americans were humourless was no longer true as she had been impressed by the satire of the first of the American 'homespun philosophers', Seba Smith, under the name of Major Downing. Yet most contemporary Americans did not see her fifth edition as some attempt at a friendlier or at least more balanced approach. She outraged most of them by devoting her new preface to an outspoken assault upon slavery in which 'every Christian and every human feeling' cried out against 'the hideous barbarities inflicted on ... our dark-skinned fellow-creatures'. She now regretted that she had not devoted a larger part of *Domestic Manners* to attacking slavery. She announced she would never set foot in America again until slavery was abolished and predicted that it would lead to the break-up of the Union.

In the years that followed this fifth edition, her book has remained controversial. When her daughter-in-law, Rose Trollope, landed in America in the 1860s, she was accused of being the author, and even in this century Fanny Trollope's great-grand-daughter, Muriel Trollope, on her own visit felt compelled to apologise for the 'naughty book' a century after its appearance. In the 1920s the distinguished American historian, Allan Nevins, called Mrs Trollope a 'censorious harridan' but did admit that much of her book had 'at the time a large degree of truth in it'. *Domestic Manners* is still read and remains the best known of English travel books on America: in 1982 BBC Radio broadcast a feature to mark the 150th anniversary of its publication and in 1984 Oxford University Press brought out a new edition, both prepared by the present writer. In the elegant words of Michael Sadleir, the book survives because it has 'precisely those qualities of piquancy and paradox most agreeable to the malice of posterity'.[55] It still provides that element of superior criticism which is so important a part of the 'love-hate' relationship between Britain and America. It is still worth reading for sheer pleasure, for Mrs Trollope could be a very good writer. Unfair she certainly could be, although her many critics have never caught her in a deliberate lie. As Dickens wrote to her, after his own book, *American Notes*, became equally controversial: 'I am convinced that there is no writer who has so well and so accurately (I need not add, so entertainingly) described it, in many of its aspects as you have done.' After reading Dickens' book Macaulay agreed: 'A reader who wants an amusing account of the United States had better go to Mrs Trollope, coarse and malignant as she is.'[56] Certainly today anyone who reads *Domestic Manners of the Americans* finishes it with a sense of enjoyment at its true humour and with an appreciation of its real insights. The reader also closes it with admiration for the courage and determination of this valiant woman who, in spite of constant reverses, managed to survive and eventually to triumph.

✳

Mrs Trollope's great success with *Domestic Manners* did not end her troubles but it did show her a way to support her family. Even before her book was published she had begun work on her first work of fiction, a three-volume novel entitled *The Refugee in America*, which drew upon many of her recent experiences. It even had an idealistic Frenchman called de Clairville, who is clearly modelled on Hervieu. In New York, Philip Hone noted in his diary: 'I have finished reading a new novel by the famous Mrs. Trollope. Like her former work, it abounds in ridiculous remarks on the national character and political institutions of the United States, and represents highly exaggerated caricatures of our domestic manners, but ... the work is written with more ability than I supposed our prejudiced visitor possessed. I paid it the compliment of devoting two or three hours to it when I ought to have been in bed.'[57] *The Refugee in America* has another distinction: it was the first 'Trollope novel'. For the rest of the century almost every year saw at least one novel by a member of the Trollope family. Mrs Trollope produced thirty-three novels – of three-volume dimensions. Her youngest son, Anthony, brought out forty-seven, while both her eldest son and his second wife wrote novels. (His first wife wrote poetry and political diatribes disguised as history.) Even Cecilia managed to write one novel before her death in 1849. Almost all the Trollopes followed the foundress of the 'family line' (as Anthony called it) by writing travel books as well as novels. Anthony eventually wrote his own book about America, a far more favourable one but without the sparkle of his mother's book. Tom Trollope wanted to publish an account of his brief visit to America, but, in spite of her support, he could not find a publisher. His view was the opposite of his mother's: 'I liked the Americans ... because some quality in their manners and behaviour had the effect of making me less shy with them than with others.'[58]

Because she wanted to continue her career as a travel writer Fanny Trollope took the opportunity provided by a visit to Germany to stay with Julia Garnett, now the wife of Professor Pertz, to produce a book on Belgium and Western Germany for John Murray. When she returned she found her husband's health and debts worse than ever; at last even his finances could get no worse. In April 1834 his landlord finally called in the bailiffs to seize what remained of the family's possessions to be auctioned for non-payment of rent. Mr Trollope fled to Belgium to avoid any possibility of imprisonment for debt. Mrs Trollope remained loyal to her husband and followed him into voluntary exile. As always in adversity her heroic side – and it was nothing short of heroic – emerged. Henry, that tragic figure who had failed in his attempt to become a barrister, died in December 1834: 'My poor boy had suffered so long and so hopelessly that his death was at last almost a blessing', she told John Murray. Within the year she was describing to another publisher the 'melancholy and unexpected' event of her husband's death.[59] A short time after that, Emily, her younger daughter, died, like Henry, a victim of the family's curse – consumption. Eventually Cecilia also died from the same disease. At times Mrs Trollope seems like one of the Brontë sisters as she carries on writing her novels in the midst of tragedy and death, rising before dawn to write so as to have the rest of the day to nurse.

Four of Mrs Trollope's novels used America as a setting, of which the most important was *The Life and Adventures of Jonathan Jefferson Whitlaw: or Scenes on the Mississippi*, published in 1836 with numerous illustrations by Hervieu. This book has a strong claim to be the first anti-slavery novel, for it appeared several months before the Massachusetts historian, Richard Hildreth, published *The Slave; or Memoirs of Archy Moore*, which he later claimed was the first novel to attack slavery.[60] (This was fifteen years before *Uncle Tom's Cabin*.) Mrs Trollope's novel was far fiercer in its portrayal of slavery than *Domestic Manners*. She made effective use of her travels to provide local colour in describing New Orleans and the pervasive forests on the Southern frontier. She was particularly horrified by the outrageous ways in which a cruel master could treat female slaves. At one point a young slave begs that Whitlaw not force her to strip before beating her, upon which he shouts: 'Strip black toad – strip d'ye hear, strip, or you will be soaked in oil and then singed.' To us today this is a good example of 'erotic brutality', as Mrs Trollope's biographer effectively puts it, but for many Victorians it was a shocking example of the novelist's tendency to 'vulgarity' or what *The Gentleman's Magazine* in its obituary called her 'coarse unfeminine style'.[61] Many of her novels horrified (and no doubt titillated) contemporary readers because she would use 'coarse' words like 'strip' which the prescribed correctness of her time forbade. In 1857 this novel was re-issued under the new title of *Lynch Law* to capitalise on the tremendous success of *Uncle Tom's Cabin*. In *The Old World and the New*, Fanny Trollope's last novel to have an American setting, she portrays an English family who emigrate to Cincinnati. Unlike the Trollopes, they stayed, and this novel does have a more hopeful view of America. By 1849 she believed that the tremendous improvement in transatlantic communications was promoting 'warm and cordial friendships between individuals who were born of the same race'.

Because *Domestic Manners of the Americans* is the only book by Fanny Trollope that is still read today, it is easy to assume that the Americans were her only target. However her novels can be equally scathing about English society: *The Vicar of Wexhill* is a fierce attack upon Evangelicalism; *Michael Armstrong, the Factory Boy* is an even fiercer assault on the evils of the Industrial Revolution, while her *Jessie Phillips* denounced the Poor Law as 'class legislation based on selfishness'.[62] The popularity of her novels provided the money to allow her a comfortable life in a villa by the city wall in Florence. Even in Italy she found some hostility because of her first book. The American feminist and revolutionary, Margaret Fuller, spotted her in Rome in the winter of 1847: 'Pensioned at the rate of two thousand pounds a year to trail her slime over the fruit of Italy ... after having violated the virgin beauty of America.' Fanny Trollope would have enjoyed this inaccurate report in the *New York Tribune*, but I suspect she would have enjoyed the two thousand pound pension even more, though she never received one. Other Americans found 'warm and cordial friendship' at the *Villino Trollopé*. She helped promote the Florentine career of Hiram Powers, the American sculptor whom she had met when he worked with her at the Western Museum in Cincinnati. From that city came another American visitor to pay tribute to the mother of the anti-slavery novel: Harriet Beecher Stowe was a welcome guest at the *Villino*. Yet another anti-slavery writer, the poet and diplomat, Bayard Taylor, heaped praise upon his elderly hostess:[63]

> That lady whose famous book on America is no gauge of her cordiality towards Americans ... Her book which, spiteful and caricaturesque as it was, did us no real harm ... we can afford now to be friendly towards a witty, cheerful and really warm-hearted woman – who having forgotten what she lost, remembers only what she admired among us.

Indeed in her last decade she returned to some of her earlier liberal views and Harriet Garnett exulted that her old friend delighted in a poem that so well expressed the hope of the age, 'The Good Time Coming'. The sentiments of this English poem by Charles Mackay appealed to a young American composer, Stephen Foster, who used it for one of his first songs. The lines that Fanny Trollope loved expressed that common transatlantic faith in progress and recalled those sentiments that had led her to follow the 'angel', Fanny Wright, to America:[64]

> There's a good time coming, boys,
> A good time coming:
> We may not live to see the day,
> But earth shall glisten in the ray,
> Of the good time coming.

Her son, Anthony, also liked this poem and quoted it in many of his novels. In 1862, he arrived in a small muddy frontier town called Rolla, Missouri where a newspaper reporter demanded, 'Air you the son of the Mrs. Trollope?' When he admitted that he was, he was told: 'Then, sir, you are an accession to Rolla.'[65]

His mother would not have heard this story, for by then she was in feeble health in Florence. Her once brilliant mind and powerful memory had slowly failed. At the end she had a sudden flash of thought about the long-dead daughter for whom she had once had to sell her possessions to buy shoes when they lived by the broad Potomac River. Her last words were 'Poor Cecilia' and then she died on 6 October 1863, at the age of eighty-three. The America she had visited and castigated also lay dying in the blood-soaked trenches of Vicksburg and on the rolling hills of Gettysburg.

4

The Fashionable Visitor:
Lady Emmeline Stuart Wortley

EARLY LIFE AND WRITING

Of all the Englishwomen who visited and wrote about America in the nineteenth century, none came with better social connexions than Lady Emmeline Stuart Wortley.* As the daughter of a Duke she not only had the courtesy title of 'Lady' but arrived with numerous letters of introduction to the leading figures in American life. These letters would assure her entry into the best houses while her title would be sure to attract further kindnesses. In addition, she was already an experienced poet and playwright – she had six plays published between 1840 and 1843; she was extremely well travelled and possessed of a quick mind and an affable personality. Her views were very much of her time and her comments reflected a large segment of English opinion. Secure in her social position, moderate in her politics, anxious to be objective and florid in her prose, Lady Emmeline provides us with one of the best accounts not just of the America she visited but of English travel, and travellers, in the period. The experience of America changed the lives of Rebecca Burlend, Fanny Wright and Fanny Trollope, and would do the same for Catherine Hopley, but for Lady Emmeline Stuart Wortley, it was simply an enjoyable chapter in a life filled with journeys and adventures. While her account of her 1849-50 American trip did not attract the attention, or the criticism, of some of the others we have looked at, it did reflect the increasingly friendly views of ordinary travellers, however far from ordinary she was herself.

Emmeline Charlotte Elizabeth Manners was born on 2 May 1806, the daughter of the fifth Duke of Rutland. She passed her childhood at her father's resplendent residence, Belvoir Castle, with its magnificent view of the Vale of Belvoir. The Duke, an important figure in Tory politics, was one of the greatest landed aristocrats in England and lived on a mediaeval scale: at one of his birthday dinners he played host to nearly 400 guests of whom 145 were retainers who roared their approval to an oration by the ducal coachman, one Mr Tapps, 'a man of great abdominal dignity', as he recounted what a jolly good chap His Grace was.[1] From her father

---

* Unlike many members of this aristocratic family, Lady Emmeline did not use a hyphen between Stuart and Wortley.

Emmeline acquired an ability to mix among all sorts of people, to gain their trust and to have a feeling for their sufferings. The Duke was known as a man to whom the humblest could present their problems and, if he rarely provided a solution, he was at least a kindly listener.

His formidable Duchess was the decisive figure in the family and the driving force behind the Castle's position as a social centre in the Tory party. According to one slightly less important Tory lady, the Duchess was 'said to be the proudest woman in England'. While she might have had rivals for this perennial honour, there was no doubt that she had become the essential companion to the Duke of York, the heir to the throne in the 1820s. One diarist observed them at a dinner at the Rutlands' London house in 1825: 'They are like a boy & girl of 17 & 15, & when one recollects that the one is 62 & the other an old grandmother, it is really disgusting.' (The 'old grandmother' was only in her mid-forties.) Less than half a year later the same observer, Mrs Arbuthnot, took a more charitable approach in her diary, for the Duchess had died suddenly. It was a dreadful loss for the Duke of Rutland for 'he did nothing himself, and his estates, his houses, his family, every thing was under her rule'. This was the powerful mother under whose sway the young Emmeline grew up, and she inherited some of her characteristics. Like her 'she was conscious of her high rank ... [but] scorned all the petty arts & nonsenses of fashion'. While her mother was generally 'hated by all the fine ladies of London', Lady Emmeline rarely aroused such extreme emotion.[2] Even so, most references to her in the diaries and letters of her aristocratic acquaintances treat her either with bemusement or with disapproval.

After Emmeline's mother died, she shared the duties of hostess with her two unmarried sisters, the Ladies Katherine and Adeliza, and their grandmother, the fourth Duchess of Rutland. This lady, who was known as 'The Beautiful Duchess', is credited with beginning the obsession with tiny waists that was to torture so many Victorian ladies and please so many Victorian men. It was said that hers was the size of one-and-a-half oranges and that to display this wonderful achievement she was given to wearing the riband of the Order of the Garter as a belt.[3] If we can credit a hostile account from 1826 by a visitor, Lady Elizabeth Belgrave, life at Belvoir Castle was not entirely happy. The Duke was a 'fig'; his late Duchess had been a 'goddess of folly'; the Dowager Duchess was only 'a fool'. Lady Elizabeth's real venom was reserved for Lady Emmeline, who, she decided, 'must be mad, saying she is the most perfect creature that ever existed. She does not trouble herself with any civility, but writes poetry all day in her room.'[4] While she was not mad, she most certainly was precocious and had been writing, in both verse and prose, for many years. Ten years earlier, in 1816, a disastrous fire had roared through the mock gothic castle when the young Emmeline was only ten and had led to her first literary effort, *The Account of the Dreadful Fire at Belvoir Castle Which Happened on the Sixth Morning of the Month of October at two o'clock 1816*. In this

juvenile production we can already see her gift for colourful writing and
interest in foreign scenes: 'There was no Moon, but the light of the Fire
illuminated the whole sky, it had a tremendous but very grand appearance
and very awful, the trees looked white like snow itself, the Castle like
Mount Etna in an Erruption.' Yet another visitor, our old acquaintance,
Mrs Arbuthnot, had a completely different reaction when she spent a week
at Belvoir in the following year. She decided that the three 'Lady Manners
are very handsome, nice girls and make the house very pleasant'.[5]

Certainly the young Emmeline was a cause of constant upset to her
family. These problems had begun shortly before her mother's death. That
imperious lady foresaw a great future for her daughter and, aided by the
Duke of York, she sought to arrange a royal marriage in 1825. The young
Prince Leopold of Saxe-Coburg had continued to live in England after the
death of his wife, Princess Charlotte, who had been heir to the throne.
Leopold was in receipt of a large income voted by Parliament and seemed
in need of a wife. Emmeline appears to have fallen in with the idea and
certainly the remarkably handsome Prince would have appealed to her
Romantic nature. However, further enquiries showed that he had installed
a mistress a mile away from his comfortable country house, Claremont, in
Surrey. After raising Emmeline's hopes, Leopold called off the idea of a
match on the grounds that his income was only for his lifetime and
therefore 'it never was my intention to marry and never will be'. If the plan
had succeeded, Lady Emmeline would have become within six years the
first Queen of the Belgians, when Leopold was elevated to that new throne.
She also would have become the aunt of Queen Victoria.[6]

In the following year, 1826, Lady Emmeline gave great concern to her
relations. It is impossible to discover exactly what she did, but whatever
it was, she horrified her family. Her former governess, the delightfully
named Miss Gooding, kept Lady Elizabeth Drummond – Emmeline's
eldest and married sister – informed of developments. It appears that
Emmeline paid little attention to conventions and struck up friendships
without being 'introduced'. (Given her mother's behaviour with the Duke
of York, it is hardly surprising that she paid little attention to rules, but a
higher standard was imposed on young unmarried ladies.) She was very
flirtatious and formed an attachment to a scandalous young aristocrat
named Henry De Ros.* We do not know what occurred, but it is surely
suspicious that she was kept in her father's London house throughout
August – a month when 'no one' remained in town. Two doctors, including
the Royal Physician, made frequent visits to the house and one lectured
her 'on the absurdity of her ideas and the wickedness of her religion'. Poor
Miss Gooding moaned: 'Would to God she were but married, and to one

* The De Ros title was one of the oldest in the peerage and the family had at one time
owned the Belvoir estate. Some years after this scandal, Lord De Ros agreed to go into
continental 'exile' after being accused of cheating at cards.

who could manage her, if such a one is to be found, for until she is I am sure there can be no peace for any one.' For the governess there was at least the consolation that De Ros would remain silent 'for his own sake'. While it is possible that her 'ill conduct' had produced what the aristocracy called a 'child of the mist', it is more likely that it only led to some temporary breakdown by the highly emotional and asthmatic Lady Emmeline.[7]

In 1831, five years after her difficulties, Lady Emmeline did as her governess had wanted and found a husband, the Hon Charles Stuart Wortley, son of the first Lord Wharncliffe and grandson of the Lord Bute who had been so hated by eighteenth-century Whigs, whether in Britain or in the American colonies.* His courtship had not been an untroubled one. The Duke recorded that his daughter had the worst 'fit' of her life when she received a letter from her brother-in-law advising her to reconsider her acceptance of Wortley. Yet within a few weeks the new husband was writing to his sister-in-law that Emmeline's devotion made up 'for all the past misery and wretchedness she has made me suffer'. One of Lady Emmeline's cousins was bemused by the marriage: 'It strikes one as the most absurd union, or more properly, the union of two most absurd people', while one Whig lady was even more caustic: 'He is a great coarse stupid creature. Her fortune will be much wasted by 22 volumes of poetry which she told me some time ago she meant to publish as soon as she was married. The Duke for long has been hoping to get rid of her and her poems and all.'[8]

Two years later, Lady Emmeline did produce a volume of poetry and she continued to bring out one volume for each of the next eleven years, which brought her half-way towards the adolescent calculation she had mentioned to her sarcastic guest. While she may have written too freely she certainly did not have to write for money, for her father had settled on her an income of £1,000 a year, a very large sum in the 1830s. (Three years later Mrs Trollope's son, Anthony, began his career as a Post Office clerk, a position for 'gentlemen', at £90 a year.) Emmeline's new mother-in-law, Lady Wharncliffe, found her 'a very nice creature, and will I think suit us *all*, especially as we get her out of some old habits of indolence and irregularity about hours etc.'. Like many a mother-in-law, Lady Wharncliffe may have exaggerated her new daughter's faults, for Lady Emmeline, rather than remaining in indolence, threw herself into literary work. As well as writing her own poetry, she edited the colourful annual, *The Keepsake*, a fashionable anthology meant to decorate the boudoirs of idle ladies. Lady Emmeline's editing must have made her one of the first daughters of a Duke to earn an annual salary.[9]

* Her marriage gave Lady Emmeline a distant connection to Lady Mary Wortley Montagu, her husband's great-great-grandmother, whose celebrated *Turkish Letters* (published in 1763) made her one of the earliest and best known of women travel writers. Some people in America confused Lady Emmeline with Lady Mary.

Her work brought her friendships with many authors such as Mary Shelley and Theodore Hook. Her writing also aroused fierce criticism when the *Quarterly Review* turned its guns on 'modern English poetesses' in 1840. (This shows that the *Quarterly* did not confine its attacks to America and its 'glorious institutions'.) The anonymous writer – modern research shows him to be Coleridge's eldest son, Hartley, who was also a poet – was 'deeply concerned' at her Byronic misery: 'We conclude from this volume that her ladyship has been from earliest youth the most wretched and broken-hearted woman in England.' The reviewer pointed to her lines:

> Sorrow is my perpetual guest,
>   The constant inmate of my mournful breast;
> Joy but an ignus fatuus light at best,
>   Just seen and gone!

He then went on: 'We are really deeply concerned at it ... Here is a lady of exalted birth, dowered from infancy with all the gifts of nature and fortune ... yet it turns out to be all an *ignis* – or as Lady Emmeline writes, *ignus* – *fatuus*, – in the vernacular, mere moonshine.'[10]

Her mother-in-law was upset when she heard of this fierce attack:

> I have not yet seen the Quarterly & am almost afraid of it, as I shall find Emmeline as well as *it* at Wortley [the Wharncliffe's Yorkshire home] when I go back, & I fear she will be much annoyed, & I shall feel *conscious*, & sorry for her poor thing, tho' I wish it may do her good ... you must read 'Eva' (*her tragedy*). It shews a great deal of cleverness & has some pretty lines & less exaggeration than usual. I wonder if the Quarterly reviews it?

The Hon Caroline Norton, Lady Emmeline's predecessor at *The Keepsake*, was another of the 'society poetesses' criticised in the *Quarterly*. She defended her friend: 'If the author of the article knew Lady Emmeline Wortley he would be too much in love with her to laugh at her. She is the truest, simplest woman that ever was bitten by romance ... Not that I defend my lady's high-flown language and starry sublimities at all times, but she is so gentle and earnest and real that I feel a little unhappy when I read the review.' Anyone who today reads Lady Emmeline's book on America would agree with Mrs Norton's assessment, and undoubtedly as a poet she was derivative. The real importance of her verse is that it reveals the characteristic features of her age: Byronic exaggeration combined with a sentimental liberalism. It was Disraeli who, perhaps, described her best after being introduced by Mrs Norton: 'her person more beautiful than her poetry.'[11]

Next to poetry, Lady Emmeline's second great passion was travel and it is not surprising that her travel books contain a great deal of verse. Her honeymoon had consisted of several months in Nice, followed by a few more in Naples. She was, however, not content with the usual circuit through

France and Italy, and ventured to less visited places such as Poland and Russia. She learnt Russian so well that she could write poetry in that language. She also carried on a long correspondence with Tsar Nicholas I whom she frequently praised in her writings. She went on a six-month tour with her husband through Hungary, the Balkans and Turkey and even visited North Africa. Throughout her travels she was always anxious to meet famous people and usually her title or family connexions helped. Thus in Rome she was able to visit Napoleon's mother, the redoubtable 'Madame Mère'. This was something of an achievement, for her hostess did not particularly enjoy meeting English people. The visit was only made possible because Lady Emmeline's husband's cousin had married Napoleon's niece. As a child Lady Emmeline had frequently argued with the Duke of York about the treatment of the fallen Emperor on St Helena. Her continuing devotion to Napoleon's memory amused 'Society' and was even the subject of a discussion between Queen Victoria and her Prime Minister.[12] In her own way the Duke's daughter was as much a rebel as Fanny Wright had been.

When they were in England, the Wortleys continued to spend many weeks at Belvoir. The Castle was always full of guests and from one of them, Fanny Kemble, Lady Emmeline had a chance to hear about America at first hand. Kemble, one of the most celebrated actresses of the age, had already published her *Journal* recounting some of her adventures in America, where its appearance created the usual outrage at yet another critical account by yet another English traveller. In a later portion of her diaries – she supplemented her career on the stage with the regular production of rather breathless journals – she recounted the splendours of Belvoir. The guests were roused for breakfast by the Duke's private band walking round the Castle playing lively music; this same ceremony was followed before dinner. In the evening a dance was held in the ballroom and the Duke not only led the dancing, but encouraged the housemaids and 'men-cooks' to dance as well. Fanny Kemble speaks highly of the kindness of the Duke and his daughters, including Lady Emmeline.* The actress appeared somewhat surprised at the way in which the servants were encouraged to enjoy the music and other pleasures. Of course some contemporaries would have been more shocked at the idea of a Duke and his daughters' entertaining an actress in their ancestral Castle. Yet this inherited ability to see servants as people and to listen to their stories would be one of the most pleasant aspects of Lady Emmeline's American books.[13]

By the time she came to America Lady Emmeline was not only an experienced traveller but an enthusiastic travel writer, though her

---

* This visit to Belvoir Castle marks a crucial moment in English social history. The Duchess of Bedford invited several other guests to her room and the ladies sat down to drink tea. This is usually cited as the first reference to that most beneficent institution, afternoon tea.

previous efforts had been almost totally confined to verse. (She even inspired her husband to make one attempt at writing: in 1833, under the flimsy guise of 'Capt. the Hon. C.S.W.' he produced a not particularly memorable book about a military expedition to Antwerp.) The passion for travel was supposed to be part of the Romantic character. This was certainly the case with Lady Emmeline, though not with her husband who soon tired of his wife's passion for movement. Her brother-in-law described this restlessness: 'The fact is that her nature and temperament are not made for the common destinies of this life, & her feelings are so vehement and exaggerated that they not only undermine her own health, but are such as to cause anxiety and unhappiness to those she loves most.' There appeared to be growing tension between husband and wife, particularly after the birth of one of the children. A member of the family wrote to her sister: 'Charles has just been declaring he would not have another child for £1000, for that her Ladyship takes no part of the management on her own shoulders and that he has to make the bed and to cook the victuals with his own hand; and that Emmeline would let it starve and sleep on the floor if *he* were to be accidentally out of the way.'[14]

Years before, during that mysterious summer when the young Emmeline was secluded in the family house in London, she had burst out to Miss Gooding, the exasperated governess: 'I shall behave well till I am married and then they shall see what I will do.'[15] The marriage of a dull and sickly man to a passionate and talented woman with a craving for travel had caused tension in the Trollope household in Harrow ten years before as it now did in the Wortleys'. These tensions no doubt undermined the husband's already weak health and Charles Stuart Wortley died on 22 May 1844. Shortly after his death their son, Adalbert, also died, and Lady Emmeline never fully recovered from this. The death of one of her sisters fuelled her melancholy still further and all these upsets only increased her passion — by this time it was a mania — for travel. She insisted that travel would help her young daughter's 'delicate' constitution. One may wonder whether it was really the best thing to take a young girl on a tour through France and Italy in the midst of the revolutions of 1848, but Lady Emmeline was undaunted.

The following year she decided that she and her twelve-year-old daughter would visit the United States in a long tour that would also include Canada, Mexico, Cuba, the West Indies, Panama, Peru and Bermuda. Her daughter had been born only a few months before Queen Victoria's accession in 1837 and had not only the future Queen but her mother, the Duchess of Kent, as Godmothers. The custom was for girls so honoured to take one of the Queen's names; in this case the Stuart Wortleys took both, but reversed the order so that the child was baptised Victoria Alexandrina. (The Queen's name before her accession was Alexandrina Victoria, but she dispensed with her first Christian name and reigned with only her mother's name, Victoria.) Like Lady Emmeline, young Victoria was a talented amateur artist and drew some charming sketches of her trip which were published when she returned to London. These illustrated her short anonymous book, *A Young Traveller's Journal of a Tour in North and South America During the year 1850*, which was mainly intended for children. Victoria Stuart Wortley, usually called in her mother's book 'V', is probably the youngest writer ever to produce a travel book on America. Her mother's book, *Travels in the United States Etc. during 1849 and 1850*, was published in three volumes in 1851 by the firm of Richard Bentley which brought out many of the travel writers so popular with the Victorians.[16] Of the three volumes, only the first deals with the United States although the other two, which described the '*Etc.*' – Latin America and the Caribbean islands – have frequent references to the United States. The book shows Lady Emmeline's usual weaknesses: verbosity, sentimentality and too frequent references to her other travels. Yet these do not mar what is actually an excellent book. One is constantly impressed with the fact that here is a well-travelled woman who is prepared to look without prejudice at a different society. She liked what she saw in America and her book is filled with praise, so much so that at times she is forced to break into enthusiastic verse. Most of the book appears to be founded on letters written at the time to her sister or her cousin and this gives it that sense of immediacy so important to the best travel writing. In this use of the epistolary method of travel writing, Lady Emmeline resembled Fanny Wright.

Two years after her *Travels in the United States Etc.*, Lady Emmeline published another book with the absurd title, *&c.* In her preface she explained, or at least sought to explain: 'I intend to avail myself of all the illimitable comprehensiveness of the invaluable little hieroglyphic, and of those much involving Latin words it stands for.' These essays on her travels – mostly her American ones – are an excuse for Victorian 'book-making' at its worst: she can waffle for a whole chapter and say little. Occasionally, however, this second book does allow her further reflection on her American experiences and her conclusions are even more favourable than in her first book.

Almost two decades had passed between the publication of Mrs Trollope's *Domestic Manners* and Lady Emmeline's *Travels in the United States Etc.*, and Anglo-American relations were changing. The 1840s had seen the United States increase its national territory to a vast extent. Britain and America had reached a peaceful settlement of the dispute over the Canadian-Oregon border. Texas had been added to the Union by annexation and California as a result of the Mexican War, the first war in which the United States had fought a country other than Britain. (It may be recalled that Rebecca Burlend's son, John, died as a result of it.) The *Spectator*, then a Liberal journal, said that the Mexicans were defeated because 'they could not resist the charge of bayonets; they have only yielded to what is almost uniformly irresistible in the "Anglo-Saxon" race'. Yet the *Spectator*'s pride was mixed with apprehension: 'We do not affect to conceal our regret at this victory.' Political disputes or economic rivalry could bring out perennial prejudices, but underneath there was a growing acceptance, indeed a glory in the acceptance, of the view which *The Times* described in 1846: 'We are two people, but we are of one family.' This common racial bond was stressed a few years later in a letter from a leading scholar in America to a similar figure in England: 'There is in our Anglo-Saxon blood more of a spirit of adventure and romance than belongs to the age.'[17] Lady Emmeline would frequently see the relationship between Britain and America as a family one, and it is possible that the wide extent of aristocratic families made this an easier concept for her.

From time to time 'the battle of the books' could overheat even Anglo-Saxon blood. Dickens' *American Notes*, published in 1842, and the American scenes in his novel, *Martin Chuzzlewit*, published in the two following years, stirred up great resentment in the country where he had recently been a welcome celebrity. Yet in spite of this resentment, Americans continued to make visiting Englishmen welcome. Settlers from the British Isles continued to pour into America, hoping to find a new and more prosperous home. (We might remember that Rebecca Burlend's book was published in 1848 as a guide to others who might wish to follow her example.) There was also a growing number of young Englishmen from aristocratic families who were 'having a run across' to see America in the same spirit in which their grandfathers had wandered through Italy. Lady Emmeline's nephew was one, while her young cousin, Lord Morpeth, had recently become probably the most popular English visitor with his admiring American hosts.[18] They were about to behold yet a new type of traveller: a wealthy lady tourist who had come not to find a new life but solely on a holiday jaunt.

Fifteen years earlier, Lady Emmeline had described her feelings when sailing from England, and no doubt she still had similar sentiments as she bade farewell to:[19]

> Thy fading shores, embracing with your skies,
> As the outskirts of an earthly Paradise!
> Well may the Wanderers, severed from thy breast,
> Proclaim thee, weeping – Fairest, First and Best!

NEW YORK AND NIAGARA

The two Stuart Wortleys, each accompanied by a maid, arrived in New York aboard the *Canada* on 16 May 1849.* Lady Emmeline also brought with her the two relics which always accompanied her. There is nothing which better shows her pure Romanticism than her devotion to the twin

---

* The two Wortleys were the only women in this book to be accompanied by maids throughout their stay. Mrs Trollope arrived with one but seems to have lost her during her difficult time in Cincinnati. Fanny Wright makes no reference to a maid. Neither Mrs Burlend nor Catherine Hopley could have afforded one.

pillars of the Romantic legend, Byron and Napoleon. One reliquary was a silver lyre inside which was a lock of the poet's hair, given to her by Augusta Leigh, 'her very affectionate friend and relation ... the Beloved Sister of our Immortal Poet'. The second relic was a lock of Madame Mère's hair which she had presumably acquired on her visit to Rome. This was almost as sacred as having a snippet from the Emperor's own receding locks.[20]

It was a particularly tense moment for anyone from England to step ashore in New York, as less than two weeks before, the city had witnessed the 'Astor Place Riot' when a mob, who favoured the American actor, Edwin Forrest, invaded the theatre where the great English tragedian, William Macready, was performing in *Macbeth*. The mob had been whipped up by the notion that New York's elite was, as usual, favouring an English import over the native American product. Macready had to flee the theatre for his life and twenty-two people were shot dead when troops fired into the raging mob. There is no better example of how dangerous latent anti-English feelings could be in America. Yet, in spite of this horrible event, there were encouraging omens that better feelings were developing between America and the Mother Country. Philip Hone – still busy with his massive diary – had noted this only a few weeks before Lady Emmeline arrived:[21]

> The tone of writing and speaking in Europe on the subject of the United States is greatly altered of late. Even in England the public press, as well as the popular orators ... speak of us with a certain degree of respect ... They may occasionally abuse us as an arrogant people, grasping at extended territory, disregarding the rights of our neighbours, invading peaceful countries ... But the language of contempt is heard no more ... [We are] growing to be a 'big boy', and must be treated with a little more respect.

Throughout her book, Lady Emmeline was careful to let the reader know of her aristocratic connexions: the work is dedicated to her cousin, the Countess of Chesterfield, while the Preface is signed from her father's residence, Belvoir Castle. Young Victoria surpassed her mother by dedicating her book to another cousin – a Marchioness. Like almost all women writers on America, Lady Emmeline was anxious to reassure readers that her book was not devoted to 'serious' topics like politics as these were better left to men:

> For the politician or philosopher these pages will, I fear, have little or no interest; written familiarly to relatives and friends at home, their staple is the gossip of travel; and if they amuse that large class to whom gossip is welcome, and tend in any way to strengthen kindly feelings in the breasts of my English readers toward the people from whom their wandering countrywoman received so much and such constant courtesy and hospitality, I shall not regret giving to the world this Work.

When her ship entered New York harbour Lady Emmeline broke into raptures about the beauty of the scenery. This was not just her Romantic nature at work for, as we have already seen, praise for the beauties of New York harbour occurs in almost all travel books of the period. The precise details which she gave about the various fortifications guarding the harbour illustrate that devotion to statistics so characteristic of Victorians, whatever their attitude to Romanticism. Of even greater interest were the 30,000 letters being unloaded off the ship by postal officials. In one of her exaggerated metaphors she called them 'white-winged messengers of peace', but despite this she saw their true significance: 'These numerous letters of business, of friendship, of mutual interest, seemed so many links uniting the two countries in a concord not to be easily, if ever, broken.'

Lady Emmeline had mixed feelings about New York, 'the Empress City of the West'. Like most other travellers of the age she was impressed with Broadway because few if any European cities had such wide, long and straight thoroughfares (which only became fashionable in Europe after the creation of the Parisian boulevards in the 1860s). It was 'a noble street' with a 'thoroughly bursting, lively, and somewhat democratic air'. Her general view of the city has been shared by later visitors: 'New York is certainly handsome, and yet there is something about it that gives one the idea of a half-finished city.' Another complaint which still applies concerned the amount of rubbish. Even Broadway 'was literally littered with all imaginable rubbish which, we should imagine from appearances, is usually shot [thrown into] in that celebrated thoroughfare ... Piles of timber, mounds of bricks, mountains of packing cases, pyramids of stones, and stacks of goods, were observable on all sides.' She found New Yorkers annoyed – as they still are – both at this and at the constant tearing up of the streets 'for sewage purposes'. She observed people continually having to remove stones from their boots because of the never-ending roadworks. She also found that the dreadful condition of the roads affected her hired carriage, much as it does the modern taxi, and was annoyed that it 'swayed from side to side and rolled and rattled ponderously along'.

Lady Emmeline was an excellent traveller who followed one simple rule: whenever possible she had the best of accommodation. Yet if she was forced to 'rough it', she accepted this as a necessary price and sometimes even a delight of travel. In New York she headed straight for the Astor House. This six-storey hotel had been built by America's wealthiest man, John Jacob Astor, and had been opened in 1836. It was one of the world's first modern hotels and surpassed anything in Europe: it boasted 300 bedrooms and plumbing on the upper floors so that each floor had its own water closet and bathroom. There were seventeen bathrooms, two showers, free soap tablets in every room and gas lighting in the public rooms. It is hardly surprising that the rooms were expensive at two dollars each. When Davy Crockett visited it he reflected on the fur trade which had given Astor his wealth: 'Lord help the poor bears and beavers! But they must be used to being skun by now.'[22] Lady Emmeline referred to the hotel as 'Astor *Town*, for the size is prodigious'. She and her daughter took a suite so that they could dine in the privacy of their own rooms: it was considered somewhat vulgar for unaccompanied – Victorians used the term 'unprotected' – ladies to dine in public. She was pleased with the hotel's service and was amused to note that the waiters, although Irish, wore 'Imperial' moustaches to give themselves a French look.

As Lady Emmeline peered down from the windows of the Astor she, like Fanny Wright and Fanny Trollope, was quick to comment on American fashion. She approved the light and cool bonnets with their long cloth at the back to shade both the neck and the shoulders, but disliked the prevalence of white shawls which gave the women a 'table-clothy' appearance. She did not just observe ladies' fashion. Her first general impression of New York was of its overwhelming energy: 'Everything around me betokens energy, industry, and prosperity, and also the impetuous go-aheadiness, which will hardly allow time for completing all that is begun, or for contriving that order and comfort which should keep pace with improvement and innovation.'

A visit to Niagara Falls, some 400 miles from New York City, was, as we have seen with Mrs Trollope, virtually obligatory for all nineteenth-century travellers and certainly for those contemplating a travel book based on their journey. Indeed, Mrs Trollope's vivid description only increased this interest. Such a trip also allowed the visitor to see the beauties of 'upstate' New York. Lady Emmeline took a 'fast and beautifully-decorated' steamer from New York City to the 'handsome town' of Albany. The fare for this journey was little more than two shillings while an extra two shillings secured her a private cabin. As she looked about at the carpets, mirrors and gilding throughout the steamer, she found it difficult to believe that it was only forty years since the first steamboats had sailed on this river, or, as she put it in &c, 'when the majestic Hudson first bore on its bosom the wonderful vessel'. As the steamer sailed along at twenty-two miles an hour, her trip was only marred by passing the wreck of another steamer, the *Empire*, which had sunk only two days before with considerable loss of life. Here she was struck for a second time by what she called the 'American indifference to human life'. (She had first worried about this trait when reading of the reactions to the Astor Place Riot.) As she reflected on the apparent indifference shown by her fellow passengers she made what was perhaps the harshest comment in her book and one she would later soften. She may have been influenced by previous writers on America, for her analysis of this 'indifference' sounds suspiciously like Mrs Trollope's. Like her, Lady Emmeline attributed it all to money:

Money-getting, which is certainly in most countries a great business, appears here to me almost a battle. It seems as if they must win, do or die ... That they are a very kind-hearted people, I fully believe; but to make money seems a sort of duty in America – the great object of living; and this paramount feeling ... swallows up all the rest.

Perhaps this criticism was heightened after her arrival at Albany where she had hoped to change to the railway journey to Niagara. She found that the railway companies had so arranged the time-tables that steamer passengers from New York were forced to spend a night in the city's hotels. This one piece of trickery was bad enough, but then her cab driver cheated her by driving first to a closed hotel so that her cab fare cost her more than the four shillings she spent on the trip up the Hudson River.

Unlike Mrs Trollope, Lady Emmeline was quick to shake off disagreeable incidents like these. When she was at last able to get under way the next day she was amused, as other travellers have been, with the somewhat pretentious, not to say presumptuous, names of the little towns she passed: Rome, Syracuse, Athens, Geneva and Egypt. (The best example was surely Basil Hall's sight of a small canal boat proudly dubbed *Cleopatra's Barge*.) She much preferred using Indian names with their musical sounds, names which have always had an attractive ring to the English ear. The fame of Niagara had grown in the years since Mrs Trollope and almost every British visitor sought for words to portray it. Lady Durham, the wife of the famous Governor-General of Canada, felt that she had seen 'the most stupendous, sublime, & beautiful spectacle in Creation'. Dickens also could not contain himself when he reached 'the very steps of Nature's greatest altar' and he 'felt ... near to my Creator ... [with] tranquillity, calm recollections of the dead, great thoughts of eternal rest and happiness.'[23] With such competition, we could hardly expect Lady Emmeline to be restrained. When she arrived at 'the audience-chamber of the great Water King' she was so overcome that she feared no words would adequately describe the spectacle. Yet anyone who has followed the good lady this far would not expect this to stem her flow of words, which sometimes seems as overwhelming as the Falls themselves:

> If one saw the sun for the first time, could one describe it? ... What a wonderful thing can water become! One feels, on looking at Niagara, as if one had never seen that element before ... now I can most truly say it is far more magnificent than I had anticipated it to be, though my expectations were of the very highest order.

At first she was worried that too much description would 'tire the readers with my rhapsodies'. Even so, she scurried back and forth from her desk to the hotel balcony to view the mighty Falls before returning to write more. She would not have been a Romantic writer of the period had she not done so. She delighted in watching the little ship, the *Maid of the Mist*, dash about under the spray with its crowd of damp tourists, much as its successor does today. She admits to being 'utterly Niagarized'.

Lady Emmeline and her daughter had settled down to draw the scene they saw before them when a 'sable gentleman' came up to Victoria and said: 'Wal, Miss! so I see you're a taking down of them nice Falls.' Lady Emmeline included her drawing as a frontispiece to &c. She was still in raptures about the Falls more than two years later when she devoted a chapter to it in &c, where she said it surpassed everything she had seen elsewhere in the world.

As we have mentioned, a trip to the Falls also allowed British visitors to cross over into British territory. Lady Emmeline spent a fortnight in Canada staying with a Colonel who had been a close friend of her father-in-law's when he was stationed in Quebec fifty years before. Unfortunately she tells us little about her reactions to Canada, except to say that she found true English comfort which she felt surpassed the luxuries of New York's hotels. (It was a standard view of Englishmen throughout the nineteenth century that 'comfort' could only be found in the British Isles. Dozens of continental hoteliers advertised in *Murray's Handbooks* on European travel that their hotels provided 'comfort'.) She was also delighted to see emigrants from the Mother Country doing so well in their new home. Always adventurous in matters of food, she tried maple sugar in her tea and coffee and claimed she could not tell any difference from cane sugar. That energetic maple sugar farmer, Rebecca Burlend, would have been pleased. Perhaps Lady Emmeline needed maple sugar, for her family heard from the wife of the Bishop of Montreal that she was looking well but somewhat thin during this Canadian visit.[24] Her quiet time in Canada also gave her time to reflect on her first weeks in the New World:

> Great injustice has been done to the Americans, and we have been accustomed too implicitly to believe the often unfair and unfounded reports of prejudiced travellers. Instead of discourteous and disobliging manners we find them all that is most civil and obliging. Amongst the less educated, no doubt, occasionally, some of the faults so unsparingly attributed to them, may be found; but they appear to me ... a generous-minded people. And then, what a noble enterprising people they are! What miraculous progress is visible on every side in the United States.

She received startling proof of the progress of 'these locomotive days', when she returned to New York City at the end of June. She found a letter awaiting her from a friend in North Africa, who had seen an announcement in *Galignani*, a newspaper compiled in Paris for the benefit of English travellers, about Lady Emmeline's American trip.

The heat in New York must have approached that of North Africa as the city was in the midst of one of the hottest summers in the early nineteenth century: the temperature soared to 100 degrees Fahrenheit in the shade. One could excuse Lady Emmeline if this had made her cross, but it seems only to have increased her regard for the country: 'I like the Americans more and more: either they have improved wonderfully lately, or else the criticisms on them have been cruelly exaggerated.' Everywhere she found people anxious that 'foreigners should carry away a favourable impression of them'. She obviously had some of Mrs Trollope's criticisms specifically in mind when she reassured her English readers that American manners were excellent: 'The superior classes here have almost always excellent manners, and a great deal of real and natural, as well as acquired refinement, and are often besides (which perhaps will not be believed in fastidious England) extremely distinguished-looking.' Because Mrs Trollope was particularly hard on the society of American steamboats, Lady Emmeline goes out of her way several times to praise both the courtesy and the efficiency of the steamboat captains she had met.

A SUMMER IN NEW ENGLAND

Lady Emmeline did not remain long in New York. She was driven on not just by the heat (and a spreading epidemic of cholera) but by her own love of travel. One great problem for travellers was that American porters were justly known as 'baggage-smashers' and were, she said, frequently guilty of 'carpet-bagacide'. By 3 July she was in Boston and once again movement allowed her time to reflect. Long before any historical theory about the American frontier had been coined she saw the impact of the country's size on the national character. Indeed, one of the strengths of her account is the way in which she continually emphasises, as a good Romantic, the influence of nature on man. The continental vastness of a Union which within the last eighteen months had been extended from the Atlantic to the Pacific was mirrored in the prevalent largeness of so much she saw about her:

> Schools, universities, manufactures, societies, institutions, appear spreading over the length and breadth of the land, and all seem on such a gigantic scale here too! Lakes, forests, rivers, electric telegraphs, hotels, conflagrations, inundations, rows, roads, accidents, tobacco, juleps, bowie knives, beards, pistols, etc! Moderation or littleness appears not to belong to America, where Nature herself leads the way and seems to abhor both, showing an example of leviathanism in everything.

Like many English visitors, Lady Emmeline was impressed with Boston, a 'very handsome, very large, and very clean town' which made her think more of England or Holland than America. Nevertheless, to arrive on the eve of Independence Day in the city which had given the spark to the American Revolution caused her some bemusement:

> To-morrow they have a grand commemorative festival, in honour of their independence, and we, poor English, must make our minds to hear them 'Yankee-doodling' and 'Hail Columbianing' all day long. I shall shut myself up pretty closely on the occasion to save my feelings of nationality, especially as I have no idea of seeing 'the Crown of England' burnt in a fire-work and consumed to ashes, as it is announced in a pompous advertisement ... for the

pleasing recreation of Brother Jonathan.* I hope, I must confess, that just at that moment it will rain in torrents, and put out their very impertinent and presumptuous pyrotechnics without loss of time: the English Crown thus may not be consumed to a cinder after all.

Obviously she took all these fervent effusions of patriotism with a grain of salt. 'Fourth of July' celebrations in America at that time still had as much an anti-English as a pro-American flavour: the teething problems of a new nation had not yet been overcome. Hostility to England had been kept alive by memories of the War of 1812 and by the debates over the border with Canada. This feeling had been increased by the arrival of thousands of Irish emigrants fleeing the horrors of the potato famine. Lady Emmeline was determined not to allow any rhetoric or even 'presumptuous pyrotechnics' to impede her growing love of America: 'Our American cousins are such a good-humoured, kindly-disposed people, that I think one could not well be sulky with them long.' So she did not really begrudge her hosts their 'seas of sherry-cobblers and cataracts of mint juleps, miles of flags, wildernesses of crackers, pyramids of edibles, mountains of lolly pops'. Like almost all her countrymen she accepted that there was no argument about the justice of the Americans' cause in 1776: 'But though I did not like their promised entertainment of fireworks, yet, when I recollect how abominably ill England behaved before she forced this country into a revolution, I can – nationality not withstanding – rejoice with them a little in their joy.'[26]

Lady Emmeline was not one to ponder over much on the quarrels of the past. As a good child of her age, she revelled in the marvellous advances of her own time. 'What a fast age we live in', she wrote, with Cunard liners arriving so frequently and quickly in Boston that she felt close to home. She found her Boston hotel was so large that the management had even provided finger-posts, hitherto reserved for public highways, to point bewildered guests to their rooms. She joked that they might perhaps also provide omnibuses to carry these weary travellers. Still, as in New York, she was careful to take a suite so that she and her daughter could eat in privacy: 'I have not yet dined one day in public since my arrival in America – it must be extremely unpleasant for ladies.'

Another characteristic of the age which Lady Emmeline shared to the full was a passion for statistics. We saw how, when she first arrived in New York, she made a detailed study of the forts that would have done credit to her friend, the Duke of Wellington. In Boston she turned her attention to the city's bridges and to the public water supply. Part of this concern can be traced to the increasing degree of civic awareness in England. This

---

* 'Brother Jonathan' was a term often used by Englishmen in the nineteenth century to refer to Americans, much as the latter employed the old term 'John Bull'. There is great debate about the term's derivation: does it come from a term for Puritans or from George Washington's frequent references to his friend, Governor Jonathan Trumbull. 'Brother Jonathan', like 'John Bull', could be used either affectionately or with disparagement. It has now been replaced by 'Uncle Sam'.

Birds of Passage

found expression in legislation in the 1830s that provided an improved framework of civic government for England's fast growing towns and cities. The problems of water supply were among the most pressing facing Britain, so it is hardly surprising that she was impressed with Boston's reservoirs. The three million dollars they had cost was money well spent: 'They will probably save that much in drugs and medicine ere many years ... The doctors must be the only people who will suffer from the liberal supply of the pure element.' She liked many of the public buildings but did feel that it was 'saying too much' to maintain, as some Bostonians did, that the dome of the State House or Capitol was one of the finest in the world.

The two Wortleys were escorted round Boston by Charles Sumner, a prominent lawyer and literary figure who had many friends in England and who would become within a few years a controversial Senator and one of the leading opponents of slavery in national politics. The young Victoria noted in her book how surprised she was to see girls younger than herself – some as young as seven – reading in the Boston Athenaeum, a private society whose large library was open to the public. Lady Emmeline was not impressed with the city's pavements: as in New York these were blocked by stacks of merchandise from the shops. She noted that this led to a considerable amount of thieving, 'not of shoplifting exactly, but side-walk-lifting'. As in New York she complained, as did almost all British tourists, about the frequency of fires and the constant noise of fire-engines.

The summer of 1849 proved to be the hottest America had experienced for twenty-four years and Lady Emmeline wisely decided to postpone any further travels until the heat wave had subsided. Perhaps it was this great heat that led to an American custom that appeared strange to her daughter, 'the habit of drinking an immense quantity of iced water'. Because she did not want to go back towards New York where cholera was still raging, Lady Emmeline decided at the end of July to seek the cooling breezes of Gloucester, Massachusetts. She avoided the more famous resort of Newport, Rhode Island because she had no desire for 'society'. She was once again enthusiastic about her hotel which fronted onto the Atlantic. As she sat looking out at the ocean she became enthralled with the effect of light and atmosphere which she found 'like that in beauteous Italy ... so exquisitely clear and transparent'. She also enjoyed the quiet company in the hotel and used the opportunity to refute the complaint of Mrs Trollope and others about American loudness:

> There is no loud talking and constant giggling, of which travellers have so often accused American young ladies, and which, I believe, wherever it is to be found, is greatly owing to their being partly educated at large public schools, which perhaps, gives them a habit of pitching their voice high in order to make themselves heard among numbers. I am happy to say I have not yet met with any who have that unrefined disagreeable habit.

One sound she was particularly pleased to hear and frequently was that of music: 'The New Englanders appear to me generally a very quiet people, and very fond of music: we hear them playing and singing a great deal. Some of them sing exceedingly well.' Young Victoria noted, however, that New England Sundays were as quiet as those in the Mother Country and utterly unlike those she had experienced in Italy.

American newspapers, however, were not as agreeable as American music. While in Gloucester Lady Emmeline found time to read and, using her experience as an editor, to analyse the country's papers. She was impressed at their cheapness and variety: in Boston alone there were thirty-six of which twelve were dailies. She admitted with tongue in cheek: 'The American newspapers amuse me much; they are so unlike anything else of their kind.' She saw both good and bad:

> Some of their more distinguished papers are admirably written, and replete with varied and extensive information and tidings from all corners of the earth: there seems in general in their tone, I think, more heartiness of feeling and more freshness and originality than in ours. What I do not like in the daily American press, is the perpetual and sometimes puerile and paltry attempt at wit and humour, which they seem to think indispensable ... They sometimes mingle this often rather ponderous pleasantry with the most serious accounts of accidents and disasters. Then their abuse of the authorities and people in office is beyond all idea violent. In the opposition papers, the most unmerciful vituperations are poured forth against some of their most eminent men; *really* if you did not see their names you would sometimes think they were speaking of the most atrocious criminals. It might almost make me imagine that three quarters of the population are in a state of perpetual irritation and disappointment at not being President themselves, or, at least, Secretary of State.

She was horrified to see the President, Zachary Taylor, called 'Journeyman Butcher', 'Nero', 'Tyrant', 'Dolt', 'Fool', 'Cypher', 'Monster' and 'Ignominious Cheat'. In the event, these words are only mildly stronger than those which English publications such as *John Bull* or that vigorous infant, *Punch*, customarily flung at British politicians who had incurred their ire.

Refreshed and cooled by their stay in Gloucester, mother and daughter returned to Boston in the middle of August to see more of the city. Here Lady Emmeline was surprised by a visit from her nephew, the Hon Edward Stuart Wortley, who was also on his own tour of America.* She explored the streets of Boston and when she came across the site of the so-called 'Boston Massacre' of 1770 her sympathy for Americans welled up within her and she wrote of 'the righteous Revolution, if ever there was one deserving to be so called; yet my English feelings make me dislike always to dwell on the details of it'. What particularly delighted her in Boston was

* The Hon Edward Stuart Wortley became the third Lord Wharncliffe in 1855. During the American Civil War, he was a leader of the Southern Independence Association, the pro-Confederate organisation in England.

an excellent law, then in force and generally obeyed, which forbade smoking in the streets. As another British visitor put it: 'You may chew until you expectorate yourself away, and may poison your dwelling with smoke to your heart's content, but a whiff in the open air is a luxury not to be enjoyed in Boston under a penalty of five dollars.'[27]

One of the factors that make Lady Emmeline's visit so interesting and so different from those of our other 'birds of passage' is her connexions, both social and literary, which gave her an *entrée* to the most famous people in America. She had brought with her, for example, a letter of introduction from the historian and current American Minister to Great Britain, George Bancroft, to the 'merchant prince' and politician, Abbott Lawrence. She was escorted round Harvard by the University's President and another former Minister to London, Edward Everett. (It was Everett, considered one of the greatest of American orators, who was the main attraction on the field of Gettysburg in 1863, though it is Lincoln's speech that is remembered.) Lady Emmeline had become quite friendly with Everett's wife and daughter, so he did all he could to return her kindness. Among the distinguished men she met at Harvard she was most impressed with the famous zoologist, Professor Jean Louis Agassiz, who turned out to be a cousin of her Swiss governess. Lady Emmeline paid a visit to Plymouth where the Pilgrim Fathers had landed in 1620: here she sat in a chair that had been brought over in the *Mayflower* and had remained in the same family ever since. She was also delighted to see some portraits by the great American portrait painter, John Singleton Copley, 'father of our greatly-distinguished Lord Lyndhurst (who was born, I think, in Boston)'.*

Among the famous writers who called on Lady Emmeline was the historian, W.H. Prescott, 'one of the most agreeable people I ever met with'. Prescott had gained considerable fame by this time for his *History of the Conquest of Mexico*. Scholars such as Prescott, Bancroft, Agassiz and Everett – to mention only those Lady Emmeline alludes to – had played a large role in raising the reputation of American literature in Europe. Prescott invited her to visit his summer home and as her party travelled there by train Lady Emmeline was surprised to see a black man as a fellow passenger. Another passenger explained that even in Massachusetts 'this could not ... have happened two years ago ... so strong then were the prejudices against any approach to, or appearance of amalgamation with the black race'. Her natural sympathy came into play and she noted: 'No one could certainly appear more humble and quiet, less presuming or forward in his new position, than did this coloured individual.'

Lady Emmeline also met the famous orator, Daniel Webster, who was then in his last years as Senator from Massachusetts. When he was Secretary of State, an office he would be called to again a year later, he

---

* Lord Lyndhurst had been Lord Chancellor in several Tory Cabinets. Although he was born in Boston, he was taken to England at the age of three at the outbreak of the Revolution.

concluded an important peace treaty with Britain and he probably was the best known American politician to most British readers. On his visit to England, he had stayed at Belvoir Castle as the guest of her father, the Duke of Rutland. Webster's appearance reminded her of a bust of Homer: 'His magnificent countenance – that prodigiously massive brow, those mighty eyes, that seem as if they were calmly looking down the depths of the ages, and that grand air of *repose*.' Like Prescott, Webster invited her to pay a visit to his country home and when she arrived there with the Everetts, she was pleased to see a portrait of her father in the dining room. During her stay she spent much time with her host and was even more impressed than at the first meeting. She was surprised to find that all the servants in Webster's house were freed blacks.[28] She asked him about this and was told that he considered them 'the best possible servants, much attached, contented and grateful, and he added he could "fearlessly trust them with *untold gold*".' She heard an anecdote about her host and his servants when she later went to visit Martha's Vineyard in Massachusetts. Webster was a very swarthy man and one evening he arrived at an inn accompanied by some of his servants. The innkeeper looked first at the dark figure in the carriage and then at his servants and told them that 'he made it a rule never to receive any *coloured persons*'. The innkeeper was aghast when he realised it was the 'Great Dan', the most famous orator in America, whom he was turning away from his door.

While Lady Emmeline normally avoided political questions, she did ask Webster why neither he nor Henry Clay, whom, along with Webster, she regarded as the greatest statesmen in America, had never become President. He replied: 'As regards the politics of their chief magistrate, they [Americans] appear universally to prefer what is called in sporting circles in England a "dark horse".' Unfortunately she gives us no other indication of Webster's conversations on political subjects because, as with so many other women writers of the time, she felt it was right to leave such discussions to 'those more conversant with such subjects'.

Lady Emmeline obviously enjoyed herself in New England, for she and her daughter stayed there until well into October. She constantly commented on the kindness and fine manners she found. Indeed, when she once encountered rudeness at a small hotel in Martha's Vineyard, she explained that this was 'a *very rare thing* in America'. At another small hotel in the same town she found the landlady upset because her son was off to hunt for gold in California as one of the 'forty-niners'. She was later to see many of these gold-seekers when she visited Panama, but her first reaction was, 'What misery has this Californian emigration brought on thousands of families – unknown, incalculable wretchedness!'

Lady Emmeline left New England to return to New York and on her way stopped in Boston to visit the city's Blind Asylum which had been made famous by Charles Dickens in his *American Notes*. Like Dickens she was most impressed with the extraordinary progress of Laura Bridgeman, a precursor of the more famous Helen Keller. She was not only blind, deaf and dumb but had no sense of smell and little of taste. Victoria Wortley wrote in her *Young Traveller's Journal* that Laura was 'very slight and delicate-looking, as almost all American women are'. On her way through Connecticut Lady Emmeline stopped to visit Yale where she recorded, 'The more I see of American society, the more I like it.' Like Fanny Wright and Fanny Trollope, her good will even extended to the Irish whom so many British travellers to America attacked. Whereas many middle-class women sneered at the poor Irish emigrants pouring into America, Lady Emmeline, secure in her own social position, spoke kindly of nearly everyone she met, including the Irish. When in Bridgeport, Connecticut, she delighted the Irish maid waiting on her by listening to tales of the 'ould country'. When Lady Emmeline gave her a tip the maid burst out: 'Och sure, my heart warmed towards ye from the first, when I found ye was from the *ould countries.*'

WASHINGTON AND KENTUCKY

The Wortleys did not remain long in New York, for their travels had already been delayed by the summer's heat. Lady Emmeline wished to move southward now that the temperatures had become more moderate. Unlike most visitors she did not particularly like Philadelphia. Her dislike seems to have arisen from that frequent source of annoyance which travellers can experience anywhere: lack of sleep. In this case it was the 'unearthly nightly noises' which someone told her came from the neighbourhood of the freed slaves. This seems the one place on her entire trip where she allowed a temporary annoyance to unbalance her wider view. What traveller can look kindly on a city in which they cannot sleep? The young Victoria, who tended to be more critical than her mother, found the train journey from Philadelphia to Baltimore an uncomfortable one. Her complaint was 'too horrible to mention here: other writers have said enough'. The twelve-year-old girl was being diplomatic about the loathsome habit of tobacco spitting. Her mother, once again contented, praised Baltimore as both a clean and an expanding city.

When Lady Emmeline reached Washington she was disappointed by the unfinished state of many of the buildings: 'Washington would be a beautiful city if it were built; but as it is not I cannot say much about it.' The principal street, Pennsylvania Avenue, was 'splendid', but the same could not be said for the houses fronting it: they were too small for its great width. Victoria Wortley was 'completely disappointed' with the Capitol building as well as the number of dogs and even pigs roaming through the streets. There was another sight that appeared unusual to her young eyes: 'the great quantity of coloured people in Washington ... It seems as if three-quarters of the population were black or mulatto.' For her mother the White House had 'altogether a noble effect' although 'it is said to be not at all in a healthy situation'. This, however, did not put her off visiting it to talk to President Zachary Taylor.

One of the most striking things in the many British travel books about America is the number of authors who were invited to the White House. In those spacious days, Presidents were less preoccupied with the minutiae of government and, of course, there was – mercifully – far less government to create work for the current tenant of the White House. Fanny Wright, as we saw, met several of the Presidents. Washington did not attract as many visitors or celebrities as New York or Boston and since Presidents rarely left the city, they were pleased to meet someone new; usually the visitors, for their part, enjoyed their visit to the President. However, there were occasions when the meeting could be difficult, as Captain Thomas Hamilton found in 1831 when he called on Andrew Jackson. He had been introduced to the President at a reception and Jackson, who asked Hamilton to sit next to him, talked with the young man for about half an hour. Hamilton noted, with his usual waspish tone, that the President 'makes sad havoc of the King's English'.* Hamilton must have kept his censures for later because Jackson not only invited him to dinner, but told him to drop in any evening. The Captain did call and send up his card. The President was ill with a headache, but he came down. 'The conversation for the first quarter of an hour, was about the state of his bowels, the failure of calomel, the success of salts etc.' After these engaging topics they proceeded to discuss European and American politics.[29]

It was not every day that a Duke's daughter, let alone a poet and playwright of some reputation, visited Washington and it was hardly surprising that she, too, was invited to the White House. Zachary Taylor had become President two months before her arrival in America. 'Old Rough and Ready' was a national hero from his victories in the Mexican War; as one historian aptly puts it, 'His political asset was mere availability.' There was also a popular hope that General Taylor, a Southern slave-owner who was opposed to slavery in the new territories, would be the best man to lessen the growing sectional controversy. At the time of Lady Emmeline's visit, tension in Washington was reaching fever pitch over the admission of California as a 'free' state: this would turn the balance in the Senate against the South. Grandiloquent fanatics in each section began to call for disunion and more conservative people feared that their country was heading for what her recent host, Webster, called 'caverns of darkness'. It is a pity that Lady Emmeline's 'self-denying' rule on political discussions meant she left us no record of the political events taking place around her – and all the more so

---

* Actually the then King, William IV, possessed the blunt vocabulary of a retired Admiral and several of his sayings are not all that dissimilar from those of General Jackson. Perhaps the President could have taken comfort in one of them: 'I know no person so perfectly disagreeable and even dangerous as an author.'

because she came from a political family. Ironically the only comment she allowed herself was one of her few mistakes. It occurred in a footnote in which she wrote that she was glad to hear that slavery was to be abolished in the District of Columbia as a result of the 'Compromise of 1850'. In fact, it was the slave trade, not slavery, that was abolished. One of the reasons for doing so was to keep foreign visitors, such as herself, from seeing a sight that was bound to cause revulsion. Slavery continued both in Washington and throughout the country for more than a decade; indeed it only ended in the midst of that 'cavern of darkness' that Daniel Webster, President Taylor and Lady Emmeline would not live to witness.[30]

Despite her self-imposed restrictions, her description of her visit to Zachary Taylor remains interesting. She was impressed with the President's demeanour: 'His manners are winningly frank, simple, and kind, and though characteristically distinguished by much straightforwardness, there is not the slightest roughness in his address. There was a quick, keen, eagle-like expression in the eye which reminded me a little of the Duke of Wellington.' With knowledge gained in his recent military campaign in Mexico, Taylor was able to advise her what to see when she visited that country. He had a pleasant discussion about flowers with young Victoria who recorded in her *Journal* that the kindly President did everything to overcome her shyness and put her totally at ease. He advised the Wortleys to visit St Louis, Missouri, which he claimed was the most interesting town in the United States and whose phenomenal growth he had witnessed himself.

Naturally Lady Emmeline was interested to hear his views on Anglo-American relations, a subject which happily stood outside her ban on political discussions:

> He spoke very kindly of England, and adverting to the approaching acceleration and extension of steam communication between her and America ... he exclaimed, 'The voyage will be made shorter and shorter, and I expect England and America will soon be quite alongside of each other, ma'am.' 'The sooner the better, sir,' I most heartily responded, at which he bowed and smiled. 'We are the same people,' he continued, 'and it is good for both to see more of each other.' 'Yes,' I replied, 'and thus all detestable old prejudices will die away.' 'I hope so,' he said, 'it will be for the advantage of both.' He continued in this strain and spoke so nobly of England, that it made one's heart bound to hear him. And he evidently felt what he said.

Taylor told his guests that he longed to return to his plantation and invited them to visit there if they went down the Mississippi. After their meeting had ended, he paid them the great compliment of accompanying them to their carriage where he handed Lady Emmeline into her seat. Etiquette prescribed that a head of state only accompany another head of state outside his residence, but Zachary Taylor was a Southern gentleman to whom courtesy to ladies outranked state etiquette.[*]

Lady Emmeline now left Washington for Kentucky. She was annoyed to hear that its famous Senator, Henry Clay, had passed her en route as she had been given a letter of introduction to him. It is a pity they did not meet because he was the man popularly identified with the Compromise of 1850 and a portrait, like that of Zachary Taylor, could also have been penned without violating her rule against politics. Lady Emmeline found her trip across the Alleghany Mountains dreadful: the roads were horrible, the horses cruelly treated, and the drivers drunk. She visited Pittsburgh, toured the factories and found the place as black as Sheffield (which was close to the Stuart Wortley family seat): both cities were famous for their iron foundries.

In Ohio Lady Emmeline stopped for a day in Cincinnati because the crowded hotels made a longer visit impossible. She does not refer to Mrs Trollope even though, like her, she found the city full of pigs and still well worthy of its name, 'Porkopolis'. The city had continued its rapid growth. In 1840 the population had been 49,338; by 1849 it had more than doubled to 110,000. She noted the large numbers of German immigrants and asked how they were regarded. She received the standard reply: 'They are the best immigrants possible: industrious, generally sober and quiet – not quarrelsome like the Irish ... but we could not do without the Irish. They build all our railroads, make our roads, canals and do all the hardest work in the country.' She was evidently stirred by thinking of the various groups that had come to America. When moved, her natural impulse was to break into verse. Some extracts from the poem composed on this occasion will give a good idea of the limit of her poetic abilities:

> Wanderers! who come from many a distant zone,
> To gaze on Nature's Transatlantic throne:-
> Wanderers! – whose feet like mine ne'er trod before,
> This proud, magnificently-various shore;
> Ne'er lightly view the thousand scenes sublime
> Of great America's resplendent clime;
> But still, in thoughtful mood's observant care
> Weigh well the many-mingling glories there
>
> . . .
>
> A large and mighty meaning seems to lurk,
> A glorious mind is everywhere at work!-
> A bold, grand spirit rules and reigns around,
> And sanctifies the lowliest herb and stone
>
> . . .

---

[*] Zachary Taylor died on 9 July 1850 after over-indulging in iced milk and cherries at a Fourth of July celebration.

America's great Mind, – *the true* New World,
Launched like the Sun, 'gainst th' elder darkness hurled;
Hung, as the Heavens are hung, above them all,
And holding their sublimest powers in thrall!

Presumably refreshed after this poetic effusion, Lady Emmeline crossed the Ohio River and entered Kentucky, thereby setting foot in the South. Here again she has Mrs Trollope in mind even if she does not mention her by name. It may be recalled that the Ohio River was one of the few things in the Union to receive praise – indeed, frequent and fervent praise – from Frances Trollope's pen. Lady Emmeline's verdict is similar: 'The Ohio exceeded my expectations: the river and the scenery are both beautiful.' Although Louisville, Kentucky, like Cincinnati, was full of pigs on their way to market, she liked this 'fine city' which she found the best lighted in America. Her more critical daughter saw another side. She was shocked to read a notice on their bedroom door in the hotel: 'Caution! to prevent robbery!! Bolt the door before going to bed.' Victoria discussed this with her hosts and her reaction was one felt by many later English visitors: 'It really would appear that you can neither sleep in peace, nor stir out of your room without being robbed. The Americans, in general, lay it *all* on the backs of the poor Negroes.'

While in Louisville the Wortleys took the opportunity to visit the famous caves near by. Like Niagara Falls, these had already become a favourite sight in nineteenth-century America.[31] Lady Emmeline, who claimed to dislike walking, nevertheless walked eight miles in one cave and fourteen miles in another on the following day. She had enough energy left to compose a poem celebrating the glories of these caves. In order to display the echo, guides sang 'Yankee Doodle Dandy' and the great 'hit' of 1849, 'Oh! Susanna', a tune she would soon grow tired of hearing. The gold recently discovered in California had attracted hordes of 'forty-niners' like the son whose mother in Massachusetts had gained her sympathy. As these men made the long journey west they sang Stephen Foster's song:

Oh, Susanna, don't you cry for me,
I'm off to California with a washbowl on my knee.

DOWN THE MISSISSIPPI TO NEW ORLEANS

Lady Emmeline had decided to follow President Taylor's advice and visit St Louis. She left Louisville by steamboat where she encounted, as had Mrs Trollope before her, 'one of the very roughest sets I had ever been among'. To add insult to injury, they were among the First Class passengers. Victoria had a good ear for conversation and shared Mrs Trollope's delight in recording choice examples. Her mother was asked by one American woman: 'Does ye live at Pittsburgh, marm?' 'No, we come from England.' 'Englarnd, marm! and where may that be? A-ah I've heerd say that's a long way off to be sure.' The trip to St Louis took almost as long as that across the Atlantic. Their boat, the *Hindoo*, was slow, but Lady Emmeline took comfort in knowing that the captain, unlike some others, was at least more concerned with safety than with speed. When she reached St Louis she found a town which, like Cincinnati, was growing fast. It had been established by the French in 1764 and expanded rapidly after Missouri was admitted to the Union in 1821 as the twenty-fourth state. Lady Emmeline found that it still attracted Frenchmen in addition to the large numbers of Germans. She was impressed with the speed and size of building in the city: 'From our hotel windows we had a long view of gigantic and gigantically-growing-up dwellings, that seemed every morning to be about a storey higher than we left them on the preceding night.'

One ill effect of all this growth was the absorption of those Romantic rural vistas Lady Emmeline longed to see. Dickens in his *American Notes* had described his visit to Looking Glass Prairie, some thirty miles from the town. Now, only seven years later, she was informed that there were no proper prairies nearby, 'for Civilization hereabouts walks with no mincing, graceful, dancing-master-like steps but great, seven-league boots, and sprawling, earth-shaking strides ... that it is all the horizon can do to get out of her way in time'. In further proof of this she was told that although a cholera epidemic had claimed almost a third of the population, enough new settlers were pouring in for the gap soon to be filled. It is interesting to note that the visitor who had been so shocked at the Americans' matter-of-fact attitude towards death when she first arrived, made no comment on this statement. She also avoided any hostile comment about the phlegmatic attitude she encountered towards steamboat wrecks, though she had been horrified at similar sights when travelling up the Hudson. The most famous wreck in recent years was an explosion on the *Louisiana* in which hundreds had been killed. Yet, as she prepared to sail down the Mississippi from St Louis, her only comment on the *Louisiana* explosion was that it would probably make her own journey safer: captains would now exercise more care. (Readers of Mark Twain's novels set on the Mississippi will recall similar attitudes among those characters who lived on the river.) Obviously she was absorbing the attitudes round her.

The most appealing aspect of Lady Emmeline's writing is the way her Romantic appreciation of nature and scenery is expressed and the way in which she conveys a sense of the beauty round her to her readers. Nowhere in the book is this more the case than in her description of her trip down the Mississippi. She had expected the river to be boring – another example of Mrs Trollope's influence – but she found herself delighted and 'watched and gazed on it day after day, and hour after hour, with ever-newly kindling interest and admiration'. When she described the nights she waxed lyrical:

By night the scene is one of startling interest and of magical splendour. Hundreds of lights are glancing in different directions, from the villages, towns, farms and plantations on shore, and from the magnificent 'floating palaces' of steamers, that frequently look like moving mountains of light and flame, so brilliantly are these enormous river-leviathans illuminated, outside and inside. Indeed, the spectacle presented is like a dream of enchantment. Imagine steamer after steamer coming sweeping, sounding, thundering on, blazing with these thousands of lights, casting long brilliant reflections on the fast-rolling waters beneath.

Victoria shared her mother's enthusiasm and wrote that the sight of the illuminated steamboats passing one another was 'almost too beautiful to be of earth'. Twice their boat was 'snagged', when floating trees or logs got caught in the blades of its large paddle-wheel. This would bring the huge ship to a sudden halt and cause noisy fright to the numerous horses and mules aboard. Despite these accidents, Lady Emmeline was as impressed with the luxury on this steamboat as she had been when she sailed up the Hudson. The menu even included 'soufflets'. The only real annoyance was the number of animals aboard: it resembled Noah's Ark, she later remarked. She complained that 'one's olfactory' nerves were assaulted by the hordes of pigs carried on the boat. Mrs Trollope would have sympathised.

In spite of travelling with two maids, Lady Emmeline must have made efforts not to appear as a *grande dame* as one American passenger asked her if she had come West to take a farm and told her how one woman from London had been successful as a frontier farmer. However Victoria noted that the two maids had overheard an American say that the two ladies must be English because they ate their pudding with a spoon and a fork rather than relying on a knife. It was Lady Emmeline's ability to mix with all sorts of people that made her such a good traveller. She never saw any need to hector, she listened and, only occasionally, smiled to herself, as when another woman told her that on the whole she approved of Queen Victoria's behaviour. Lady Emmeline wrote home to her family – who were presumably perplexed as to why she was going so far from the settled East – that she was 'very well contented with the choice I made in visiting the West and the great rivers; these mighty rivers are worlds in themselves'.[32]

At Natchez, in Mississippi, the Wortleys left the boat to visit President Taylor's plantation, Cyprus Grove. Young Victoria was amazed that no one seemed to know where the President's plantation was. The estate was about two thousand acres and the 'hands' or 'servants' – the Taylors did not use the word 'slave' – were said to be worth $50,000. Lady Emmeline arrived with the customary English view about slavery: she was opposed to it and hoped to see its gradual abolition, but she was not really all that interested in it. While she had seen both freed blacks on her visits to Webster's home and elsewhere in the North, and slaves in Washington, Maryland and Kentucky, this visit was her first real experience of 'slavery' on a large plantation. Once again Lady Emmeline was lucky with her guide; the President's son, Richard, was a well educated and cosmopolitan man, who had studied in Edinburgh, Paris and at Yale. Although he had shown no inclination to follow in his father's military footsteps, he became a Lieutenant-General in the Confederacy, and, according to the wife of the Confederate President, Jefferson Davis, was 'one of the most gallant and daring heroes of an army that was "the admiration of one continent and the wonder of the other" '. (Given that Richard Taylor's sister had been President Davis' short-lived first wife, the tribute of the second wife is perhaps all the more remarkable.) Richard Taylor would live to write one of the best Confederate memoirs of the war, a book that would be highly praised by Edmund Wilson, the literary critic and Marxist, who was no admirer of the South. To use a modern term, Lady Emmeline had come from the heart of the English 'Establishment' to that of the South.[33]

Young Taylor 'mustered and marshalled' all the slaves for the two English visitors. Victoria Wortley made a point of writing in her *Journal* that Richard Taylor had had no idea that they were coming and therefore he had no time to try to disguise anything from prying English eyes. She noted that each of the 'servants' was given one pound of meat a day as well as flour, milk, coffee, butter and vegetables. Certainly some of the agricultural labourers near Belvoir Castle would have envied that diet. Lady Emmeline found them 'as well fed, comfortably clothed, and kindly cared for in every way as possible'; they 'seemed thoroughly happy and contented'. She asked to see round the interior of one of the quarters or cabins, which impressed her: 'The dwelling-house we went to look at was extremely nice: it was a most tastefully decorated and an excellently furnished one; the walls were covered with prints, and it was scrupulously clean and neat.' Young Victoria asked to see some of the children and her mother wrote: 'Such a congregation of little smiling, good-natured raven roly-polies, I never saw collected together before.' Lady Emmeline noticed only one difference between the slave children and the white – their exceptional quiet. Perhaps she did not consider the effect on the children of a visit by a titled English lady, her young daughter and two attendant maids. (Almost certainly the ladies' maids were a more exotic sight than the two ladies.) Richard Taylor also introduced the Wortleys to one man who was 100 years old. In a typical comment she wrote that the man 'reminded me a little in his courteous salutation of dear old Marquis de l'Aigle, who used to tell me ... of his dancing minuets with poor Marie Antoinette'. On a more practical level her host told her that the man raised his own poultry which he then sold to his master and added: 'He invariably charges the very highest prices for them.' Taylor also told her of his valet who had taught himself to read at night when his work was done.

Lady Emmeline was aware that she was seeing one of the most favourable examples of plantation slavery but she also believed that the whole question was incredibly complex and could not be solved by the moral

outrage of English and Northern intellectuals who substituted vague
compassion and novelists' fiction for concrete understanding. Her conclusions are worth quoting:

> Alas! there are too many interests involved – even those of the slaves
> themselves – to permit the immediate extinction of slavery. I am quite aware
> that on plantations such as the one I have been writing about, one sees
> entirely the *coleur de rose* of the business; but I believe it is very rarely the
> negroes are ill-treated, except as I am told by an American, by small farmers.

She was also aware of the somewhat odd position occupied by the English
who had, after all, ruled America when the 100-year-old slave she met was
born: 'Of all people in the world, the English have the least right to find
fault with the Americans for retaining still the legacy which they had from
England, that melancholy and dangerous keepsake that was her gift – a
gift forced on their acceptance too.' Finally, she warned her readers that
emancipation was not desired by the slaves: 'Of one thing I feel quite
certain, from many observations I have made, if you had the power to
liberate all the slaves in the United States, you would not find a tenth, not
even a twentieth – perhaps not a hundred part of them – would accept their
freedom from your hands.'

Zachary Taylor's modern biographer, Holman Hamilton, was greatly
impressed with Lady Emmeline's account and found it 'the best description' of Cyprus Grove. Professor Hamilton concludes:[34]

> If Lady Emmeline Stuart Wortley did not overdraw her picture, and the
> deduction from Taylor's own writings are faithful to the situation as it really
> was, slavery at Cyprus Grove was perhaps as idyllic as it ever became. It was
> the antithesis of what would be printed on page after page of *Uncle Tom's
> Cabin* ... Jefferson Davis, whom Taylor admired, has long enjoyed a reputa-
> tion as one of the most humane of masters. Now Zachary Taylor himself can
> be portrayed in a similar role ... If Harriet Beecher Stowe had gone with Lady
> Emmeline to Cyprus Grove, one wonders whether she would have written
> the volcanic tale that shook the world.

After her visit to the plantation Lady Emmeline boarded another
steamboat bound for New Orleans. 'No longer', she reflected, 'does New
Orleans seem a place far out of the world.' Now that they were connected
by telegraph to New York, they could receive news of the latest Paris
fashions as quickly as the eastern cities. When the Wortleys arrived in
December they found the city unusually hot and crowded, so much so that
they could not find any room at the St Charles, the largest hotel in America.
They had to make do with a smaller hotel whose verandah reminded her
of Paris. Here she was amused when it turned out that her waiter was a
Swede who happened to have been a neighbour of the famous singer, Jenny
Lind. As with the Irish waitress in Connecticut, Lady Emmeline delighted
the man by talking about his homeland and told him that she had both

heard and admired the 'Swedish Nightingale'. Even the friendly waiter was unable to comply with her desire to taste exotic food such as alligator, though he did bring her 'wild ros bief ' which turned out to be buffalo. Lady Emmeline was willing to try anything: she had already eaten bear meat, which she found 'excellent', and was soon to attempt wild raccoon. Victoria, who tended to see more practical problems than her poetic mother, complained that New Orleans suffered dreadfully from mosquitoes.

New Orleans was the largest cotton port in America at a time when cotton was not only America's most important export but the basis of her national wealth. The docks were 'so covered with huge bales of cotton (though it is far from a productive year) that the ground was literally strewn with little lumps of it, fallen from the bales in moving them. It almost looked as if it had been snowing in large flakes.'[35] Once again she was struck with the vastness of everything in America: 'I shall want a microscope when I return to England; so miserably small and petty will seem its rivers, its hills.' As she sat in her hotel room in the stifling heat and watched cotton being carried everywhere through the streets, she thought about the future of the country. Again, she emphasised the close connection between Nature and the people who inhabited the land:

> What a future! what a country! and what a noble people, to work out the grand destiny, and to fill up magnificently the magnificent designs of Nature. It is all petty malice and jealousy which make people talk of the exaggerated expressions and ideas ... What would be exaggerations in other countries, is here the simplest moderation, and in all probability lags behind the reality. The fact is, they feel their destiny, and their country's destiny, and they would be stocks and stones if they did not; and if, in England, we are disposed to think they 'greatly daring' talk [*sic*], we should remember a little what a prospect lies before them. Nature, their present, their future – all is in such an exaggerated mood here, all on such a stupendous scale.

Before leaving New Orleans, Lady Emmeline took a short railway journey and was able to see at first hand the older America that was being replaced by the new. She saw an Indian tribe on the move and was fascinated by the sight, especially the differences between the men and women: 'The men seemed a magnificent-looking set, splendidly rigged out in very brilliant and picturesque habiliments ... They stalked along with extreme dignity ... as upright as their own arrows.' The same could not be said for their 'unlucky squaws, who followed after, bowed under the weight of papooshes, lodge-poles, pots, pans, kettles, all sorts of luggage and lumber'.

REFLECTIONS AT MOBILE, ALABAMA

In January 1850 Lady Emmeline felt it was time to end her eight-month journey through America. She left New Orleans by boat for Mobile, Alabama, then the second largest cotton port. Here she hoped to get a Royal

Mail steamer to take her party to Mexico but the ship was late and all who wished to take it had to be ready to board whenever it should arrive, regardless of the hour. (The California gold rush had had a tremendous effect upon shipping and it was often difficult to get a passage.) Fortunately she had an English friend in Mobile with whom she and Victoria could stay. This woman had recently lost two of her daughters to scarlet fever. This created a bond with Lady Emmeline who was still grieving over the death of her son. With this new 'chosen sister of my soul' she paid several visits to cemeteries to seek inspiration for her poetry.

> Courage, sad heart! fan all they heaven-born fires!
> See death-freed myriads take their sunward flight!
> Eternity advances! Time retires!
> The grave's dark gate but leads to life and light!

She made use of her extra time by visiting a settlement of Choctaw Indians near the city, where she was struck by their 'pride'. Naturally her Romantic sensibilities were stirred: 'How much they must have suffered.' Yet she was anxious to defend her friend President Taylor from rumours that he had used bloodhounds to hunt down Indians in war.[36] She also used her time for a few final thoughts about slavery. One of the slaves in her friend's house told how she had once seen George Washington. The memory of the meeting was at least fifty years old as Washington had died in 1799 and all the servant could recall was seeing an elderly man riding by in a carriage. Even so, 'E might fine man as ebber I seen'. Several people told her – as a few years later similar people would tell Catherine Hopley – that Southern slaves were miserable if they were taken on a visit to the North as they met much more racism there. She decided that 'what one says in black and white about white and black in these days' was a 'delicate subject' and passed on to other topics with evident relief.

With her usual good fortune, Lady Emmeline met the newly appointed American Minister to Mexico and he invited her party to accompany him aboard the warship taking him to his new post. As the ship made its way out of Mobile Bay – which in the next decade would see one of the greatest naval battles in American history – she was busy with two poems, one of farewell to America and another, more personal one, to the 'sister of my soul'. After these melancholy chores she settled down to enjoy the voyage. She was delighted with the way that the sailors referred to each other by their states, so that there were cries of 'Tennessee, give us a song'. The ship seemed altogether very musical, which led her to wonder if Americans were not more musical than Britons. The music, however, had one drawback:

> It was a gallant and goodly company on board, and pleasant was it to hear them singing in merry chorus in the evening, when the water was compara- tively calm (very much *comparatively*, I assure you), 'O Susanna!' which

rather whimperingly-inclined lady seems really to be the 'undying one', and also the universal and ubiquitous one; for go where you may, you will hear her invoked. I am told they harpoon whales to this cheering tune in the Atlantic.

Some of the best general reflections in her book were written during her enforced stay in Mobile and on board ship. Many of her forecasts have come true in this century. Lady Emmeline was always anxious to defend Americans against the criticisms of those who singled out the swaggering boastfulness that was so common in this pre-war era of rapid growth and seemingly endless 'progress'. While she rarely mentions this trait, she knew that her readers would know Mrs Trollope's and similar books, and made this prediction:

> As this people progress and advance more and more, they will gain the humility of true greatness. They will feel more the vast responsibilities that rest upon their Titanic shoulders ... They will feel more and more that their past and present colossal greatness does not make future improvement and progress ... impossible, but imperative, – absolutely indispensable. Nature has done so much for them, that to be commensurate with her, to keep pace with their giant opportunities, they *must* act as giants.

However, Lady Emmeline did endorse a frequently heard opinion about American family life. 'The one point, perhaps, in which I most concur with other writers on the United States, is there being no real child-like children here.' She found the children were too serious and too opinionated; perhaps this is a strange view by one who began writing when she was ten and whose own twelve-year-old daughter was writing a book. Mrs Trollope had attacked 'the total want of subjection and discipline' of American children. Her son, Anthony, in his travel book thirty years later, made similar comments and said he believed that this produced many 'wretched and uncomfortable' children. Normally, when English travellers concurred in a general criticism of America, American travel writers returned the compliment by saying the same thing about Britain. However, American visitors tended to accept this particular criticism. A 'Wall Street Bear', who visited England about the same time that Lady Emmeline was wandering about America, commented: 'English children ... are much better trained than ours; conducting themselves like little gentlemen and ladies, and not dragging their weak and affectionate parents around as if *they* were the children.' Lydia Sigourney – 'the Connecticut poetaster ... [whose] lugubrious preoccupation with death caused her to look at every sick child as a potential angel' in the delightful phrase of *The Oxford Companion to American Literature* – agreed that English children enjoyed 'subordination, the privilege of childhood'.[37]

Lady Emmeline realised that the seriousness she observed in the children of America reflected the earnest urgency of their parents. 'No drones', she wrote, 'are admitted into the great Transatlantic hive. There is no time to spare; they must be ready, as soon as possible, to take their places and run in the great race.' Once again American travellers were ready to admit that this was a valid criticism of their homeland. When Harriet Beecher Stowe looked round the dinner tables of London, she was amazed how young so many famous people appeared: 'Generally speaking, our working minds seem to wear out their bodies faster.' She agreed that climate might be one factor, but she also pointed to 'the intense stimulus of our political *régime*, which never leaves anything long at rest'.[38] Indeed, Stowe herself would be a good example: after wearing out her 'working mind' on *Uncle Tom's Cabin* and its profitable side-lines, she retired to Florida.

In his *Democracy in America* Alexis de Tocqueville had predicted the future power and greatness both of America and of Russia: 'Each of them', he wrote at the end of the first volume, 'seems to be marked out by the will of Heaven to sway the destinies of half the globe.'[39] This opinion, which has frequently decorated leading newspaper articles and ornamented the orations of the more literate politicians of the late twentieth century, was also held by Lady Emmeline. While, unlike Tocqueville, she rarely attempted analysis, she did, again unlike Tocqueville, possess a considerable knowledge of the expanding Russian Empire, its language, its peoples and its ruler. She frequently wrote in Russian and also displayed in her books and her life a sympathy with the problems facing the Tsar and his Empire.[*] Her comparison of what would become the two 'super powers' – or what she called 'giant powers' – therefore deserves further consideration. She observed that she had met various other foreign travellers in America but noted that there was one strange omission among those she encountered:

There are but few Russian visitors here it seems; but I am very much struck by the apparent *entente cordiale* that exists between Russia and the United States. There seems an inexplicable instinct of sympathy, some mysterious magnetism at work, which is drawing by degrees these two mighty nations into close contact. Napoleon, we know, prophesied that the world, ere long, would be either Cossack or Republican. It seems as if it would first be pretty equally shared between these two giant powers ... Russia is certainly the grand representative of despotic principles, as the United States are the representatives of democratic ones ... Russia and the United States are the two young, growing, giant nations of the world – the Leviathans of lands! They enjoy extraordinary advantages; the older nations seem to have paved and prepared the path before them ... science and knowledge have shone the most surprising light ... Man almost seems a second time to have been hailed master of the creation – civilization has penetrated the uttermost corners of the earth – time and space and the lightning are his familiars and his

---

[*] A few years later, her friend the Tsar told a visiting American Senator, Stephen Douglas, that the United States and Russia were the only two 'proper governments' in the world and that they would eventually absorb all other nations.

servants. With all these advantages, those two grand young nations are strong to the race ... Far off, in the future, centuries and ages beyond the present hour, is their culminating point.

Lady Emmeline then passed on to praise her friend, the autocratic Tsar Nicholas I. She argued that the basis of Russian policy was continued expansion and direct influence throughout the world, but the United States had only expanded into neighbouring lands such as Texas and California, which were improved by their absorption. America's 'stupendous work is at home, but her influence is felt to the farthest ends of the earth, and her shadow is spreading from pole to pole. Like a colossal tree, she *stands*, and firmly stands, while she grows and spreads, and her roots are deepening while her branches are expanding.' She contrasted Russian and American foreign policies and, despite her sympathy for Russia and for Nicholas I, she analysed the essential differences between Russian and American diplomacy:

Russia is anxious to foment contentions and jealousies between other nations, for her own ulterior purposes and profit. America would merely incline towards a constitutional propagandism and that chiefly from a generous desire felt by all her people, from her loftiest statesman to her lowliest citizen, – that others should participate in what, with a thorough straightforward conscientiousness, they firmly believe to be the most precious of benefits and advantages – their free institutions and popular forms of political organization.

Lady Emmeline joined her concern over the one great danger facing America to those of many observers at the time. We should remember that she was writing when some rather dubious manoeuvring by government officials over the admission of California to the Union as a free state had produced a raging argument. We should also remember that Lady Emmeline had spent the final months of her visit in the South and that she was probably writing her conclusions in Mobile. As the Mobile *Daily Register* put it when she was in the city, the demands of Northern politicians were threatening 'the catastrophe of a dissolution of the Union'.[40] If she had been in Boston she would have found the same worries, except that there the blame would have been laid on Southern politicians. Writing in January 1850 she warned her English audience:[41]

There are symptoms of grave disorder threatening there [in California] and strange signs of the dissolution of the great federal compact. Nothing more convinces the uninitiated stranger of the fact, than the incessant denunciation thundered against disunion ... I think they exaggerate the evil that would arise, in the event of dissolution.

LATIN AMERICA AND THE CARIBBEAN

It is not within the compass of this book to follow Lady Emmeline's wanderings after she left the United States, except so far as they illustrate her remarkable character as a true Romantic or as they brought her into further contact with aspects of American life. The fact that the title page of her book calls this part of her trip '*Etc.*' reflects the true importance it occupied in her mind. She enjoyed her trip through Mexico, where she met its current President, General Herrara. She found a ship that was going to Cuba and its route gave her another brief time in Mobile. On her first voyage from Mobile she had grown weary of the Americans' constant singing of 'Oh! Susanna'. It must have given her some wry amusement, which she was too polite or kind to record, to meet on this return trip an American organ-grinder who had gone to Mexico hoping to '"O Susanaize" and "Yankee-doodleize" the whole country'. The Mexicans had ignored him and he now told Lady Emmeline that this neglect of music was undoubtedly a cause of the frequent revolutions in Mexico! Her ladyship would, no doubt, have allowed herself some small ironic pleasure if she had heard the parody that many unsuccessful miners sang on their return from the gold fields:

> Oh California! this is the land for me;
> A pick and shovel, and lots of bones,
> The golden land of dross and stones.
> Oh Susanna, don't you cry for me
> I am living dead in Californee.

After she and Victoria travelled about Cuba – one of the last outposts of the once great Spanish Empire in the western hemisphere – they found yet another ship, this time bound for Panama where there were said to be 1,300 Americans, mostly dressed in red flannel shirts, on their way across the isthmus on the way to California. She also noted that already there was considerable hostility between Americans and Panamanians. After this she went to South America to visit Peru and afterwards made her way to Jamaica. Before leaving that island, she visited a slave ship, the *Clementina*, which had recently been captured by the Royal Navy. She was quite horrified at the conditions and was particularly shocked to see that most of the Africans were young men; this allowed more to be squeezed into the foetid ship, which was smuggling slaves to Latin America. Once this dreadful vessel had been brought into British territory the slaves were released and became free workers in Jamaica. Fortunately this horrible spectacle was not the Wortleys' final experience in the Americas. According to Victoria's *A Young Traveller's Journal*, she and her mother then sailed to New York, and before leaving for England they retraced their steps northward to have another sight of Niagara Falls and to revisit their friends in Canada.[42]

As much as Lady Emmeline enjoyed her hectic travels through Latin America and the Caribbean, thoughts of the United States were never far from her mind and she frequently interrupted long passages about the floral or other natural beauties of the southern nations to break into a sermon on the potential power of the Great Republic to the north. She longed for an understanding between the two Anglo-Saxon countries: 'If all illiberal prejudice and antagonizing influences and unfortunate jealousies could be annihilated, and the United States and England would fairly go hand-in-hand', the 'work of regeneration' would be accomplished. She was perceptive in her belief that England would need the younger nation in the future. Britain's economic vulnerability in light of growing American and German power would not become evident for another forty years, but Lady Emmeline pointed to the danger long before public discussion became common:

> But England is too calculating; beginning now, – not to decline, I do not think or believe that, – but to lose some portion of that vigorous and restless energy, which *must* advance – and to be more anxious about retaining than gaining; and her object is, perhaps, yet more to check and interdict others from snatching at coveted prizes, than to seize them herself.

She knew that many would argue that the Americans' preoccupation with materialism would keep them from ever having a genuine concern for the Mother Country in any hour of need. Yet she was perceptive and saw that beneath the materialism, which she disliked, there was an older, idealistic strain, which she praised:

> If the true hero-nature lives anywhere it is in the American: if the age of chivalry is *not* past – though Burke declared it was, in the Old World of Europe, – if, in short, chivalry still exists on earth, it is in the great and mighty West. I think I see a satirical smile on the reader's lips ... I know if I were in a London drawing-room what a chorus would be raised of 'dollars and cents'! etc., but I boldly write what I most conscientiously believe: and how absurd it is to keep harping on one fault (and it really seems almost their only one), as if either a nation or an individual could be absolutely perfect!

Two years later in her next book, *&c*, she was even more fervent in advising her countrymen to abandon 'any lingering and unworthy prejudice or dislike against our enterprising Transatlantic relations'. Now that Cunard steamships made it possible to cross the Atlantic in two weeks, she urged her readers to go and 'see with their own eyes ... our noble-hearted, wonder-working cousins, in their gigantic and glorious country'. Lady Emmeline dismissed any lingering suspicions about American manners; speaking with the authority of a Duke's daughter, she proclaimed herself 'delighted' with them.

One of the most important aspects of Lady Emmeline's two books on America is the stress she gives to themes that were to be increasingly heard by later English visitors and writers. 'What friends', she asks, 'can be kinder or more generous' than American ones. She is also one of the first to proclaim that far from being a land of rough frontier conditions, America was becoming a land of luxury with its hotels and steamboats far surpassing anything in Europe. She pointed to the 'laws, lineage, language' that would promote closer bonds between the two great English-speaking nations. She saw, decades before Bismarck, what the effect of this would be on the twentieth century: 'Let America and England thoroughly cooperate, and the world, in the next century, will be whatever they have chosen to make it.' For her, the irresistible rise of American power was a source not of fear but of satisfaction: 'Let us say, with a fitting pride, "we laid the foundations of this mighty nation".' She expressed her feelings in her poem, 'Farewell to America':

> Onward! with changeless stateliest cheer,
> The Universe shall follow. Lead!
> On! on! Columbia.
> Scorn not your English sister's tones,
> Scorn not your English sister's tears,
> For they are truths, and trusty ones,–
> And each a world of feeling bears
> For your Columbia!

Absolutely perfect America may not have been, but Lady Emmeline had enjoyed and had been impressed by the rising giant of the West. Her holiday had been a success and she announced: 'America will evermore seem a second country to me.'

LATER TRAVELS

Once back in England, Lady Emmeline reached an agreement with the publisher, Richard Bentley. She would produce two volumes 'of the usual size'. In the end, like so many patient publishers, he found that his author had produced enough material for three volumes. Bentley agreed to print 750 copies, and if 600 of these were sold she would receive £200. The reason there was such a small print run was because books of travel were rarely bought by readers. They borrowed them, as they did novels, from circulating libraries. *Travels in the United States Etc.* was greeted with a condescending review in the *Athenaeum*: 'A style more gaily-tinselled ... could hardly be found.' Anyone who reads her book would have to agree that 'epithets, neologisms, superlatives, exclamations, allusions are huddled together in a profusion'. Yet the male reviewer who sneered at this 'march of female' prose, did admit the book had many good parts. He was certainly correct when he predicted a warm welcome for it in the United

States. The book was rapidly reprinted in America where few English travel writers received such warm praise as Lady Emmeline. 'With the exception of De Tocqueville, no European has ever visited the United States who has done such justice to their present prospective greatness as Lady Emmeline has', claimed the *Albany Dutchman*. It lauded the 'brilliancy' of her style, but gave even more praise to one unusual virtue: 'There is one peculiarity in which Lady Emmeline differs from every other English writer, and that is, she knows what gratitude is.' Few things annoyed – and continue to annoy – people on either side of the Atlantic more than the way in which a traveller expected to be entertained and then returned home to sneer at his recent hosts. Americans believed that Dickens was guilty of this, just as Englishmen said the same of the American travel writer, Nathaniel Parker Willis. Lady Emmeline was careful to heap praise and thanks on her former hosts. Another American publication, the *Home Journal*, proclaimed its view of her book in the headline to its favourable review: 'A Noble Lady Differing From a Trollope.' While the *Albany Dutchman* believed her book would do 'an incalculable amount of good', it left little lasting impression on Americans. Perhaps that is because people remember criticism much longer than praise. Young Victoria's book, which was published by an obscure publisher, did not attract as much attention, although the *Athenaeum* praised her 'surprising precocity'.[43]

Lady Emmeline was as anxious to make money from her book as Mrs Trollope had been. Within a few weeks of the book's being published, she wrote to Bentley to ask if her volumes 'have sold well, and what likelihood there is of my receiving ere long the sum of £200'. The publisher looked over his accounts and found that so far, 204 copies had been sold and another thirty-two presented for review. Three and a half years later Bentley was able to tell Lady Emmeline that 462 copies had been sold. If she wanted any money for the book, she would have to buy 120 copies and then she would receive £65 for her efforts. This sum would not even have paid the transatlantic fares for the two Wortleys and their maids.[44]

After completing their American books, the mother and the daughter did not long remain in England. In October 1851 they sailed to Portugal and Spain and once again Lady Emmeline produced a book of her travels, *A Visit to Portugal and Madeira*, which appeared in 1854. Even there she often recalled her recent stay in America: for example, as her ship approached Madeira, she thought of the sad sight of the Indians near Mobile.[45] (Her book on Spain, *The Sweet South*, was published privately in 1856.) Despite the Crimean War, in which Britain and France were allied with the Ottoman Empire against Russia, the young Victoria and her mother set out in January 1855 to visit Lady Emmeline's surviving son, Henry, who was serving with the Grenadier Guards in the Crimea. Her father, the Duke, disapproved of this venture as he had in general disliked all her extensive travels.[46] Yet these indomitable travellers were not put off by the difficulties of wartime travel: they went by train from

Paris to Lyons and by boat down the Rhone. At Marseilles they boarded a ship filled with French soldiers bound for Constantinople. Once there, Lady Emmeline was able to use her Russian by visiting wounded Russian soldiers in hospital. She offered them a choice: they could have either an orange or a crucifix, and she was delighted when they chose the latter. After seeing her son, she and Victoria set off again, this time for Egypt and the Holy Land. Just outside Jerusalem she happened to meet her brother-in-law, Lord Wharncliffe and his wife, who were just leaving the city. Wharncliffe was – quite naturally – at work on his own travel book. (Six years earlier she had come across their son in Boston.) These encounters provide a microcosm of the wanderings of the Victorians.

When the young Victoria saw the Holy City she said that she hoped the 'signs of the Mohammedan rule, which is a disgrace to Christendom, were removed'. At the Gate of Zion, Lady Emmeline was kicked by her daughter's horse and had to be carried into the city where she was taken to the roof of a harem. From here she could gaze out onto the sacred sites while the shrieks of peacocks in a nearby garden reminded her of her youth amid the splendours of Belvoir Castle. Although considerably weakened by loss of blood she insisted on being carried about Jerusalem on a litter. In spite of the pain, she did not lose her observant eye and noted that the costumes worn by the Jews in their ancestral city were the same as she had seen in the Warsaw ghetto.

Having followed these restless Victorians so far, it should come as no surprise to us that she met yet another relative in Jerusalem. Her nephew turned up unexpectedly, having just completed a forty-eight-day camel ride across the desert in an attempt to follow the route of the Israelites under Moses. Perhaps this meeting increased her desire to resume her travels, even though she had not fully recovered from her injury. In her *&c* she had spoken of how she had been fascinated with camels since she was a child in the nursery at Belvoir looking through travel books. She and Victoria now set out with an escort of Bedouins to see Jericho, the Valley of the Jordan and Damascus. After Damascus her party started a trek north to Aleppo. The journey turned into a nightmare in the fierce heat and eventually their dragoman abandoned them. Their maid died from sunstroke and both Lady Emmeline and Victoria came down with dysentery. Victoria said her mother 'never recovered' from the death of her maid. The two ladies were abandoned in the middle of the desert and the ill Victoria had to crawl to her mother's side to give her water. Lady Emmeline was depressed because all her papers had been lost or stolen so there would be no possibility of producing another travel book. Victoria felt that her mother was 'dying, alas! … of a heart gradually broken by her many trials'.

On 30 October in the desert near Beirut, Lady Emmeline Stuart Wortley died, a victim of that Romantic restlessness and love of travel to which she had dedicated her life.[47] Victoria was left to crawl for help, which she finally obtained. In Beirut she was nursed back to health by the British Consul and his wife. After she recovered she accompanied her mother's body back to England for burial in the Mausoleum at Belvoir, that splendid castle where in Lady Emmeline's youth the Duke's private band had awakened guests for breakfast and summoned them to dinner.*

※

Lady Emmeline's life from Belvoir to Beirut had involved much travel and she had given considerable pleasure to others through her colourful writing and often through the genuine kindness of her personality. She had lived the life of the true Romantic and even her end, miserable though it was, had a certain Byronic quality to it. That cruel comment about her poetry in the *Quarterly Review* in 1840 had come true in a horrible way: 'How even handed Providence is ... a lady of exalted birth, dowered from infancy with all the gifts of nature and fortune, clothed in purple and fine linen and faring sumptuously every day – yet it all turns out to be an *ignis fatuus.*' Lady Emmeline's restlessness may have been at times foolish; it certainly was, in the end, fatal. Yet it gave her the ability to understand and to depict that unique American restlessness that was making a great nation out of a vast wilderness.

* Victoria Stuart Wortley was taken into the Royal Household by her Godmother, Queen Victoria, who made her a Maid of Honour. She eventually married Sir William Welby and went on to write some notable articles on philosophy and language for the *Encyclopaedia Britannica.*

5

The Tragic Observer:
Catherine Hopley

Ten years after Lady Emmeline Stuart Wortley sailed happily out of Mobile Bay, the America that she had visited and celebrated received a rude shock. On the night of 16 October 1859 the fanatical abolitionist, John Brown, led his famous armed raid on the US Armory at Harper's Ferry on the Potomac River, the border between Virginia and Maryland. His aim was to gather enough weapons to lead an armed uprising of slaves. Much ink has been spilled over the question of his sanity, but today, having witnessed scores of similar figures on television, we can see that in many ways he was the world's first terrorist – complete with glazed eyes, bristling beard and a direct communication with the Almighty. After the farcical failure of the raid, he was tried and executed on 2 December. Three days later Congress assembled. Feelings were running so high that members came armed with revolvers: when one Congressman accidentally dropped his gun a near riot ensued. In many Northern states there was an exodus of Southerners: in Pennsylvania alone over 200 Southern students left for home. From the South came troubling stories about visiting Northerners being forced to flee for safety. The agitation of those like Fanny Wright and the novels of those like Mrs Trollope had borne fruit, but the taste was bitter – the dissolution of the Union they had come to praise or to criticise.

During these same months of turmoil and wild rumours, a middle-aged Englishwoman who had been living in Ohio was planning to move south to Virginia. In 1863, in the middle of the Civil War, she brought out an anonymous book, *Life in the South*, which gave a vivid portrayal of the last year of peace and the first two years of the war which ended slavery. When I first read her book, I realised that it provided the perfect finish to this procession of Englishwomen who had written about America in these formative decades. Behind all the others' accounts loomed this crucial issue of slavery. Yet who was this woman? The full title of her book describes her as 'a blockaded British subject' and the Introduction only gives the additional nugget of information that her initials were S.L.J. Inside the book there is a reproduction of a Federal Army pass issued to her in 1862 which gives her name as 'Miss Sarah L. Jones'. It is, of course, a daunting task to search for a Miss Jones in the overflowing records of nineteenth-century Britain and America. Swayed, no doubt, by the prospect of such a labour, I began to wonder whether 'Miss Jones' had ever existed. It occurred to me that her book could have been a clever piece of Confederate propaganda. The Confederacy had some remarkably able writers in its service in London: anyone who reads the well-known *Memoirs of the Confederate War of Independence* by the dashing Prussian officer, Heros von Borcke, can see that this scintillating account could not have sprung unaided from the pen of a gigantic German cavalryman who had fought as a volunteer for the Southern cause. Major von Borcke actually existed and he was a genuine hero, but he had a Virginian novelist as his ghostwriter in London. Might not a similar feat have been performed with 'Miss Jones'?

Then, on a visit to Washington, I decided to look at a copy of the Jones book in the Rare Books Room of the Library of Congress. Two decades after its publication, 'Miss Jones' had noted on this copy in her careful handwriting that her real name was Catherine Hopley. I began to take heart at finding out something about her. Finding a Hopley is certainly easier than finding a Jones. I had one diversion when I was misled by an article about one of her employers, the wartime Governor of Florida, which claimed that her name was Miss Hapley, but this soon proved to be a typographical error. I was still puzzled as to the reasons why she had taken such pains to hide her identity. Of course it was easy to understand why she was discreet about the names of her Southern friends in the midst of a rancorous war, when *habeas corpus* had been suspended and Federal fortresses closed round outspoken critics,[*] but why should an English governess, safe in London, be concerned if her name appeared on the title page of a book published in her own country? The answer came – as such historical answers often do – by pure chance. While doing some research on another topic, I happened to be looking through a book about life in mid-Victorian Britain when I saw a reference to the 'Hopley Divorce Case and Scandal'.

Once I had read the newspapers from the spring and summer of 1860, I realised why Catherine Hopley had taken such pains to hide her name. In the 1860s the name of Hopley meant only one thing: the sensational story of a schoolmaster who flogged a boy to death. The name was kept in the news by a controversial divorce case that developed from the tragedy. It still proved difficult to find out any details about Catherine Hopley herself or her connection with this case. Anyone – particularly a woman on her own – who wished to remain anonymous in the nineteenth century, an age in which the average person rarely was confronted by the form-

---

[*] Catherine Hopley's book appeared in 1863, by which time large parts of Virginia were occupied by Federal troops. She had no idea what had happened to her friends and it was safer not to give their names.

filling beloved of modern bureaucrats, did not have to take any special pains. Fortunately I discovered that late in her life, in the last years of the nineteenth century and the first years of the twentieth, Catherine Hopley did fill in a form when she applied to the Royal Literary Fund for help. The few facts I found in the Fund's files at last proved that 'the blockaded British subject' was a real person and an author of some distinction.[1] Her first book, *Life in the South*, is a tribute to the heroism of others, but there is something heroic in her own life, both in Britain and in America. There were thousands of single women in both countries who, like Catherine Hopley, devoted themselves to education and to writing, women who received little reward and no fame for their tireless work. By uncovering the basic outline of such a life as Catherine Hopley's, some small tribute can be paid to those who did so much and yet received so little in return.

FIRST TRIP TO AMERICA

Catherine Cooper Hopley was born near Canterbury on 5 October 1817. She came from a family that produced several other talented people. Edward William John Hopley, who was, I believe, her elder brother, achieved some fame as an artist of those domestic scenes that delighted the Victorians. He was also the inventor of a mathematical system of measuring faces for portraits. Another of her brothers, Thomas, was the author of pamphlets on educational reform which campaigned for a wider curriculum and the importance of exercise, although his real fame came from his trial for manslaughter. She spent much of her early life in Lewes, a prosperous market town in Sussex. We know nothing of her education but she was certainly of a bookish disposition throughout her life. She must have received some training in art as she contributed sketches to the *Illustrated London News* in the 1860s and later provided illustrations for a history of the United States. Throughout her life she had a strong interest in natural history, and she eventually made a name for herself in the field of insect studies. Perhaps some of this interest came from her brother, Edward, who, before he became an artist, was also interested in science and planned to become a doctor. All of this would have meant that the family had some access to money. Catherine Hopley seems to have been an active member of the Church of England. This fact, and the attainments of herself and her brothers, indicate a prosperous middle-class background.

Certainly she was well off enough to book a first-class fare when, at the age of thirty-six, she sailed for America at the end of June 1854. This is the earliest episode of her life of which I have managed to find any account. She dropped a few meagre facts about the first of her many transatlantic voyages in an anonymous article she wrote for a religious publication called *The Sunday at Home: A Family Magazine for Sabbath Reading*, which was meant to provide inspiration and discreet entertainment for people who would not open a novel or newspaper on a Sunday. Catherine Hopley's 'Two

Sabbaths on the Atlantic' shows how religious services on transatlantic crossings were often a source of tension. The travel books of other voyagers frequently allude to these services at sea and, human nature being what it is, one reads more complaints than compliments. American travellers and some English Dissenters were thrown into fanatical fury at the idea of the ship's captain reading Morning Prayer from the Book of Common Prayer. One American lady insisted this was a perfect instance of 'English impertinence which ought to be steadfastly resisted by all Americans'.* Cunard's most famous captain was even said to swear when hunting for his prayer book: 'Damn it, why wasn't this put where it belongs!' Sometimes, if there was a clergyman on board, he would be asked – or even forced – to take the service, as is still the case on the few passenger ships that cross the Atlantic. When Catherine Hopley appeared at her first shipboard service she was startled to see an American passenger push himself forward. He was a 'rationalist' minister from Massachusetts (presumably of some Unitarian sect) and he began a harangue that went on so long that some passengers fell asleep and others of even greater sense left. This 'rationalist' had a fixation on the number seven, and a great deal of his discourse revolved round this magic number. Naturally much of his sermon was devoted to broadcasting his own political theories, and he spent much happy time describing which prominent politicians were on their way to the seventh ring of hell.[2] For Catherine Hopley this was a shock because in those days Anglican clergymen were not as inclined as they are today to haul their political nostrums into the pulpit. This spectacle was a good introduction to the increasingly divided country on whose shores she was about to step.

Unlike all the other women in this book, Catherine Hopley already had family settled there. Her sister had married an American and they had been living in Indiana for some time. In her *Life in the South* she also mentions that she had numerous relatives 'scattered throughout the Northern states'. One of them, John Hopley, probably her brother, was a journalist in Ohio. He became the editor of a newspaper which supported the rising Republican party. By 1858 Catherine Hopley was settled in Cleveland, Ohio, where she earned her living by taking pupils. Four years after her arrival in America she received the offer of a position to teach music and to head the Arts Department at the nearby Western Reserve Eclectic Institute, which later became Hiram College. When this offer

---

* There were always vigilant, and one hopes dyspeptic, busybodies prowling round transatlantic ships in the nineteenth century. One American lady-evangelist, Phoebe Palmer, on her way to 'Evangelistic Labor' in Britain in 1859 was horrified to see 'a duly accredited Congregational minister and a Baptist minister together at a game of *chess* in the presence of a score of beholders'. Another busybody, the Rev. Robert Breckinridge of Baltimore, already annoyed at having to drink four different wines at each dinner, was aghast to spot an Anglican clergyman with a chess board. Naturally Breckinridge felt compelled to offer his advice: 'I do not believe that Saul of Tarsus ever traveled with a chess board in *his luggage.*'

arrived she was torn between the idea of remaining in Cleveland or becoming a teacher in an eastern city or in Canada 'where I might perhaps be better understood or appreciated'. Here we see the several characteristics she would show throughout her life: restlessness, indecisiveness and a resentment of those who failed to appreciate her. Yet she also showed a strong sense of independence. Her reply to James A. Garfield, the Institute's President, did not have the deferential tone of a nineteenth-century governess. Her letter is that of an independent woman, aware of her abilities and anxious to use them. She asked for further details about the Institute and told Garfield that she would wish to teach drawing and painting as well as music. By the next week she was clearly turning against the idea of moving to Hiram in spite of a letter urging her to do so from Lucretia Rudolph who was teaching there. Catherine Hopley remained in Cleveland, and Lucretia Rudolph married James Garfield within a few months: the beginning of a marriage that would end in the White House when he became the twentieth President of the United States. Although he is the least important President in American history – he was assassinated three months after taking office in 1881 – Garfield had one staggering accomplishment, which as far as is known has not been inherited by any of his successors: he could write in Latin with one hand while at the same time writing in Greek with the other. No doubt such ambidextrous skill is fertile training for any politician. Although she did not take up the position at Hiram, Catherine Hopley became friendly with the Garfields and eventually became the governess to their children.[3]

At the time of the raid on Harper's Ferry in the autumn of 1859, Catherine Hopley was visiting friends in some other mid-western state; she heard many people discussing the great topic of the day even though she had long given up 'in despair' any attempt to understand American politics. Like most of the other women in this book she had a restless temperament and a love of travel which would take her back and forth across the Atlantic several times in her life and even to South Africa in her seventies. 'It is astounding', she writes in her book, 'how quickly a zest for travelling grows upon you in such a country as the United States where you soon learn to measure distances by hundreds of miles, instead of by tens.' Although she felt 'at home' in America, she had one great problem, 'too expensive taste'. When she heard people discussing life in the South, an idea began to form in her mind that she could become a governess in a Southern family where she would enjoy a comfortable life in a warm climate. She had heard some of her friends saying that Southerners were renowned for their hospitality. However 'a whole posse of my relatives in the North' warned her that this was not a sensible idea at such a dangerous time. Of course, of all the women in this book only Mrs Burlend's travel to America could be classified as 'sensible'. Probably Catherine Hopley's relatives' opposition only stimulated her desire for a new adventure as she says that she was 'anxious to preserve my independence'. She went ahead with her plan 'to take up my abode in a Southern family, and give lessons in the "ornamental branches", as all accomplishments are called'. This would 'afford delightful opportunities of at once enjoying a home, benefiting by the climate, and seeing the South'.

Anyone with some knowledge of nineteenth-century England or with some familiarity with Victorian novels could well think this was nothing out of the ordinary. Yet in this, as in so many other aspects, the American South was different from the rest of the English-speaking world. There were relatively few governesses in Southern homes, where the few girls who received any formal education were usually sent to small local 'academies' or 'ladies' seminaries' or, sometimes, to convent schools in larger cities like Charleston or New Orleans. Sometimes they were sent to Northern schools. In the smaller towns scattered throughout the mainly rural South, clergymen and their wives or any widow with a vague pretence to learning could set up a small school. Here they provided the rudiments of education as well as what Catherine Hopley called the 'ornamental branches', by which she meant such lady-like accomplishments as French, music and drawing. Among the wealthy planters there had been a long tradition of employing men as tutors, some of whom were Englishmen or Europeans down on their luck. Governesses were an entirely different affair, particularly on a plantation with many slaves. Some of the Virginian planters, anxious as in so many other things to preserve their attachment to English traditions, continued to employ governesses. Yet these ladies normally had to be imported and women from the North or, even worse, from England were assumed to be fiercely anti-slavery. Thus John Washington, the last member of the family to live at Mount Vernon, expressed the worry felt by many other planters when he wrote to a clergyman who had recommended a governess: 'I presume that Miss N. is sound (according to Southern Views) on the subject of Slavery. This is indispensable, as I would not on any consideration, have the views of "Higher Law Abolitionists" instilled into the minds of my children.'[4]

When Catherine Hopley placed her advertisement as 'an English lady' in newspapers in Richmond, Virginia, no doubt several planters would have shared Colonel Washington's fears, fears all the stronger after the John Brown raid. Nevertheless she received seven replies and after three months in negotiations she made her choice, little suspecting 'the singular and lamentable chain of circumstances' which would lead to a 'long, frightful and perhaps lasting separation' from her family in the North and in England. Any planter who feared an advertisement from 'an English lady' would have found some justification in the fact that Catherine Hopley was, indeed, an opponent of slavery. She admits that she had read and been influenced, as had so many people in England, by Harriet Beecher Stowe's novel, *Uncle Tom's Cabin*, a book that was even more popular in Britain than it had been in America.[5] She expected to see 'lacerated figures ... toiling to their daily task, with the cruel task-master and his frightful whip bringing up the rear'. However she was resolved 'to judge for myself' and what she would see would surprise and amaze her.

In the spring of 1860 – exactly a year before the war began – she crossed from Ohio, into the western parts of Virginia. She followed the route Mrs Trollope had taken thirty years before and stopped at Wheeling where she was not impressed by the 'dirty, desolate, half-built villages, where the inhabitants would seem to live in coal and *upon* coal, to build with coal, and vie with it in blackness'. One assumes she had never visited the valleys of South Wales or the villages of the West Riding of Yorkshire. Yet she took heart from the splendid mountain scenery, vibrant with the colours of spring. As a good child of her age she found a moral message in what she saw: 'Nature is preaching to us her majesty in lessons of philosophy.'

She stopped at Harper's Ferry, still today a place of spectacular scenery where the mountains part to allow the Shenandoah River to join the Potomac. Here her thoughts turned to recent events and what she called 'that woeful and mistaken enterprise' which had taken place less than six months before. She carried on to Washington, which she found a 'city of gardens, monuments, and marble palaces; honoured in appellation, favoured by nature, distinguished in authority, and great in responsibility'. As she looked about the city she 'was full of pride and sympathy for a great and promising republic, and felt an interest in its future welfare almost equally that towards my own country'. 'It is impossible for a foreigner', she continued, 'to visit Washington without being struck with the liberality and courtesy displayed in the arrangement of all the public buildings to accommodate visitors, and more particular in the Capitol.' While she was impressed by the Library of Congress, still in the Capitol building, and by the 'quiet dignity' of the Senate, she shared the revulsion of so many of her predecessors at the vile effects of tobacco chewing. It was impossible, she said, 'to stir without kicking' the spittoons and she was sickened at the circles of brown spit deposited round them by those whose aim was somewhat faulty. Although she had a friend 'whose husband held an important public office which brought her into acquaintance with all the notorieties of the season' she decided not to go to any of the weekly receptions given in the White House: the 'motley crowd' that descended on the building was too much for a 'woman's curiosity'. This is unfortunate as she could have provided a portrait of President Buchanan, as Lady Emmeline had of President Taylor.

In the Senate she attended a debate about the route of the first transcontinental railway. This also increased sectional tensions as each region wanted it to pass through their states. In the House of Representatives she listened to the debate on the strange activities of the Mormons in the territory of Utah, another vexed subject that seemed likely to lead to military intervention. The political atmosphere around her spurred her to state her own view about a woman's role in politics, a view similar to those of all the other women in this book except Fanny Wright.

In Catherine Hopley's opinion, a woman should 'exercise her true "women's rights", not by usurping the power and office of the other sex, but by informing and cultivating her mind to increase her influence in her true sphere, the sphere of HOME'. The planter in the Southern home to which she was making her way would have breathed a sigh of relief at such a traditional sentiment.

A VIRGINIA PLANTATION

Apparently Catherine Hopley was not hurrying to meet her new employer as she now turned north and went to Baltimore where she boarded a steamer, the *William Selden*, on one of its twice weekly journeys to the 'northern neck' of Virginia. Unlike Mrs Trollope and Rebecca Burlend, she thoroughly enjoyed steamboat travel. On board she was waited on by a black woman who was 'exceedingly gracious, not to say patronizing, but overwhelmingly polite, yet with so much of self-respect'. This behaviour confused her, as had a similar attitude by a black waiter in Maryland: neither fitted the caricatures she had seen in Mrs Stowe. They must, she felt, be freed blacks. She contented herself with walking on the ladies' deck, relaxing in the spacious state room, doing crochet work, recording her expenses and, of course, writing her impressions as the boat moved through Chesapeake Bay. Then it turned into the Rappahannock River, where for two centuries giant hogsheads of tobacco had been rolled down to landing places to be loaded onto ships for Britain: it was at one of these landing places that her new employer had arranged to meet her. At this point in her book, she begins to disguise names and places: thus she tells us she was met by 'the venerable Dr. W., the dreaded "slaveholder", whose house was to be my home'.[6] He was portly, about forty-five years old and polite. He removed his hat, bowed, and greeted her. In her book we are told that Dr W. said, 'Miss Jones from S., I presume?', but I suspect she was still using her real name of Catherine Hopley. He ordered his servants to sort out her luggage and gave her the back seat of his carriage. This was an honour she appreciated because the back seat was preferable to the front, not just because one was not travelling backwards but because one was safe from any 'embarrassment' due to the horses. The rule applied even when the carriage was closed.

Catherine Hopley was perplexed and quite frankly displeased to see so many black people round her. Like young Victoria Wortley, it was a sight that was new to her and she was frightened. She was positively annoyed at Uncle Ike, the coachman whose manner to Dr W. seemed 'disrespectful' to her English feelings. The relationship between 'slave' and 'master' was one that would perplex her for months to come. Seated next to her in the carriage was the sixteen-year-old girl who would be her pupil. 'Cinta', as she is called in the book, was a tall, handsome girl 'of a fine well-developed form, with the exception of the stooping shoulders which more or less disfigure all American girls'.

After a journey of ten miles Catherine Hopley found herself at the plantation of 'Forest Rill', which would be her home until July. Most of her time in the South would be spent on large plantations or in hotels in Richmond. It might be thought, therefore, that her experience of Southern life was confined to the wealthy and to slave-holders. After all, the 1860 Census showed that only some 346,000 people out of a population of eight million in the thirteen Southern states actually owned any slaves. Of the minority who did own slaves, the largest group (189,000) owned from two to fifty while 77,000 Southerners owned only one. The plantation life experienced by Catherine Hopley was that which would be immortalised in novels and Hollywood films. Yet plantation slavery was the exception, not the norm. Likewise, life in Virginia was not the same as on the farms of the South's rapidly expanding frontier in states such as Florida, Arkansas, Mississippi or Texas. Having said all this, Catherine Hopley would travel a great deal through the South and would meet a wide cross-section of people. Even so, her conclusions, as she readily admitted, were based only on what she had seen or heard from reliable sources. It is the size of the homes she visited, not the life or attitudes she described, that was unusual.

Forest Rill was a two-storey building with a large hall, originally the same 'run' that Mrs Burlend had found in Illinois cabins, that divided the house through the middle with rooms on both sides. She found that the plantation was almost a self-contained world. While groceries were bought once a year from 'up North' – which normally meant Baltimore – all else was produced or killed at home. She was surprised at the farm's 'want of finish, and untidiness' and the 'impudence' of blacks towards Dr W. After she had been introduced to 'Aunt Ailsey' who greeted her with a curtsey and a 'Howdy' she was shown to her room by Mrs W. and Cinta.[7] Here she was amazed to see 'servants' enter and leave at will to deposit her luggage or lay a fire. Her hostess 'expressed no surprise to see the invasion of negroes in my apartment, neither were the Topsies at all abashed by their presence, and continued their undisturbed study of my physiognomy'. It would take her several days to get used to the fact that black servants had the run of the house and entered rooms whenever they wanted, without knocking. She soon learned, as Lady Emmeline had done, that the term 'slave' was rarely used as Southerners preferred 'servant' or 'people'. She was assigned a young girl named Flora as her own maid and was shocked when she offered to sleep on the floor in front of the fire if the English lady wanted it: the English lady did not want it.

Once seated at the tea-table another illusion vanished. Dr W. did not employ an overseer for, as he told Catherine Hopley, 'I superintend my own plantation ... and I prefer to look after my own people; and then I know they are properly treated.' (It was only then that she realised that the blacks she had seen about the place actually *were* slaves: their lack of deference, their friendliness and their habit of shaking her hand when introduced had made her think they were free.) Just as the new English governess listened to Dr W. describe his relationship with 'his people' so she listened to Uncle Cassius, the old butler to Dr W.'s brother, Colonel W. His story, which she tried to render in dialect, is worth quoting at length:

I b'long'd to ole Massa Harry ebber sin' he [Colonel W.'s father] was married. He an' me was jes' about of an age 'n' I tended him all his life, an' when he married Miss Molly, my ole massa [Colonel W.'s grandfather] gie'd me to him. I allers 'tended to him when he was a boy, an' went out hunting and shooting wid him in vacations; 'n' I trabbled wid him all over de Norf, an' down to New Orle*ee*ns, an' wharebber Massa Harry went he allers took *me*. Den he married, an' my ole massa gave me to him 'long wid my wife an' family, an' some o' th'others dat b'longed to dis heah estate, all to young Massa Harry ... So he took me into de house, an' my wife, Miss Molly took *her* into de house, an' all our children was bringed up in de house to be house-servants too, till dey married. Dat ar leetle yellow boy in de dining-room now, he's my gran'son; his muvver was my younges' daughter, and she married a servant what b'longed to old Capp'n Planter over to Caroline [County]; so de Capp'n bought her, an' she went and libbed 'long'd her husband over thar. Den I outlib ole Massa Harry ... but young Massa Harry [Colonel W.] he's boun' to take care o' me, an' he *will* too; an' I lib an' die on dis heah place whar I b'longs to.

This was not the world of Mrs Stowe. Catherine Hopley was, she admitted, 'greatly reassured, and with an immense dread off my mind, that so far as my immediate home was concerned, no very harrowing scenes were likely to endanger my position in the slaveholder's family'. She still had no doubt that there were 'harrowing scenes': it was just that they were elsewhere, waiting to shock her in due course.

Catherine Hopley was not as impressed with the appearance of the slave 'quarters' or cabins on this Virginia plantation as Lady Emmeline had been on her visit to the Taylor plantation. While several of the cabins had gardens, pigs and chickens, none was very neat. She was, however, impressed by the manners of her hosts and of their friends and relations who lived on nearby farms and whose children would also come to her for lessons. She heard for the first time the letters 'F.F.V.' – 'First Families of Virginia' – and she was made aware that it was a 'coveted distinction'.[8] If the people she met were not 'over-much given to intellectual pursuits' they were 'home-loving, easy, contented beings, unsullied by contact with the world, simple-minded and guileless more than any other people under the sun'. She soon was full of praise for people who had inherited 'a natural and graceful dignity of character and deportment from long standing associations, and [who] combine in their sentiments and habits a singular mixture of the genuine aristocrat, with the stanch yeoman of England'. It may be remembered that Mrs Trollope had specifically exempted

Virginians from her description of the loutish behaviour she had observed
among Congressmen. Catherine Hopley noted with evident pleasure that
'all deferred to me with great politeness', but she soon grew tired, as
many English visitors still do, at the cross-questioning she had to
endure regarding England. 'You English ladies walk a great deal? Why
is it? ... Have you ever seen the Queen? What is she like? How tall is
she? Pretty? etc.'

This new world in which she found herself never ceased to amaze,
interest, amuse and infuriate her. She found it difficult to understand
why white people were called by their Christian names – Massa Harry
– by their slaves, and elderly blacks by the honorific title of Aunt or
Uncle. Nor could she understand the carefree attitude towards locking
doors or windows despite all the talk of a possible 'slave uprising'. She
was also puzzled by the all-night parties and religious meetings that
went on in the cabins and she noted that this led to bad food and poor
service the next day. Even on ordinary days she found it difficult to
adjust to the constant interruptions by the 'people' asking 'massa', even
at meal times, to come and look at a servant who was ill. Of course much
of this behaviour resembled that of late medieval or Tudor England. If
a visitor from sixteenth-century England could have been wafted to the
nineteenth-century South (as Mark Twain's Connecticut Yankee was
wafted to the court of King Arthur), he would not have been shocked by
this exotic mixture of formality and informality. Another custom that
was strange to her Victorian propriety was the never-ending shaking of
hands: 'In the course of visiting about the neighbourhood, one discovered so many unexpected uncles and aunts who presented their ebony
palms to the stranger, that I confess that my philanthropy was somewhat tried by this perpetual shaking of hands.' She was astounded later
when staying in a Richmond hotel to see guests shake hands with Negro
waiters and used her observation to make a point about Southern life
to her fellow Englishmen: 'Yes, dear reader, strange as it may appear
to us to think of shaking hands with the footman in attendance at table,
it is by no means uncommon in the land of slavery.' Servants not only
entered rooms at will but would peep in at windows while the family sat
down to dinner. Black children would be called to the table by the
daughter of the house and given portions of food, and if it was raining
outside the children would come in and curl up before the fire on the
floor of the dining room during meal times. At night, while the family
read or played games in the sitting room or listened to someone playing
the piano, Negro children would gather round the open windows to enjoy
the music: 'No one', she noted, 'takes any notice of them.'

Like other English visitors to the South, Catherine Hopley was not
impressed by the quality of the slaves' work: 'Never in a hurry, never with
any sense of responsibility; one good English or Irish labourer would have
done the work of any three of them in the same time, and much more

efficiently ... "How can the Virginians endure it!" I exclaimed a thousand times.' Thackeray, who visited the South twice in the 1850s, had come to a similar conclusion: 'It is the dearest and worst kind of service.'[9] Of course what both the English novelist and the English governess forgot was that most of the slaves they saw lacked the power and therefore the incentive to improve their condition that Lady Emmeline had seen with Daniel Webster's free black servants in Massachusetts. Furthermore, both Catherine Hopley's and Thackeray's main experience was with 'servants' in houses or hotels; they had relatively little contact with those who worked in the fields.

Religion caused some difficulties, though not nearly as great as those faced by Mrs Trollope. Like her, Catherine Hopley was a loyal member of the Church of England, but the nearest Episcopal Church was twelve miles away while the Methodist Chapel was ten miles closer. Furthermore, her employers were Methodists. When she joined them on Sunday morning she was not much more pleased with American Methodism than Rebecca Burlend had been. Catherine Hopley had mistaken the Methodist Chapel for a barn on her first trip to Forest Rill and was surprised on entering to find a gallery for blacks and two doors, one for men and one for women.* The order of worship and sermon seemed vulgar to her and, not surprisingly, left her unmoved: 'The next sabbath might be passed as profitably in my own room, in the event of having no other church to attend.' She was interested to know that the chapel had been built through the generosity of one planter and was struck when watching families arrive for church to see that they largely told the time by reference to the sun. There were simply very few clocks about. (Of course this was true of many English villages as well.)

The prim English governess was staggered at 'so great a want of discipline and good training' as regards the slaves and wondered how order was maintained. In the wake of Harper's Ferry and the threat of a 'slave uprising', were Southerners not afraid? The militia was, after all, already drilling. A young girl living only a few miles from Catherine Hopley was full of fear and when she wrote her memoirs as an old woman she recalled: 'We knew John Brown was dead, [but] we knew Mamma was still afraid of him, so we were too.'[10] Colonel W., Catherine Hopley's employer's brother, laughed at such fears: 'We only think our servants dangerous when the Yankees come among them.' On reflection, the Englishwoman noted that there was little Southerners could do given the fact that blacks made up at least a third of a population thinly spread over a vast region. The whites' security, she felt, had two sources. There was 'a natural reverence and awe of "white folks" ' among blacks, combined with a

---

*In the new churches being built in England's expanding suburbs, parish churches had free seating instead of the eighteenth-century system of rented box pews. While not having two doors they did divide the nave into two sections, one for men and one for women.

'devotion to their owners which seems instinctive'. She was beginning to learn, however, that this reverence and devotion did not extend to white people outside the family. She was outraged to see her maid rifling through her private things. When challenged neither the girl nor her mother, Aunt Ailsey, indicated any feeling of guilt. Their argument was that the girl had not 'troubled' – stolen – anything and that therefore the Englishwoman's outrage was out of place.

Catherine Hopley soon discovered that life in rural America had other drawbacks. There was only one post a week, on Saturday, at Tappahannock, a small town ten miles away on the Rappahannock River. Each family had to go to the post office to collect their letters and newspapers. (They could also go on Wednesday to Creek Landing if it were urgent to post or collect letters.) Virginia, like most states, was sparsely populated, at least by English standards: the 1850 census showed that even after 231 years of settlement there were only twenty-three people to the square mile. Richmond was the only city of any size and there were few towns. As in the rest of America, forests, whose extent had only shrunk by twenty-five per cent since the first settlers arrived from England, still dominated the landscape. These, combined with periodic flooding, made travel difficult and frequently impossible. The woods, despite their drawbacks when it came to travel, fascinated the English visitor with their dogwoods, azaleas, rhododendrons, tulip and magnolia trees. She, in turn, fascinated her hosts and their servants by her devotion to long walks in the woods: later when she was in Florida one slave told her, 'You be allers a hunting weeds, ain't you, missus?' She already had a great knowledge of plants and animals and later in her life would be acknowledged as something of an expert. On her walks she was intrigued by an entire network of footpaths created by blacks as they walked between farms and plantations on errands or to visit friends.

Like all English visitors to America, Catherine Hopley was intrigued at the differences in language. In her notes she carefully listed words and phrases which were unknown to her: 'bluffs' for cliffs; to 'build' a fire rather than to 'lay' one; 'howdy', usually confined to blacks and a corruption of 'how do you do'; to 'come by' meaning to visit; 'mighty' as an adverb for 'very' (a seventeenth-century survival which had died out in England); 'right smart' for large amount of ('Done right smart knitting today'); a 'heap' for a large amount of; 'done' used for the past tense of a verb, normally confined to slaves ('I done go [I went] to town yesterday'); to 'buy up'; a 'spell' meaning a period, like a 'spell of bad weather'; 'overshoes' for galoshes; 'to take an interest'; a 'cord of wood'; to 'save my life' used to express an excessive degree of something ('I couldn't stop laughing to save my life'); to 'take a holiday'; a 'fine man' (meaning one of estimable mental qualities); 'sold out' and to 'sell out'; 'thrilling' as an adverb meaning 'exciting' ('a thrilling article in the newspaper'); 'cold spell'; the 'boss' (from Dutch settlers); 'ugly' to mean bad mannered; 'along' meaning 'stops at'

('The boat comes along tomorrow') and 'shoot' meaning a wooden slide such as those used for cotton.

By the summer of 1860, however, things began to change. Cinta became ill and her mother took her and a slave, whom the local doctor had not been able to help, to Baltimore for expert medical attention. It appears that while Catherine Hopley was happy at Forest Rill, the arrangement was not working out. The position of a governess was not an easy one, particularly for someone as old as she was – forty-three was a far more advanced age than it is now – and someone as set in her ways. One Southern girl commented about this time: 'I never see a governess that my heart does not ache for her. I think of the nameless, numberless, insults and trials she is forced to submit to; of the hopeless, thankless task that is imposed on her, to which she is expected to submit without a murmur; of all her griefs and agony shut up in her heart, and I cry Heaven help a governess.'[11]

TROUBLE AT HOME

In July 1860 both Catherine Hopley and the country she was living in were going through 'griefs and agony'. Troubling news had arrived from England and she decided that she must go home. As she made her way to New York City she would have seen the signs of the impending presidential election. The last great bond of Union, the Democratic Party, had split, like so many other organisations and even churches, into Northern and Southern wings. Now four candidates were competing for the Presidency and people feared that the least known of the four, Abraham Lincoln – who had grown up in Illinois in a log cabin such as Mrs Burlend had known – would be elected and thus precipitate the secession of the Southern states. As Catherine Hopley boarded her ship in New York on 14 July she had two strange companions on the voyage home: a pair of mockingbirds in their cage. These Southern birds were unknown in England. Their sprightly sounds may have distracted her somewhat as did the thrilling sight of HMS *Hero* and her two accompanying warships bringing the Prince of Wales on the first official visit of a member of the Royal Family to Canada and the United States. In contrast to her experience on her first transatlantic voyage, she derived comfort from the religious services on her trip eastward. In her article on Sunday aboard ship she spoke warmly of the Virginian minister, a Presbyterian, who conducted the service. She could not help but contrast him to the ranting fanatic from Massachusetts who had subjected his fellow passengers to a political harangue disguised as a sermon on her first crossing in 1854.[12]

In her book she adopted a coy manner when speaking of herself, and of the reason for this visit she only tells us that 'duty seemed to recall me to my native land, from which I began to feel quite an alien, and my return to the Western continent was doubtful'. Behind this prim façade lay a dreadful tragedy. Thomas Hopley, Catherine's brother, had become a schoolmaster and was, according to the *Annual Register*, 'a person of high attainments and irreproachable character'. He was a man of definite views about education and, as we have seen, he had a strong belief in the value of physical education. He appears to have been an efficient schoolmaster. In mid-Victorian England the rapidly expanding ranks of prosperous business and professional men demanded more schools to educate their sons. Private schools sprang up to prepare young boys for traditional public schools or to equip older boys for university or a profession. Thomas Hopley catered for this growing demand and his school at Eastbourne had the added attraction of benefiting from sea air, which Victorians believed the perfect environment, especially for sickly youths. The fees at Hopley's school for 'the sons of persons of a high rank in life' were large: £180 a year, a sum far above the yearly income of many government clerks as well as most curates in the country.

Among Hopley's pupils was a fifteen-year-old boy named Reginald Channell Cancellor, whose father was one of the Masters of the Court of Common Pleas. According to Hopley's barrister, young Reginald was of 'weak intellect' and Hopley himself, again according to his own barrister, was 'distorted'. The schoolmaster could not understand young Cancellor's inability to learn and he attributed this – as Victorians were all too apt to do – to laziness and obstinacy. In fact the boy suffered from what Victorians called 'water on the brain'. There could be only one cure: young Cancellor was subjected to continual punishment. On the night of 21 April 1860 the other boys at the school at 22 Grand Parade, Eastbourne were awakened by harrowing screams. It appears that Hopley got carried away in an excessive flogging of the boy with a rope. This went on for at least two hours. As Hopley explained at his trial: 'When I brought the rope and inflicted punishment for the last time I burst into tears and Cancellor then placed his head on my breast and asked to be allowed to say his lesson. I afterwards prayed with him and I left him saying, "Heaven knows I have done my duty to that poor lad".' When the boy was found dead the next morning, servants began to gossip and Hopley's wife's attempt to cover the horrific injuries with long stockings and kid gloves proved useless. The police were soon summoned.

Hopley's brother, Edward, was by this time moderately successful with his painting. For years he had been working on a vast canvas, 'The Building of a Pyramid by an Early Egyptian Queen', which he had exhibited in 1859. He now sold this to raise money for his brother's defence and went to one of the leading counsels of the day, Serjeant Ballantine. Ballantine described the artist, whom he had known for some time, as a man 'with some genius, but eccentric'. Presumably the family must have written to Catherine to tell her of the tragedy, but the two weeks required for the letter to reach America and the lengthy delays it took for the post to reach her in the Virginia countryside no doubt explain why she complained so bitterly about the delays in getting her mail at Forest Rill. It must have been early June before she knew of the 'Eastbourne Tragedy', as the press were calling it. Within a month she had severed her links with Forest Rill to hurry to New York to get a passage. No doubt all the time she must have been in dread that American newspapers, who took much of their news from the English press, would play up the story. Southern editors might well be particularly anxious to have their revenge for the numerous stories about the flogging of slaves.

Catherine Hopley may have reached England just in time for the trial which began in Lewes on 23 July. If they had favourable weather, ships could now cross the Atlantic within a fortnight – the Prince of Wales' had done just that. Hopley's barrister said in his memoirs that 'the plea of insanity was not set up, although for the credit of human nature I could wish that it should have been'. Thomas Hopley was found guilty of manslaughter and sentenced to four years penal servitude. He spent some of his time in prison drawing up a plan for a 'grand model educational establishment' where he would, of course, be the master and his wife who had been trained by him for the purpose would be 'the model Christian mistress'. Hopley was pleased to hear that 'Aunt Katie' (Catherine) had visited his wife who had retired to a country cottage.[13]

RICHMOND, VIRGINIA

The disgrace and ruin of the most prosperous member of the Hopley family no doubt left the others in a dreadful state. Suddenly there was at least some glimmer of hope from America. Catherine received a letter from Virginia from a man she calls Dr Rowell, who had been one of those who had replied to her advertisement in the Richmond newspapers a year earlier. She had, of course, chosen Dr W., but now that Rowell had heard she had left Forest Rill, he offered her the position of governess in his household. This at least would give her some employment: few households in England would want a Hopley in charge of its children in 1860. It may well be that her visit to her unhappy sister-in-law had been to bid farewell. Her ship, the *Fulton*, arrived in New York at the beginning of November 1860 after a rough crossing lasting twelve days. She stepped ashore to find herself in the midst of the presidential campaign with its four parties competing in political parades and torch-light processions. She set off almost immediately for Virginia by ship. On this trip she complained about the heat on board as temperatures soared to 100 degrees Fahrenheit and there was no fresh air.

The ship sailed up the James River – where the first English settlers had landed more than two and a half centuries before and where the first slaves had been sold to them a decade later – to Richmond, Virginia's capital, where she disembarked two days before voting began. Catherine Hopley's first task was to meet Dr Rowell, but when she found him she was horrified to hear that he had never received her acceptance of his offer and had consequently sent his daughters away to school. 'Well!', she wrote, 'this was a time for actions, not regrets.' She was a 'lady travelling alone' and knew no one in a strange city. Her first task was to find a boarding-house which would be cheaper than her hotel. This accomplished, she was able to get 'a stray pupil or two' and planned to spend the winter in Richmond. That she was able to settle into a strange city, particularly at a time of great tension, and find not only a place to live but a way to support herself, shows what a resourceful woman she was. As regards her future, things seemed more secure. For Richmond, however, this was not the case: 'a funeral cloud seemed to hang over the city' as people realised that the next President would be Abraham Lincoln. The reaction she encountered was muted: 'We will see what his policy is.' This meant waiting until March when the inauguration would take place.

Richmond was a large city, at least by Southern standards, with a population of 37,910 of whom 11,699 were slaves and 2,576 were freed blacks. Unusually for a Southern city it boasted manufacturing industries which included a famous ironworks that would soon be working round the clock forging cannons. Catherine Hopley genuinely liked Richmond and the surrounding area where there were many old houses and churches; these gave it something of an English atmosphere. However she did not care for the city's principal industry, processing tobacco. While some thirty factories prepared tobacco for shipment there was still plenty for home consumption. Like almost all English visitors she was disgusted with its most glaring result. The city, she said, was 'redolent of tobacco' and 'filthy with it' as men walked about chewing their wads of tobacco. Pavements or side-walks – the terms were then interchangeable – were uniformly marked by spit as today they are by chewing-gum: '*In toto*, the streets of Richmond are simply disgusting.'

As she picked her way round this vile detritus, she thought about Lincoln's election and how the growing talk of disunion might affect her personally. She had found that while Northerners were jealous and envi-ous of England, her industrial might and expanding empire, Southerners were different. They were 'more cordial ... in their welcome to the descen-dants of their ancestral England'.* However, the atmosphere now changed somewhat. She now had to be careful because, as her relatives in the North

*The value placed on ancestral links with England by Virginians of old families is best illustrated in *Recollections Grave and Gay* by Mrs Burton Harrison, the wife of President Davis's personal secretary. Throughout her memoirs she mentions numerous connexions with England and how 'British lined ladies' in her childhood home in Alexandria loved to read all the accounts of Queen Victoria's daily activities in the *Illustrated London News*. Mrs Harrison was the grand-daughter of the ninth Lord Fairfax, who had lived in Virginia, but who had not normally used his title. After the end of the war, she and her mother, the Hon Monimia Cary, paid their first visit to England. As the mother stepped ashore she announced: 'Thank God, I have at last set foot upon the soil of home!' Another Virginian, John S. Wise, son of a former Governor, well summarises this attitude in the index entry in his memoirs, *The End of An Era*: 'English ancestors the best.'

had warned, people suspected she was an abolitionist. While fellow guests were happy to welcome the Englishwoman to their conversations about 'slavery', they would cease talking if she drew near when they were discussing any story of mistreatment of blacks. For her part she admits she was horrified when she saw advertisements in the newspapers for slave auctions and notices by those seeking information about runaway slaves. Southerners were always very sensitive about these two aspects of slavery. A few years before, Thackeray's secretary was lucky to escape without injury when he attempted to sketch the horrors of a slave auction, and in his *American Notes* Dickens had included many such notices. [14]

Even more than auctions and notices about runaway slaves, the breaking up of families, if one member was sold, caused understandable outrage in England and in the North. Catherine Hopley talked to 'Uncle Pete', the butler-handyman at her boarding-house, 'Warneford House', about this. He told her about his own separation from his father and brother and of the pain it still caused him. She noted down his story and included it in her book. While her aim was openly to show aspects of Southern life unknown to Englishmen and to encourage sympathy for the Confederacy, she also wanted to be truthful and show the bad as well as the good. This is what makes *Life in the South* so valuable, unlike some other accounts which are nothing but Confederate propaganda. She cited this case as it was 'the *only* case I met with during my whole residence in the South where I heard a negro speak so feelingly on the subject'.

Catherine Hopley used these winter months to observe life in a Southern city as before she had observed it on farms and plantations. She was especially fascinated by the lives of slaves in an urban setting. In her discussions and observations she discovered that owners frequently hired out their slaves on a year's contract if the slaves agreed. The blacks paid a percentage of their wages to their owners, kept the rest and lived as if they were free workers. If they were not happy the arrangement was not renewed. Their employers had to give them a written contract, provide adequate medical attention, food, lodging, two entire suits of clothes per year and 'every protection'. In Richmond, although some worked as domestic servants, many others worked in shops and in the tobacco factories. [15] She found that many of these blacks were guaranteed a 'servants' holiday' over Easter and Christmas and these tended to last two-and-a-half days and about ten days respectively – far longer than workers would get in England. They were also entitled to Christmas boxes or gifts. She was surprised to learn that Richmond's merchants regarded blacks as their best customers for clothes, sweets and 'finery' in general. She also visited one of the 'African Churches' where she was impressed by the numbers of 'very wealthy' members and by the beautiful singing, though she found the worship too 'demonstrative'.

One of Catherine Hopley's fellow lodgers told her that one of his 'people' worked as a waiter and was doing extremely well, so well that he could have bought his freedom. That he had no desire to do so amazed her but, she added, 'I discovered from time to time, that almost as many who are freed, either by will or by purchase, sell themselves back into slavery, as those whom we hear of as having run away'. There was a logical explanation for this strange behaviour: if free, they had no one to act as their protector, to provide free medical care, food, lodging and clothes or to look out for them in old age. Also, if they were hired out and earned their own living, their way of life would basically not alter if they were free. There was another factor, as Fanny Wright had discovered decades earlier: there was a deep fear of freed blacks in the slave states and the suspicion had been growing in recent years that they would either help slaves to escape or provide leadership in any slave uprising.

As December wore on, anxiety in Virginia began to turn into near panic. New laws were passed which expelled any newly freed slave from the state. Any freed black convicted of a crime was to be sold into slavery. Blacks could not congregate on street corners. Finally it became illegal for white men to harbour meetings of blacks. There were also new regulations regarding railway travel. 'Home Guards' were being formed throughout Virginia and this militant atmosphere was causing some businesses to fail. At last, on 20 December the telegraph lines brought the news: South Carolina, the most fanatical of the Southern states, had officially seceded from the American Union. Everyone knew this was the prelude to an unparalleled crisis, and Christmas was a muted affair. On Christmas Eve guests gathered for an 'oyster supper' (Virginia was famous for her oysters), but in the midst of the meal most of the men were called away as there was a rumour of a slave insurrection in a suburb of Richmond: it turned out to be some dozen blacks who were hoping for help from Northern contacts. Rumours and exaggerated accounts of small incidents like this had played a tremendous role in bringing the crisis to the boiling point. The South in 1860 resembled France in 1789 when 'the Great Fear' swept through the countryside arousing a terrified peasantry to storm the châteaux. At Warneford House there was a more immediate upset on Christmas Day when the landlady's nursemaid, one of those slaves hired by the year, handed in her notice and left for her holidays. Catherine Hopley wondered 'how my friends in systematic and deferential England would tolerate the slightest approach to such "freedom" even in a country of free white servants'. It is hardly surprising that, given all these tensions, she came down with a miserable cold. Nevertheless she struggled to St Paul's Episcopal Church near the Virginia Capitol Building to enjoy the comfort of hearing the familiar Christmas service.

The fourth day of the new year was observed in Virginia as a Day of Fasting and Prayer as requested by President Buchanan, but in some Northern states many Republican ministers ignored the President's request. They were led from Brooklyn by Harriet Beecher Stowe's brother, Henry Ward Beecher. He was the infamous 'political parson' of

Plymouth Church. (His hypocrisy in maintaining segregated seating in his church had infuriated Charles Dickens when he visited New York.) The level of public anxiety continued to rise: there were reports of acts of incendiarism and of cotton pouring into ports for export. In New Orleans alone some 2,480 bales, valued at over one million dollars, arrived in 36 hours over 2-3 January. As Virginia's legislature was called to consider the future, legislators poured into Richmond. At Warneford House there was a group from Virginia's western counties. Each stood over six feet in height, and the short English governess judged them to be 'remarkably fine specimens of humanity'. In these men Catherine Hopley met Southerners who owned no slaves – the overwhelming majority – and those who were against secession:

> The advocates for secession were the better educated and more polished among them; others appeared to be easy, quiet, jog-trotting sort of men, who had been born and bred in the Union, and who loved the Union for its own sake, as a principle, without ever having troubled themselves to ascertain how much of principle prevailed therein; and who came determined to uphold the Union for no particular reason.

She also observed that some were beginning to change their minds as the subject was debated. Yet many moderate Virginians struggled to find a compromise that could avoid disunion and war.

WAR COMES TO VIRGINIA

All these public affairs could not completely distract Catherine Hopley from worries about her own future. She was, therefore, delighted to receive an unexpected offer of a position as governess at 'Millbank', a plantation some fifty miles north of Richmond in Caroline County, near the village of Crossroads and not all that far from her former home at Forest Rill. Her new employer was a Baptist minister with the somewhat grandiose name of the Reverend Lafayette Quince. Catherine Hopley admits that she had an English prejudice 'in favour of our Established Church and regular clergy'. Yet she was in need of a position and an offer of five months' work as governess to four children could not be rejected. Her time there was unhappy from the start . Quince was 'gruff' and his slaves were 'very irregular', especially with meals. The Quinces were suspicious of her as an Englishwoman and as someone with a regular correspondence with family and friends 'up North'. Ironically, her own letters were filled with information about the South and with requests for her correspondents not to believe what they read in the newspapers. The suspicions grew to hatred on Mr Quince's part and Catherine Hopley admitted, 'The truth is, no silly woman ever was *so silly* in trying to heal up the affairs of a country as was Miss Sarah Jones' in her suspect letters.

If Catherine Hopley found the Quinces difficult she had better luck with
their servants, even if Mrs Quince worried about her friendship with the
slaves. The English governess visited their cabins and became especially
friendly with Uncle Junius and Aunt Ony, but she was amazed at the state
of the cabins. Given all the workmen she saw about the plantation, she
was astounded 'that people should be so regardless of comfort as to
countenance shabby fences, leaky apartments, and a thousand other minor
miseries'. The house had rats and the doors and windows did not fit
properly. 'On the whole, my life at Millbank was not extremely delightful;
and the daily increasing alarms in public affairs did not tend to improve
matters.' She was horrified at Lincoln's refusal to declare his policy – 'so
unequal to the hour, so unsuited to the crisis' was her sensible judgment.
She was, however, able to get to Richmond to attend St Paul's on Easter
Sunday and therefore, as a devout Anglican, to make her 'Easter Duty'.

Despite her dislike of the Quinces she did admire the efforts they and
their neighbours made to provide for old servants. When one neighbour
asked her the question that had plagued so many English visitors: 'What
do you think of our domestic institutions?' she replied, 'I wish our own
working classes were as well provided for and protected as your slaves, Mr
Tyler. It is almost provoking to witness their grinning faces and light-
hearted indifference at this season of anxiety and alarm.' She now heard
of freed slaves actually selling themselves as families back into slavery to
get the protection it offered and presumably to be able to remain in
Virginia: the lot of freed blacks in the North was often a miserable one.
This same Mr Tyler who had asked her view about America's 'institutions'
told her a story of a freed slave named Tim. Mr Tyler had been on a trip
to Philadelphia and on the train he met a black porter who turned out to
have been one of his father's 'people' and one of his own boyhood friends.
'Oh, Massa John, gim me your hand, sah! Oh it does my heart good to shake
the hand of a white man; I've bin heah forty-three year, an' I never so much
as touched a white person's hand all that time.' He begged his old master's
son to take him back to Virginia, which he did. Lady Emmeline Stuart
Wortley had heard similar stories a decade earlier.[*]

By April as the flowers were appearing throughout Virginia, horrifying
news arrived from farther South. Southern forces had opened fire on Fort
Sumter, one of the few symbols of federal authority in the seceded states.
The North was horrified that Southern 'fire-eaters' had 'fired on the flag'.
Lincoln demanded 75,000 volunteers to put down the 'rebellion' and
proclaimed a blockade of Southern ports. Virginians were not prepared to
make war on their fellow Southerners. Many of the moderates, whom
Catherine Hopley had admired, were particularly outraged. One wrote to

* The idea that the blacks who lived in the North were anxious to return to the South was
a popular one in Southern mythology. Indeed, this is the meaning of some of the words in the
original version of 'Dixie'. It continued to be a popular idea up to the days of Al Jolson's singing
'Mammy'.

a Northern Senator: 'The time of *war* is on hand. And may the God of battles *crush to the earth and consign to eternal perdition*, Mr Lincoln, [and] his cabinet.'[16] Virginia, which, more than any other state, had created the American Union, now seceded and soon became a member of the Confederate States of America. Virginian officers such as Colonel Robert E. Lee sadly resigned their commissions in the United States Army. Catherine Hopley could not view this tragedy as an ordinary Englishwoman. She had now lived in America, mainly in the North, for over six years. Her relations and her friends were each flocking to their separate colours. James Garfield, whom she had known in Ohio, abandoned his teaching and volunteered for the Federal Army where soon he would become the youngest Union general. The English governess had to decide what to do as the American world she had known fell apart.

At Millbank the Quinces had other problems to face as spring floods swept away roads and bridges. There was now not even a weekly post and currency was growing scarce. Catherine Hopley felt herself totally cut off: if Virginia were invaded, Millbank was frighteningly near the rail line to Washington. Catherine had endured and overcome many troubles in the year since tragedy had struck the Hopleys in England but now, exactly twelve months later, she felt almost hopeless: 'I felt beset on all sides with dangers without one friend.' The world she knew was disintegrating: 'It seemed impossible in civilized America, that favoured land, so lately teeming with prosperity, [that] brethren were thirsting for each others' blood.' She wrote to friends in Washington for advice and then discovered that Quince had opened her letter to what was now the enemy capital: 'I despised him at heart.' She also wrote to the British Consul in Richmond to ask him for proof that she was a British Subject, in effect a passport, to forward letters to relatives in the North and to give her information as to how she could join them in what was now another country. The Consul was able to give her a pass dated 29 April 1861 but could do nothing else.

With war fever gripping the South one of the favourite ceremonies was the 'raising of a Secession Flag' and Mr Quince invited Catherine Hopley to such a ceremony at his Baptist Church. While waiting for the festivities to begin she was prevailed upon to join the young ladies in target practice with pistols. She took up 'an elegant little Colt revolver' and did not disgrace herself. She looked about to find a flagpole and finally noticed a tree whose top branches had been sawn off. Suddenly the Confederate banner was raised on the makeshift pole. 'How unreal, how dreamlike and incredible, did all this farce appear as we rode homewards through the woods and lanes, glorious with floral beauty.' Finally, by the middle of May, four letters arrived, two from Washington and two from New York. All urged her to flee the Confederacy, but it was not that simple. She now needed a pass which only the Governor of Virginia, John Letcher, could issue to those wishing to leave the state.

While Catherine Hopley was trying to decide what to do, news came that Federal troops were planning to invade Virginia. From the uncompleted dome of the Capitol, which she had so admired only a year before, outraged Federal officers peered across the broad Potomac River to the small town of Alexandria where they could see a large 'banner of secession' floating from the hotel. The town where Fanny Wright's hero, Lafayette, had enjoyed one of his many triumphal welcomes and where Mrs Trollope, recuperating from an illness, had written her reflections about slavery had now become the nearest outpost of the 'rebellion'. To Catherine Hopley, however, Alexandria was something quite different: it was the end of the railway line going north and the means of escape to the quiet homes of her relatives. Suddenly word arrived from Quince's sister, who lived closer to Washington, that she had heard gunfire from that direction. After some time Mr Quince hurried in with the latest news: a colourful group of Northern volunteers, mainly firemen, had set out under the command of a braggart Colonel for Alexandria. This man was a close personal friend of Lincoln and had promised his leader that he would remove the offending banner. Quince exulted:

> Colonel [Ephraim] Ellsworth insisted on taking down a Secession flag from an hotel and the landlord shot him dead – *shot him dead on the spot*! Mrs Quince cried out, 'Good God! and the man?' Her husband lowered his voice: 'He was shot too, madam; and he died a *hero* to his country. A noble instance of fidelity. The first Virginian gone.'

With his pulpit training, the Baptist minister raised his voice and continued, 'but not the last *Yankee* though … nor the last by thousands'. Catherine Hopley had heard a reasonably accurate account of the first minor fray and reached her own conclusion when she referred to 'two reckless men'. Mr Quince, while accurate in his account, had not been so in his prediction: in the next four years hundreds of thousands of Southerners, as well as Yankees, would die.*

On 1 June postal communication between the two countries ceased and the Confederate Post Office began work.† Catherine Hopley wanted to send two letters home, one to her mother and one for publication in England. This second 'letter' was a defence of the South. Ironically neither was sent

---

* A marker recording this event was placed on the Marshall Hotel in Alexandria to honour the bravery of the innkeeper, James Jackson. It can still be seen as it was re-erected on the modern Holiday Inn that occupies the site. Not far away is the remarkably evocative statue of a Confederate soldier commemorating Alexandria's young men who marched South to take up arms for their cause on the same day as the Ellsworth incident; few were left to return in 1865. James Jackson's name was added to this monument.

† Postage was five cents for 'ordinary' letters, i.e. within 500 miles, and ten cents for letters going over 500 miles. The Confederate Post Office proved the most successful department of the Southern government; it even made a profit. Mrs Hopley in Lewes would probably have had to pay the postage when she received her daughter's letters as that was the normal practice with international post.

because her employer kept them from the post. Even if they had been mailed they would have been opened and confiscated in Washington. Frustrated at getting her letters sent, she then heard that post was going 'viâ Nashville', which meant that letters would go down the Mississippi to New Orleans, thereby avoiding censors in the Federal capital. Once again delay by the Quinces meant she failed a second time. The only chance left was to send them via Richmond. Twelve years earlier, Lady Emmeline had been full of enthusiasm at the sight of all the 'white winged messengers of peace' when she saw the piles of transatlantic post. Now there was neither peace nor 'white winged messengers'.

With her escape route through Alexandria closed, Catherine Hopley hoped that she might go towards Harper's Ferry where she could cross the Potomac. But Northern troops soon poured into that area and another of her plans collapsed. At least she was able to use her continued stay at Millbank to study the 'domestic manners' of the South and how whites and blacks behaved towards one another. She admits that 'It was a long time before I became accustomed to this freedom of manner in the negroes. No white servant in England would ever dare to venture an approach to it.' Her explanation of this intimacy is worth recording:

> It is tolerated from the slaves, partly, perhaps, because the line is so distinctly marked by colour and position, that there is no fear of encroachment beyond a certain limit; although the relationship existing between master and slave induces it still further. There is that peculiar tie, 'I belong to you,' so very hard to comprehend by us English, the servants looking upon their masters as their natural protectors, and being themselves so free from all responsibilities. The masters on their part grow up with corresponding sentiments.

Time only encouraged the bond because the parents and grandparents of slaves had in their turn nursed, fed, worked for and been protected by the parents and grandparents of the 'masters'. (Of course, this was only the case among slaves in the older, settled regions like Virginia; in the deep South, particularly on its western borders, this generational bond was unusual.) In these unique relationships she found much good emerging: 'Not humanity alone, but patience, kindness, forbearance and many other Christian virtues are developed.' She acknowledged that a critic might say that 'it is to the interest of planters to maintain a community of healthy, cheerful, faithful servants' and that 'selfishness alone necessitates care', but 'humanity goes further, and affection further still'. She also felt that the relationship between master and slave accounted for 'the peculiar urbanity of the Southern character' which continued to fascinate her.

As full-scale war grew nearer, Catherine Hopley was impressed at what she called 'the unanimity of the South, so long doubted by those beyond the confines of the Confederacy, and so hard to be credited by her enemies ... [which] became a fixed fact in the minds of those who dwelt there, from the earliest stages of the war'. (Actually there was considerable opposition in parts of the South to secession: the western part of Virginia would secede from Virginia to form a new state, West Virginia.) The Englishwoman felt a surge of patriotism when she saw 'with what confidence the Southerners trusted in the integrity of England' to come to their aid. At last the Quinces realised that they had at least one English ally. Their suspicion of her motives and her absorption in letter-writing evaporated when a family friend asked the governess if he could read one of her letters. It was then read aloud to the Quinces, who found that it was an appeal to Englishmen to support the Southern cause. Quince urged her to send it to the *Richmond Enquirer*. This was the beginning of her career as a writer. 'I little dreamed then', she wrote in her first book, 'what a weighty matter, to me, rested on the fate of that letter.'

In the first week of June two letters finally arrived, one from her sister and brother-in-law in Indiana and one from her mother in England. Her brother-in-law, a strong supporter of the Union, assured her that the North was not motivated by any desire to free the slaves. He told her that it was 'the loss of the best States of the *ci-devant* Union that was galling and goading on the North to their fearful war'. A letter from England, of course, stirred her concern for her own country. Catherine Hopley saw this war not only from a Southern point of view, but from an English one. She knew that the federal blockade would keep Southern cotton from the textile factories of England. While English workers were being laid off from mills in Lancashire, 'so-called *slaves*', she wrote in anger, were parading to church in their silks. She insisted that at least in the South 'selfishness alone secures aid to the enfeebled slave', but in England only the work-house awaited the elderly who could no longer earn a living.

BACK TO RICHMOND

By the beginning of June it was obvious that, even with her employer's new attitude, her days at Millbank were numbered. Federal forces were moving closer and there were rumours of impending battle. Millbank stood close to an obvious route which the 'Yankees' might follow in an attack upon Richmond, which had become the capital of the Confederacy. In the third week of June, Catherine Hopley left Millbank, determined to find a way to her family in the Northern states. After much fretting as to how to travel she set out for Richmond, perhaps hoping to find a boat still going north. The roads were already busy with carriages of Southern sympathisers fleeing from Maryland where any editor or legislator who opposed the Washington government was imprisoned without trial. Once in Richmond she called at Governor Letcher's office to obtain the necessary permit to leave Virginia. Then she went to the British Consul's office where she met other stranded Englishmen without money and Marylanders who had families confined in their home state with no way to contact them. Mr Moore, the Consul, urged her to change her plans but she stood her ground and he promised an escort to Washington in company with four other Englishmen and two escorts carrying consular post under a flag of truce. She began packing her belongings as well as some letters that people had asked her to take to their friends in the North. Then the Consul told her that he had had to give up the plan as it had proved impossible. She now thought of trying to leave the Confederacy by making her way directly west and then turning north towards Ohio, but this route was cut off when Federal troops marched into the area to aid the opponents of secession.

When it became apparent that she could not easily or quickly join her family, 'the blockaded British subject' found herself more and more caught up in the Southern cause, 'this second great American revolution'. On a slightly defensive note, because she feared her objectivity might be questioned, she added: 'One must take an interest in something in order to live at all, and I am sorry to confess that each day found me less and less a "neutral" British subject.' Like others in the American Hotel she would jump up when she heard the cry, ' "Live Yankees! Live Yankees! Prisoners are passing!" and then such a rush as there would be to the windows of the hotels on Main street when the Yankee prisoners were marshalled through town'. She met Samuel Phillips Day, the correspondent for the London *Herald* and saw a group of Choctaw Indians arrive from Texas to join the 'Wise Brigade', named after the former Governor of Virginia. These exotic troops became the excuse for fantastic stories of atrocities in Northern papers. This was, she accurately observed, due in part to Southerners' 'loose and objectionable mode of expressing themselves in violent and extravagant language'. One did not like, but 'love'; one did not dislike, but 'hate', and so on.

Catherine Hopley had an opportunity to see troops assembling for war when two Southern women asked her to accompany them to a camp of soldiers at Yorktown. The women were planning to set up a hospital for ill and injured soldiers. At this stage of the war illness was a great problem, particularly for boys from the rural South who had little experience of being confined among large groups of men. The word 'Yorktown' had an immediate meaning for Catherine Hopley: here eighty years before, in 1781, the surrender of Lord Cornwallis and his besieged army led to the recognition of American Independence. She had to get permission from the military authorities to visit this camp which was close to a bastion of Federal power, Fortress Monroe. From there enemy troops were menacingly close to the Confederate capital. Even with her increasing commitment to the Confederate cause, she was somewhat shocked at what she saw at Yorktown. The sight brought home the 'peculiar character of the war, and those who fought it'. She had had little previous experience of the military, but she naturally thought in terms of highly disciplined troops in scarlet uniforms, performing intricate manoeuvres and obedient to every command of imperious officers. Now she suddenly beheld a 'citizen army', 'an army of "sovereigns," the husbands, sons, and brothers of those unused to be controlled, but on the contrary educated to control others'. She was given a room at Nelson House, once the headquarters of the ill-fated Lord Cornwallis. Some suspected her of being a spy, particularly when they saw her sketching the camp and its fortifications. She was probably making a drawing to send to the *Illustrated London News*, which was anxious for the latest pictures and stories from America.

Once she had dealt with the suspicions that she was a spy she could help the two women unpack supplies and establish a hospital routine. She regarded the soldiers' bravery and patience in their suffering with 'speech-less astonishment'. She recalled one man who had just had an arm amputated: before the severed arm was carried away he called for it to be returned so that he could take a treasured ring from one of the now lifeless fingers. When the Englishwoman was asked to stay on as a nurse she declined. Catherine Hopley was no Florence Nightingale and she wrote with amazing candour: 'I am sorry to confess that army rations did not quite suit my palate, nor the excitement and harrowing scenes by which we were surrounded; and I felt that health was my only safeguard at such a time.'

Her return to Richmond became something of an adventure in itself. She had to cross the peninsula that was to play such an important role in the war by means of a closed carriage. When the passengers reached the James River they waited for a steamer and while waiting could, by using a telescope, 'easily distinguish the Federal blockade ships at the mouth of the river in the Hampton Roads, and also the fortress'. Luckily her ship, like so many others, was able to evade the blockade and reach Richmond. On board she heard the first news of the South's great victory at Manassas or Bull Run, the first major battle of the war. By the time she landed in the city more details were arriving:

> Who can ever forget the scenes of those two following days! ... Oh! how that information spread like wild-fire through the large and crowded hotel ... 'Oh, my only son!' 'My husband!' 'My brother!' 'My two sons!' – and then the fearful suspense of the speakers, the rush to the telegraph office, the craving for more information, the eager looks and restless fever of impatience cannot be described ... the hurrying off of mothers, fathers and sisters to the battle-field ... added to all this the flood of arrivals by every train, of persons from all parts of the Confederacy, who had just received the tidings.

The pandemonium had been increased when Jefferson Davis, who was at the battle, sent a telegram to his wife: 'We have won a dearly-bought but signal victory; night closes on the enemy in full retreat, and we are in full pursuit.'[17]

Catherine Hopley was totally caught up in the feverish activity that seized Richmond. She talked to men fresh from the battlefield and a week later on 28 July she, like thousands of others, made the journey to Manassas where she talked to farmers who regaled her with stories of the

Yankees' panic as they fled back to Washington. Before that she had volunteered as an amanuensis for a newspaper correspondent who was also an officer and whose hand had been injured at Manasses. On the Sunday after the battle she was in St Paul's Church for the Day of Thanksgiving proclaimed by President Davis and saw him and his family in their pew and General Robert E. Lee in the pew that had been used by the Prince of Wales. She quickly became one of the President's staunchest supporters: 'Character is stamped upon his features. A broad, full, prominent forehead, nose somewhat aquiline, lips thin, firm and delicate. Mildness and gentleness are the prominent expression; kindness, benevolence, then a touch of sadness strikes you: the least shadow of bitterness melting into sorrow.' Lest her reader think she had portrayed an irresolute leader she added: 'But there is plenty of resolution, and dignity combined with conscientiousness.' She was touched to see the President sharing his Prayer Book with his young son. (This little boy, Joseph Davis, was later to die tragically in a fall from a balcony of the Confederate White House.)

The fear of spies and abolitionists was greater than ever and Catherine Hopley was aware that 'people were taking so much trouble to watch me, and judge harshly of my actions'. Their fear also undermined her efforts to raise money for the Yorktown hospital. She therefore resolved to trace the letter she had sent to the *Richmond Enquirer* to have it published: this would establish her loyalty to the new nation. When she found that the editor had joined the army she decided to rewrite the article and submit it to a second editor. Then she found that he, too, had 'joined up'. Still she remained undaunted and chose a third man, the editor of the *Richmond Whig*. This time she took no chances, took the article to him personally and refused to leave his office till he had read it. Her 'letter' was published the next day.

Catherine Hopley's reputation among her fellow guests rose. People told her that her article had 'exonerated' her from suspicion of being a spy, at which 'my English blood was boiling'. Her fury was short-lived and she was soon full of more commendations for Southerners. She turned their former suspicions of her into a cause for praise: 'The fact is, the Southern people are not diplomatists. Honest and straight-forward themselves, with no disposition for intrigue, they are slow to detect those qualities in others; while a plain, open spoken body, such as myself, who did not disguise that I took an interest in all that was going on, was more likely to be suspected of sinister designs.' Once again she was able to join in the numerous discussions that filled the parlours and lobbies. She heard of one group of Marylanders who had made a large kite of Northern newspapers with wings and tails made up of letters and messages and, when the wind was from the north, set it free to cross the Potomac and come to earth in Virginia, which it did. Her hotel was home not only to Marylanders who had 'refugeed south' but to soldiers and their wives and to Members of the Confederate Congress.

Five of these Congressmen were from the deep Southern states of Alabama and Georgia. From them she heard what was a common Southern view: if the 'slave states' had not been vilified and isolated by abolitionists, they would eventually have come to abolition on their own. (Any eventual emancipation might have occurred in states like Virginia, but in the expanding 'cotton states' that stretched from Georgia to Texas, it was unlikely to have occurred in the short term. Slave labour was essential to the large-scale production of cotton which Southern states exported and the cotton exports were, in turn, essential to maintain the American balance of trade.) She made the criticism that Southerners did not educate their 'people' for eventual freedom, a criticism they rejected. She stuck to her guns and made one of her most telling criticisms of the South, one which did not fit easily with her previous comments on the conditions of blacks:

> I know from many persons, as well as from observation, that the condition of the slaves had become worse and worse for many years, on account of increased rigour; but that previously their condition had been gradually improving for the last fifty years.

Before her English critics might feel too smug, she added, 'just as we find an improvement in the discipline of institutions and asylums in England'. (One wonders if she was here thinking of her brother who was still in prison, and perhaps one of his sons who was in a mental asylum.) Catherine Hopley's dislike of slavery as an 'institution' was equalled by a dislike of its effects on Southerners, and in this she reflected the views of many moderate people: 'Perhaps the chief cause of half the discomforts and miseries of the country [the Confederacy] might be attributed to the "Institution," which renders labour derogatory, and the white class dependent.' By the time she was preparing her book for publication a year later, Lincoln had issued his 'Emancipation Proclamation'. She wrote dismissively:

> Intercourse with the polished world beyond, and the improvement of the country [the South] by commerce and travelling, will do more towards the amelioration, or the abolition of slavery, than a twenty years' war, and all the Proclamations of all the Presidents that may be elected, so long as the Federal States continue to exist.

Catherine Hopley had settled into a pleasant enough routine in Richmond. She began her day with an early walk. Her favourite spot was the beautiful Hollywood Cemetery above the James River, laid out in the 1850s and eventually the final resting place of many of her Confederate heroes, including President Davis. After her walk she read the newspapers and then devoted an hour or more to giving lessons in music and French to the hotelier's daughter. For the rest of the day she drew, wrote up her notes and, along with everyone else, waited like Mr Micawber for something to 'turn up'. The lack of specie – the hotelier may well have given her free room and board in return for the teaching – meant that she, too, was finding that the falling value of the new 'paper money' and the shortage of goods due to the blockade were making life more difficult. In addition it was becoming obvious that the blockade would not be lifted and that British recognition of the Confederacy was not coming. As a result British subjects 'now began to find themselves at a discount'. While she wanted to return to England she simply did not have enough money even if a ship were available and she had 'no choice but to become reconciled to' another winter in the South. In this she resembles Mrs Trollope, who was forced to stay in America until money for the passage arrived from England.

In August 1861 Catherine Hopley therefore placed advertisements in the papers, hoping to find 'new ground to visit' and an increased income. Some prospective employers, knowing she did not want all her income in Confederate money, offered to make up the difference or pay her entire salary in bales of cotton. Although she considered offers from Virginia, Alabama and Tennessee, she wanted to travel further south to get away from the war zone. She had various offers from Florida and Mississippi but was more attracted by an offer to teach the children of Governor Milton of Florida, the 'land of flowers and orange groves'. Once again slow posts meant that by September nothing had been decided. She therefore accepted another offer from a college or ladies' seminary in Warrenton, about eighty miles north-west of Richmond. There was only one drawback: 'They were Baptists again!'

Despite Catherine Hopley's 'prejudice against Baptists and colleges' she accepted the offer and went to the War Office for a pass to Warrenton. At first this was refused as the town was too near the front line, but the influence of a friend won the day. She set out despondently in the first week of October for the College and its 'troop of silly girls'. The rail journey was a nightmare as trains were constantly being shunted to make room for trains full of wounded and dying: at the sight of these men lying on beds of maize-shucks on open cattle cars she burst into tears and contrasted them with the 'negroes fat and happy in the crowded city' while 'my countrymen were harping on the misery of slavery!' 'Would my philanthropic country never learn the truth?' Once in Warrenton she was pleasantly surprised. From the College she could see the Blue Ridge Mountains in the distance and, on a clear day, the camps at Manassas and Centreville. She loved the startling autumn colours of the maple gum, oaks and sumac, the brilliant sunsets and the lovely countryside. Best of all, these Baptists were not like Mr Quince: they were civilised. There were only some dozen girls in residence and her teaching, confined to music, only took up four hours a day. She could not get the girls to practise classical pieces: all they wanted to learn was 'Dixie', the 'Jeff Davis Waltz' and 'General Beauregard's March'. With so much free time she could once again take her long walks. Sadly few of the girls could accompany her. This was not because they were lazy but because their 'war-shoes' could not stand the wear and tear of walking outside.

Catherine Hopley's hope that in Warrenton she might get away from the war was an absurd one: she had moved almost to the front line. She could distinctly hear the cannon fire during minor battles; there were enemy troop movements all round the town; orders to evacuate were frequent; Warrenton was filled with hospitals and on average six or seven men died each day. The blockade increasingly affected daily life: shops closed early because there was no oil for lamps and churches had to give up evening services. She had another outing to Manassas and spent an evening with some of her girls in the camp of the 17th Virginia Regiment. Once again she left, impressed with the great courtesy she was shown and the 'unsuspicious' nature of the men. She was amazed at their 'free and easy' attitudes which allowed them to go home for a few days between stints of picket duty.

FLORIDA

As autumn came on, Catherine Hopley must have realised that she had made yet another mistake in choosing where to spend the war, but suddenly she had another chance. At last the letter from the Governor of Florida arrived, and on Christmas Eve she set off for Richmond. This was her second Christmas in the city, but St Paul's Church was very different: the organist had 'gone North' and with him the Christmas anthem. Although the promised advance did not arrive from the Governor, she had her salary from Warrenton. She used her brief time in the city to arrange a position as the Florida correspondent for a Richmond paper. This was quite an achievement for any woman in the 1860s, but for an English-woman to find this in a country in the midst of a civil war shows how resourceful Catherine Hopley could be. She may have been helped by the fact that in late December 1861 England seemed on the verge of war with the United States after a Federal warship had removed two Confederate diplomats from the *Trent*, a Royal Mail ship, on 8 November. (The American ship was commanded by Charles Wilkes, a kinsman of the Wilkes who, it may be recalled, was so kind to Fanny Wright and Fanny Trollope.) Catherine Hopley read about this in the *Richmond Enquirer* of 19 November and she heard someone say, 'Why they [the Yankees] might as well have walked into Queen Victoria's drawing room to arrest them.'

The diplomatic incident was still smouldering when, on 2 January 1862, Catherine Hopley left for the long journey south to Florida. As before, she found herself in a train crowded with soldiers and she thought that many 'were merely going home to be nursed, some probably to be buried, who had not much hope of surviving even the journey; some certainly to be buried, for there were the same coffin-like looking cases standing on the platforms ... sad scenes and sorrow wherever we go'. When she found herself in South Carolina, she despaired of her surroundings: 'Pines, pines, nothing but pines – when shall we ever behold the now historical palmetto?' The palmetto had figured on one of the earliest Southern flags. As the war went on the palmetto had more prosaic uses, as a popular song testified:

> My homespun dress is plain, I know.
> My hat's palmetto, too;
> But then it shows what Southern girls
> For Southern rights will do.

Catherine Hopley eventually saw one of 'the historical palmettoes' in Charleston, surrounded by a protective fence. She did not know that these trees grow mainly along the coast.

As always on train journeys, she began to talk to the people she met, among whom was a Major Yancey, the brother of a Confederate diplomat who had been sent to England. The Major, a well-travelled man, amused her with stories of English prejudice against the South, one of which deserves retelling. Yancey was returning from a visit to England when a young Englishwoman on the ship asked, 'Oh, Mr. Yancey, they tell me there is a "slave-driver" on board. I have heard so much of slave-drivers that I am most anxious to see one.' The Major told her he knew the man she wanted to see and asked her to look round until she spotted him. 'She was a long time in deciding; but at last selected a heavy-browed, dark-eyed, bushy-haired man ... She had selected a plodding, phlegmatic, metaphysical German, about the last man on board to whom the qualities she had mentioned were likely to be applicable.' When the young girl learned the truth she apologised profusely only to be told by Major Yancey, 'My dear young lady do not for one moment distress yourself, we are so accustomed to hear ourselves spoken of in this manner, that we take no notice of it at all. It is no consequence to us what people choose to call us; we understand ourselves, and that is enough.'

Catherine Hopley was as interested in the appearance of Southerners as in their attitudes and speech. With her artist's eye she saw a general look of 'mild, quiet, guileless expression of countenance' when people, especially older men, heard ill-informed comments about the South. Her time in the Confederacy had been spent mainly among the well-to-do, more refined section, people who could afford an English governess, and not among farmers or shopkeepers. She admitted that the stereotype of the violent Southerner who 'always carried loaded revolvers and bowie-knives' had, like most stereotypes, some foundation in fact. She told her English readers that this type of man may well exist in 'the recently settled, and more Western States' of the Confederacy, where

the inhabitants have been inured to a life of almost lawless ferocity, engendered in them by living within dangerous proximity of savage Indians, wild

animals, and the refuse of society who have repaired to those far-off States
to fly from justice or prosecute their roving pursuits as hunters and trappers.
Parts of Mississippi, Arkansas, Western Missouri, and Texas are still in this
pioneer condition.

Like many Victorians she was exasperated by the pace of life in hot
climates: 'A long time must elapse before you can induce the Southerners
to be in a hurry.' This was a fault she found in all parts of Southern society:
'You never see a negro in a hurry and the master and mistress are inured
to slowness. They are learned and educated in slowness.'

During her brief visit to Charleston, Catherine Hopley was impressed
not only with the city, but with its people. Charlestonians 'belong to a race
of heroes' and their city was 'one of the most finished, substantial, and
well-kept towns in the American States. There was an air of refinement
and exclusiveness that distinguished Charleston.' She was also impressed
that before a fire which had devastated much of the town less than a month
before her arrival, there had been eleven Episcopal churches, whereas in
Richmond, with a somewhat larger population, there were only four. 'This
fact', she wrote as a devout Anglican, 'speaks loudly for the orthodox
principles of the Palmetto city.' She found in Charleston that love for
England which she had noted in Virginia:

'That came from London.' 'That house was built by an English architect.'
Strange yet true, one never detected in the Southerner that lingering spirit
of envy and ill-will that might almost be expected in a people who had fought
so hard and suffered so much from the parent-country; but on the contrary,
a sort of veneration and affection remained for everything English. To be
English was almost a passport to society.

She also took an opportunity to visit Fort Sumter, where the first shot of
the war had been fired nine months before. The fort was in Confederate
hands but subjected to frequent bombardment from the Federal fleet which
was blockading the harbour. She noticed that Dante's well-known and
timely lines, *'Lasciate ogni speranza, voi ch' entrata'* ('Abandon hope, all ye
who enter here') had been carved above the main entrance to the battered
fort where the Confederate flag was kept flying in spite of the hellish
shelling. Neither Catherine Hopley nor her friends had yet abandoned
hope in the Southern cause in January 1862, but as she peered out to sea
through a borrowed telescope at the powerful fleet she must have experienced some fright. She could see the force that was keeping her in the South
and that was slowly strangling her friends.

From Charleston she moved further south to another blockaded port,
Savannah, on the Georgia coast. On the way she travelled just west of the
coastal strip already occupied by Northern troops, through swamps and
fields of rice and sugar cane. While in Savannah she had the benefit of a
Confederate officer as an escort, and in a hotel lobby he introduced her to

General Robert E. Lee. General Lee was spending an unhappy time supervising the fortifications along the coast. Unfortunately he was called away before Catherine could have a conversation with him. While she much enjoyed Savannah, she was once again amazed at the Southerners' informality regarding the war despite the presence of so many Northerners: she could overhear General Lee giving orders concerning fortifications and so too could a Northern woman who was 'listening eagerly'. Perhaps she forgot that only a few months before many people in her Richmond hotel feared that she too was a spy! The Charleston hotel had been managed by a Northerner, as were several shops (these were often German immigrants) while telegraph workers and, in some cases, even newspaper editors, were 'Yankees'. Regarding this last group she added that if a Southern-born editor in the North had said even half of what these men had, 'he would have been quickly handed off to Fort Warren'. On the train, conductors seemed almost always to be from the North. Catherine Hopley so enjoyed her visit to Savannah that she extended her stay by an extra day. She used the time to visit a Negro school which she later described in an article.[18]

She was soon on her way to Florida, where she would be among the first of what has since become a mighty wave of British visitors to the 'sunshine state'. She had to transfer to a stage-coach to travel west across the top of the state to the small town of Madison where she met her new employer, Governor John Milton. She was not terribly impressed: 'His manner was not particularly cordial' she wrote. One rather suspects he may have been over-burdened with the demands of the war particularly as his sparsely settled state with its long coastline was an easy prey for any sea-borne invaders. Milton had stood for Governor in 1860 as a convinced 'states' righter' and had taken office in October 1861, so he had only been Governor for a few months when she met him. Unlike 'Dr W.' and 'the Rev. Mr Quince' we know something about her third and final employer. Milton was a lawyer by training but in the 1840s had set himself up as a cotton-planter in Jackson County, Florida and by 1861 was a wealthy man.* The 1860 Census shows that both his real and his personal estates were each valued at $40,000, considerable sums. His plantation, Sylvania, had 52 slaves working 7,326 acres.[19]

Following the meeting in Madison, Catherine Hopley carried on west to the Governor's plantation near the small town of Marianna. She passed through the capital, Tallahassee, which she pronounced 'a pretty place, though not a "city", according to our ideas'. Finally she reached Jackson County where the temperature stood at eighty degrees Fahrenheit although it was January. As if that were not bad enough she discovered that

---

* Milton was related to the seventeenth-century poet: he was the great-great-great-grandson of the poet's brother, Sir Christopher Milton. Sir Christopher's grandson emigrated to Virginia in the 1730s.

there were ten children of whom six were to be pupils: 'Ten children are all very well, but where an inmate in a family is concerned, experience had shown that, as a general thing, comforts naturally diminish in proportion as a family increases.' The plantation house was a long, low building with a 'piazza' or verandah along the front. Once again she was amazed at the relationship between whites and blacks. The children – Caroline at sixteen was the eldest and Jeff Davis, the youngest at not much more than a year old – ran out not to see their new English governess but to greet the black coachman. The house stood in a clearing amidst dogwood, plum, sassafras, azaleas, verbena, oxalis, violets and white lilies. She was not impressed with the level of education of her charges although the 1860 census showed that all the older children had some education, probably from a school-mistress from New York who is listed as residing in the Milton household before the war. Her English successor found the Milton girls lazy and uninterested in books but always very amiable. They were a 'type of Southern girls generally, who have fortunes spent on their education, or rather upon the routine of getting "through" books, but who rarely are educated at all, in the true sense of the word'. Caroline Milton, the Governor's wife, was the niece of one of the most famous Southern politi-cians of the time, Howell Cobb.* She quickly won the affection of the English governess, who described Mrs Milton as 'one of the most good tempered people in the Confederacy'.

In many things Sylvania reproduced the same pattern of life as the two Virginia plantations on which Catherine had been employed. There was a weekly post, weather permitting, and disorder reigned: the children were 'perfectly happy, contented, and smiling, accustomed to gratify every wish, with no thought of care or sorrow, and no sense of responsibility'. The buildings were badly constructed and the weather was atrocious. She was introduced to the 'norther', that sudden blast of cold air that can sweep through those parts of the South unprotected by mountain ranges, causing the temperature to fall dramatically. In Catherine Hopley's case the fall was some twenty degrees in three minutes and forty degrees within a few hours. As if this were not bad enough, when the temperature did drop that winter, the pig-killing began. 'These killing days were horrible. You could not look out of a door or window without beholding cart-loads of slaugh-tered pigs.' Because Florida earned large sums in supplying Charleston and Savannah with salted meat, the scale of slaughtering and salting at large plantations like Sylvania was truly enormous.

Catherine Hopley was furious, as any nineteenth-century English visi-tor would have been, to see lemons, oranges and limes rotting on the trees because no one would pick them. Farmers were more concerned with

* Englishmen, who often made great sport with nineteenth-century American names, would have delighted in the Milton family: Mrs Milton's mother was called Obedience Dutiful Bugg while the Governor's father had the poetic name of Homer Vergil Milton.

cotton, rice, sugar and tobacco. Families lived on their thousands of acres without garden plots and fresh vegetables. Instead they relied on an

> ordinary diet of corn bread ... and hard salted meats, with cabbages and sweet potatoes for vegetables, and poultry for variety; they have plenty of horses and carriages, plenty of ready money ... but slovenliness, disorder, incompleteness, and discomfort may be witnessed everywhere.

The cause could be traced partly to the 'peculiar institution' and partly to the climate. In her analysis she was equally scathing about black and white alike:

> The negroes are too indolent and stupid to do anything unless compelled. The masters and mistresses tolerate any amount of confusion rather than exert themselves to remedy it, and indeed, having been reared in this same confusion, they do not often observe it. The further southward one goes, the more this is seen to be the case, where the relaxing and enervating influences of climate are also more perceptible.

In an article she wrote two years later she described how families often spent days camping out in the woods: 'The inhabitants of Florida enjoy life in a manner which, in our dewy and misty England, we should scarcely associate with health or comfort.'[20]

'The resources of the South', Catherine Hopley fumed, 'are not even half known, much less developed.' When she heard from Governor Milton that land was being sold at ten cents an acre she asked a friend to buy her between 200 and 300 acres. To let the land to 'some enterprising Englishman – a horticulturist, for instance – would be so very charming.' Unfortunately her friend never got her message and the acreage remained unbought. 'It was a pity, as nothing would have been so interesting as to persuade some English people to run the blockade, and go and cultivate my estate in Florida.' Her idea was for a new infusion of English blood on a wide scale:

> While so many of our English poor are being supported in idleness, and doing incalculable moral harm to the country, *there* is a land where all that is required is labour, and intelligence combined with it. And what an opening there is for emigrants ...

In her discussions of life at Sylvania she turned to that most emotive topic, flogging. Englishmen had been raised for three decades on novels which presented gruesome scenes of flogging. As we saw, Mrs Trollope had created this fictional theme and of course it had culminated in *Uncle Tom's Cabin*. Some English visitors to the South, most notably Fanny Kemble, insisted in her *Journal of a Residence on a Georgia Plantation*, based on her fifteen-week stay, that floggings were a regular occurrence.[21] Catherine Hopley had a different experience in her stay of almost three years.

She claims that she had personal knowledge of only one whipping, when the normally kind Mrs Milton threatened to have the maid who looked after the governess beaten for slovenliness: 'This was the first case of private whipping I had ever known or heard of, during my residence in the South.' When the threat produced no improvement, Mrs Milton, who normally punished the smaller children, black and white together, sent the girl to be beaten by the overseer. Afterwards the young slave told the relieved Englishwoman that the overseer had let her off with only a threat. Perhaps Catherine Hopley may have reflected privately at the far worse brutality suffered by boys at her brother's school in Eastbourne.

By the spring of 1862 Catherine Hopley's health had given way under the heat, the monotonous diet and the isolation. Often there was no rice to eat, no white sugar, very little molasses, little baking soda, no tea and no imported fruits. Quinine was selling at $20 an ounce. There were troubling reports of Confederate defeats, including one at Columbus, Georgia, the nearest and most important large town to Sylvania. There was also news that Manassas had been evacuated and this meant that her friends in Virginia might now be forced to flee their homes. Even worse, New Orleans, the largest city in the South, fell to Northern troops in April 1862 and the city was placed under martial law by General 'Beast' Butler. Catherine lived in dread that Yankee gunboats would ascend nearby rivers and cut Florida off from the rest of the Confederacy.

If all this were not enough, Catherine had a falling-out with Mrs Milton. Like so many English travellers of the period, she always came equipped with a bottle of brandy. She had learned from past experience on plantations that brandy was frequently given to ill slaves, but she wanted to make sure she had enough for her own use. One day Mrs Milton sent a message by the maid who looked after the governess. A neighbour had a slave who was ill and she needed some brandy: could Miss Hopley let the neighbour have her bottle? 'This was an embarrassing sort of message.' She knew she would probably not be able to buy any more; she knew she needed it for her own health and she doubted whether it was the best medicine for a young, feverish child. She therefore sent the girl to Mrs Milton to say that the brandy was almost gone and would her bottle of whisky do. At dinner that night the lady of the house was silent and finally was forced to say that her friend 'was likely to lose her little negro girl, to whom she was very much attached: and that she had felt quite hurt at my message this morning'. When questioned further Mrs Milton told her that the servant girl had said that Catherine Hopley 'thought brandy too good to give to a nigger'. 'We don't consider anything too good for our niggers', said the Governor's wife, 'and give them whatever we have ourselves, when they are sick, and need it.' The Englishwoman was suitably abashed.

Occasionally there was some relief from the tensions and tedium of wartime isolation. A nephew of Governor Milton arrived from Texas and entertained her with stories of the recklessness and bravery of the Texas

Rangers against the wild animals that roamed that state. Catherine Hopley often describes handsome young men in her book and she was clearly taken with, or taken in by, these stories. 'It is by such training, foresight, skill and courage, that the Texans have become the daring soldiers whose feats have been frequently recounted, since the commencement of the war.' She would recall many of these stories in yet another article she did after she returned home.[22] Perhaps the restlessness of the Texan soldiers appealed to a similar streak in her own character. She never stayed long in any one place and by the spring she was anxious to be on the move yet again. She had only come to Florida on the assumption that the blockade would be lifted by the spring of 1862. Far from being lifted, it was getting tighter. Governor Milton had advised her to try to get into New Orleans to see if she would be allowed to sail to England, but she was terrified when she heard of 'Beast' Butler's infamous proclamation that any lady who showed open disrespect to Northern soldiers would be treated as 'a woman of the town, plying her avocation'. She shared the general revulsion of her countrymen at this order and did not wish to place herself under Butler's power.[23]

Catherine therefore decided to retrace her steps to Richmond, if she could raise enough money. Governor Milton could not find the specie to pay her but offered instead a draught drawn on his Liverpool cotton factors, who owed him money. She could cash this when she got to England. This plan fell through and in the event he was able to find specie for a large portion of her salary. He made up the rest in Confederate currency, which would at least pay for her trip to Richmond. She left Sylvania in July 1862 and admitted to feeling 'cowardly' at leaving her Florida friends. As she got into the carriage the Milton's youngest son ran up: 'Little Jeff Davis [Milton] had the last kiss; little laughing Jeff – *he* knew nothing of these sorrows.' (One wonders if she ever learnt that an exhausted and depressed Governor Milton retired to Sylvania in the first week of April 1865, as the Confederacy collapsed, and there took his own life.)

ESCAPE FROM THE SOUTH

The chaotic nature of Southern transport compelled her to follow a roundabout route as she took a steamer up the Chattahoochie River as far as Eufaula in Alabama where she boarded a train eastwards for Macon in the centre of Georgia. From there she got another train to Augusta, on the Georgia-South Carolina state line. While she was in Georgia she paid a brief visit to Mrs Milton's family, the Cobbs. As she continued her protracted travel she met a refugee from New Orleans whose passport had cost her eighty-five dollars; some had to pay as much as five hundred to get out of the occupied city. The money was pocketed by Northern soldiers.

When she reached Richmond Catherine found a city much changed from the one she had left six months before. Only a few weeks before her return an enormous Federal Army had marched up to the outskirts. The Confederate capital seem doomed until General Robert E. Lee, whom Catherine Hopley had met in Savannah, took command of the Army of Northern Virginia. By brilliant tactical fighting in the Seven Days' Battles he drove the vastly more powerful Federal forces into a retreat, or what the Northern commander called a 'change of base'. Richmond was now under martial law and crowded with wounded soldiers and continual funeral processions to Hollywood Cemetery, where Catherine Hopley had taken her morning walks in happier days. The Confederate victories meant that the war was likely to continue for some time and a surge of supplicants now besieged the small War Office and the nearby Executive building. (The Confederate government was basically run from two buildings.) One of the most annoying tasks for the few clerks was dealing with desperate people who wanted permission to leave the Confederacy. Many men tried to claim that they were British subjects and therefore not liable for military service. Catherine Hopley found that even a letter from a Governor could not get her an interview with the Secretary of State, Judah Benjamin, or other Cabinet officials.*

Confronted with pushing people and weary clerks, Catherine Hopley burst into tears. As so often this weapon worked and she was taken into the office of an old friend, Albert Bledsoe. He had been Professor of Mathematics at the University of Virginia, but now was an official at the Bureau of War: indeed he was in charge of issuing the pass that she needed.[24] She was so pleased that she again burst into tears – this time of relief. She now had her precious paper: 'Pass Miss Catherine Hopley, a British subject, beyond the lines, by flag of truce, subject to the military control of the general in command. 26 July, 1862.' In the midst of all her battles with bureaucracy she had one sight that she treasured. As she wandered round the Confederate offices, she passed an open door and saw President Davis working at his table. No vignette in her book shows better the state of the South at war than this: a visitor could simply peer through a doorway and see the Confederate President at work.

Catherine Hopley was now so committed to the Confederate cause that she offered, as she makes plain in her book, to smuggle official dispatches, but it appears that she was not asked to do so. On 2 August 1862, after bidding farewell to her friends, she joined seventeen other people in a party led by a Provost Marshal. They had a short journey to City Point on the James River. This was the spot where prisoners of war could be exchanged by both sides and where a few people were allowed to pass between the

---

* Ironically, Judah Benjamin himself would eventually make use of his claim to be a British subject. He was one of the two members of the Confederate Cabinet to escape capture in 1865. He found his way through the Florida swamps and discovered a small boat which took him to the West Indies, where he had been born. He then sailed for England and at the age of fifty-five began his studies in the Inns of Court. Within a few years he was a QC and one of the best paid barristers in England.

lines. Her first sight of Union officers did not impress her: 'Ah, those faces reveal much truth: your hearts are not in the cause; you are making a good thing of this war, you, who take care not to be killed, and are driving such a profitable trade. What cold, hard faces, and unyielding manners they had! One felt, at the moment, that it was meeting a different race of people.' While she was furious that she, an Englishwoman, had to ask their permission to go home (forgetting that she had needed similar permission to leave the Confederacy) she was astounded that the Provost Marshal handed over letters from prisoners of war and copies of Confederate papers and received similar material from his Union counterpart. He even joked with his *'friendly enemies'*, which caused Catherine Hopley to burst out, not for the first time, 'Oh, what a singular war.'

A steamer for Baltimore lay waiting and the time of departure was now at hand. She went up to the Provost Marshal to shake the hand of her last Southerner, well aware that she was under suspicion:

> Many pairs of eyes were watching us, for we were now in the presence of people who think it their privilege to arrest and imprison women for doing less than shaking hands too kindly with a rebel. It was a silent parting, with that last 'good old Virginian'. .

As they sailed down the James she carefully saved her Union pass 'in remembrance of the revolution'. The version of the pass she gave in her book changed not only her name (to her new pen-name) but her age:

Age ... 30
Height ... Four feet 11 inches
Complexion ... Florid
Hair ... Carroty
Eyes ... Hazel
Build ... Robust

Either Miss Hopley was lying to the Union officer or 'Miss Jones' was not telling her readers the truth, at least in regard to her age. She was not thirty but within two months of her forty-fifth birthday. There is no way of knowing how accurate the other descriptions were. The pass also carried the text of an oath that passengers were normally required to take: 'In availing myself of the benefits of the within Pass, I do solemnly affirm that I am a true and loyal citizen of the United States, and that I will give no aid, comfort, or information to the enemies of the United States Government in any manner.' However in her book she added: 'N.B. – *Not* "solemnly affirmed," by a British subject.' Her outrage at being forced to give such personal information was shared by one of the reviewers of her book, who wondered how 'a Federal officer (and gentleman?) had the brutality to impose on a lady'. The reviewer said she had shown 'no ordinary moral courage in publishing it'.[25] Such attitudes say more about the civilities and civilisation of Victorian Britain than anything else. Who else but a Victorian could have thought it beyond the pale for an officer to ask a few facts of a hostile visitor in the midst of a horrible civil war that was tearing his country in two?

During the journey on the steamer Catherine Hopley was interrogated regarding her movements, first by a Northern officer on his own, and then by a group, but she was able to restrain herself. Some of the passengers were sent back to Virginia and one elderly man who was going North to bring home two orphaned sisters from school simply disappeared. She had to transfer to two further ships before she reached Baltimore and en route she heard soldiers talking about the recent destruction of the house of Edmund Ruffin, the fanatical secessionist who had fired the first cannon-shot to bombard Fort Sumter. She was appalled that 'A spirit of revenge seemed to possess them', a spirit she had not seen among Confederate troops. En route they sailed past Fortress Monroe, where three years later her hero, Jefferson Davis, would be imprisoned in chains without trial for two years.

In Baltimore Catherine Hopley had to move quickly, for her pass only ran for three days. She telegraphed to her sister in Indiana that she would be on her way soon. Baltimore was a city with widespread Southern sympathy and Anthony Trollope, a supporter of the North, was somewhat shocked when he saw how it was held in check by Northern soldiers and the ever-present threat of a long stay in a Federal prison.[26] When she boarded the train the proprietor of the hotel where she had stayed came up to her. After much manoeuvring she established that he was a Southern sympathiser. He had with him an old man with tears in his eyes who grabbed her hand and shook it. 'God bless you, madam! God bless you! you feel for us, I know.' The hotelier then explained that the man had a son in the Confederate army and could not get any news of him. 'You have just come from there', the old man continued, 'and it does me good to look at you.' This was the last Southern sympathiser she would meet. Indeed, as she travelled west through Pennsylvania she discovered just how hostile her new environment could be. She had already heard street urchins in Baltimore singing 'We'll hang Jeff Davis to an old apple tree'. When she halted over-night at Cressons Springs she went out walking and stopped under the corner of a balcony to watch the sunset and to reflect. Inadvertently she began humming the tune of 'Maryland, My Maryland', whose most famous line was 'The despot's heel is on thy shore'. It naturally had a deep appeal to someone who had just visited Baltimore. She was unaware of the crowd that had gathered round her until she heard the whispered cry of 'Secesh' which meant secessionist or supporter of the Southern cause. After that she tried to be more careful.

Once in Indiana, her sister warned her to be quiet for fear of arrest. Despite her wariness, her feelings must have been known for she was described in a local paper as a 'rank Secesh'. She was furious at the invented stories in the Indiana papers of Southern 'atrocities', especially those made up about women who were supposed to have mistreated wounded prisoners, and she recalled the untold acts of kindness she had seen at first hand. She was also appalled at the cries for wholesale revenge on the South and the demand that 'We must annihilate them.' It was fairly obvious that she could not remain with her sister, for her brother-in-law was as ardent a Unionist as she was a Confederate, and she soon left for New York where she found a ship sailing for England. It was the same ship that had brought her from England in November 1860.

PUBLICATION IN ENGLAND

Catherine Hopley returned to England in the autumn of 1862 and found a great interest in the war in America. In October, William Gladstone, the Chancellor of the Exchequer, made his famous speech in Newcastle in which he said that Jefferson Davis had not only made an army and a navy but also a nation. This was widely – and incorrectly – interpreted as a hint that the Government were about to recognise the Confederacy. The British and French Cabinets were actively considering mediation in a war that was causing so much bloodshed on one side of the Atlantic and so much misery on the other. The war was causing particular distress in Lancashire where thousands were on the verge of starvation as factories closed for the lack of Southern cotton. Books about the war were pouring forth from English publishers. She was soon in touch with the publishers Chapman and Hall, best known for launching Dickens upon the world. They had also recently published Anthony Trollope's *North America* which was almost completely concerned with the Northern states; Catherine Hopley could offer the other half of the picture.[27] She wrote hurriedly, completing the book in ten weeks. Her Introduction was dated December 1862, but she may have added a few details later as she mentions the death of the Confederate General, Thomas Cobb, at the battle of Fredricksburg, news of which would only have reached her in the last days of the year. She had stayed with his family in Georgia.

'This book', she wrote, 'has nothing but *truth* to recommend it; and of melancholy truth, and sad reality, so much must be recorded.' Later she insisted that it was not 'a disquisition on slavery, which is a subject better left in the hands of those more capable of arguing. My business is only to state facts, and tell the truth.' She also admitted a growing admiration for the Southern Confederacy. This feeling increases with every chapter of her book. When, in the summer of 1861, she had seen the rows of wounded soldiers in the Yorktown hospital, scores of whom died from lack of medicine which could not get through a blockade which England could have raised, she took a vow: 'I did resolve to do all I could for those same "rebels," not only in Richmond but in England.' Writing her book was the way she chose to honour her vow.

By the time she wrote, Lincoln had issued his Emancipation Proclamation which would abolish slavery in the Southern states (though not in
some of the border states) provided the North won the war. For decades
there has been a pious legend that English workers, particularly in
Lancashire, gladly endured starvation to abolish slavery and to support
'Honest Abe'. But a careful study of the English press and public meetings
shows this to be totally false: 'The real heroes of the weaving towns were
Jefferson Davis, Robert E. Lee, and the other leaders of the dying Confederacy.'[28] There was a widely held view in England that Lincoln's conversion
to abolition was just a trick designed to gain English support. Britons had
read in the books of Fanny Wright, Fanny Trollope and Lady Emmeline
Stuart Wortley that blacks were treated far worse in the North than in the
South. Catherine Hopley recalled the conversation she had had with the
first Northern officer she met as she crossed from Confederate lines. He
had told her – only weeks before the Emancipation Proclamation was
issued – 'To tell the truth there are very few of our people who approve of
the scheme.'

In spite of the favourable picture she drew of the actual life of the slaves
whom she had seen, Catherine Hopley was anxious to stress that she did
not approve of slavery. 'Reader, English reader,' she pleads in her Introduction, 'do not for a moment suppose that your countrywoman approves
of slavery, though she has been very careful to relate the exact truth,
leaving it to others to decide, how far it is just to denounce a people, who
preserve an institution entailed upon them by our own ancestors.' She
explained:

> Much as I had hesitated in going to the South, through a dread of witnessing
> the sufferings of the slaves, not once had I seen serious reason for pitying
> them. I had known them in houses and fields, domestic servants and
> "plantation hands"; had come upon them unexpectedly and suddenly in the
> midst of their labour; and in the two years and a half between six of the Slave
> States, exclusive of Maryland, I had never seen nor heard of corporeal [sic]
> punishment, excepting such as has been mentioned in these pages.

Her book about Southerners would not have been 'written in vain, if those,
who have not before so thought of them, should be induced, through these
imperfect pages, to regard with more leniency and justice the people of the
Southern Confederacy'.

Catherine Hopley's book is not a work of propaganda. It made many
criticisms of the South and of the effect of slavery upon it, but it gave its
readers a generally favourable picture of a courageous people at war. Given
her commitment to the Southern side, how accurate are her observations
on American life? As has been said earlier, she, like all visitors to any
country, only saw certain aspects. Her life was spent mainly among
wealthy people, people who owned 'plantations', or at least large farms,
and people who could afford to stay in hotels. But these were the same

people who gathered information, debated issues and took a more general view of life than the less educated or less well-off farmers or labourers. They were also the people who owned slaves and as such were in a minority. But since slavery was the American issue which most interested Englishmen, this was a boon, not a detraction. While she remained opposed to slavery, 'the most calamitous and unmerciful infliction that could befall both master and servant, would be the *sudden* emancipation of the slaves of the Southern States'. She accepted that 'horrible scenes have undeniably occurred in the Slave States, as in other countries' although she never saw or heard of any. But, she added,

> let any upright reader judge, whether it would be a fair representation of English society, to collect from a year's, or even a week's newspapers, the terrible list of crimes and sufferings, and concentrating them in one volume, to send it forth to the world, saying, 'Such is England.'

As we have seen, Catherine Hopley frequently criticised aspects of American behaviour in the same manner as Frances Trollope and Rebecca Burlend had done. She always tried to remain detached. She did not like most aspects of American religion; she despised tobacco; she had little regard for American education, at least of the wealthy; she shared the general English distaste for American newspapers; she most decidedly did not like the presumption of equality and the lack of discipline even among bodies, such as the Confederate army, which she admired. She never could fully reconcile herself to democratic manners among people who were legally 'slaves'. Her picture of large parts of American life balances those painted by the other four women in this book and, like theirs, the limitations on her work are obvious. While women like Rebecca Burlend and Fanny Trollope painted a picture of America in the making, it was Catherine Hopley's task to paint the American Union in dissolution.

She never went into the arguments for or against states' rights, the right of secession or the nature of the American Union, nor did she discuss politics save to dismiss Lincoln and praise Jefferson Davis. In this she was hardly unique, for one contemporary journalist said, with only some exaggeration, that the general English view about the political 'worthies of the North' was that they were 'low speculators, dishonest politicians, pettyfogging tyrants, unhanged murderers, and strong-minded women, for whose conduct insanity is the only possible excuse'.[29] *Life in the South* by the anonymous 'Blockaded British Subject' was published at the beginning of March 1863 at twenty-one shillings. It was not a good week in which to launch a new book as the country was in a frenzy about the marriage of the Prince of Wales.[30] A few weeks later the book was reviewed in the *Athenaeum*, the most important literary journal of the time. The reviewer praised it as a very good book, but commented that it had appeared too late since the English people had already formed 'a just appreciation of the good as well as the evil features of those whom Northern partisans have systematically misrepresented'. The review did emphasise that aspect of her book which still makes it worth reading: 'The governess photographs much which a man would either not observe or would erroneously pass over as unworthy of narration.' Another publication, the *Press*, praised the book as a good portrayal of 'the present condition of the New Confederacy'.[31]

Catherine Hopley had discovered a new cause and a new profession in the American South and for the next few years she would unite them. By writing for Richmond newspapers, the *Illustrated London News* and the *Southern Literary Messenger*, she had become, as she said, an 'authoress'. Within months she was busy on another anonymous book. This was a short life of the great Confederate hero, 'Stonewall' Jackson, which she rushed out when word of his death reached England. She began to write for *All the Year Round*, founded and edited by Dickens. In 1864 she wrote about Florida and in 1865, as her beloved Confederacy was collapsing, she wrote an article praising the Texans: 'I have been an Englishwoman among the Texans.' Here her developing skill as a periodical writer is evident: the casual reader could easily assume that she had spent years in Texas or indeed that she might actually have been writing from there. Her knowledge came from the stories told to her by Governor Milton's Texan nephew. In other articles she also used letters and publications sent to her by Southern friends.[32]

Her family difficulties in England continued as her imprisoned brother became involved in a notorious divorce case with his wife. Catherine appears to have divided her time between caring for her mother in Lewes and researching at the British Museum. The Florida slave who had noticed her pleasure in 'weeds' was quite prophetic as she increasingly devoted her writing to scientific subjects. The Superintendent of the Reading Room at the British Museum said no reader was as constant and as hard working as she was. She also won the admiration of the distinguished scientist, Sir Richard Owen. For the next three decades she contributed articles to periodicals and encyclopaedias about bugs and snakes. Her first article was based directly on her American experiences: 'The Entomologist Goes South' was written for Dickens' *All the Year Round*.[33] Throughout the 1870s, she was busy writing children's books which drew upon her knowledge of American animal life. *Aunt Jenny's American Pets*, which was mainly about birds, was more widely reviewed and praised than any of her other books. 'Miss Hopley', said *The Times*, 'writes lightly and brightly, and knows how to make knowledge interesting.' This book, which like all her later books appeared under her own name, even bridged the formidable religious divisions of Victorian Britain: the Catholic *Tablet* called it a 'charming book for children' while the *Nonconformist* said that 'Aunt Jenny is a lovable sort of creature, and will interest as much in herself as in her pets'. Her American theme continued with *Rambles and Adventures in the*

Wilds of the West and *Stories of Red Men from Early American History.*
She did not neglect her artistic abilities. As well as illustrating some of her
own works, she contributed sketches to *Cassell's History of the United
States.* She also wrote widely for periodicals including a series of articles
about America in the magazine *Golden Hours* in 1878.

Three years later, when she was living in Camden Square, London, she
was delighted to receive a letter from her old friend, Lucretia Garfield, who
was about to move to Washington following her husband's election as
President. Catherine Hopley's lengthy reply – the reader has to revolve
the pages to try to make out all the comments squeezed into every corner
– provides our best insight into her personality. As always there is a strong
note of self-pity: 'I live alone and very much alone.' 'My means are very
narrow ... I am becoming a feeble old lady.' Along with the self-pity comes
humour: 'I am reading Mark Twain "just for fun".' Above all the letter
exalts in pride in her own achievements as a writer and the success of her
friends. Mindful of Mrs Garfield's new position, she said how helpful it
would be if the American government would donate some of its scientific
publications to the British Museum. This led her to recall her Florida
experiences of two decades before as she remembered that Governor
Milton had given her two volumes of the Pacific Exploration Reports and,
she boasted, 'I am proud of them.' She had 'an immense hope for the
interest in America, though I lost much money there, partly through bad
investment and again through [the] failure of a Va [Virginia] Bank.'
Realising that she was writing to the wife of a man who had been the
youngest Northern general, she joked: 'Serves me right! for being a partizan of the South.' Yet she had a ready excuse: 'I am always a partizan of
those who are kind to me.' She concluded with a message for 'our most
scholarly and intellectual President as yet', and she stressed the use of
'our' as she wished him 'a happy and truly satisfactory reign'. Yet just as
Mrs Garfield was preparing to reply to her friend in London, word arrived
that the new President had been shot. He died after only a few months
'reign'.[34]

There are some indications that Catherine Hopley revisited America to
see her family and friends there. We do know that three years after
Garfield's assassination she signed the copy of her book, *Life in The South,*
that is now in the Library of Congress. After writing her name on the title
page, where she was described as a 'blockaded British subject' she wrote
in pencil, 'Catherine Cooper Hopley alias Catherine C. Hopley'. At the end
of her Introduction to the first volume she added: 'For any errors &
misconceptions discoverable in this work, the authoress would plead the
hasty preparation of it, demanded of her immediately on her return to
England. It was only the work of ten weeks.' She dated her note 'June 3
1884'.[35] (One wonders if she knew that this was the seventy-sixth birthday
of her old hero, Jefferson Davis – a day that would soon be celebrated as a
holiday in the old states of the Confederacy.)

✳

Catherine Hopley's old restlessness persisted throughout her long life; her few surviving letters rarely have the same address. She continued to support herself by writing and she became a correspondent for newspapers in London and Philadelphia. By 1887, as she was approaching her seventieth birthday, the years of toil were taking their toll. With her old fondness for hiding her identity, she wrote a letter to the *Globe*, signed 'An Elderly Spinster', to suggest that the Golden Jubilee of Queen Victoria's reign should be celebrated by establishing a home for elderly women writers. At the same time she applied to the Royal Literary Fund, a charity which had been established to help authors in distress. Her application says that she was 'a spinster' and that her literary earnings in the last year had amounted to only £12 or £13; fortunately she also had a small annuity which gave her another £24 a year. In addition, she received small sums from investments. She said she was very ill and needed 'rest from brain work'. The Fund gave her a grant of £50 to allow her to have a rest. For the next twenty years she continued to apply to the same body almost every other year and they normally gave her a grant of about £50. All her applications were strongly supported by prominent figures in the world of scholarship who attested to her contribution to entomology. In spite of what Victorians called 'her reduced circumstances', she was able to maintain a maid for part of the time. In 1892, when she was eighty-five, she even went to South Africa for a visit and became acquainted with Cecil Rhodes. Her last years were spent in desperate efforts to finish another book which seems to have been on a scientific topic. In 1904 she reported to the Secretary of the Royal Literary Fund: 'Literary earning nil! but some chapters written.' Appropriately for someone who so loved 'weeds' and flowers, she spent her final years in Kew, where she died at the age of ninety-three on 29 April 1911.[36] It was just fifty years since she had seen the outbreak of the war that changed forever the America that she, like the four other Englishwomen in this book, had gone to find.

Epilogue

If Catherine Hopley returned to the re-United States after the horrors of the Civil War, she would have found a country far different from the one she had first visited in 1854, let alone the innocent young Republic that Fanny Wright discovered in 1818. The most obvious change was the abolition of slavery – that part of American life that had most appalled and intrigued English visitors. The new problems that had arisen to take its place did not seem so exotic to travellers from England. The slums of American cities were not all that different from the slums of Britain. The vulgar display of great wealth differed only slightly from that in London or in the vast country houses that industrial magnates were building in the English countryside. The growth of radicalism and of trade unions was hardly unfamiliar to any British traveller. Of course certain minor points of etiquette or language could still trouble a sensitive soul, but these no longer seemed as important as they had in the days of Mrs Trollope.

To return to the metaphor Fanny Kemble had used: America, if still a daughter, was nearing maturity, and to the mother this process could occasionally be troublesome. Daughters, of course, can be a source of great pride and minor annoyance at the same time, particularly when they exhibit some of the same traits as their mothers. At the beginning of this book we saw how the young Queen Victoria had been perplexed by the 'manners' of an American diplomat's wife. The Queen, it may be recalled, thought this proved the account from books that had been 'lately written'. A quarter of a century later she was quite annoyed when her nineteen-year-old daughter, the Princess Royal, made a similar comment. The Queen, glowing with delight at the reception that her eldest son had received in the United States, rebuked her daughter: 'We are somewhat shocked at your speaking of those "horrid Yankees" – when Bertie was received everywhere in the United States as no one has ever been received anywhere, primarily from the (to me incredible) like they have for my unworthy self.' She commanded: 'Don't therefore abuse the "Yankees".' The Queen was once again expressing the changing views of her subjects. When she came to the throne, Britons took their image of America from travel books; by the mid-point of her long reign, personal contacts and friendships were beginning to replace the accounts of travel writers. Yet the travel writers had left a rich legacy upon which to draw.

In our own century Lady Emmeline Stuart Wortley's prediction has come true: 'Let America and England thoroughly co-operate, and the world in the next century will be whatever they have chosen to make it.' Most

Britons would also agree with her view of America: 'Let us say, with a fitting pride, "we laid the foundations of this mighty nation".' Our five women guides have shown us that nation in the making. Each of them saw aspects that still endure today and each provided a delightful introduction to that strange relationship between the two great English-speaking nations, a relationship which has had no parallel since the days of Greece and Rome.

Our five women discovered in their American adventures that their native land and what Lady Emmeline called her 'second country' shared not only a common language but a common set of values. These two bonds remain in spite of fashionable chatter about America's turning towards 'the Pacific' and Britain's turning towards 'Europe.'

There is a third bond, and it is one as strong as language and values. This is the bond of kinship and friendship. Some years ago I wrote a BBC programme about the adventures of Rebecca Burlend in her pioneer log cabin. I received a letter from Mr John Burlend in Pinner. He was the last member of the family in England and wanted to know if there was some way he could get in touch with Rebecca's descendants in America. I suggested he contact the Pike County Historical Society in Illinois. It may be recalled that it was at Philips Ferry in Pike County that Rebecca and John Burlend, along with their frightened children, landed with their few possessions on a dark night in 1831. Mr Burlend kindly wrote to tell what happened on his visit to his cousins:

> Despite the fact that my relationship with the American Burlends was somewhat remote – fifth cousins – we were able to talk about family matters. We also found that we had characteristics in common ... It meant that though they were farmers and I am a townsman I fitted into their lives easily and felt very much at ease with them. They were most hospitable and seemed very proud of their English relative. At a reunion in a public park on my last evening, there were between sixty and seventy descendants of John and Rebecca to meet me. I tried and found it easy to talk to most of them. It was interesting that Rebecca's great-great-great-grandson flew me over Philips Ferry in his own Cessna plane.

The flight of the private Cessna aeroplane seems a long way from that of a 'Bird of Passage', but each was on its own voyage of discovery.

Notes

Unless stated otherwise, the place of publication of all books cited is London. To reduce the number of footnotes, individual page references to the seven American travel books referred to throughout the text are not given. Those books are:

Anon [Rebecca Burlend], *A True Picture of Emigration: or Fourteen Years in the Interior of North America; Being a Full and Impartial Account of the Various Difficulties and Ultimate Success of an English Family who Emigrated from Barwick-in-Elmet near Leeds, in the Year 1831* (G. Berger, 1848, 1 vol.).

An Englishwoman [Frances Wright], *Views of Society and Manners in America; in a Series of Letters from that Country to a Friend in England, during the Years 1818, 1819, and 1820* (Longman, Hurst, Rees, Orme, and Brown, 1821, 1 vol.).

Frances Trollope, *Domestic Manners of the Americans* (Whittaker, Treacher, 1832, 2 vols).

Lady Emmeline Stuart Wortley, *Travels in the United States Etc. during 1849 and 1850* (Richard Bentley, 1851, 3 vols).

Lady Emmeline Stuart Wortley, *&c.* (T. Bosworth, 1853, 1 vol.).

Anon [Victoria Stuart Wortley], *A Young Traveller's Journal of a Tour in North and South America During the year 1850* (T. Bosworth, 1852, 1 vol.).

Anon [Catherine Hopley], *Life in the South; From the Commencement of the War by a Blockaded British Subject. Being a Social History of Those who took part in the Battles, from a Personal Acquaintance with Them in their Homes. From the Spring of 1860 to August 1862* (Chapman and Hall, 1863, 2 vols).

Introduction

1. Diary entry for 2 August 1837, Carola Oman, *The Gascoyne Heiress: The Life and Diaries of Frances Mary Gascoyne-Cecil, 1802-1839* (1968), 253. It is not clear what the Queen particularly disliked in Mrs Stevenson. Perhaps it was something similar to Lady Holland's complaint after entertaining her to dinner a few months previously: 'She is rather pleasing, but diverted Mr Hallam whom she sat next to at dinner, by lamenting that the people in this country did not speak English, only a bad jargon. In the meantime she is often herself unintelligible from her accent and very strange *locutions*.' Lady Holland to Lord Holland, 27 Dec. 1836 in the Earl of Ilchester [ed.], *Elizabeth, Lady Holland to Her Son, 1821-45* (1946), 163-4. Mrs Stevenson's own account of her time in England makes most interesting reading. See Edward Boykin [ed.], *Victoria, Albert and Mrs Stevenson* (1957).

2. Edmund Quincy, *Life of Josiah Quincy* (Boston, 1874), 458.

3. Although there is no complete list of British travellers to America who wrote up their experiences, Allan Nevins has a large selection in his anthology, *America Through British Eyes* (New York, 1948). See also: Max Berger, *The British Traveller in America, 1836-60* (Gloucester, Mass., 1964) and Jane Robinson, *Wayward Women: A Guide to Women Travellers* (Oxford, 1990).

4. Mill's comment in his review of the second volume of Tocqueville's *Democracy in America* in the *Edinburgh Review* was reprinted as an introduction to the 'Schocken' edn. of *Democracy in America* (New York, 1961), II.vi.

5. *Athenaeum*, 18 April 1863, 521.

6. Mrs Trollope's MS. Notebooks, Lilly Library, University of Indiana.

7. q. in Richard M. Ludwig, 'American Literature' in *The Princeton University Library Chronicle* XXXVIII (winter-spring, 1977), 195.

8. q. in Nevins, *America Through British Eyes*, 140. See Harriet Martineau's autobiography in which she maintained that her *Society in America* (1837, 3 vols) is not a 'favourable specimen' of her writings. (Harriet Martineau, *Biographical Sketches, 1852-75* (1888, new edn.), xxv.)

9. Anon., 'American Orators and Statesmen' in *Quarterly Review* LXVII (Dec. 1840), 45.

10. Ben Macintyre, 'The Wretched Refuse of a Teeming Shore' in *The Times Saturday Magazine*, 31 Oct. 1992, 4.

11. q. in Frances Wright, *Views of Society and Manners in America* (1821), 46.

12. q. in J.C. Furnas, *Fanny Kemble: Leading Lady of the Nineteenth-Century Stage* (New York, 1982), 385.

13. Winston Churchill, *Richard Carvell* (New York, 1899), 299. *The Times*, 3 Jan. 1846.

14. Anon., 'American Orators and Statesmen', 45.

15. Alexis de Tocqueville, diary entry for 13 Jan. 1832 in J.P. Mayer [ed.], *Journey to America* (1959), 177.

16. Alistair Cooke, Introduction to Richard Kenin, *Return to Albion: Americans in England, 1760-1940* (Washington, 1979), xiv.

1. The Settler: Rebecca Burlend

1. A second, expanded edition appeared in 1856 under the title, *Wesleyan Christianity Tested and Exemplified being an Authentic Narrative of Striking Events in the History of a Wesleyan Family of Yorkshire Emigrants in the Back Woods of America*. The author is given as Edward Burlend. The 1848 edition was reprinted in America in 1937 in the 'Lakeside Classics' with an introduction by M.M. Quaife who drew on recollections of some of the Burlends' descendants. In 1968 Citadel Press (New York) reprinted the 1937 edition and this is the edition I have used.

2. J. Deacon, 'A Story Linked With Barwick: *Amy Thornton or the Curate's Daughter* by Edward Burlend' in *The Barwicker Journal of Barwick-in-Elmet Historical Society* (July 1987), no. 6, 24-7.

3. John Cassell [ed.], *The Emigrant's Handbook: Being a Guide to the Various Fields of Emigration in All Parts of the Globe* (1852), 60, 6-7. Herman Melville, *Redburn*, ch. xxix; Oliver Macdonagh, *A Pattern of Government Growth, 1800-1860: The Passenger Acts and Their Enforcement* (1961), 31-9.

4. Robert W. Johannsen, *Stephen A. Douglas* (New York, 1973), 19-21.

5. See James Munson, *The Nonconformists: In Search of a Lost Culture* (1991), 186-203.

6. Cassell [ed.], *The Emigrant's Handbook*, 21.

7. Sarah Mytton Maury, *An Englishwoman in America* (1848), cxvii.

8. J. Deacon, 'A Story Linked With Barwick', 24.

2. The Enthusiast: Frances Wright

1. 15 May 1784, James Boswell [G.B. Hill & L.F. Powell, eds], The *Life of Samuel Johnson* (Oxford, 6 vols, 1979), IV.275.

2. Celia Morris, *Fanny Wright: Rebel in America* (Urbana, Illinois, 1992), 6-8.

This is the best biography and is founded upon extensive research. It was originally published under the name of Celia Morris Eckhart in 1984 by Harvard University Press. See also A.J.G. Perkins & Theresa Wolfson, *Frances Wright: Free Enquirer, The Study of a Temperament* (1939), 14-15.

3. Daniel J. Boorstin, *The Americans: The National Experience* (Harmondsworth, 1969), 458-9. Boorstin also quotes the comment by William Hart, biographer of Patrick Henry, about Botta's habit of 'making too free with the sanctity of history' (q. on 446).

4. [Frances Wright], *Biography, Notes, and Political Letters of Frances Wright D'Arusmont* (Dundee, 1844), 8.

5. William R. Waterman, *Frances Wright* (New York, 1924), 16.

6. A second edn followed almost immediately. There is a modern edn in the 'John Harvard Library' ed. by Paul R. Baker (Cambridge, Mass., 1963) and this is the edition used here.

7. Lady Blessington, after visiting an American ship at Naples in 1824, wrote that no fair person 'could deny that our trans-atlantic brethren have made a wonderful progress as a nation' q. in Edith Clay [ed.], *Lady Blessington at Naples* (1979), 110-11. The *Amity* was one of four 500-ton packet ships of the American Black Ball Line, whose monthly sailings, starting in 1816, made Liverpool into the main transatlantic port.

8. Capt. Basil Hall's wife speaks constantly of his help to them. See Una Pope-Hennessy [ed.], *The Aristocratic Journey: Being the Outspoken Letters of Mrs Basil Hall Written during a Fourteen Months Sojourn in America 1827-28* (1931), *passim*.

9. Morris, *Fanny Wright*, 24.

10. q. in Morris, *Fanny Wright*, 27-8.

11. q. in Waterman, *Frances Wright*, 36. Thomas Jefferson to Fanny Wright, 22 May 1820 in W.C. Ford [ed.], *Thomas Jefferson Correspondence* (Boston, 1916), 254.

12. An exiled French aristocrat, Hyde de Neuville, noted in the 1790s of American women: 'When they marry, they so to speak, divest themselves of all their vivacity, and become grave and silent.' *Memoirs of Baron Hyde de Neuville* (n.d., 2 vols) I.232. He was a close friend of John Garnett, who played an important role in Fanny Wright's life.

13. For Dickens' racial views see William Oddie, 'Dickens and the Indian Mutiny' in *The Dickensian* (Jan. 1972), LXVIII/366, 3-15. Robert W. Johannsen [ed.], *The Lincoln-Douglas Debates of 1858* (New York, 1965), 321, 316.

14. See Capt. Basil Hall's *Travels in North America in the Years 1827 and 1828* (1829, 3 vols), II.338.

15. See also [Wright], *Biography ...*, 27.

16. In her *Biography*, Fanny is tolerant enough to allow that Royalists and even Christians may be sincere and honourable though wrong (16-17).

17. Waterman, *Frances Wright*, 58.

18. Critics of America paid a great deal of attention to violence among American legislators. The story of the 1805 fist-fight between Congressmen Leib and Nicholson was still being cited in Dickens' *Household Words* (XIV) on 19 July 1856. There was also much violence in Parliament and in 1829 the Prime Minister, the Duke of Wellington, fought a duel after another peer impugned his motives.

19. Boorstin, *The Americans*, 197.

20. Lonnelle Airman, *We the People: The Story of the United States Capitol* (Washington, D.C., 1978), 32-3. I wish to thank my friend, Mr Louis Stark, for calling this source to my attention.

21. W.P. Cresson, *James Monroe* (Chapel Hill, North Carolina, 1946), 340.

22. Other writers were interested in the question of continued emigration from

England: Henry Fearon came to America to collect information for a group of potential emigrants who financed his trip. See his book, *A Narrative of a Journey Through America* (1818). I have shortened the title of Fearon's book and that of some others in these notes as travel writers seemed to compete to have the longest title: Fearon's full title comprised 25 words.

23. His home, 'The Whitehouse', is now the Buccleuch Mansion Museum.

24. Some of this hostility waned as she aged. See, for example, her *England the Civilizer*, published in 1848. Some of her views were also based on her Scottish background and she often calls herself 'an Englishwoman', as in her *Views of Society and Manners*. The letter about England's 'retrograde' state and all following letters to Julia and Harriet Garnett come from the 33 letters in the Garnett-Pertz MSS. in the Houghton Library at Harvard University. Two-thirds of these have been published by Cecilia Helena Payne-Gaposchkin as 'The Nashoba Plan for Removing the Evil of Slavery: Letters of Frances and Camilla Wright, 1820-29' in the *Harvard Library Bulletin* XXIII/3-4 (July & Oct. 1975), 221-51 & 429-61. Professor Payne-Gaposchkin, who donated the MSS. to Harvard is the great-great-grand-daughter of Julia Garnett Pertz. Any books about Frances Wright or Frances Trollope that were written before this source became available are of limited use.

25. *The Works of the Rev. Sidney Smith* (2 vols, 1859), I.286-92

26. Fearon, *A Narrative*, 49-50.

27. T.A. Trollope, *What I Remember* (New York, 1888-90, 2 vols), I.106-7.

28. [Wright], *Biography* ..., 12.

29. Anon, *Quarterly Review* (Mar. 1832) XLVII, 49. The article, which was actually by Capt. Basil Hall, was a review of Mrs Trollope's *Domestic Manners of the Americans*.

30. Morris, *Fanny Wright*, 49. See also Margaret Lane, *Frances Wright and the 'Great Experiment'* (Manchester, 1972), 14-15.

31. q. in Morris, *Fanny Wright*, 52.

32. [Henri Beyle] Stendhal [T.W. Earp, trans.], *Memoirs of An Egoist*, (1949), 37-9. The final part of the passage about the Portuguese girl relates to 1832 when Lafayette was 75.

33. Fanny Wright's letter of 18 July 1822 and Lafayette's of 26 Apr. 1824 q. in Waterman, *Frances Wright*, 65-6, 79. See Stendhal, *Memoirs*, 12, regarding the height of women.

34. Fanny Wright to Jeremy Bentham, 12 Aug. 1822, Bentham MS., B.L. Add. MSS. 33545 *f* 588. See also letter of 11 Aug. 1822, Add. MSS. 33545 *f* 585. For the radical circle in which Fanny Wright was involved at this time see Richard Mullen, *Anthony Trollope: A Victorian in his World* (1990), 42-9.

35. Morris, *Fanny Wright*, 82. Eleanor Custis Lewis was really only the grand-daughter of Martha Washington, as she was descended from her grandmother's first marriage. However George Washington always treated her as his grand-daughter. Celia Morris thinks that Eleanor Custis Lewis' dislike of Fanny Wright was increased by the fact that Wright paid a private visit to the lodgings of a Haitian diplomat in Philadelphia (81).

36. Fanny Wright to the Garnetts, 30 Oct. 1824, Garnett-Pertz MS.

37. Morris, *Fanny Wright*, 81.

38. In her letter to the Garnetts of 12 Nov. 1824, Fanny Wright also spoke of the 'deep melancholy' of seeing such a brilliant mind as Jefferson's in its decline (Garnett-Pertz MS.).

39. q. in Morris, *Fanny Wright*, 84-5.

40. Scotsmen played an enormous role in the history of the Owenite movement. See John F.C. Harrison, *Quest for the New Moral World* (New York, 1969), *passim*. The *Washington Gazette*, 9 Dec. 1824 q. in Waterman, *Frances Wright*, 88. Camilla

Wright to the Garnetts, ? Dec. 1824, Garnett Pertz MS. Frances Trollope [Richard Mullen, ed.], *Domestic Manners of the Americans* (Oxford, 1984 edn), 190. Bernard, Duke of Saxe-Weimar, *Travels through North America During the Years 1825 and 1826* (1828), *passim.*

41. James Madison to Fanny Wright, 1 Sept. 1825 in Marvin Mayers [ed.], *The Mind of the Founder: Sources of the Political Thought of James Madison* (New York, 1973), 415-220.

42. F.M. Brodie, *Thomas Jefferson; An Intimate History* (New York, 1974), 463.

43. Clement Eaton, *A History of the Old South* (1966), 339. See James E. Roper, 'Marcus Winchester and the Earliest Years of Memphis' in *Tennessee Historical Quarterly* (1962), 326-51.

44. Trollope, *What I Remember*, I.106. Fanny Wright to Jeremy Bentham, 4 Nov. 1827, Bentham MS., B.L. Add. MSS. 33546 *f* 173.

45. Camilla Wright to the Garnetts, ? Nov. 1829, Garnett Pertz MS. Waterman, *Frances Wright*, 131.

46. Frances Trollope [Mullen, ed.], *Domestic Manners*, 59. Mrs Trollope to Mary Mitford, 20 Jan. 1829 q. in A.G. L'Estrange, *The Friendships of Mary Russell Mitford* (1882, 2 vols), I.191-3.

47. Thomas L. Nichols, *Forty Years of American Life* (1864, 2 vols), II.22. Whitman q. in Horace Traubel, *With Walt Whitman in Camden* (New York, 1908, 2 vols), I.80. Martha Saxton, *Louisa May: A Modern Biography of Louisa Alcott* (1978), 61-2.

48. Frances Wright to Camilla Wright Whitby, 21 Feb. 1829 q. in Waterman, *Frances Wright*, 146, 174. Manufacturing had been developed in Paterson to take advantage of the water power from the Passaic Falls.

49. 3 July 1830, Allan Nevins [ed.], *The Diary of Philip Hone, 1828-51* (New York, 1970), 25-6. The support of such a prominent atheist and feminist did not help Jackson, who was himself a practising Christian. See A.P. Stokes, *Church and State in the United States* (New York, 1950, 3 vols), I.702. Thomas Carlyle to John A. Carlyle, 17 June 1834 in C.R. Sanders et al. [eds], *The Collected Letters of Thomas and Jane Welsh Carlyle* (Durham, N. Carolina, 1960-), VII.218.

50. [Hall], *Quarterly Review* XLVII, 49.

51. J.F. Beard [ed.], *The Letters and Journals of James Fenimore Cooper* (Cambridge, Mass., 1960-), II.72.

52. Morris, *Fanny Wright*, 249-50.

53. 20 June 1839, Hone, *Diary*, 402. The Loco-focos were the radical wing of the Democrats; the name comes from a type of match they used to light a meeting place when the party bosses had ordered the lights extinguished.

54. Frances Wright MS., Envelope C, Library of Congress. This is reason number 13 in the petition.

55. Richard J. Carwardine, *Evangelicals and Politics in Antebellum America*. (1993), 95-6. Fanny Wright apparently played no part in the British anti-slavery movement. See Clare Midgley, *Women Against Slavery: The British Campaigns, 1780-1870*, (1992), 83.

56. Robert Dale Owen in *Atlantic Monthly* (July 1874), 75. The younger Owen's wife had boarded for some time with the D'Arusmonts. Owen eventually became a Congressman and an American diplomat in Italy.

57. q. in Morris, *Fanny Wright*, 290.

58. Madison to Lafayette, in Gaillard Hunt [ed.], *The Writings of James Madison* (New York, 1900-10), XI.311. Jane Welsh Carlyle to Thomas Carlyle, 5 Aug. 1845 in Trudy Bliss [ed.], *Jane Welsh Carlyle: A New Selection of Her Letters* (1949), 162. Van Wyck Brooks, *Fenelossa and His Circle, with Other Essays* (New York, 1962), 106. This essay on Fanny Wright is the first to use the Garnett letters, which he discovered by talking – appropriately on a transatlantic liner – to a descendant of Julia Garnett Pertz.

59. q. in Waterman, *Frances Wright*, 219-20. Mother [Ann] Lee was the foundress of the 'Shakers', the religious sect particularly hated by Fanny Wright.

3. The Critic Abroad: Frances Trollope

1. Frances Trollope to Thomas Anthony Trollope, 12 March 1810, Sadleir MS. Don C 5 vol. 12, f129. T.A. Trollope to Lord Northwick, 18 Dec. 1830, Northwick MS., ACC 76/2274, Greater London Record Office. For the background to Mrs Trollope's life before her departure see Mullen, *Anthony Trollope*, chs. 1 and 2.

2. Frances Trollope, 'Journal of a Visit to La Grange', Trollope MS. University of Illinois. F.E. Trollope, *Frances Trollope: Her Life and Literary Work from George III to Victoria* (1895, 2 vols), II.68-9. Frances Eleanor Trollope was Mrs Trollope's daughter-in-law and the second wife of Thomas Adolphus Trollope.

3. Anthony Trollope, *An Autobiography* (1953 edn.), 18-19. One wonders if the 'French Prolétaire' was a reference to Mrs Trollope's painter-friend, Jean Auguste Hervieu? The 'archduchess' who later befriended Mrs Trollope in Vienna was Archduchess Sophie (1805-1872), daughter of King Maximilian I of Bavaria and wife of Archduke Francis of Austria. Her son reigned as Emperor Franz Joseph from 1848 to 1916. Thomas Adolphus Trollope, Anthony's elder brother, took issue with his brother's recollection whereas in fact Anthony played down her involvement with radicals. See Trollope, *What I Remember*, I.490-4.

4. Trollope, *An Autobiography*, 22. Frances Trollope to Harriet Garnett, 8 Oct. 1827; Fanny Wright to Julia Garnett, 8 June 1825, Garnett-Pertz MS.

5. Harriet Garnett to Julia Garnett Pertz, 19 Aug. 1828, Garnett-Pertz MS. Fanny Wright to Harriet Garnett, 26 Dec. 1827, Garnett-Pertz MS. Fanny Wright to Harriet Garnett, 20 March 1828, Garnett-Pertz MS. Lafayette to Charles Wilkes, 8 Nov. 1827 q. in Perkins and Wolfson, *Frances Wright*, 180-1. Fanny Wright to Harriet Garnett, 20 March 1828, Garnett-Pertz MS. Fanny Wright to Jeremy Bentham, 4 Nov. 1827, Bentham MS., British Library, Add. MSS. 33546 *f* 173. Robt. Dale Owen to ?, 2 Nov. 1827, Bodleian Library, English letters, MS. Eng. Lett. b. 32 *f* 101. In her letter of 26 Dec. 1827 Wright referred to 'my sudden departure' and said that the captain had only given her 'but one day's warning' as to the time of sailing.

6. Frances Trollope [Mullen, ed.], *Domestic Manners*, 11, 41. Hereinafter all unattributed quotes can be assumed to come from this edn of Mrs Trollope's book. Frances Trollope to Charles Wilkes, 14 Feb. 1828, Cincinnati Historical Society MS. q. in Helen Heineman, *Mrs Trollope: The Triumphant Feminine in the Nineteenth Century* (Athens, Ohio, 1979), 269. Fanny Wright to Julia Garnett Pertz, 26 Dec. 1827, Garnett-Pertz MS. There is in this letter a reference to Mrs Trollope's need to close their 'pretty place and large establishment'.

7. Frances Trollope, 1st draft of *Domestic Manners* q. in introductory essay, 'Mrs. Trollope in America' in Donald Smalley [ed.], *Domestic Manners of the Americans* (New York, 1949), xvii.

8. Smalley, 'Mrs. Trollope in America', xvii-xviii. Frances Trollope to Charles Wilkes, 14 Feb. 1828, q. in Heineman, *Mrs Trollope*, 269. Fanny Wright to Julia Garnett, 20 Mar. 1828, Garnett-Pertz MS. On Hervieu see J.F. McDermott, 'Mrs Trollope's Illustrator ...' in *Extrait de la Gazette des Beaux-arts* (March 1958), 169-90.

9. Pope-Hennesy [ed.], *Aristocratic Journey*, 285-6.

10. Charles Ambler, *A History of Transportation in the Ohio Valley* (Glendale, California, 1932), 30-1. See 'Parade of Painted Ladies in Porkopolis', *Wall Street*

Journal, 27 Oct. 1988. I would like to thank Mrs Muriel Lass of Cincinnati for bringing this to my attention.

11. q. in Smalley [ed.], 'Mrs. Trollope in America', xxvii-xxviii. F.E. Trollope, *Frances Trollope*, I.113. Cincinnati takes its name from the Order of Cincinnatus, a society designed to honour officers in the War of Independence.

12. Mrs Trollope to Harriet Garnett, 27 Apr. 1828, Garnett-Pertz MS. For Wilkes see Trollope, *What I Remember*, I.114, 130. Carl Abbott, 'The Location and External Appearance of Mrs Trollope's Bazaar' in *Journal of the Society of Architectural Historians* (1970), 256-60.

13. Anthony Trollope, MS. of his *Autobiography*, British Library, B.L. Add. MS Autogr. 42856. Henry Sedgwick, *Francis Parkman* (Boston, 1904), 145. [Capt. Thomas Hamilton], *Men and Manners in America* (New York, 1968 edn), 169-70. The book was first published in two volumes in Edinburgh, 1833.

14. Michael Chevalier, *Society, Manners and Politics in the United States ...* (New York, 1969 edn), 203. Mrs Trollope to Julia Garnett Pertz, 22 Aug. 1831, Garnett Pertz MS. More than a century later, family legend maintained that the responsibility for 'the crackbrained enterprise of the Bazaar was as much her husband's as hers' according to her great-grand-daughter, Muriel Trollope, in 'What I was Told' in *Trollopian* (March 1948), 223-4.

15. Sedgwick, *Parkman*, 144-5. The Rev. C.C. Jones to Charles C. Jones & Joseph Jones, 23 June 1857 in Robert Manson Myers [ed.], *The Children of Pride: A True Story of Georgia and the Civil War* (1972), 335-6.

16. Mark Twain's comments on Mrs Trollope occur in marginalia in his copy of *Domestic Manners* and were reproduced in Frances Trollope [Mullen, ed.], *Domestic Manners*, 369. (Hereafter 'Mark Twain's Marginalia'.) Ironically this copy of *Domestic Manners* was preserved in New York Public Library's Arents Collection because the founder wanted a copy of every book that mentioned tobacco.

17. q. in Smalley [ed.], *Domestic Manners*, 60n.

18. E.M. Butler [ed.], *A Regency Visitor* (1957), 83. The original translator of Prince Pückler-Muskau, Sarah Austin, was annoyed when Mrs Trollope's book was 'hailed with enthusiasm by the same people who detest yours', i.e. English Tories. See Lotte and Joseph Hamburger, *Contemplating Adultery: The Secret Life of a Victorian Woman* (1992), 239. Nichols, *Forty Years of American Life*, 112. Henry T. Tuckermann, *America and her Commentators ...* (New York, 1970 edn), 225. Flint is q. in Smalley, 'Mrs. Trollope in America', xxxviii-xl. Flint's review was first published in *The Knickerbocker* in 1833. Parts of his description were reprinted in England as late as 1855 in John Cassell's *The Popular Educator* (VI.778-80).

19. Trollope, *What I Remember*, I.46. Richard Carwardine, *Trans-atlantic Revivalism ...* (1978), 67-9.

20. The review appeared in Sept. 1832 and was reprinted in *American Criticisms of Mrs. Trollope*, 1-23.

21. This view survived until the present century. In *The King's English*, H.W. and F.G. Fowler wrote: 'If any one were asked to give an Americanism without a moment's delay, he would be more likely than not to mention I guess.' (Oxford, 3rd edn, 1934, 33). They pointed out, however, that 'I guess' was an old English usage dating back to Chaucer's 'I gesse'. Like many 'Americanisms' it was a survival of a form which had died out in England.

22. Frances Trollope to Tom Trollope, 30 June 1828 q. in F.E. Trollope, *Frances Trollope*, II.114-15. Frances Trollope to Charles Wilkes, 18 June 1828, Parrish Collection, Princeton University, AM 20408. Mrs Trollope as a foreigner would have had no way to protect her copyright in America. Frances Trollope to Mary Russell Mitford, 20 Jan. 1829 in Alfred Guy l'Estrange [ed.], *The Friendships of Mary Russell Mitford*, II.193.

23. Anthony Trollope, *North America* (New York, 1951 edn), 372-3. Frances Trollope to Julia Garnett Pertz, 12 Mar. 1830, Garnett-Pertz MS.

24. Hamilton, *Men and Manners*, II.15. James Fenimore Cooper [D.A. Ringe & K.W. Staggs, eds], *Gleanings in Europe: England* (Albany, N.Y., 1982), 78-9.

25. Frederick Law Olmstead, *Walks and Talks of an American Farmer in England* (Ann Arbor, 1967 edn.), 41-2.

26. Trollope, *An Autobiography*, 22. Frances Trollope, *Paris and the Parisians* (Gloucester, 1985 edn), 394-5.

27. The anecdote about Brougham is from Lord Hatherton's MS. Journal in his papers at Staffordshire Record Office, q. in R.F. Mullen, *The House of Lords and the Repeal of the Corn Laws* (Oxford D. Phil Thesis, 1974), 77. Cooper, *England*, 104. Nathaniel Parker Willis, *Pencillings By the Way*, (1942 edn), 197.

28. Frances Trollope to Tom Trollope, summer 1830 q. in Trollope, *Frances Trollope*, I.131.

29. Ibid.

30. General Lee's comment on slavery in the 1830s was included in his remarks to a visiting Englishman in 1866, q. in R.E. Lee, Jnr. *Recollections and Letters of General Robert E. Lee* (Garden City, N.Y., 1924), 231-2.

31. Journal entry for 16 May, 1831, Harriet Arbuthnot [Francis Bamford and the Duke of Wellington, eds], *The Journal of Mrs. Arbuthnot 1820-32* (1950, two vols), II.419.

32. Alexis de Tocqueville to Ernest de Chabrol, 9 June 1831 from New York City in Roger Boesche [ed.], *Alexis de Tocqueville: Selected Letters on Politics and Society* (1985), 40.

33. Frances Eleanor Ternan, the second wife of Mrs Trollope's eldest son, Thomas Adolphus, was born on an American paddle-steamer in August, 1835, while her parents were making a theatrical tour of America. See Claire Tomalin, *The Invisible Woman* (Penguin edn, 1991), 34.

34. Van Wyck Brooks, *The World of Washington Irving* (1947), 316-17.

35. Op. cit., 1-18.

36. *Mirror and Ladies' Parterre*, 18 Aug. 1832.

37. Mark Twain's Marginalia.

38. Trollope, *Paris*, 57-8. Thomas Hamilton, *Men and Manners*, I.325. 'Jefferson and His Slave', *New York Times*, 22 Nov. 1987. To put the Jefferson story into perspective see Catherine Clinton, *The Plantation Mistress* (New York, 1982), especially ch. XI, 'The Sexual Dynamics of Slavery' which is most useful.

39. Christ Church, the Episcopal Church in Alexandria was begun in 1767 and is the same building that Mrs Trollope would have known. The Roman Catholic parish, St Mary's, was founded in 1790, but the current building was built several decades after Mrs Trollope's visit. I wish to thank my sister, Nora Mullen, for her help with this research.

40. The children of Presbyterian ministers frequently found this custom of the 'Donation Party' a humiliating experience. See John Morgan Richards, *With John Bull and Jonathan: Reminiscences of Sixty Years of an American's Life in England and in the United States* (1905), 9-11. For Cassell's description of a similar event in an Episcopal Church see Article V, 'American Character and Manners ...' in 'America as It Is' in *Cassell's Illustrated Family Paper*, 26 Jan. 1861.

41. Frances Trollope to Julia Garnett Pertz, 22 Aug. 1831. Garnett-Pertz MS.

42. For Tom's and Mr Trollope's visit to Trenton Falls see Trollope, *What I Remember*, I.129.

43. Walter Stirling to George Harrison, 20 July 1832, q. in Heinemann, *Mrs Trollope*, 73.

44. Frances Trollope to Julia Garnett Pertz, 22 August, 1831. Garnett Pertz MS.

Mr Trollope said he was under great obligation to Hervieu. This letter was written after Mrs Trollope's return to England.

45. Frances Trollope to Julia Garnett Pertz, 22 Aug. 1831. Garnett-Pertz MS. Frances Trollope to Mary Mitford, 18 Sept. 1831, Mitford MS., Berkshire County Record Office. Mary Mitford had recently begun a literary side-line in editing American stories for Whitaker, who had published her well-known book, *Our Village*.

46. Frances Trollope to Tom Trollope, n.d. [Mar./Apr. 1832] q. in Trollope, *Frances Trollope*, I.131. Both ladies had good reason to dislike America: Lady Louisa was the daughter of Lord Bute and Lady Charlotte, the daughter of Lord North. Bute and North were the most hated British politicians in the American colonies in the 1770s and 1780s.

47. Entry for 8 May 1832 in John Quincy Adams' Diary in Marc Friedlander & L.H. Butterfield [eds], *Diary and Autobiography of John Quincy Adams* (Cambridge, Mass., 1962, 4 vols), IV.294.

48. *American Criticism of 'Mrs. Trollope's Domestic Manners of the Americans'*, *passim*.

49. E.T. Coke, *A Subaltern's Furlough Descriptive of Scenes in Various Parts of the United States, Upper and Lower Canada, New Brunswick and Nova Scotia in the Summer and Autumn of 1832* (1833), 167-8. Henry B. McLellan, *Journal of a Residence in Scotland and a Tour Through England ...* (Boston, 1834), 353. Charles Stewart, *Sketches of Society in Great Britain and Ireland* (Philadephia, 1834, 2 vols), I.214. Stanley T. Williams, *The Life of Washington Irving* (New York, 1935, 2 vols), II.28. *The Lion of the West* was by James K. Paulding. The Rev. Isaac Fidler's *Observations ...* was a critical account of his American tour. The cartoons appeared in D.C. Johnston, *Trollopania*. Frederick Shelton, a New York Episcopalian clergyman, published a poem called *The Trollopiad, or, Travelling Gentlemen in America: A Satire by Nil Admirari* in 1837. It has been called 'the most savage attack ever made by an American on the European traveler' by Warren S. Tryon, *My Native Land* (Chicago, 1961), ix.

50. *New York Constellation*, 14 July 1832. For the full text of the poem see Trollope [Smalley ed.], *Domestic Manners*, 340.

51. Hone, *Diary*, 633 (14 Nov. 1842). C. Vann Woodward [ed.], *Mary Chesnut's Civil War* (1981), 744 (5 March 1865).

52. Sir Augustus Foster to Josiah Quincy, 30 Sept. 1833. Josiah Quincy to Sir Augustus Foster, 7 Mar. 1834. Sir Augustus Foster to Josiah Quincy, 12 July 1834 in Quincy, *Life of Josiah Quincy*, 457-60. Isaac Fidler and Thomas Hamilton, referred to above, both published books on their travels in America. Hamilton also visited Cincinnati and praised Mrs Trollope. For Foster's earlier hostile views of America see his letters to his mother in Vere Foster [ed.], *The Two Duchesses* (1898), *passim*.

53. Thomas L. Nichols, *Forty Years of American Life*, 112. Twain q. in Trollope [Mullen ed.], *Domestic Manners*, 369, xxviii.

54. Anthony Trollope told the Louis Philippe anecdote to his first biographer, T.H.S. Escott. See T.H.S. Escott, *Anthony Trollope* (New York, 1967 edn.), 34. Chevalier, Society, *Manners ...*, 190.

55. Trollope [Michael Sadleir ed.], *Domestic Manners of the Americans* (1927), xi.

56. Charles Dickens to Frances Trollope, 16 Dec. 1842 in Madeline House et al. [eds], *Letters of Charles Dickens* (Oxford, 1965-), III.395. T.B. Macaulay (19 Oct. 1842) in Thomas Pinney [ed.], *The Selected Letters of Thomas Babington Macaulay* (Cambridge, 1974-1981, 6 vols), IV.61.

57. Hone, *Diary*, 87-8 (1 Feb. 1833).

58. Tom Trollope to Richard Bentley, 16 Sept. 1838, Taylor MS. Collection,

Princeton University. For Tom Trollope's view of America, see his memoirs, *What I Remember*, I.117-18. For an assessment of Anthony Trollope's debt to his mother's *Domestic Manners* see Mullen, *Anthony Trollope*, 65-8.

59. Frances Trollope to John Murray, 20 Jan. 1835, John Murray MS. (courtesy of Miss Virginia Murray). Frances Trollope to Richard Bentley, 7 Nov. 1835, Taylor MS.

60. Tocqueville's companion, Gustave de Beaumont, published his *Marie, ou l'Esclavage aux Etas-Unis* in 1835. It is not really a novel but what a later generation would call 'faction', the first of many such works in the study of slavery.

61. Heineman, *Mrs Trollope*, 148. *Gentleman's Magazine* (Dec. 1863).

62. See Helen Heineman, 'Frances Trollope's *Jesse Phillips*: Sexual Politics and the New Poor Law' in *International Journal of Women's Studies* (Jan. 1978), 60-80.

63. L.J. Reynolds and S.B. Smith, '*These Sad But Glorious Days*' (1991), 171-2. Bayard Taylor, *At Home and Abroad* (New York, 1860), 40.

64. For the background to 'Good Time Coming' see Mullen, *Anthony Trollope*, 380-1. Harriet Garnett to Julia Garnett Pertz, 12 Dec. 1847 and 24 April. 1848. Garnett Pertz MS.

65. Anthony Trollope, *North America*, 394.

4. The Fashionable Visitor: Lady Emmeline Stuart Wortley

1. Henry Reeve [ed.], *The Greville Memoirs: A Journal of the Reigns of King George IV, King William IV, and Queen Victoria* (1888, new edn, 8 vols), IV.45 (Journal entry for 4 Jan. 1838). E.T. Coke, whose *A Subaltern's Furlough* was quoted in an earlier chapter about the American reception of Mrs Trollope's *Domestic Manners*, dedicated his book of American travels to the Duke of Rutland.

2. Frances Bamford & the Duke of Wellington [eds], *The Journal of Mrs. Arbuthnot 1820-1832* (1950, 2 vols), I.196, 407, 430 (11 Nov. 1822, 9 July 1825, 20 Dec. 1825).

3. Mrs Henry [Emmeline] Cust, *Wanderers: Episodes From the Travels of Lady Emmeline Stuart-Wortley and her Daughter Victoria, 1849-1855* (1927). This work, by Lady Emmeline's grand-daughter, is the only book about her and provides basic information.

4. Gervas Huxley, *Lady Elizabeth and the Grosvenors* (1965). Lady Elizabeth Belgrave eventually became the Marchioness of Westminster and the Grosvenor family, into which she had married, were prominent Whigs. Thus political hostility to the Tory Manners family may have played some role in her hostility towards Lady Emmeline. Lady Emmeline endeavoured to remain friendly with the Grosvenors. See an undated letter in the Bodleian Library to one of them inviting the recipient to a comedy she had written for the Haymarket (MSS. Eng. Lett. c 441, *ff* 123-4).

5. Bamford & Wellington [eds], *Journal of Mrs. Arbuthnot*, II.230 (11 Jan. 1829).

6. Drummond of Cadland MSS., Hampshire County Record Office, B6/78/33 and B6/79/21 (letters from the Duchess of Rutland to her daughter, Lady Elizabeth Drummond). See also B5/A27 for a letter of November 1825 re. negotiations over the marriage of Lady Emmeline to Prince Leopold. The Record Office does not have the bulk of the personal letters in this collection as they remain in private hands. They do have an extensive and detailed catalogue with summaries of the contents and quotations from the letters. Unless otherwise noted, all letters cited from this collection were sent to Lady Elizabeth Drummond, Lady Emmeline's elder sister, who married Andrew Drummond.

7. Drummond of Cadland MSS., B6/39/31 (letter, n.d.) and B6/39/34 (letter of 12 Aug. 1826). B6/39/36 (letter of 4 Sept. 1826). B6 90/25 (letter of Charles Stuart-Wortley to Lady Elizabeth Drummond, 7 June 1831).

8. Drummond of Cadland MSS., B6/78/33 (letter from the Duke of Rutland). AR/23/1 (draft of the letter from Andrew Drummond to Lady Emmeline). B6/90/25 (letter of 7 June 1831 from Charles Stuart Wortley). Lady Georgiana Ellis to the Countess Gower, 25 Jan. 1831 q. in Maud, Lady Leconfield [ed.], *Three Howard Sisters* (1955), 183.

9. Lady Wharncliffe to her mother, Lady Erne, 21 Apr. 1831 q. in. Hon. Caroline Grosvenor and Charles Beilby, Lord Stuart of Wortley, *The First Lady Wharncliffe and Her Family, 1779-1856* (1927, 2 vols), II.71. (The editor, Lord Stuart of Wortley, was Lady Emmeline's nephew, who married Mrs Trollope's grand-daughter, Beatrice Trollope.)

10. *Quarterly Review* LXVI (Sept. 1840), 397.

11. Lady Wharncliffe to the Hon. Mrs J. C. Talbot, 8 Oct. 1840 q. in Grosvenor and Wortley [eds], *First Lady Wharncliffe*, II.309. Benjamin Disraeli to Sarah Disraeli, 8 July 1833 in Ralph Disraeli [ed.], *Home Letters Written By Lord Beaconsfield, 1830-1852* (1928, 'Pocket Edition'), 124. Disraeli was introduced to her by Caroline Norton.

12. Her superb account of the meeting with Madame Mère was printed in *The Keepsake* in 1837 and re-printed in Mrs Cust, *Wanderers*, 337-40. See also Lady Emmeline's book, &c., 155-61. [Reginald] Viscount Esher [ed.], *The Girlhood of Queen Victoria* (1912, 2 vols), I.396 (the Queen's Journal for 29 Aug. 1838). No more details of this conversation are reported; it flows from a discussion of Lady Holland's fascination with Napoleon. The Queen may also have been anxious to know something about her beloved Uncle Leopold and Lady Emmeline.

13. Frances Anne Kemble, *Records of Later Life* (1882, 3 vols), II.185-7. This visit was in March, 1842.

14. The Hon. James Stuart Wortley to Lady Wharncliffe, 28 Nov. 1842 q. in Grosvenor and Wortley [eds], *The First Lady Wharncliffe*, II.324. Drummond of Cadland MSS., B6/50/87 (letter of Earl Jermyn [husband of Lady Emmeline's sister, Lady Katherine], 11 July 1835). For the context see Judith S. Lewis, *In the Family Way: Childbearing in the British Aristocracy* (New Brunswick, N.J., 1986), 213.

15. Drummond of Cadland MSS., B6/39/33 (Aug. [?] 1826).

16. Bentley published Mrs Trollope's travel books on Austria, France, and Italy as well as several of her novels.

17. *Spectator*, 20 June 1846. *The Times*, 3 Jan. 1846 in a lead article urging peaceful settlement of the Oregon dispute. Ticknow to Sir Charles Lyell, 15 May 1849 in George S. Hillard, *Life, Letters, and Journals of George Ticknor* (Boston, 1877, 6th edn, 2 vols), II.241. Lyell, the President of the Geological Society, twice visited America and, naturally, produced travel books about each visit.

18. Lord Morpeth, one of the best Lords Lieutenant of Ireland in the nineteenth century, succeeded as the seventh Earl of Carlisle in 1848. Lady Emmeline's mother was the daughter of the fifth Earl. Among the many diarists to record his triumphant visit was Philip Hone (Nevins [ed.], *Diary of Philip Hone*, 575). A good example of the way in which prominent British visitors were seen as potential allies is given in the diary of the South Carolina politician, James Henry Hammond: 'I did all I could to give him a favourable idea of our slave institutions.' (Carol Blesser [ed.] *Secret and Sacred: The Diaries of James Henry Hammond, a Southern Slaveholder* (Oxford, 1988), 87. The wife of another South Carolina Governor remembered almost twenty years later the difficulties of one American politician with British titles. 'Shall I call Lord Morpeth [the courtesy title for the eldest son and heir to the Earldom of Carlisle], "My Lord," "The Lord," or "Oh, Lord"?' (Woodward [ed.], *Mary Chesnut's Civil War*, 23.)

19. *Travelling Sketches in Rhyme* (1835), 'Farewell to England', 13.

20. The Leigh quotation is from the dedication of Lady Emmeline's *Impressions of Italy*.

21. Nevins [ed.], *Diary of Philip Hone* (9 Feb. 1849), 862.

22. q. in Virginia Cowles, *The Astors* (1979), 54.

23. Patricia Godsell [ed.], *Letters & Diaries of Lady Durham* (place of publication not given, 1979), 55. Charles Dickens, *American Notes*. See chapters XIV and XV for Dickens' account of Niagara.

24. Drummond of Cadland MSS., B6/36/25. Mary Fulford was related to Lady Elizabeth Drummond by marriage.

25. Drummond of Cadland MSS., B5/AR 23/7. (This letter from Lady Emmeline to her sister is the only one from America to survive in this collection.) See also the account in *&c.*, 200-4. Lady Emmeline had suffered a great shock when a cousin died from cholera in 1832. See B5/14/7.

26. Lady Emmeline's grandfather, the fifth Earl of Carlisle, had been sent on a peace mission to the rebellious colonies in 1778.

27. Alexander Mackay, *The Western World; or, Travels in the United States in 1846-7* q. in Clement Eaton [ed.], *The Leaven of Democracy* (New York, 1963), 131.

28. Webster and the Duke of Rutland were both interested in agriculture. On 27 Mar. 1851 he gave a Baptist minister who was visiting the Great Exhibition to study agricultural improvements a letter of introduction to the Duke. In this letter Webster recalled his visit to Belvoir and sent 'kind remembrance to your daughter Lady Emeline [*sic*]'. in C.H. Van Tyne [ed.], *The Letters of Daniel Webster* (New York, 1902), 634. Webster had also entertained Lady Emmeline's father-in-law when he visited America in 1824. For details of how Webster bought slaves and then emancipated them and their subsequent lives as his servants see Claude Fuess, *Daniel Webster* (Boston, 1930, 2 vols), II.334-5.

29. Hamilton, *Men and Manners in America*, xxiii. These details about the Presidential bowels are given in a private letter to his brother that Hamilton included as a Preface.

30. Avery O. Craven, *The Growth of Southern Nationalism, 1848-61* (Baton Rouge, La., 1953), 729.

31. She gave a fuller account in *&c.*, 27-31. For another contemporary description see Myers [ed.], *Children of Pride*, 72-7.

32. *&c.*, 6.

33. Richard Taylor, *Destruction and Reconstruction: Personal Experiences of the Late War* (New York, 1879). Varina Davis, *Jefferson Davis: A Memoir* (Baltimore, 1990 reprint, 2 vols), II.94. Edmund Wilson, *Patriotic Gore: Studies in the Literature of the American Civil War* (1987, 'Hogarth Edition'), 299-307. Christopher Mulvey (*Transatlantic Manners* [Cambridge, 1990], 92-4) is somewhat scathing about her visit.

34. Holman Hamilton, *Zachary Taylor: Soldier in the White House* (Indianapolis, 1951), 32-3.

35. In this period Britain and America were overwhelmingly each other's main trading partners. The US supplied 81.13 per cent of Britain's cotton imports, while 50.71 per cent of US exports went to the UK. Norman Buck, *The Development and Organisation of Anglo-American Trade* (Newton Abbot, 1969 reprint), 36,2. A bale of cotton could weigh up to 300 lbs.

36. *&c.*, 230-5.

37. In predicting the eventual success of a Panama Canal, Lady Emmeline was quite prophetic. An attempt by the French to build a canal in the 1880s was a disaster, but an American-built canal was opened in 1914. The fifty-mile canal connecting the Atlantic to the Pacific saved a 6,000-mile trip round South America. Many other contemporary observers, like Anthony Trollope, believed that it would never be possible to build such a waterway (Mullen, *Anthony Trollope*, 336).

38. Allison Lockwood, *Passionate Pilgrims: The American Traveler in Great Britain, 1800-1914* (New York, 1981), 450.

39. Tsar Nicholas I told this to Douglas, when the latter visited Russia in 1853. Johannsen, *Stephen A. Douglas*, 385-6.

40. *Mobile Daily Register*, 9 Jan. 1850 q. in Craven, *The Growth of Southern Nationalism*, 86.

41. It may be a sign of her recent residence in the South that she uses the term 'compact' to describe the American Constitution. This was the term favoured by the proponents of State's Rights.

42. *&c.*, 335-61. Travellers frequently found that the quickest way from the West Indies to England was to go to New York first.

43. Bentley MSS., British Library Add. MSS. 46615 *f* 309, agreement dated 27 February 1851. *Athenaeum*, 10 May 1851. American reviews q. in Mrs Henry Cust, *Wanderers*, 355-6. Much of the review of Victoria Wortley's book is found in the advertisements of her publisher, Thomas Bosworth, which is in a brochure at the end of her mother's book, *&c.* Tuckerman, in his *America and her Commentators*, never mentioned Lady Emmeline because he was anxious to include only hostile English writers.

44. Bentley MSS., Add. MSS 46615 *ff* 312-14, letter dated either 15 or 17 Oct. 1851; the two accounts of her book are *ff* 313-14 of which the final account is dated 31 March 1855.

45. *A Visit to Portugal and Madeira* (1854), 202.

46. Drummond of Cadland MSS., B6/78/242-3 (letters from the Duke of Rutland, 16 & 18 Nov. 1855).

47. The brief notice in *The Times* of 24 Nov. 1855 says she died on 29 October, but the letters in the above footnote and also B6/78/248 indicate it was on 30 Oct. *The Gentleman's Magazine* (1855, II.183) was anything but gentlemanly in its obituary. According to this, Lady Emmeline 'was a poetess, or at least a writer of verses'.

5. The Tragic Observer: Catherine Hopley

1. The basic sources used in unravelling Catherine Hopley's background are: the archives of the Royal Literary Fund (Catherine Hopley's file is no. 2263), a microfilm of which is available in the Manuscript Room of the British Library; the *Annual Register* for 1860 (1861), 58-60; Daisy Parker, 'John Milton, Governor of Florida' in *The Florida Historical Quarterly* XX (April 1942); the *Dictionary of National Biography* under Edward John Hopley; Thomas Hopley, *The Hopley Divorce Case. A Cry to the Leading Nation of the World for Justice: and for the Souls of my Wife and Children: Dedicated to Lord Brougham* (privately published, 1864); William [Serjeant] Ballantine, *Some Experiences of a Barrister's Life* (1882, 6th edn), 397-8. The original reference to the Hopley case was in W.L. Burn, *The Age of Equipoise* (New York, 'The Norton Library', 1965), 42-3. See also references in footnotes 2, 3, 6, 13, 18-20 and 22 below.

2. The date of birth may be found in the MSS. of the Royal Literary Fund. Anon. [Catherine Hopley], 'Two Sabbaths on the Atlantic' in *The Sunday at Home*, IX (8 Nov. 1862). (The magazine was published by the Religious Tract Society.) Lockwood, *Passionate Pilgrims*, 161-3.

3. Catherine Hopley to James Garfield, 31 May and 2 June 1850, Garfield MSS., Library of Congress, vol. 002/332; vol. 002/346. One of her letters of reference in the Royal Literary Fund MSS. says that she was a governess in the family of the 'late president Garfield'.

4. q. in Evelyn D. Ward, *The Children of Bladensfield* (New York, 1978), 118. The Abolitionists made frequent appeal to a 'higher law' than the American Constitution. For the death of 'the pious Christian and gallant gentleman, Col.

John Washington' early in the war see Walter H. Taylor, *Four Years With General Lee* (New York, reprint, n.d.), 29. It is amusing to compare the reactions of an eighteenth-century New Jersey tutor on a Virginia plantation with Catherine Hopley's almost a century later. See Hunter Farish [ed.], *The Journal and Letters of Philip Vickers Fithian, 1773-4* (Williamsburg, Virginia, 1957). Fithian was told that a college-bred tutor was given the social status of a gentleman with an estate worth £10,000.

5. See J.E.B. Munson, 'Uncle Tom in England' in *Civil War Times*, XXI (Jan. 1983).

6. Dr W.'s name may well have been Wright as the Wright family was an important local family, many of whose members were landowners. Like 'Dr W.' they were Methodists and one of their homes was called Forest. This information was kindly sent to me by Virginia Wright Durrett and Martha C. Carter of the Spotsylvania Historical Association.

7. 'Howdy' seems to have been a standard usage from and to slaves. For the frequent use of it see Myer, *Children of Pride, passim.*

8. The *Athenaeum* review (18 Apr. 1863) of the Hopley book assumed that their readers would know the term 'F.F.V.'

9. W.M. Thackeray to his daughter Anne, 3 Mar. 1853 from Richmond, Virginia in Gordon N. Ray [ed.], *The Letters and Private Papers of William Makepeace Thackeray* (1945-6, four vols), III.223.

10. Ward, *Children of Bladensfield*, 16-17.

11. Charles East [ed.], *Sarah Morgan: The Civil War Diary of a Southern Woman* (New York, 1992), 153.

12. [Hopley], 'Two Sabbaths ... ' in *The Sunday at Home*, 8 Nov. 1862.

13. *Annual Register* for 1860, 58-60. Ballantine, *Some Experiences of a Barrister's Life*, 397-8. Burn, *Age of Equipose*, 42-3; *The Times*, 30 July 1860. The fact that Thomas Hopley's wife's family lived in London's highly respectable Gloucester Crescent is another sign of middle-class status. There was a recent reference to the case in *The Times* of 13 April 1993.

14. See Dickens, *American Notes*, ch. XVII for numerous examples.

15. Dickens describes his visit to the tobacco factories in *American Notes*, ch. IX. See also W.M. Thackeray to Albany Fonblanque, 4 Mar. 1853 in Ray, *Letters and Private Papers*, III.229.

16. Thomas H. Gilmer to Sen. Stephen Douglas, 17 Apr. 1861 q. in Johannsen, *Stephen A. Douglas*, 861.

17. The report in *The Times* by the celebrated war correspondent, W.H. Russell, became famous. In America he became known as 'Bull Run' Russell.

18. In her application forms to the Royal Literary Fund, Catherine Hopley had to provide a list of her books and other writings. She listed an article on 'a Negro School in Savannah' in *The Sunday at Home* in 1863. A close examination of this periodical revealed no article by her on that topic. Catherine Hopley did say in one application form that she no longer had copies of all her writings and that she was not sure of the details.

19. The 1860 Florida Census Returns for Jackson County, Schedule 1, 132-3 in the Florida State Archives, Tallahassee, Florida. See also W.L. Gammon, *Governor John Milton of Florida, Confederate States of America*, unpublished MA Thesis (1948), Univ. of Florida at Gainesville, and Daisy Parker, 'John Milton ... ' in *The Florida Historical Quarterly* XX (April 1942). Governor Milton was described as 'an enlightened patriot' by the historian, Clement Eaton, because, unlike most Confederate governors, he did not wage battles over states' rights with the Richmond government (*A History of the Southern Confederacy* [New York, 1954], 151).

20. [Catherine Hopley], 'In A Sinking State' in *All The Year Round* XII (17 Sept. 1864).

21. Kemble, *Journal of Residence on a Georgia Plantation*, 74, 85-6, 240-1.

22. [Catherine Hopley], 'Young Texas' in *All the Year Round* XII (1 Jan. 1865).

23. For Palmerston's reaction see Jasper Ridley, *Palmerston* (1970), 555-6. For one example of how exaggerated versions of Palmerston's outrage circulated in the Confederacy and gave hope to Southerners, see East [ed.], *Sarah Morgan: The Civil War Diary*, 151.

24. R.G.H. Kean, *Inside the Confederate Government* ... (New York, 1957), xxv-xxvi.

25. *Athenaeum*, 18 Apr. 1863.

26. Anthony Trollope, *North America*, 453. For life in occupied Baltimore see the diary of Trollope's friend, William Glenn: B.E. Marks & M.N. Schatz [eds], *Between North and South: A Maryland Journalist Views the Civil War: The Narrative of William Wilkins Glenn 1861-1869* (1976), *passim*. For a summary of the 'despotic measures' prepared by occupying Federal troops and dated on the day of Catherine Hopley's arrival, see 319-23.

27. See Mullen, *Anthony Trollope*, 378. It is unlikely that Catherine Hopley got a tenth of this sum for her book. She must have returned by late October at the latest as her article, 'Two Sabbaths', was published in the 8 Nov. issue of *Sunday at Home*.

28. Mary Ellison, *Support for Secession: Lancashire and the American Civil War* (1972), 175.

29. This summary of of English opinion was reported by the Paris correspondent of the *Spectator* in 1863. It was sent to Richmond and was quoted in J.D. Richardson [ed.], *A Compilation of Messages and Papers of the Confederacy, 1861-5* (Nashville, Tennessee, 1906, 2 vols), II.491.

30. *The Publishers' Circular*, 16 Feb. 1863, said it would be published 'in a few days'. A Chapman and Hall advertisement in the 2 March 1863 issue lists it as published.

31. *Athenaeum*, 18 Apr. 1863. The comment in the Press is quoted in the Chapman and Hall advertisement for the Hopley book in *The Publishers' Circular*, 16 Feb. 1863.

32. [Catherine Hopley], 'Young Texas' in *All the Year Round* XII, 1 Jan. 1865. Another article, 'A Waif from Dixie' in *All the Year Round*, 29 Oct. 1864 is also probably by Catherine Hopley.

33. [Catherine Hopley], 'The Entomologist Goes South' in *All the Year Round* XI (18 June 1864), 440-4.

34. Letters in the Bentley MSS. in the British Library show that she was living in England in 1867. She had written to George Bentley on 20 May 1867 concerning three articles she had proposed for his magazine, *Temple Bar*. One of these was on South Carolina. (Bentley Papers, Add. MSS. 46654 *ff* 23-4.) See her letters of 17 January 1881 and 2 July 1881 (the day Garfield was shot) to Mrs Garfield in the Garfield MSS., Library of Congress.

35. Library of Congress, Rare Book Collection E487-H79.

36. Records at Somerset House, London show that Catherine Hopley died intestate and that her only relative, a nephew named John Edward Hopley, who was a publisher, was given the administration of her small estate which stood at £652 19s 9d net of tax.

Index

Abbreviations: C.H. = Catherine Hopley; C.S.A. = Confederate States of America; E.S.W. = Lady Emmeline Stuart Wortley; F.T. = Frances Trollope; F.W. = Frances Wright; J.B. = John Burlend; R.B. = Rebecca Burlend; V.W. = the Hon Victoria Stuart Wortley.

22; 'Illinois mange', 20; Illinois River,
journey up, 17-18; illness, 20, 23, 25; interest rates on frontier, 25; land, purchase of
on frontier, 19, 27, 30; law on land
purchase, R.B. denounces, 28; laziness on
frontier, 27; legal battles, 25-6, 27-8; Liverpool, journey to & stay in, 11- 12; livestock
on frontier, 20, 25, 26, 27, 30; maize, importance of, 20, 21, 26; maple sugar,
19-20, 22, 26; meat, 19, 20, 24; Methodists, 10, 13, 16, 25, 29; Methodist church
in Illinois, 22, 29, 31; Mississippi River,
journey to St Louis on, 16-17; money, lack
of, on frontier, 22, 24, 25, 26; mosquitoes,
22-3; 'Mr. B.' [Charles Bickerdike], 10, 19,
25, 30; natural beauty of America, 24-5;
New Orleans, 15-16; optimism, 21-2; patriotism, 12; Philips Ferry, landing at, 17,
218; Philips, hospitality of, 18-19; pigs,
importance of, 21, 24; pirates, 15, 15n;
ploughing, 22, 26, 27; pregnancy, 27;
pride, 15; provisions, 13; rainstorms, 22;
rattlesnakes, 26; religion on frontier, 29-
30; religious faith, 12, 13-14, 17-18, 28; St
Louis, 17; slavery, 16; smoking [pipe], R.B.
takes up in old age, 31; sowing, 22, 26;
steamboat, trips on, 16-17; steerage,
conditions in, 13-15; theft on steamboat,
attempted, 17; tobacco, grown on frontier,
19, 24; transatlantic crossing, 12-15; vegetables, dearth of, 20, 26; wheat, 23-4; *see
also* frontier; Pike characters; *True
Picture of Emigration*
Butler, General B.F. [Beast] (1818-93), 206
Byron, Lord (1788-1824), 79, 108, 120, 134,
139, 169

California, 137, 149, 151, 160, 163, 164
Canada: attitudes toward show English visi-
tors' opinions, 48; border disputes with
U.S., 145; E.S.W. visits, 143, 165; F.T.
argues better for poor than U.S., 103; F.T.
visits & praises, 114; F.W. on, 48
Cancellor, Reginald Channel: *see* Hopley,
Thomas
Capitol, U.S.: C.H. visits, 176; E.S.W. visits,
150; F.T. visits, 98; F.W. visits, 53
Carlisle, 5th Earl of [E.S.W.'s grandfather]
(1748-1825), 230 n.26
Carlisle, 7th Earl of [E.S.W.'s cousin] (1802-
64), 229 n.18
Carlyle, Jane Welsh (1801-66), 76
Cassell, John (1817-65), 3, 112
Carlyle, Thomas (1795-1881), 71, 72
Charles X (1757-1836), 104
Charleston [S. Carolina], 31, 175, 201-2, 204
Chateaubriand, Vicomte de (1768-1848), 106
Chesapeake Bay, 98, 177
Chesapeake & Delaware Canal, 105
Chesnut, Mary (1823-86), 124, 229 n.18
Chevalier, Michael (1806-79), 92
Church of England: *see* England, Church of

Churchill, Winston [U.S. novelist] (1871-
1947), 7
Cincinnati: background to, 83-4; Bazaar,
F.T.'s, 85-6; Beecher family &, 73-4;
E.S.W. visits, 153-4; F.T. &, 83-95, 108,
122, 129; F.W. settles & dies in, 75; Hall,
Mrs Basil on, 83-4; Jones, the Rev C.C. on,
86; location for F.T.'s novel, *The Old
World and the New*, 128; meat, cost &
availability of, 8, 88; origin of name, 225
n.11; Parkman, Francis on, 86; pigs, 84,
86, 123; shopping, 88; theatres, 88
Cincinnati Gazette, 84
City Point [Virginia], 208
Clay, Henry (1777-1852), 57, 59, 153
Cobb, General Thomas, 211
Cobden, Richard (1805-65), 7-8
Coke, E.T., 123
Coleridge, Hartley (1795-1849), 134
Columbus [Georgia], 206
Combe, George, 3
Commons, House of, 100
Confederate States of America: atrocities,
invented stories in North of, 211; blockade, effect of, on England, 194, 199; & on
South, 206, 207, 211; British recognition,
199; C.H. defends, 192-3, 195; Congressmen in Richmond, 198; cotton, embargo of,
211; cotton, use of, as money, 199, 207;
egalitarianism in C.S.A. army, 195; England, C.S.A. enjoys popular support in,
212; 'flag of Secession', 191; flags of, 201;
'friendly enemies' with U.S., 209; illness in
army, 195; inflation, 199, 206; Manassas,
196-7, 200; medicine, lack of due to blockade, 206; Northerners in, 203; oath
required of C.S.A. citizens to enter U.S.,
209; Post Office, 192; slavery, effect of on,
198; specie, lack of, 199, 207; spies &
abolitionists, fears of, 197; Trent Affair,
38, 200; unanimity over war, C.H. on, 193-
4; U.S. prisoners of war in Richmond, 195;
Yorktown, Virginia, army camp at, 195-6;
see also C.H.; South & Southerners
Congress: behaviour in, debated, 100; F.T.
visits, 99-100; F.W. on, 50; F.W. visits, 53,
65; petitions over reform of land law, 74;
Sylva Wright appears before Committee
of, 75; referred to, 99
Congress, Library of, 70n, 171, 215
Cooke, Alistair (1908-), 8
Cooper, James Fenimore (1789-1851), 73, 95,
98, 100, 108
Copley, John Singleton (1737-1815), 148
Cornwallis, Charles, 1st Marquess (1738-
1805), 195, 196
cotton: embargo of by C.S.A. hurts England,
211; E.S.W. on, 159; floods market in Jan.
1861, 189; importance to U.K.-U.S. trade,
230 n.35; money, used as, 199, 207
Cowper, William (1731-1800), 25
Crockett, Davy (1786-1836), 140